JIDDU KRISHNAMURTI was born in South India in 1896, and adopted in his teens by Dr. Annie Besant, president of the Theosophical Society. Educated privately in England and in France, where he attended the Sorbonne, Krishnamurti was proclaimed to be a vehicle of the "World Teacher," who, according to various scriptures, takes possession of a human from time to time in history and brings spiritual enlightenment to mankind. Then, more than forty years ago, Krishnamurti renounced his role as a new messiah and dispersed his followers, declaring, "Truth is a pathless land ... You cannot approach it by any religion, any sect." Since then, he has traveled in many countries, speaking and writing not as a guru but as a lover of truth.

Other Avon Discus Books by
J. Krishnamurti

TALKS AND DIALOGUES

THE AWAKENING OF INTELLIGENCE

J. KRISHNAMURTI

A DISCUS BOOK/PUBLISHED BY AVON BOOKS

Cover photograph by Mark Edwards.

AVON BOOKS
A division of
The Hearst Corporation
1790 Broadway
New York, New York 10019

Copyright © 1973 by Krishnamurti Foundation Trust Ltd.
London, England
Published by arrangement with Harper & Row, Publishers, Inc.
Library of Congress Catalog Card Number: 73-6328
ISBN: 0-380-00462-3

First Discuss Printing, January, 1976

DISCUS TRADEMARK REG. U.S. PAT. OFF. AND IN
OTHER COUNTRIES, MARCA REGISTRADA,
HECHO EN CANADA

Printed in Canada

UNV 10 9 8 7

QUOTATIONS

"Intelligence is not personal, is not the outcome of argument, belief, opinion or reason. Intelligence comes into being when the brain discovers its fallibility, when it discovers what it is capable of, and what it is not. Now what is the relationship of intelligence with this new dimension? . . . The different dimension can only operate through intelligence: if there is not that intelligence it cannot operate. So in daily life it can only operate where intelligence is functioning"—*Part VIII, page 385.*

"When (thought) sees that it is incapable of discovering something new, that very perception *is* the seed of intelligence, isn't it? That *is* intelligence: 'I cannot do'. I thought I could do a lot of things, and I can in a certain direction, but in a totally new direction I cannot do anything. The discovery of that is intelligence"—*Part VIII, page 384.*

"Thought is of time, intelligence is not of time. Intelligence is immeasurable"—*Part VII, page 350.*

"Intelligence comes into being when the mind, the heart and the body are really harmonious"—*Part VIII, page 420.*

"Is there the awakening of that intelligence? If there is . . . then it will operate, then you don't have to say, 'What am I to do?' Perhaps there have been a thousand persons here during these three weeks who have listened. If they really live that, do you know what's going to happen? We should change the world"—*Part VIII, page 421.*

"When there is that supreme energy, which is intelligence, is there death?"—*Part VII, page 338.*

EDITORS' NOTE

DURING RECENT YEARS J. Krishnamurti has continued to speak to audiences of all sorts, as well as to individuals and to smaller groups, in America, Europe and India. The present book has been planned as a more comprehensive record of his teaching over this period, that is since 1967, than has appeared in previous publications. As the Talks are always extempore, with interchange of question and answer, the reports printed here are taken from tapes, so that the exact words and phrases are accurately recorded. They are edited sufficiently to present a readable page, with some elimination of redundancies.

Several of the themes in these chapters are taken up in a different way in Conversations with four notable people interested in Krishnamurti's ideas. These personal interviews are also reported from tapes recorded at the time.

A word should be said about the Dialogues and the small group Discussion in Chapter 10. The Dialogues are not discussions in the sense of debates or arguments, but are free exchanges between people with a common aim who are intent on understanding together with Krishnamurti fundamental problems. For instance, the five Dialogues at Saanen follow a series of seven Talks and continue the themes there initiated, clarifying or probing the issues further. It is at Saanen, Switzerland, that for the last eleven years there have been gatherings each Summer with people coming from all over the world to share some weeks with Krishnamurti.

The small group Discussion (Chapter 10) took place at Brockwood Park in Hampshire, England, where there is an educational centre and school for young people founded by Krishnamurti. This discussion was with people for the most part long connected with Krishnamurti in his work.

The illustrations show Krishnamurti at some of the main

centres associated with him: Saanen in Switzerland, Rishi Valley and Rajghat, Banares, in India (the two schools in India founded in his name and visited by him) and Brockwood Park Educational Centre in England.

We are indebted to a number of helpers in the recording, transcribing and editing of this book.

George and Cornelia Wingfield Digby

CONTENTS

AMERICA

Part I
Two Conversations:
J. Krishnamurti and Professor Jacob Needleman

Part II
Three Talks in New York City

The need to change. A process in time or instantaneous? The conscious and the unconscious; dreams. The analytical process. To see the content of consciousness without the separation of observer and observed. Noise and resistance. "When there is complete cessation of division between the observer and the observed, then 'what is' is no longer what is."
QUESTIONS: Observer and observed; fragmentation; resistance.

Relationship. "You are the world". The separate self; corruption. To see what actually "is". What love is not. "We have no passion; we have lust, we have pleasure." To understand what death is. Love is its own eternity.
QUESTIONS: The concept of good and bad; sharing; pain and fear: how to be free of the past?

energy. "The mature mind has no comparison . . . no measure." The validity of "the life that you lead every day . . . without understanding it you will never understand love, beauty, or death". Through negation, that thing which alone is the positive comes into being.

Ploughing, never sowing. Ideation. Sensitivity lacking in daily life. Attention and intelligence. Disorder in ourselves and the world: our responsibility. The question of *seeing*. Images and direct contact. The sacred. "When you have that love you can put away all your sacred books."

Part VI
Four Dialogues in Madras

Images: are we aware that we see through images? Concepts; the gap between concepts and daily living; resulting conflict. "To get illumination you must be able to *look*." To live without conflict, but not to go to sleep."

Self-interest and self-dedication. Demand for satisfaction. Levels of gratification. Has psychological gratification any meaning? "A whirlpool of mischief and misery inwardly." Aggression. Pursuit of pleasure. "There are no roots of heaven in pleasure—there are only roots of indifference and pain." Watching is its own discipline.

The ideal, the concept, and "what is". Need to understand suffering: pain, loneliness, fear, envy. The ego-centre. The space and time of the centre. Is it possible not to have an ego-centre and yet live in this world? "We live within the prison of our own thinking." To see the structure of the centre. To look without the centre.

What is clear thinking in relation to daily living? Meeting the present with the past. How to live with memory and technological knowledge and yet be free of the past? Double life: temple, office. How to live without fragmentation?—to answer from a concept is further fragmentation. Silence before the immensity of a fundamental question. "Can you live so completely that there is only the active present now?"

EUROPE

Part VII

Seven Talks in Saanen, Switzerland

tions. Can the mind enter into the immeasurable?
What is the factor of illusion? Physical and mental fear and escapes. The mind that is constantly learning.
QUESTIONS: Can one observe without judgment and evaluation? Is perception seeing something totally? Can words be used to describe a nonverbal state?

Great energy needed; its wastage. Will is resistance. Will as assertion of the "me". Is there action without choice, which is not motivated? "To look with eyes that are not conditioned." Choiceless awareness of conditioning. To see and reject the falseness. What love is not. To face the question of death. "The ending of energy as the 'me' is the capacity to look at death." Energy to look at the unknown: supreme energy is intelligence.
QUESTIONS: We understand intellectually, but can't live it; is a man capable? How to listen? Are not feelings and emotions the cause of violence?

Different meanings of space. The space we think and act from; the space that thought has built. How is one to have immeasurable space? "To carry our burden and yet to seek freedom." Thought which does not divide itself is moving in experiencing. The meaning of intelligence. Harmony: mind, heart and organism. "Thought is of time, intelligence is not of time." Intelligence and the immeasurable.
QUESTIONS: Hatha Yoga. Is there separation of observer and observed in technological work? Awareness and sleep.

Part VIII
Five Dialogues in Saanen

Are we aware that we look at life fragmentarily? The conditioning of consciousness. Do we really know its content? Is there a division into conscious and unconscious? The observer is part of the content of consciousness. Is there any agent outside this conditioned content? "Tricks I play upon myself." What is action? Since the self is fragmented, "I" cannot see life as a totality.

What is the relationship between intelligence and thought? The limitations of conditioned thinking. No new movement can take place if the "old brain" is constantly in operation. "I have been going South, thinking I was going North." The perception of the limitations of the old is the seed of intelligence. Is the "new" recognisable? The different dimension can only operate through intelligence.

The link between pleasure and fear; the role of thought. Thought cannot reduce the uncertain unknown to terms of knowledge. Need to see the structure of fear. Psychologically, tomorrow may not exist. What does, "To live wholly in the present" imply?

Chronological and psychological time. The dilemma of knowledge. The dilemma of thought and the image. Can one find the root of fear? "The mind that can never be hurt."

What is a religious life? Relationship between meditation and the quiet mind. Thought as measure; the action of measurement. How can the immeasurable be understood? Intelligence as the relationship between the measurable and immeasurable. The awakening of intelligence. Choiceless awareness. Learning, not accumulating knowledge.

ENGLAND

Part IX
Two Talks at Brockwood

The uses and limitations of thought. Images: the authority of the image. "The more sensitive one is, the greater the burden of images." Analysis

and images. Psychological order; causes of disorder: opinion, comparison, images. Possible
dissolution of images. Formation of images. Attention and inattention. "It is only when the
mind is inattentive that the image is formed."
Attention and harmony: mind, heart, body.

"Meditation is the total release of energy." Western world built on measurement, which is *maya*
for the East. Schools of meditation useless. Energy depends on self-knowledge. Problem of self-
observation. To look "without the eyes of the
past". Naming. The hidden in oneself. Drugs.
The hidden content and the impossible question.
"Meditation is a way of putting aside altogether
everything that man has conceived of himself
and the world." A radical revolution in one
affects the whole world. What takes place when
the mind is quiet? "Meditation is . . . seeing the
measure and going beyond the measure." Harmony and a "totally different life".
QUESTIONS: Intuition; awareness; awareness and
sleep; teacher and disciple.

Part X
A Discussion with a small group at Brockwood

Does change imply violence? To what extent do
we reject violence? Violence and energy: observing violence. What is the root of violence? Understanding the "me"; the "me" that wants to
change is violent. Does the "me" or intelligence
see? The implications of *seeing*.

Part XI
Conversation:
J. Krishnamurti and Professor David Bohm

Thought is of the order of time; intelligence is of
a different order, different quality. Is intelligence
related to thought? Brain the instrument of intelligence; thought as a pointer. Thought, not
intelligence, dominates the world.

Problem of thought and the awakening of intelligence. Intelligence operating in a limited framework can serve highly unintelligent purposes.

Matter, thought, intelligence have a common source, are one energy; why did it divide? Security and survival: thought cannot consider death properly.

"Can the mind keep the purity of the original source?" Problem of the quietening of thought. Insight, the perception of the whole, is necessary. Communication without the interference of the conscious mind.

LIST OF ILLUSTRATIONS

Photographs by Mark Edwards

Plates following page 244

At Rishi Valley, January 1970
Krishnamurti talking to students at Rajghat School, December 1969
Talking at Rishi Valley School, January 1970
View of Rishi Valley
View of Saanen and Gstaad, Switzerland
Outside the Conference Tent at Saanen, July 1968
Talking to students and staff at Brockwood Park, October 1972
View of Brockwood Park, Hampshire, England
With students at Brockwood Park, October 1972
Krishnamurti, *Photograph by Cecil Beaton*
At Saanen, Summer 1968
Krishnamurti, Saanen, Summer 1968
Talking at Brockwood, October 1972
Krishnamurti, June 1972
Talking to students and staff at Brockwood Park, October 1972

THE AWAKENING OF
INTELLIGENCE

AMERICA

I

Two Conversations:
J. Krishnamurti and Professor Jacob Needleman

1

THE ROLE OF THE TEACHER

*Conversation between J. Krishnamurti
and Professor J. Needleman*

Needleman.[1] There is much talk of a spiritual revolution among young people, particularly here in California. Do you see in this very mixed phenomenon any hope of a new flowering for modern civilisation, a new possibility of growth?

KRISHNAMURTI: For a new possibility of growth, don't you think, Sir, that one has to be rather serious, and not merely jump from one spectacular amusement to another? If one has looked at all the religions of the world and seen their organised futility, and out of that perception seen something real and clear, perhaps then there could be something new in California, or in the world. But as far as I have seen, I am afraid there is not a quality of seriousness in all this. I may be mistaken, because I see only these so-called young people in the distance, among the audience, and occasionally here; and by their questions, by their laughter, by their applause, they don't strike me as being very serious, mature, with great intent. I may be mistaken, naturally.

Needleman: I understand what you are saying. My question only is: perhaps we can't very well expect young people to be serious.

KRISHNAMURTI: That is why I don't think it is applicable to the young people. I don't know why one has made such an extraordinary thing out of young people, why it has be-

[1] Jacob Needleman is Professor of philosophy at San Francisco State College; author of *The New Religions*, and editor of the Penguin Metaphysical Library.

3

come such an important thing. In a few years they will be the old people in their turn.

Needleman: As a phenomenon, apart from what is underneath it all, this interest in transcending experience—or whatever one wants to call it—seems to be a kind of seedground from which certain unusual people aside from all the phoneyness and all the deceivers, certain Masters perhaps, may spring up.

KRISHNAMURTI: But I am not sure, Sir, that all the deceivers and exploiters are not covering this up. "Krishnaconsciousness" and Transcendental Meditation and all this nonsense that is going on—they are caught in all that. It is a form of exhibitionism, a form of amusement and entertainment. For something new to take place there must be a nucleus of really devoted, serious people, who go through to the very end. After going through all these things, they say, "Here is something I am going to pursue to the end."

Needleman: A serious person would be someone who would have to become disillusioned with everything else.

KRISHNAMURTI: I would not call it disillusioned but a form of seriousness.

Needleman: But a pre-condition for it?

KRISHNAMURTI: No, I wouldn't call it disillusionment at all, that leads to despair and cynicism. I mean the examination of all the things that are so-called religious, so-called spiritual: to examine, to find out what is the truth in all this, whether there is any truth in it. Or to discard the whole thing and start anew, and not go through all the trappings, all the mess of it.

Needleman: I think that is what I tried to say, but this expresses it better. People who have tried something and it has failed for them.

KRISHNAMURTI: Not "other people". I mean one has to discard all the promises, all the experiences, all the mystical assertions. I think one has to start as though one knew absolutely nothing.

4

Needleman: That is very hard.

KRISHNAMURTI: No, Sir, I don't think that is hard. I think it is hard only for those people who have filled themselves with other people's knowledge.

Needleman: Isn't that most of us? I was speaking to my class yesterday at San Francisco State, and I said I was going to interview Krishnamurti and what question would you like me to ask him. They had many questions, but the one that touched me most was what one young man said: "I have read his books over and over again and I can't *do* what he says." There was something so clear about that, it rang a bell. It seems in a certain subtle sense to begin in this way. To be a beginner, fresh!

KRISHNAMURTI: I don't think that we question enough. Do you know what I mean?

Needleman: Yes.

KRISHNAMURTI: We accept, we are gullible, we are greedy for new experiences. People swallow what is said by anybody with a beard, with promises, saying you will have a marvellous experience if you do certain things! I think one has to say: "I know nothing." Obviously I can't rely on others. If there were no books, no gurus, what would you do?

Needleman: But one is so easily deceived.

KRISHNAMURTI: You are deceived when you want something.

Needleman: Yes, I understand that.

KRISHNAMURTI: So you say, "I am going to find out, I am going to enquire step by step. I don't want to deceive myself." Deception arises when I want, when I am greedy, when I say, "All experience is shallow, I want something mysterious"—then I am caught.

Needleman: To me you are speaking about a state, an attitude, an approach, which is itself very far along in understanding for a man. I feel very far from that myself,

5

and I know my students do. And so they feel, rightly or wrongly, a need for help. They probably misunderstand what help is, but is there such a thing as help?

KRISHNAMURTI: Would you say: "Why do you ask for help?"

Needleman: Let me put it like this. You sort of smell yourself deceiving yourself, you don't exactly know . . .

KRISHNAMURTI: It is fairly simple. I don't want to deceive myself—right? So I find out what is the movement, what is the thing that brings deception. Obviously it is when I am greedy, when I want something, when I am dissatisfied. So instead of attacking greed, want, dissatisfaction, I want something more.

Needleman: Yes.

KRISHNAMURTI: So I have to understand my greed. What am I greedy for: Is it because I am fed up with this world, I have had women, I have had cars, I have had money and I want something more?

Needleman: I think one is greedy because one desires stimulation, to be taken out of oneself, so that one doesn't see the poverty of oneself. But what I am trying to ask—I know you have answered this question many times in your talks, but it keeps recurring, almost unavoidably—the great traditions of the world, aside from what has become of them (they have become distorted and misinterpreted and deceptive) always speak directly or indirectly of help. They say "The guru is yourself too", but at the same time there is help.

KRISHNAMURTI: Sir, you know what that word "guru" means?

Needleman: No, not exactly.

KRISHNAMURTI: The one who points. That is one meaning. Another meaning is the one who brings enlightenment, lifts your burden. But instead of lifting your burden they impose their burden on you.

6

Needleman: I am afraid so.

KRISHNAMURTI: Guru also means one who helps you to cross over—and so on, there are various meanings. The moment the guru says he knows, then you may be sure he doesn't know. Because what he knows is something past, obviously. Knowledge is the past. And when he says he knows, he is thinking of some experience which he has had, which he has been able to recognise as something great, and that recognition is born out of his previous knowledge, otherwise he couldn't recognise it, and therefore his experience has its roots in the past. Therefore it is not real.

Needleman: Well, I think that most knowledge is that.

KRISHNAMURTI: So why do we want any form of ancient or modern tradition in all this? Look, Sir, I don't read any religious, philosophical, psychological books: one can go into oneself at tremendous depths and find out everything. To go into oneself is the problem, how to do it. Not being able to do it one asks, "Would you please help me?"

Needleman: Yes.

KRISHNAMURTI: And the other fellow says, "I'll help you" and pushes you off somewhere else.

Needleman: Well, it sort of answers the question. I was reading a book the other day which spoke of something called "Sat-san."

KRISHNAMURTI: Do you know what it means?

Needleman: Association with the wise.

KRISHNAMURTI: No, with good people.

Needleman: With good people, Ah!

KRISHNAMURTI: Being good you are wise. Not, being wise you are good.

Needleman: I understand that.

7

KRISHNAMURTI: Because you are good, you are wise.

Needleman: I am not trying to pin this down to something, but I find my students and I myself, speaking for myself when we read, when we hear you, we say, "Ah! I need no one, I need to be with no one"—and there is a tremendous deception in this too.

KRISHNAMURTI: Naturally, because you are being influenced by the speaker.

Needleman: Yes. This is true. (*Laughter.*)

KRISHNAMURTI: Sir, look, let's be very simple. Suppose, if there were no book, no guru, no teacher, what would you do? One is in turmoil, confusion, agony, what would you do? With nobody to help you, no drugs, no tranquillisers, no organised religions, what would you do?

Needleman: I can't imagine what I would do.

KRISHNAMURTI: That's it.

Needleman: Perhaps there would be a moment of urgency there.

KRISHNAMURTI: That's it. We haven't the urgency because we say, "Well, somebody is going to help me."

Needleman: But most people would be driven insane by that situation.

KRISHNAMURTI: I am not sure, Sir.

Needleman: I'm not sure either.

KRISHNAMURTI: No, I am not at all sure. Because what have we done up to now? The people on whom we have relied, the religions, the churches, education, they have led us to this awful mess. We aren't free of sorrow, we aren't free of our beastliness, our ugliness, our vanities.

Needleman: Can one say that of all of them? There are differences. For every thousand deceivers there is one Buddha.

8

KRISHNAMURTI: But that is not my concern. Sir, if we say that it leads to such deception. No, no.

Needleman: Then let me ask you this. We know that without hard work the body may get ill, and this hard work is what we call effort. Is there another effort for what we might call the spirit? You speak against effort, but does not the growth and well-being of all sides of man demand something like hard work of one sort or another?

KRISHNAMURTI: I wonder what you meant by hard work? Physical hard work?

Needleman: That is what we usually mean by hard work. Or going against desires.

KRISHNAMURTI: You see, there we are! Our conditioning, our culture, is built around this "going against". Erecting a wall of resistance. So when we say "hard work", what do we mean? Laziness? Why have I to make an effort about anything? Why?

Needleman: Because I wish for something.

KRISHNAMURTI: No. Why is there this cult of effort? Why have I to make effort to reach God, enlightenment, truth?

Needleman: There are many possible answers, but I can only answer for myself.

KRISHNAMURTI: It may be just there, only I don't know how to look.

Needleman: But then there must be an obstacle.

KRISHNAMURTI: How to look! It may be just round the corner, under the flower, it may be anywhere. So first I have to learn to look, not make an effort to look. I must find out what it means to look.

Needleman: Yes, but don't you admit that there may be a resistance to that looking?

9

KRISHNAMURTI: Then don't bother to look! If somebody comes along and says, "I don't want to look", how are you going to force him to look?

Needleman: No. I am speaking about myself now. I want to look.

KRISHNAMURTI: If you want to look, what do you mean by looking? You must find out what it means to look before you make an effort to look. Right, Sir?

Needleman: That would be, to me, an effort.

KRISHNAMURTI: No.

Needleman: To do it in that delicate, subtle way. I wish to look, but I don't wish to find out what it means to look. I agree this is much more to me the basic thing. But this wish to do it quickly, to get it over, is this not resistance?

KRISHNAMURTI: Quick medicine to get it over.

Needleman: Is there something in me that I have to study, that resists this subtle, much more delicate thing you are speaking about? Is this not work, what you are saying? Isn't it work to ask the question so quietly, so subtly? It seems to me it is work to *not* listen to that part that wants to do it . . .

KRISHNAMURTI: Quickly.

Needleman: For us particularly in the West, or maybe for all men.

KRISHNAMURTI: I am afraid it is all over the world the same. "Tell me how to get there quickly."

Needleman: And yet you say it is in a moment.

KRISHNAMURTI: It is, obviously.

Needleman: Yes, I understand.

KRISHNAMURTI: Sir, what is effort? To get out of bed in the morning, when you don't want to get up, is an effort.

10

What brings on that laziness? Lack of sleep, over-eating, over-indulging and all the rest of it; and the next morning you say, "Oh, what a bore, I have to get up!" Now wait a minute, Sir, follow it. What is laziness? Is it physical laziness, or is thought itself lazy?

Needleman: That I don't understand. I need another word. "Thought is lazy?" I find that thought is always the same.

KRISHNAMURTI: No Sir. I am lazy, I don't want to get up and so I force myself to get up. In that is so-called effort.

Needleman: Yes.

KRISHNAMURTI: I want that, but I shouldn't have it, I resist it. The resistance is effort. I get angry and I mustn't be angry: resistance, effort. What has made me lazy?

Needleman: The thought that I ought to be getting up.

KRISHNAMURTI: That's it.

Needleman: All right.

KRISHNAMURTI: So I really have to go into this whole question of thought. Not make out that the body is lazy, force the body out of bed, because the body has its own intelligence, it knows when it is tired and should rest. This morning I was tired; I had prepared the mat and everything to do yoga exercises and the body said "No, sorry". And I said, "All right". That is not laziness. The body said, "Leave me alone because you talked yesterday, you saw many people, you are tired." Thought then says, "You must get up and do the exercises because it is good for you, you have done it every day, it has become a habit, don't relax, you will get lazy, keep at it." Which means: thought is making me lazy, not the body is making me lazy.

Needleman: I understand that. So there is an effort with regard to thought.

KRISHMURTI: So no effort! Why is thought so mechanical? And is all thought mechanical?

11

Needleman: Yes, all right, one puts that question.

KRISHNAMURTI: Isn't it?

Needleman: I can't say that I have verified that.

KRISHNAMURTI: But we can, Sir. That is fairly simple to see. Isn't all thought mechanical? The non-mechanical state is the absence of thought; not the neglect of thought but the absence of it.

Needleman: How can I find that out?

KRISHNAMURTI: Do it now, it is simple enough. You can do it now if you wish to. Thought is mechanical.

Needleman: Let's assume that.

KRISHNAMURTI: Not assume. Don't assume anything.

Needleman: All right.

KRISHNAMURTI: Thought is mechanical, isn't it?—because it is repetitive, conforming, comparing.

Needleman: That part I see, the comparing. But my experience is that not all thought is of the same quality. There are qualities of thought.

KRISHNAMURTI: Are there?

Needleman: In my experience there are.

KRISHNAMURTI: Let's find out. What is thought, thinking?

Needleman: There seems to be thought that is very shallow, very repetitive, very mechanical, it has a certain taste to it. There seems to be another kind of thought which is connected more with my body, with my whole self, it resonates in another way.

KRISHNAMURTI: That is what, Sir? Thought is the response of memory.

Needleman: All right, this is a definition.

12

KRISHNAMURTI: No, no, I can see it in myself. I have to go to that house this evening—the memory, the distance, the design—all that is memory, isn't it?

Needleman: Yes, that is memory.

KRISHNAMURTI: I have been there before and so the memory is well established and from that there is either instant thought, or thought which takes a little time. So I am asking myself: is all thought similar, mechanical, or is there thought which is non-mechanical, which is non-verbal?

Needleman: Yes. thats right.

KRISHNAMURTI: Is there thought if there is no word?

Needleman: There is understanding.

KRISHNAMURTI: What, Sir. How does this understanding take place? Does it happen when thought is functioning rapidly, or when thought is quiet?

Needleman: When thought is quiet, yes.

KRISHNAMURTI: Understanding is nothing to do with thought. You may reason, which is the process of thinking, logic, till you say, "I don't understand it"; then you become silent, and you say, "Ah, I see it, I understand it." That understanding is not a result of thought.

Needleman: You speak of an energy which seems to be uncaused. We experience the energy of cause and effect, which shapes our lives, but what is this other energy's relationship to the energy we are familiar with? What is energy?

KRISHNAMURTI: First of all: is energy divisible?

Needleman: I don't know. Go on.

KRISHNAMURTI: It can be divided. Physical energy, the energy of anger and so on, cosmic energy, human energy, it can all be divided. But it is all one energy, isn't it?

13

Needleman: Logically, I say yes. I don't understand energy. Sometimes I experience the thing which I call energy.

KRISHNAMURTI: Why do we divide energy at all, that is what I want to get at; then we can come to it differently. Sexual energy, physical energy, mental energy, psychological energy, cosmic energy, the energy of the businessman who goes to the office and so on—why do we divide it? What is the reason for this division?

Needleman: There seem to be many parts of oneself which are separate; and we divide life, it seems to me, because of that.

KRISHNAMURTI: Why? We have divided the world into Communist, Socialist, Imperialist, and Catholic, Protestant, Hindu, Buddhist, and nationalities, linguistic divisions, the whole thing is fragmentation. Why has the mind fragmented the whole of life?

Needleman: I don't know the answer. I see the ocean and I see a tree: there is a division.

KRISHNAMURTI: No. There is a difference between the sea and the tree—I hope so! But that is not a division.

Needleman: No. It is a difference, not a division.

KRISHNAMURTI: But we are asking why the division exists, not only outwardly but in us.

Needleman: It is in us, that is the most interesting question.

KRISHNAMURTI: Because it is in us we extend it outwards. Now why is there this division in me? The "me" and the "not me". You follow? The higher and the lower, the Atman and the lower self. Why this division?

Needleman: Maybe it was done, at least in the beginning, to help men to question themselves. To make them question whether they really know what they think they know.

KRISHNAMURTI: Through division will they find out?

14

Needleman: Maybe through the idea that there is something that I don't understand.

KRISHNAMURTI: In a human being there is a division—why? What is the "raison d'être", what is the structure of this division? I see there is a thinker and thought—right?

Needleman: I don't see that.

KRISHNAMURTI: There is a thinker who says, "I must control that thought, I must not think this, I must think that". So there is a thinker who says, "I must", or "I must not".

Needleman: Right.

KRISHNAMURTI: There is a division. "I should be this", and "I should not be that". If I can understand why this division in me exists—Oh look, look! Look at those hills! Marvellous, isn't it?

Needleman: Beautiful!

KRISHNAMURTI: Now, Sir, do you look at it with a division?

Needleman: No.

KRISHNAMURTI: Why not?

Needleman: There wasn't the "me" to do anything with it.

KRISHNAMURTI: That's all. You can't do anything about it. Here, with thought, I think I can do something.

Needleman: Yes.

KRISHNAMURTI: So I want to change "what is". I can't change "what is" there, but I think I can change "what is" in me. Not knowing how to change it I have become desperate, lost, in despair. I say, "I can't change", and therefore I have no energy to change.

Needleman: That's what one says.

15

KRISHNAMURTI: So first, before I change "what is", I must know who is the changer, who it is that changes.

Needleman: There are moments when one knows that, for a moment. Those moments are lost. There are moments when one knows who sees "what is" in oneself.

KRISHNAMURTI: No sir. Sorry. Just to see "what is" is enough, not to change it.

Needleman: I agree. I agree with that.

KRISHNAMURTI: I can see "what is" only when the observer is not. When you looked at those hills the observer was not.

Needleman: I agree, yes.

KRISHNAMURTI: The observer only came into being when you wanted to change "what is". You say: I don't like "what is", it must be changed, so there is instantly a duality. Can the mind observe "what is" without the observer? It took place when you looked at those hills with that marvellous light on them.

Needleman: This truth is absolute truth. The moment one experiences it one says, "Yes!" But one's experience is also that one forgets this.

KRISHNAMURTI: Forget!

Needleman: By that I mean one continually tries to change it.

KRISHNAMURTI: Forget it, and pick it up again.

Needleman: But in this discussion—whatever you intend— there is help coming from this discussion. I know, as much as I know anything, it could not happen without the help that is between us. I could look at those hills and maybe have this non-judging, but it wouldn't be important to me; I wouldn't know that *that* is the way I must look for salvation. And this, I think, is a question one always wants to bring. Maybe this is the mind again wanting to grab and hold on to something, but nevertheless it seems that the human condition . . .

KRISHNAMURTI: Sir, we looked at those hills, you couldn't change that, you just looked; and you looked inwardly and the battle began. For a moment you looked without that battle, without that strife, and all the rest of it. Then you remembered the beauty of that moment, of that second, and you wanted to capture that beauty again. Wait Sir! Proceed. So what happens? It sets up another conflict: the thing you had and you would like to have again, and you don't know how to get it again. You know, if you think about it, it is not the same, it is not that. So you strive, battle. "I must control, I mustn't want"—right? Whereas if you say, "All right, it is over, finished", that moment is over.

Needleman: I have to learn that.

KRISHNAMURTI: No, no.

Needleman: I have to learn, don't I?

KRISHNAMURTI: What is there to learn?

Needleman: I have to learn the futility of this conflict.

KRISHNAMURTI: No. What is there to learn? You yourself see that that moment of beauty becomes a memory, then the memory says, "It was so beautiful I must have it again." You are not concerned with beauty, you are concerned with the pursuit of pleasure. Pleasure and beauty don't go together. So if you see that, it is finished. Like a dangerous snake, you won't go near it again.

Needleman: (Laughs) Perhaps I haven't seen it, so I can't say.

KRISHNAMURTI: That is the question.

Needleman: Yes, I think that must be so, because one keeps going back again and again.

KRISHNAMURTI: No. This is the real thing. If I see the beauty of that light, and it is really extraordinarily beautiful, I just see it. Now with that same quality of attention I want to see myself. There is a moment of perception which is as beautiful as that. Then what happens?

Needleman: Then I wish for it.

KRISHNAMURTI: Then I want to capture it, I want to cultivate it, I want to pursue it.

Needleman: And how to see that?

KRISHNAMURTI: Just to see that is taking place is enough.

Needleman: That's what I forget!

KRISHNAMURTI: It is not a question of forgetting.

Needleman: Well, that is what I don't understand deeply enough. That just the seeing is enough.

KRISHNAMURTI: Look, Sir. When you see a snake what takes place?

Needleman: I am afraid.

KRISHNAMURTI: No. What takes place? You run, kill it, do something. Why? Because you know it is dangerous. You are aware of the danger of it. A cliff, better take a cliff, an abyss. You know the danger of it. Nobody has to tell you. You see directly what would happen.

Needleman: Right.

KRISHNAMURTI: Now, if you see directly that the beauty of that moment of perception cannot be repeated, it is over. But thought says, "No, it's not over, the memory of it remains." So what are you doing now? You are pursuing the dead memory of it, not the living beauty of it—right? Now if you see that, the truth of it—not the verbal statement, the truth of it—it is finished.

Needleman: Then the seeing is much rarer than we think.

KRISHNAMURTI: If I see the beauty of that minute, it is over. I don't want to pursue it. If I pursue it, it becomes a pleasure. Then if I can't get it, it brings despair, pain and all the rest of it. So I say, "All right, finished." Then what takes place?

Needleman: From my experience, I'm afraid that what takes place is that the monster is born again. It has a thousand lives. *(Laughter.)*

KRISHNAMURTI: No Sir. When did that beauty take place?

Needleman: The place when I saw without trying to change.

KRISHNAMURTI: When the mind was completely quiet.

Needleman: Yes.

KRISHNAMURTI: Wasn't it? Right?

Needleman: Yes.

KRISHNAMURTI: When you looked at that, your mind was quiet, it didn't say, "I wish I could change it, copy it and photograph it, this, that, and the other"—you just looked. The mind wasn't in operation. Or rather, thought wasn't in operation. But thought comes immediately into operation. Now one has asked, "How can thought be quiet? How can one exercise thought when necessary, and not exercise it when it is not necessary?"

Needleman: Yes, that question is intensely interesting to me, Sir.

KRISHNAMURTI: That is, why do we worship thought? Why has thought become so extraordinarily important?

Needleman: It seems able to satisfy our desires; through thought we believe we can satisfy.

KRISHNAMURTI: No, not from satisfaction. Why has thought in all cultures with most people become of such vital concern.

19

Needleman: One usually identifies oneself as thought, as one's thoughts. If I think about myself I think about what I think, what kind of ideas I have, what I believe. Is this what you mean?

KRISHNAMURTI: Not quite. Apart from identification with the "me", or with "not me", why is thought always active?

Needleman: Ah. I see.

KRISHNAMURTI: Thought is always operating in knowledge, isn't it? If there was no knowledge, thought would not be. Thought is always operating in the field of the known. Whether mechanical, non-verbal and so on, it is always working in the past. So my life is the past, because it is based on past knowledge, past experience, past memories, pleasure, pain, fear and so on—it is all the past. And the future I project from the past, thought projects from the past. So thought is fluctuating between the past and the future. All the time it says, "I should do this, I should not do that, I should have behaved." Why is it doing all this?

Needleman: I don't know. Habit?

KRISHNAMURTI: Habit. All right. Go on. Let's find out. Habit?

Needleman: Habit brings what I call pleasure.

KRISHNAMURTI: Habit, pleasure, pain.

Needleman: To protect me. Pain, yes pain.

KRISHNAMURTI: It is always working within that field. Why?

Needleman: Because it doesn't know any better.

KRISHNAMURTI: No. No. Can thought work in any other field?

Needleman: That sort of thought, no.

20

KRISHNAMURTI: No, not any thought. Can thought work in any other field except in the field of the known?

Needleman: No.

KRISHNAMURTI: Obviously not. It can't work in something I don't know; it can only work in this field. Now why does it work in this? There it is, Sir—why? It is the only thing I know. In that there is security, there is protection, there is safety. That is all I know. So thought can only function in the field of the known. And when it gets tired of that, as it does, then it seeks something outside. Then what it seeks is still the known. Its gods, its visions, its spiritual state—all projected out of the known past into the future known. So thought always works in this field.

Needleman: Yes, I see.

KRISHNAMURTI: Therefore thought is always working in a prison. It can call it freedom, it can call it beauty, it can call it what it likes! But it is always within the limitations of the barbed-wire fence. Now I want to find out whether thought has any place except in there. Thought has no place when I say, "I don't know." "I really don't know." Right?

Needleman: For the moment.

KRISHNAMURTI: I really don't know. I only know this, and I really don't know whether thought can function in any field at all, except this. I really don't know. When I say, "I don't know", which doesn't mean I am expecting to know, when I say I really don't know—what happens? I climb down the ladder. I become, the mind becomes, completely humble.

Now that state of "not knowing" is intelligence. Then it can operate in the field of the known and be free to work somewhere else if it wants to.

MALIBU, CALIFORNIA
26 MARCH 1971

2

ON INNER SPACE; ON TRADITION
AND DEPENDENCE

*Conversation between J. Krishnamurti
and Professor J. Needleman*

Needleman: In your talks you have given a fresh meaning
to the necessity for man to become his own authority. Yet
cannot this assertion easily be turned into a form of hu-
manistic psychology without reference to the sacred, tran-
scendent dimension of human life on earth in the midst of
a vast intelligent Cosmos? Must we not only try to see
ourselves in the moment, but also as creatures of the Cosmos? What I am trying to ask about is this question of
cosmic dimension.

KRISHNAMURTI: As soon as we use that word "dimension", it implies space, otherwise there is no dimension,
there is no space. Are we talking about space, outward
space, endless space?

Needleman: No.

KRISHNAMURTI: Or the dimension of space in us?

Needleman: It would have to be the latter, but not totally
without the former, I think.

KRISHNAMURTI: Is there a difference between the outer
space, which is limitless, and the space in us? Or is there
no space in us at all and we only know the outer space?
We know the space in us as a centre and circumference.
The dimension of that centre, and the radius from that
centre, is what we generally call that space.

Needleman: Inner space, yes.

KRISHNAMURTI: Yes, inner space. Now if there is a centre, the space must always be limited and therefore we divide the inner space from the outer space.

Needleman: Yes.

KRISHNAMURTI: We only know this very limited space but we think we would like to reach the other space, have immense space. This house exists in space, otherwise there could be no house, and the four walls of this room make its space. And the space in me is the space which the centre has created round itself. Like that microphone ...

Needleman: Yes, centre of interest.

KRISHNAMURTI: Not only centre of interest, it has its own space, otherwise it couldn't exist.

Needleman: Yes, right.

KRISHNAMURTI: In the same way, human beings may have a centre and from that centre they create a space, the centre creates a space round itself. And that space is always limited, it must be; because of the centre, the space is limited.

Needleman: It is defined, it is a defined space, yes.

KRISHNAMURTI: When you use the words "cosmic space" ...

Needleman: I didn't use the words "cosmic space"; I said cosmic, the dimension of the Cosmos. I wasn't asking about outer space and trips to the planets.

KRISHNAMURTI: So we are talking of the space which the centre creates round itself, and also a space between two thoughts; there is a space, an interval between two thoughts.

Needleman: Yes.

KRISHNAMURTI: And the centre having created that space round itself, there is a space outside the limit. There is a space between thinking, between thoughts; and also a space round the centre itself, and the space beyond the barbed-wire. Now what is the question, Sir? How to expand space? How to enter a different dimension of space?

Needleman: Not how to but ...

KRISHNAMURTI: ... not how to. Is there a different dimension of space except the space round the centre?

Needleman: Or a different dimension of reality?

KRISHNAMURTI: Space, we are talking about that for the moment, we can use that word. First I must see very clearly the space between two thoughts.

Needleman: The interval.

KRISHNAMURTI: This interval between two thoughts. Interval means space. And what takes place in this interval?

Needleman: Well. I confess I don't know because my thoughts overlap all the time. I know there are intervals, there are moments when this interval appears, and I see it, and there is freedom there for a moment.

KRISHNAMURTI: Let's go into this a bit, shall we? There is space between two thoughts. And there is space which the centre creates round itself, which is the space of isolation.

Needleman: All right yes. That is a cold word.

KRISHNAMURTI: It is cutting itself off. I consider myself important, with my ambition, with my frustrations, with my anger, with my sexuality, my growth, my meditation, my reaching Nirvana.

Needleman: Yes, that is isolation.

KRISHNAMURTI: It is isolation. My relation with you is the image of that isolation, which is that space. Then having created that space there is space outside the barbed-wire. Now is there a space of a totally different dimension? That is the question.

24

Needleman: Yes, that embraces the question.

KRISHNAMURTI: How shall we find out if the space round me, round the centre, exists? And how can I find out the other? I can speculate about the other, I can invent any space I like—but that is too abstract, too silly!

Needleman: Yes.

KRISHNAMURTI: So is it possible to be free of the centre, so that the centre doesn't create space round itself, build a wall round itself, isolation, a prison—and call that space? Can that centre cease to be? Otherwise I can't go beyond it; the mind cannot go beyond that limitation.

Needleman: Yes, I see what you mean. It's logical, reasonable.

KRISHNAMURTI: That is, what is that centre? That centre is the "me" and "non-me", that centre is the observer, the thinker, the experiencer, and in that centre is also the observed. The centre says, "That is the barbed-wire I have created round myself."

Needleman: So that centre is limited there too.

KRISHNAMURTI: Yes. Therefore it separates itself from the barbed-wire fence. So that becomes the observed. The centre is the observer. So there is space between the observer and the observed—right Sir?

Needleman: Yes, I see that.

KRISHNAMURTI: And that space it tries to bridge over. That is what we are doing.

Needleman: It tries to bridge it over.

KRISHNAMURTI: It says, "This must be changed, that must not be, this is narrow, that is wide, I must be better than that." All that is the movement in the space between the observer and the observed.

Needleman: I follow that, yes.

KRISHNAMURTI: And hence there is conflict between the observer and the observed. Because the observed is the barbed-wire which must be jumped over, and so the battle begins. Now can the observer—who is the centre, who is the thinker, who is the knower, who is experience, who is knowledge—can that centre be still?

Needleman: Why should it wish to?

KRISHNAMURTI: If it is not still, the space is always limited.

Needleman: But the centre, the observer, doesn't know that it is limited in this way.

KRISHNAMURTI: But you can see it, look. The centre is the observer, let's call him the observer for the moment— the thinker, the experiencer, the knower, the struggler, the searcher, the one who says. "I know, and you don't know." Right? Where there is a centre it must have a space round itself.

Needleman: Yes, I follow.

KRISHNAMURTI: And when it observes, it observes through that space. When I observe those mountains there is space between me and the mountains. And when I observe myself there is space between me and the thing I observe in myself. When I observe my wife, I observe her from the centre of my image about her, and she observes me with the image which she has about me. So there is always this division and space.

Needleman: Changing the approach to the subject entirely, there is something called the sacred. Sacred teachings, sacred ideas, the sacred, which for a moment seems to show me that this centre and this space you speak about is an illusion.

KRISHNAMURTI: Wait. One has learnt this from somebody else. Are we going to find out what is the sacred, then? Are we looking because somebody has told me, "That is sacred", or that there is a sacred thing? Or is it my imagination, because I want something holy?

26

Needleman: Very often it is that but there is ...

KRISHNAMURTI: Now which is it? The desire for something holy? The imposition on my mind by others who have said, "This is sacred?" Or my own desire, because everything is unholy and I want something holy, sacred? All this springs from the centre.

Needleman: Yes. Nevertheless ...

KRISHNAMURTI: Wait. We will find this out, what is sacred. But I don't want to accept tradition, or what somebody has said about the sacred. Sir, I don't know if you have experimented? Some years ago, for fun, I took a piece of rock from the garden and put it on the mantelpiece and played with it, brought flowers to it every day. At the end of a month it became terribly sacred!

Needleman: I know what you mean.

KRISHNAMURTI: I don't want that kind of phoney sacredness.

Needleman: It's a fetish.

KRISHNAMURTI: Sacredness is a fetish.

Needleman: Granted. Most of it is.

KRISHNAMURTI: So I won't accept anything that anybody says about what is sacred. Tradition! As a Brahmin one was brought up in a tradition which would beat anybody's tradition, I assure you!

What I am saying is: I want to find out what is holy, not man-made holiness. I can only find out when the mind has immense space. And it cannot have that immense space if there is a centre. When the centre is not in operation, then there is vast space. In that space, which is part of meditation, there is something really sacred, not invented by my foolish little centre. There is something immeasurably sacred, which you can never find out if there is a centre. And to imagine that sacredness is folly—you follow what I mean?

Can the mind be free of this centre—with its terribly limited yardage of space—which can be measured and expanded and contracted and all the rest of it? Can it? Man has said it can't, and therefore God has become another centre. So my real concern is this: whether the centre can be completely empty? That centre is consciousness. That centre is the content of consciousness, the content *is* consciousness; there is no consciousness, if there is no content. You must work this out ...

Needleman: Certainly what we ordinarily mean by it, yes.

KRISHNAMURTI: There is no house if there are no walls and no roof. The content is consciousness but we like to separate them, theorise about it, measure the yardage of our consciousness. Whereas the centre is consciousness, the content of consciousness, and the content is consciousness. Without the content, where is consciousness? And that is the space.

Needleman: I follow a little bit of what you say. I find myself wanting to say: well, what do you value here? What is the important thing here?

KRISHNAMURTI: I'll put that question after I have found out whether the mind can be empty of the content.

Needleman: All right.

KRISHNAMURTI: Then there is something else that will operate, which will function within the field of the known. But without finding that merely to say ...

Needleman: No, no, this is so.

KRISHNAMURTI: Let's proceed. Space is between two thoughts, between two factors of time, two periods of time, because thought is time. Yes?

Needleman: All right, yes.

KRISHNAMURTI: You can have a dozen periods of time but it is still thought, there is that space. Then there is the space round the centre, and the space beyond the self, beyond the barbed-wire, beyond the wall of the centre. The space between the observer and the observed is the space

28

which thought has created as the image of my wife and the image which she has about me. You follow, Sir?

Needleman: Yes.

KRISHNAMURTI: All that is manufactured by the centre. To speculate about what is beyond all that has no meaning to me personally, it's the philosopher's amusement.

Needleman: The philosopher's amusement ...

KRISHNAMURTI: I am not interested.

Needleman: I agree. I am not interested sometimes, at my better moments, but nevertheless ...

KRISHNAMURTI: I am sorry, because you are a philosopher!

Needleman: No, no, why should you remember that, please.

KRISHNAMURTI: So my question is: "Can the centre be still, or can the centre fade away?" Because if it doesn't fade away, or lie very quiet, then the content of consciousness is going to create space within consciousness and call it the vast space. In that there lies deception and I don't want to deceive myself. I don't say I am not brown when I am brown. So can that centre be absorbed? Which means, can there be no image, because it is the image that separates?

Needleman: Yes, that is the space.

KRISHNAMURTI: That image talks about love, but the love of the image is not love. Therefore I must find out whether the centre can be completely absorbed, dissolved, or lie as a vague fragment in the distance. If there is no possibility of that, then I must accept prison.

Needleman: I agree.

KRISHNAMURTI: I must accept there is no freedom. Then I can decorate my prison for ever.

Needleman: But now this possibility that you are speaking about, without searching for it consciously ...

KRISHNAMURTI: No, don't search for it!

Needleman: I say, without searching for it consciously, life or something suddenly shows me it is possible.

KRISHNAMURTI: It is there! Life hasn't shown me. It has shown me, when I look at that mountain, that there is an image in me; when I look at my wife I see that there is an image in me. That is a fact. It isn't that I have to wait for ten years to find out about the image! I know it is there, therefore I say: "Is it possible to look without the image?" The image is the centre, the observer, the thinker and all the rest of it.

Needleman: I am beginning to see the answer to my question. I begin to see—I am speaking to myself—I am beginning to see that there is no distinction between humanism and sacred teachings. There is just truth, or non-truth.

KRISHNAMURTI: That's all. False and true.

Needleman: So much for that. (*Laughter*)

KRISHNAMURTI: We are asking: "Can the consciousness empty itself of its content?" Not somebody else do it.

Needleman: That is the question, yes.

KRISHNAMURTI: Not divine grace, the super-self, some fictitious outside agency. Can the consciousness empty itself of all this intent? First see the beauty of it, Sir.

Needleman: I see it.

KRISHNAMURTI: Because it must empty itself without an effort. The moment there is an effort, there is the observer who is making the effort to change the content, which is part of consciousness. I don't know if you see that?

Needleman: I follow. This emptying has to be effortless, instantaneous.

30

KRISHNAMURTI: It must be without an agent who is operating on it, whether an outside agent, or an inner agent. Now can this be done without any effort, any directive—which says, "I will change the content"? This means the emptying of consciousness of all will, "to be" or "not to be". Sir, look what takes place.

Needleman: I am watching.

KRISHNAMURTI: I have put that question to myself. Nobody has put it to me. Because it is a problem of life, a problem of existence in this world. It is a problem which my mind has to solve. Can the mind, with all its content, empty itself and yet remain mind—not just float about?

Needleman: It is not suicide.

KRISHNAMURTI: No.

Needleman: There is some kind of subtle ...

KRISHNAMURTI: No, Sir, that is too immature. I have put the question. My answer is: I really don't know.

Needleman: That is the truth.

KRISHNAMURTI: I really don't know. But I am going to find out, in the sense of not waiting to find out. The content of my consciousness is my unhappiness, my misery, my struggles, my sorrows, the images which I have collected through life, my gods, the frustrations, the pleasures, the fears, the agonies, the hatreds—that is my consciousness. Can all that be completely emptied? Not only at the superficial level but right through?—the so-called unconscious. If it is not possible, then I must live a life of misery, I must live in endless, unending sorrow. There is neither hope, nor despair, I am in prison. So the mind must find out how to empty itself of all the content of itself, and yet live in this world, not become a moron, but have a brain that functions efficiently. Now how is this to be done? Can it ever be done? Or is there no escape for man?

Needleman: I follow.

31

KRISHNAMURTI: Because I don't see how to get beyond this I invent all the gods, temples, philosophies, rituals—you understand?

Needleman: I understand.

KRISHNAMURTI: This is meditation, real meditation, not all the phoney stuff. To see whether the mind—with the brain which has evolved through time, which is the result of thousands of experiences, the brain that functions efficiently only in complete security—whether the mind can empty itself and yet have a brain that functions as a marvellous machine. Also, it sees love is not pleasure; love is not desire. When there is love there is no image; but I don't know what that love is. I only want love as pleasure, sex and all the rest of it. These must be a relationship between the emptying of consciousness and the thing called love; between the unknown and the known, which is the content of consciousness.

Needleman: I am following you. There must be this relationship.

KRISHNAMURTI: The two must be in harmony. The emptying and love must be in harmony. And it may be only love that is necessary and nothing else.

Needleman: This emptying is another word for love, is that what you are saying?

KRISHNAMURTI: I am only asking what is love. Is love within the field of consciousness?

Needleman: No, it couldn't be.

KRISHNAMURTI: Don't stipulate. Don't ever say yes or no; find out! Love within the content of consciousness is pleasure, ambition and all that. Then what is love? I really don't know. I won't pretend any more about anything. I don't know. There is some factor in this which I must find out. Whether the emptying of consiousness with its content is love, which is the unknown? What is the relationship between the unknown and the known?—not the mysterious unknown, God or whatever name you give it. We will come to God if we go through this. The relationship

32

between the unknown, which I don't know, which may be called love, and the content of consciousness, which I know, (it may be unconscious, but I can open it up and find out)—what is the relationship between the known and the unknown? To move between the known and the unknown is harmony, is intelligence, isn't it?

Needleman: Absolutely.

KRISHNAMURTI: So I must find out, the mind must find out, how to empty its content. That is, have no image, therefore no observer. The image means the past, or the image which is taking place now, or the image which I shall project into the future. So no image—no formula, idea, ideal, principle—all that implies image. Can there be no formation of image at all? You hurt me or you give me pleasure and therefore I have an image of you. So no image formation when you hurt me or give me pleasure.

Needleman: Is it possible?

KRISHNAMURTI: Of course it is. Otherwise I am doomed.

Needleman: You are doomed. In other words I am doomed.

KRISHNAMURTI: We are doomed. Is it possible when you insult me to be completely watchful, attentive, so that it doesn't leave a mark?

Needleman: I know what you mean.

KRISHNAMURTI: When you flatter me—no mark. Then there is no image. So I have done it, the mind has done it: which is, no formation of image at all. If you don't form an image now, the past images have no place.

Needleman: I don't follow that. "If I don't form an image now. . . ?"

KRISHNAMURTI: The past images have no place. If you form an image, then you are related to it.

Needleman: You are connected to the past images. That is right.

33

KRISHNAMURTI: But if you don't form any?

Needleman: Then you are free from the past.

KRISHNAMURTI: See it! See it!

Needleman: Very clear.

KRISHNAMURTI: So the mind can empty itself of images by not forming an image now. If I form an image now, then I relate it with past images. So consciousness, the mind, can empty itself of all the images by not forming an image now. Then there is space, not space round the centre. And if one delves, goes into it much further, then there is something sacred, not invented by thought, which has nothing to do with any religion.

Needleman: Thank you.

* * *

Needleman: I have another question which I wanted to ask you. We see the stupidity of so many traditions which people hallow today, but aren't there some traditions transmitted from generation to generation which are valuable and necessary, and without which we would lose the little humanity that we now have? Aren't there traditions that are based on something real, which are handed down?

KRISHNAMURTI: Handed down ...

Needleman: Ways of living, even if only in an external sense.

KRISHNAMURTI: If I hadn't been taught from childhood not to run in front of a car ...

Needleman: That would be the simplest example.

KRISHNAMURTI: Or to be careful of fire, be careful of irritating the dog which might bite you, and so on. That is also tradition.

Needleman: Yes, that certainly is.

KRISHNAMURTI: The other kind of tradition is that you must love.

Needleman: That is the other extreme.

KRISHNAMURTI: And the tradition of the weavers in India and other places. You know, they can weave without a pattern and yet they weave in a tradition which is so deeply rooted that they don't even have to think about it. It comes out with their hands. I don't know if you have ever seen it? In India they have a tremendous tradition and they produce marvellous things. Also there is the tradition of the scientist, the biologist, the anthropologist, which is tradition as the accumulation of knowledge, handed over by one scientist to another scientist, by a doctor to another doctor, learning. Obviously that kind of tradition is essential. I wouldn't call that tradition, would you?

Needleman: No, that is not what I had in mind. What I meant by tradition was a way of living.

KRISHNAMURTI: I wouldn't call that tradition. Don't we mean by tradition some other factor? Is goodness a factor of tradition?

Needleman: No, but perhaps there are good traditions.

KRISHNAMURTI: Good traditions, conditioned by the culture in which one lives. Good tradition among the Brahmins used to be not to kill any human being or animal. They accepted that and functioned. We are saying: "Is goodness traditional? Can goodness function, blossom in tradition?"

Needleman: What I am asking then is: are there traditions which are formed by an intelligence either single, or collective, which understands human nature?

KRISHNAMURTI: Is intelligence traditional?

Needleman: No. But can intelligence form, or shape a way of living which can help other men more readily to find themselves? I know that this is a self-initiated thing that you speak of, but are there not men of great intelligence who can shape the external conditions for me, so that I will not have quite as difficult a time to come to what you have seen?

KRISHNAMURTI: That means what, Sir? You say you know.

Needleman: I don't say I know.

KRISHNAMURTI: I am taking that. Suppose you are the great person of tremendous intelligence and you say, "My dear son, live this way."

Needleman: Well I don't have to say it.

KRISHNAMURTI: You exude your atmosphere, your aura, and then I say, "I'll try it—he has got it, I haven't got it." Can goodness flower in your ambience? Can goodness grow under your shadow?

Needleman: No, but then I wouldn't be intelligent if I made those my conditions.

KRISHNAMURTI: Therefore you are stating that goodness cannot operate, function, flower in any environment.

Needleman: No, I didn't say that. I was asking, are there environments which can be conducive to liberation?

KRISHNAMURTI: We will go into this. A man who goes to a factory every day, day after day, and finds release in drink and all the rest of it . . .

Needleman: This is the example of a poor environment, a bad tradition.

KRISHNAMURTI: So what does the man who is intelligent, who is concerned with changing the environment, do for that man?

Needleman: Perhaps he is changing the environment for himself. But he understands something about man in general. I am talking now about a great teacher, whatever that is. He helps, he presents a way of life to us which we don't understand, which we haven't verified ourselves, but

36

which somehow acts on something in us to bring us a little together.

KRISHNAMURTI: That is *satsun,* which is the company of the good. It is nice to be in the company of the good because we won't then quarrel, we won't fight each other, we won't be violent; it is good.

Needleman: All right. But maybe the company of the good means that I will quarrel, but I'll see it more, I'll suffer it more, I'll understand it better.

KRISHNAMURTI: So you want the company of the good in order to see yourself more clearly?

Needleman: Yes.

KRISHNAMURTI: Which means you depend on the environment to see yourself.

Needleman: Well perhaps in the beginning.

KRISHNAMURTI: The beginning is the first step and the last step.

Needleman: I don't agree.

KRISHNAMURTI: Let's go into it a little bit. See what has happened. I go with good men because in that ambience, in that atmosphere I see myself more clearly, because they are good I see my idiocies.

Needleman: Sometimes it happens that way.

KRISHNAMURTI: I am taking this.

Needleman: That is one example, right?

KRISHNAMURTI: Or I am also good, therefore I live with them. Then I don't need them.

Needleman: No we don't need them then. All right.

KRISHNAMURTI: If I am good I don't need them. But if when I am not good and come into their presence, then I can see myself clearly. Then to see myself clearly I must have them. This is what generally takes place. *They* become important, not my goodness. This happens every day.

Needleman: But is there not such a thing as weaning the baby by blackening the breast? It happens that I do need these men, maybe in the beginning.

KRISHNAMURTI: I am going to question it, I want to find out. First of all, if I am good I don't need them. I am like those hills and birds which have no need.

Needleman: Right. We can rule that out.

KRISHNAMURTI: When I am not good I need their company, because in their company I see myself clearly; I feel a breath of freshness.

Needleman: Or how bad I am.

KRISHNAMURTI: The moment I have a horror of myself, in the largest sense of the word, I am merely comparing myself with them.

Needleman: No, not always. I can expose the image I have of myself as a lie.

KRISHNAMURTI: Now I am questioning whether you need them to expose yourself as a liar.

Needleman: In principle, no.

KRISHNAMURTI: No, not in principle. Either it is so, or it is not.

Needleman: That is the question.

KRISHNAMURTI: Which means if I need them. then I am lost. Then I will for ever hang on to them. Sir, this has happened since human relationships began.

Needleman: Yes it has. But it also happens that I hang on for a while and then I right it.

38

KRISHNAMURTI: Therefore why don't you, the good man, tell me: "Look, begin, you don't need me. You can watch yourself now clearly."

Needleman: Maybe if I told you that, you would take it utterly wrongly and misunderstand me completely!

KRISHNAMURTI: Then what shall I do? Go on hanging onto you, run after you?

Needleman: Not what shall you do, but what do you do?

KRISHNAMURTI: What they generally do is run after him.

Needleman: They generally do, yes.

KRISHNAMURTI: And hold on to his skirts.

Needleman: But that is perhaps because the teacher is not intelligent.

KRISHNAMURTI: No. He says, "Look, I can't teach you my friend, I have nothing to teach. If I am really good I have nothing to teach. I can only show."

Needleman: But he doesn't say it, he does it.

KRISHNAMURTI: I say, "Look, I don't want to teach you, you can learn from yourself."

Needleman: Yes, all right. Suppose he says that.

KRISHNAMURTI: Yes, he says learn from yourself. Don't depend. That means you, being good, are helping me to look at myself.

Needleman: Attracting you.

KRISHNAMURTI: No. You are putting me in a corner so that I can't escape.

Needleman: I see what you are saying. But it is the easiest thing in the world to escape.

KRISHNAMURTI: I don't want to. Sir, you tell me, "Don't depend, for goodness has no dependency." If you want to be good you cannot depend on anything.

39

Needleman: Anything external, yes all right.

KRISHNAMURTI: On anything, external or inward. Don't depend on anything. It doesn't mean just don't depend on the postman, it means inwardly don't depend.

Needleman: Right.

KRISHNAMURTI: That means what? I depend. He has told me one thing: "Don't depend on me or on anybody, wife, husband, daughter, politician, don't depend." That's all. He goes away. He leaves me with that. What shall I do?

Needleman: Find out if he is right.

KRISHNAMURTI: But I do depend.

Needleman: That's what I mean.

KRISHNAMURTI: I do depend on my wife, on the priest, on some psychoanalyst—I do depend. Then I begin. Because he tells me the truth—you follow. Sir? It is there, I have to work it out. So I have to find out if it is the truth, or if it is a falsehood. Which means I must exercise my reason, my capacity, my intelligence. I must work. I can't just say, "Well he has gone". I depend on my cook! So I have to find out, I have to see the truth and the false. I have seen it. That doesn't depend on anybody.

Needleman: Right.

KRISHNAMURTI: Even the company of the good doesn't teach me what is good and what is false, or true. I have to see it.

Needleman: Absolutely.

KRISHNAMURTI: So I don't depend on anybody to find what is true and what is false.

MALIBU, CALIFORNIA
26 MARCH 1971

AMERICA

II

Three Talks in New York City

1

INNER REVOLUTION

The need to change. A process in time or instantaneous? The conscious and the unconscious; dreams. The analytical process. To see the content of consciousness without the separation of observer and observed. Noise and resistance. "When there is complete cessation of division between the observer and the observed, then 'what is' is no longer what is."

Questions: *Observer and observed; fragmentation; resistance.*

KRISHNAMURTI: We are going to examine together the question of what is hidden in the consciousness, in the deeper layers of the mind—which is generally called the unconscious. We are concerned with bringing about a radical revolution in ourselves and so in society. The physical revolution which is advocated all over the world at the present time does not bring about a fundamental change in man.

In a corrupt society, such as this, in Europe, India and elsewhere, there must be fundamental changes in the very structure of society. And if man remains corrupt in himself, in his activity, he will overcome whatever the structure be, however perfect; therefore it is imperative, absolutely essential that he change.

Is this change to be brought about through the process of time, through gradual achievement, through gradual change? Or does the change take place only in the instant? That is what we are going to examine together.

One sees that there must be change in oneself—the more sensitive, the more alert and intelligent one is, the more one is aware that there must be a deep, abiding, living change. The content of consciousness is consciousness—the two are not separate. What is implanted in consciousness makes up consciousness. And to bring about a change in consciousness—both in the obvious and in the hidden—does it depend on analysis on time, on environmental pressure? Or is the change to take place totally independent of any pressure, of any compulsion?

You know, this question is going to be rather difficult to go into, because it is quite complex and I hope we shall be able to share what is being said. Unless one goes into this matter very seriously, really taking trouble, with deep interest, with passion, I am afraid one will not be able to go very far; far in the sense not of time or space, but very deeply within oneself. One needs a great deal of passion, great energy and most of us waste our energies in conflict. And when we are examining this whole business of existence, we need energy. Energy comes with the possibility of change; if there is no possibility of change, then energy wastes away.

We think we cannot possibly change. We accept things as they are and thereby become rather dispirited, depressed, uncertain and confused. It *is* possible to change radically and that is what we are going to examine. If you will—do not follow exactly what the speaker is saying, but use his words as a mirror to observe yourself and enquire with passion, with interest, with vitality and a great deal of energy. Then perhaps we can come to a point where it will be obvious that without any kind of effort, without any kind of motive, the radical change takes place.

There is not only the superficial knowledge of ourselves, but there is also the deep, hidden content of our consciousness. How is one to examine it, how is one to expose the whole content of it? Is it to be done bit by bit, slowly gradually?—or is it to be exposed totally and understood instantly, and thereby the whole analytical process comes to an end?

Now we are going to go into this question of analysis. To the speaker, analysis is the denial of action; action being always in the active present. Action means not "having done" or "will do", but *doing*. Analysis prevents that action in the present, because in analysis there is involved time, a gradual peeling off as it were, layer after layer, and examining each layer, analysing the content of each layer. And if the analysis is not perfect, complete, true, then that analysis being incomplete, must leave a knowledge which is not total. And the next analysis springs from that which is not complete.

Look, I examine myself, analyse myself and if my analysis is not complete, then what I have analysed becomes the knowledge with which I proceed to analyse the next layer. So in that process each analysis becomes incomplete and leads to further conflict, and so to inaction. And in analysis there is the analyser, and the analysed, whether the analyser is professional, or yourself, the layman; there is this duality, the analyser analysing something which he thinks is dfferent from himself. But the analyser, what is he? He is the past, he is the accumulated knowledge of all the little things he has analysed. And with that knowledge—which is the past—he analyses the present.

So in that process there is conflict, there is the struggle to conform, or to force that which he analyses. Also there is this whole process of dreaming. I don't know whether you have gone into all this yourself, or probably you have read other people's books, which is most unfortunate; because then you merely repeat what other people have said, however famous they are. But if you don't read all those books—as the speaker does not—then you have to investigate yourself, then it becomes much more fascinating, much more original, much more direct and true.

In the process of analysis there is this world of dreams. We accept dreams as necessary, because the professionals say, "You must dream, otherwise you go mad", and there is some truth in that. We are enquiring into all this because we are trying to find out whether it is possible to change radically, when there is so much confusion, so much misery, such hatred and brutality in the world; there is no compassion. One must, if one is at all serious, enquire into all this. We are enquiring not merely for intellectual entertainment but actually trying to find out if it is possible to change. And when we see the possibility of change, whatever we are, however shallow, however superficial, repetitive, imitative, if we see that there is a possibility of radical change, then we have the energy to do so. If we say it is not possible, then that energy is dissipated.

So we are enquiring into this question, whether analysis does produce a radical change at all, or whether it is merely an intellectual entertainment, an avoidance of action. As we were saying, analysis implies entering into the world of dreams. What are dreams, how do they come into being? I don't know if you have gone into this; if you have, you will see that dreams are the continuation of our daily life. What you are doing during the day, all the mischief, the corruption, the hatred, the passing pleasures, the ambition, the guilt and so on, all that is continued in the

45

world of dreams, only in symbols, in pictures and images. These pictures and images have to be interpreted and all the fuss and unreality of all that comes into being.

One never asks why should one dream at all. One has accepted dreams as essential, as part of life. Now we are asking ourselves (if you are with me) why we dream at all. Is it possible when you go to sleep to have a mind that is completely quiet? Because it is only in that quiet state that it renews itself, empties itself of all its content, so that it is made fresh, young, decisive, not confused.

If dreams are the continuation of our daily life, of our daily turmoil, anxiety, the desire for security, attachment, then inevitably, dreams in their symbolic form must take place. That is clear, isn't it? So one asks, "Why should one dream at all?" Can the brain cells be quiet, not carry on all the business of the day?

One has to find that out experimentally, not accepting what the speaker says—and for goodness sake don't ever do that, because we are sharing together, investigating together. You can test it out by being totally aware during the day, watching your thoughts, your motives, your speech, the way you walk and talk. When you are so aware there are the intimations of the unconscious, of the deeper layers, because then you are exposing, inviting the hidden motives, the anxieties, the content of the unconscious to come into the open. So when you go to sleep, you will find that your mind, including the brain, is extraordinarily quiet. It is really resting, because you have finished what you have been doing during the day.

If you take stock of the day, as you go to bed and lie down—don't you do this?—saying, "I should have done this, I should not have done that", "It would have been better that way, I wish I hadn't said this"—when you take stock of the things that have happened during the day, then you are trying to bring about order before you go to sleep. And if you don't make order before you go to sleep, the brain tries to do it when you are asleep. Because the brain functions perfectly only in order, not in disorder. It functions most efficiently when there is complete order, whether that order is neurotic or rational; because in neurosis, in imbalance, there is order, and the brain accepts that order.

So, if you take stock of everything that has been happening during the day before you go to sleep, then you are trying to bring about order, and therefore the brain does

46

not have to bring order while you are asleep: you have done it during the day. You can bring about that order every minute during the day, that is if you are aware of everything that's happening, outwardly and inwardly. Outwardly in the sense of being aware of the disorder about you, the cruelty, the indifference, the callousness, the dirt, the squalor, the quarrels, the politicians and their chicanery—all that is happening. And your relationship with your husband, your wife, with your girl or boyfriend, be aware of all that during the day, without correcting it, just be aware of it. The moment you try to correct it, you are bringing disorder. But if you merely observe actually what is, then what is, *is* order.

It is only when you try to change "what is" that there is disorder; because you want to change according to the knowledge which you have acquired. That knowledge is the past and you are trying to change "what is"—which is not the past—according to what you have learnt. Therefore there is a contradiction, therefore there is a distortion, therefore this is disorder.

So during the day, if you are aware of the ways of your thoughts, your motives, the hypocrisy, the double-talk—doing one thing, saying another, thinking another—the mask that you put on, the varieties of deception that one has so readily at hand, if you are aware of all that during the day, you don't have to take stock at all when you go to sleep, you are bringing order each minute. So when you do go to sleep you will find that your brain cells, which have recorded and hold the past, become totally quiet, and your sleep then becomes something entirely different. When we use the word "mind", we include in that the brain, the whole nervous organism, the affections, all the human structure; we mean *all* that, not something separate. In that is included the intellect, the heart, the whole nervous organism. When you go to sleep then, the process has totally come to an end, and when you wake up you see things exactly as they are, not your interpretation of them or the desire to change them.

So analysis, for the speaker, prevents action. And action is absolutely essential in order to bring about this radical change. So analysis is not the way. Don't accept, please, what the speaker is saying, but observe it for yourself, learn about it, not from me, but learn by watching all these implications of analysis: time, the analyser and the analysed—the analyser *is* the analysed—and each analysis

47

must be complete, otherwise it distorts the next analysis. So to see that the whole process of analyses, whether it is introspective or intellectual analysis, is totally wrong! It is not the way out—maybe it is necessary for those who are somewhat, or greatly, unbalanced; and perhaps most of us are unbalanced.

We must find a way of observing the whole content of consciousness without the analyser. It is great fun if you go into this, because you have then rejected totally everything that man has said. Because then you stand alone; when you find out for yourself, it will be authentic, real, true, not dependent on any professor, any psychologist, any analyst and so on.

So one must find a way of observing without analysis. I'm going to go into that—I hope you don't mind my doing all this, do you? This is not group therapy! (*Laughter*) This is not an open confession, it is not that the speaker is analysing you, or making you change and become marvellous human beings! You have to do this yourself, and as most of us are second-hand or third-hand human beings, it is going to be very difficult to put away totally all that has been imposed on your minds by the professionals, whether by religious or scientific professionals. We have to find out for ourselves.

If analysis is not the way—and it is not, as far as the speaker is concerned, as he has explained—then how is one to examine or to observe the total content of consciousness? What is the content of consciousness? Please don't repeat what somebody else has said. What is your total content? Have you ever looked at it, considered it? If you have, is it not the various recorded incidents, happenings, pleasurable and non-pleasurable, various beliefs, traditions, the various individual recollections and memories, the racial and family memories, the culture in which one has been brought up—all that is the content, isn't it? And the incidents that take place every day, the memories, the various pains, the unhappiness, the insults, all that is recorded. And that content is your consciousness—you, as a Catholic, or Protestant, living in this western world with the search for more and more and more, the world of great pleasure, entertainment, wealth, incessant noise of the television, the brutality—all that is you, that's your content.

How is all that to be exposed?—and in the exposing of it, is each incident, each happening, each tradition, each

48

hurt, each pain to be examined one by one? Or is it to be looked at totally? If it is to be examined bit by bit, one by one, you are entering into the world of analysis and there is no end to that, you will die analysing—and giving a great deal of money to those who analyse, if that's your pleasure.

Now we're going to find out how to look at these various fragments, which are the content of consciousness, totally—not analytically. We are going to find out how to observe without any analysis at all. That is, we have looked at everything—at the tree, at the cloud, at the wife and the husband, at the girl and the boy—as the observer and the observed. Please do give a little attention to this. You have observed your anger, your greed or your jealousy, whatever it is, as an observer looking at greed. The observer *is* greed, but you have separated the observer because your mind is conditioned to the analytical process; therefore you are always looking at the tree, at the cloud, at everything in life as an observer and the thing observed. Have you noticed it? You look at your wife through the image which you have of her; that image is the observer, it is the past, that image hasbeen put together through time. And the observer *is* the time, *is* the past, *is* the accumulated knowledge of the various incidents, accidents, happenings, experiences and so on. That observer *is* the past, and he looks at the thing observed as though he were not of it, but separate from it.

Now can you look without the observer? Can you look at the tree without the past as the observer? That is, when there is the observer, then there is space between the observer and the observed—the tree. That space is time, because there is a distance. That time is the quality of the observer, who is the past, who is the accumulated knowledge, who says, "That is the tree", or "That is the image of my wife."

Can you look, not only at the tree, but at your wife or your husband, without the image? You know, this requires tremendous discipline. I am going to show you something: discipline generally implies conformity, drill, imitation, conflict between what is and what should be. And so in discipline there is conflict: suppressing, overcoming, the exercise of will and so on—all that is implied in that word. But that word means to learn—not to conform, not to suppress, but to learn. And the quality of the mind that learns has its own order which is discipline. We are learning now to observe, without the observer, without the past, without the image. When you so observe, the actual "what is", is a living thing, not a thing looked upon as dead, recognisable by the past event, by past knowledge.

Look, Sirs, let's make it much simpler than this. You say something to me which hurts me, and the pain of that hurt is recorded. The memory of that continues and when there is further pain, it is recorded again. So the hurt is being strengthened from childhood on. Whereas, if I observe it completely, when you say something which is painful to me, then it is not recorded as a hurt. The moment you record it as a hurt, that recording is continued and for the rest of your life you are being hurt, because you are adding to that hurt. Whereas to observe the pain completely without recording it, is to give your total attention at the moment of the pain. Are you doing all this?

Look, when you go out, when you walk in these streets, there are all kinds of noise, all kinds of shouting, vulgarity, brutality, this noise is pouring in. That is very destructive—the more sensitive you are the more destructive it becomes, it hurts your organism. You resist that hurt and therefore you build a wall. And when you build a wall you are isolating yourself. Therefore you are strengthening the isolation, by which you will get more and more hurt. Whereas if you are observing that noise, are attentive to that noise, then you will see that your organism is never hurt.

If you understand this one radical principle, you will have understood something immense: that where there is an observer separating himself from the thing he observes, there must be conflict. Do what you will, as long as there is a division between the observer and the observed, there must be conflict. As long as there is division between the Muslim and the Hindu, between the Catholic and the Protestant, between the Black and the White, there must be conflict; you may tolerate each other, which is an intellectual covering of intolerance.

As long as there is division between you and your wife, there must be conflict. This division exists fundamentally, basically, as long as there is the observer separate from the thing observed. As long as I say, "Anger is different from me, I must control anger, I must change, I must control my thoughts", in that there is division, therefore there is conflict. Conflict implies suppression, conformity, imitation, all that is involved in it. If you really see the beauty of this, that the observer *is* the observed, that the two are not separate, then you can observe the totality of consciousness without analysis. Then you see the whole content of it instantly.

The observer is the thinker. We have given such tremendous importance to the thinker, haven't we? We live by thought, we do things by thought, we plan our life by thought, our action is motivated by thought. And thought is worshipped throughout the world as the most extraordinarily important thing, which is part of the intellect.

And thought has separated itself as the thinker. The thinker says, "These thoughts are no good", "These are better", he says, "This ideal is better than that ideal", "This belief is better than that belief". It is all the product of thought—thought which has made itself separate, fragmented itself as the thinker, as the experiencer. Thought has separated itself as the higher self and the lower self—in India it is called the atman, the higher. Here you call it the soul, or this or that. But it is still thought in operation. That's clear, isn't it? I mean, this is logical, it is not irrational.

Now I am going to show you the irrationality of it. All our books, all our literature, everything is thought. And our relationship is based on thought—just think of it! My wife is the image which I have created by thinking. That thinking has been put together by nagging, by all the things which go on between husband and wife—pleasure, sex, the irritations, the exclusions, all the separative instincts that go on. Our thought is the result of our relationship. Now what is thought? You are asked that question, "What is thought?" Please don't repeat somebody else—find out for yourself. Surely thought is the response of memory, isn't it—memory as knowledge, memory as experience which has been accumulated, stored up in the brain cells. So the brain cells themselves are the cells of memory. But if you did not think at all, you would be in a state of amnesia, you would not be able to get to your house.

Thought is the response of the accumulated memory as knowledge, as experience—whether it is yours, or the inherited, the communal experience and so on. So thought is the response of the past, which may project itself into the future, going through the present, modifying it as the future. But it is still the past. So thought is never free—how can it be? It can imagine what is freedom, it can idealise what freedom should be, create a Utopia of freedom. But thought itself, in itself, is of the past and therefore it is not free, it is always old. Please, it is not a question of your agreeing with the speaker, it is a fact. Thought organises our life, based on the past. That thought, based on the past, projects what should be tomorrow and so there is conflict.

From that arises a question, which is, for most of us, thought has given a great deal of pleasure. Pleasure is a guiding principle in our life. We are not saying that it is wrong or right, we are examining it. Pleasure is the thing that we want most. Here in this world and in the spiritual world, in heaven—if you have a heaven—we want pleasure in any form—religious entertainment, going to Mass, all the circus that goes on in the name of religion. And the pleasure of any incident, whether it is of a sunset, or sexual, or any sensory pleasure, is recorded and thought over. So thought as pleasure plays a tremendous part in our life. Something happened yesterday which was a most lovely thing, a most happy event, it is recorded; thought comes upon it, chews it and keeps on thinking about it and wants it repeated tomorrow, whether it be sexual or otherwise. So thought gives vitality to an incident that is over.

The very process of recording is knowledge, which is the past, and thought is the past. So thought, as pleasure, is sustained. If you have noticed, pleasure is always in the past; or the imagined pleasure of tomorrow is still the recollection projected into the future, from the past.

You can also observe that where there is pleasure and the pursuit of pleasure, there is also the nourishing of fear. Haven't you noticed it? Fear of the thing I have done yesterday, fear of the physical pain which I had a week ago; thinking about it sustains the fear. There is no ending of that pain when it's over. It is finished, but I carry it over by thinking about it.

So thought sustains and gives nourishment to pleasure as well as to fear. Thought is responsible for this. There is fear of the present, of the future, fear of death, fear of the unknown, fear of not fulfilling, fear of not being loved, wanting to be loved—there are so many fears, all created by the machinery of thought. So there is the rationality of thought and the irrationality of thought.

There must be the exercise of thought in doing things. Technologically, in the office, when you cook, when you wash dishes—knowledge must function perfectly. There is the rationality, the logic of thought in action, in doing. But also thought becomes totally irrational when it sustains pleasure or fear. And yet thought says, "I cannot let go of my pleasure"; yet thought knows, it is at all sensitive or aware, that there is pain coming with it.

So to be aware of all the machinery of thought, of the complicated, subtle movement of thought! This is really not at all difficult once you say, "I must find out a way of living that is totally different, a way of life in which there is no conflict." If that is your real, your insistent, passionate demand—as is your demand for pleasure—to live a life, inwardly and outwardly in which there is no conflict whatsoever—then you will see the possibility of it. Because, as we have explained, conflict exists only when there is division between "me" and "not me". Then if you see that, not verbally or intellectually—because that is not seeing—but when you actually realise that there is no division between the observer and the observed, between the thinker and the thought, then you see, then you observe actually "what is". And when you see actually "what is", you are already beyond it. You don't stay with "what is", you stay with "what is" only when the observer is different from the "what is". Are you getting this? So when there is this complete cessation of division between the observer and the observed, then "what is" is no longer what is. The mind has gone beyond it.

Questioner: How can I change this identification of the observer with the observed? I can't just agree with you and say "Yes, it's true", but have to do something about it.

KRISHNAMURTI: Quite right. Sir, there is no identification at all. When you identify yourself with the observed, it is still the pattern of thought, isn't it?

Questioner: Precisely, but how do I get out of that?

KRISHNAMURTI: You don't get out of it, I'll show it to you, Sir. Do you see the truth that the observer is the observed?—the fact of it, the logic of it. Do you see that? Or don't you?

Questioner: It is still only a comment which arises; the truth does not exist.

KRISHNAMURTI: The fact does not exist?

Questioner: No, a comment of agreement arises.

KRISHNAMURTI: But you see that fact, don't you? Don't agree or disagree, this is a very serious thing; I wish I could talk about meditation, but not now, for this is implied in it. Sir, see the importance of this. The truth is that "I am anger"—not "I" am different from anger. That is the truth, that is a fact, isn't it? I am anger; not "I" separate from anger. When I am jealous, I am jealousy; not "I" am different from jealousy. I make myself separate from jealousy because I want to do something about it, sustain it or get rid of it or rationalise it, whatever it is. But the fact is, the "me" is jealous, isn't it?

Now how am I to act when I am jealous, when "me" is jealousy? Before, I thought "I" could act when I separated myself from jealousy, I thought I could do something about it, suppress it, rationalise it, or run away from it— do various things. I thought I was doing something. Here, I feel I am not doing anything. That is, when I say "I am jealousy", I feel I can't move. Isn't that right, Sir?

Look at the two varieties of activity, at the action which takes place when you are different from jealousy, which is the non-ending of jealousy. You may run away from it, you may suppress it, you may transcend it, you may escape, but it will come back, it will be there always, because there is the division between you and jealousy. Now there is a totally different kind of action when there is no division, because in that the observer is the observed, he cannot do anything about it. Before, he was able to do something about it, now he feels he is powerless, he is frustrated, he can't do anything. If the observer *is* the observed, then there is no saying, "I can or can't do anything about it"—he is what he is. He is jealousy. Now, when he is jealousy, what takes place? Go on, Sir!

Questioner: He understands . . .

KRISHNAMURTI: Do look at it, take time. When I think I am different from my jealousy, then I feel I can do something about it and in the doing of it there is conflict. Here on the other hand, when I realise the truth of it, that I am jealousy, that "I", the observer, am the observed, then what takes place?

Questioner: There is no conflict.

KRISHNAMURTI: The element of conflict ceases. There conflict exists, here conflict does not exist. So conflict *is* jealousy. Have you got it? There has been complete action, an action in which there has been no effort at all, therefore it is complete, total, it will never come back.

Questioner: You said analysis is the deadly tool to thought or consciousness. I perfectly agree with you and you were about to say that you would develop the argument that there are fragments in the brain or in thought or in consciousness which will be anti-analysis. I should be grateful, Sir, if you would continue to develop that part of the argument.

KRISHNAMURTI: Of what, Sir?

Questioner: You mentioned the fragments will not constitute any conflict or struggle, they will be anti-analytical.

KRISHNAMURTI: I just explained, Sir, there must be fragmentation when there is the observer and the observed, as two different things. Sir, look, this is not an argument, there is nothing to develop. I have gone into it fairly thoroughly, we can spend of course lots more time, because the more deeply you go into it the more there is. We have broken up our life into many fragments, haven't we? —the scientist, the businessman, the artist, the housewife and so on. What is the basis, what is the root of this fragmentation? The root of this fragmentation is the observer being separate from the observed. He breaks up life: I am a Hindu and you are a Catholic, I am a Communist, you are a bourgeois. So there is this division going on all the time. And I say, "Why is there this division, what causes this division?"—not only in the external, economic, social structure, but much more deeply. This division is brought about by the "me" and the "not me"—the me that wants to be superior, famous, greater—whereas "you" are different.

So the "me" is the observer, the "me" is the past, which divides the present as the past and the future. So as long as there is the observer, the experiencer, the thinker, there must be division. Where the observer is the observed, conflict ceases and therefore jealousy ceases. Because jealousy is conflict, isn't it?

Questioner: Is jealously human nature?

KRISHNAMURTI: Is violence human nature? Is greed human nature?

Questioner: I wanted to ask you another question, if I may. Am I right or wrong, according to what you've been telling us, to say, as a man thinketh in his heart, so is he? So we must watch our thoughts and profit from experience.

KRISHNAMURTI: That's just it. As you think, what you think, you are. You think you are greater than somebody else, that you are inferior to somebody else, that you are perfect, that you are beautiful or not beautiful, that you are angry—what you think you are. That's simple enough, isn't it? One has to find out whether it is possible to live a life where thought has its rational function, and see where thought becomes irrational. We'll go into that tomorrow.

Questioner: To continue with jealously: when the jealously is "me", and "me" is the jealousy, the conflict ends, because I know it's the jealousy and it disappears. But when I listen to the noises in the street and the "me" is the noise, and the noises are "me", how can conflict end when that noise will go on forever?

KRISHNAMURTI: It's fairly simple. Madam. I walk down the street and that noise is terrible. And when I say that noise is "me", the noise does not end, it goes on. Isn't that the question? But I don't say the noise is me, I don't say the cloud is me, or the tree is me, why should I say the noise is me? We pointed out just now, that if you observe, if you say, "I listen to that noise", listen completely, not with resistance, then that noise may go on for ever, it does not affect you. The moment you resist, you are separate from the noise—not identify yourself with the noise—I don't know if you see the difference. The noise goes on, I can cut myself off from it by resisting it, putting a wall between myself and that noise. Then what takes place, when I resist something? There is conflict, isn't there? Now can I listen to that noise without any resistance whatsoever?

Questioner: Yes, if you know that the noise might stop in an hour!

56

KRISHNAMURTI: No, that is still part of your resistance.

Questioner: That means that I can listen to the noise in the street for the rest of my life with the possibility I might become deaf.

KRISHNAMURTI: No, listen, Madam, I am saying something entirely different. We are saying, as long as there is resistance, there must be conflict. Whether I resist my wife, or my husband, whether I resist the noise of a dog barking, or the noise in the street, there must be conflict. Now, how is one to listen to the noise without conflict—not whether it will go on indefinitely, or hoping it will come to an end—but how to listen to the noise without any conflict? That is what we are talking about. You can listen to the noise when the mind is completely free of any form of resistance—not only to that noise, but to everything in life—to your husband, to your wife, to your children, to the politician. Therefore what takes place? Your listening becomes much more acute, you become much more sensitive, and therefore noise is only a part, it isn't the whole world. The very act of listening is more important than the noise, so listening becomes the important thing and not the noise.

NEW YORK CITY
18 APRIL 1971

2

RELATIONSHIP

Relationship. "You are the world." The separate self; corruption. To see what actually "is". What love is not. "We have no passion; we have lust, we have pleasure." To understand what death is. Love is its own eternity.

Questions: *The concept of good and bad; sharing; pain and Fear; how to be free of the past?*

KRISHNAMURTI: I would like to talk about relationship, about what love is, about human existence in which is involved our daily living, the problems one has, the conflicts, the pleasures and the fears, and that most extraordinary thing one calls death.

I think one has to understand, not as a theory, not as a speculative, entertaining concept, but rather as an actual fact—that we are the world and the world is us. The world is each one of us; to feel that, to be really committed to it and to nothing else, brings about a feeling of great responsibility and an action that must not be fragmentary, but whole.

I think we are apt to forget that our society, the culture in which we live, which has conditioned us, is the result of human endeavour, conflict, human misery and suffering. Each one of us is that culture; the community is each one of us—we are not separate from it. To *feel* this, not as an intellectual idea or a concept, but to actually feel the reality of this, one has to go into the question of what is relationship; because our life, our existence, is based on relationship. Life is a movement in relationship. If we do not understand what is implied in relationship, we inevitably not only isolate ourselves, but create a society in which human beings are divided, not only nationally, religiously, but also in themselves and therefore they project what they are into the outer world.

I do not know if you have gone into this question deeply for yourself, to find out if one can live with another in total harmony, in complete accord, so that there is no barrier, no division, but a feeling of complete unity. Because relationship means to be related—not in action, not in some project, not in an ideology—but to be totally united in the sense that the division, the fragmentation between individuals, between two human beings, does not exist at all at any level.

Unless one finds this relationship, it seems to me that when we try to bring order in the world, theoretically or technologically, we are bound to create not only deep divisions between man and man, but also we shall be unable to prevent corruption. Corruption begins in the lack of relationship; I think that is the root of corruption. Relationship as we know it now is the continuation of division between individuals. The root-meaning of that word individual means "indivisible". A human being who is in himself not divided, not fragmented, is really an individual. But most of use are not individuals; we think we are, and therefore there is the opposition of the individual to

58

the community. One has to understand not only the meaning of that word individuality in the dictionary sense, but in that deep sense in which there is no fragmentation at all. That means perfect harmony between the mind, the heart and the physical organism. Only then an individuality exists.

If we examine our present relationship with each other closely, be it intimate or superficial, deep or passing, we see it is fragmented. Wife or husband, boy or girl, each lives in his own ambition, in personal and egotistic pursuits, in his own cocoon. All these contribute to the factor of bringing about an image in himself and therefore his relationship with another is through that image, therefore there is no actual relationship.

I do not know if you are aware of the structure and the nature of this image that one has built around oneself and in oneself. Each person is doing this all the time, and how can there be a relationship with another, if there is that personal drive, envy, competition, greed and all the rest of those things which are sustained and exaggerated in modern society? How can there be relationship with another, if each one of us is pursuing his own personal achievement, his own personal success?

I do not know if one is at all aware of this. We are so conditioned that we accept it as the norm, as the pattern of life, that each one must pursue his own particular idiosyncrasy or tendency, and yet try to establish a relationship with another in spite of this. Isn't that what we are all doing? You may be married and you go to the office or to the factory; whatever you are doing during the whole of the day, you pursue that. And your wife is in her house, with her own troubles, with her own vanities, with all that happens. Where is the relationship between those two human beings? Is it in bed, in sex? Is a relationship so superficial, so limited, so circumscribed, not in itself corruption?

One may ask: how then are you to live, if you do not go to the office, pursue your own particular ambition, your own desire to achieve and to attain? If one does not do any of this, what is one to do? I think that is a wrong question altogether, don't you? Because we are concerned, are we not, in bringing about a radical change in the whole structure of the mind. The crisis is not in the outer world, but in consciousness itself. And until we understand this crisis, not superficially, not according to some philosopher, but actually deeply understand it for ourselves by looking into it and examining it, we shall not be able to bring about a change. We are concerned with psychological revolution and this revolution can only take place when there is the right kind of relationship between human beings.

How is such a relationship to be brought about? The problem, is clear, isn't it? Please, share this problem with me, will you? It's your problem, not my problem; it's your life, not my life, it's your sorrow, your trouble, your anxiety, your guilt. This battle is one's life. If you listen merely to a description, then you will find that you are only swimming on the surface and not resolving any problem at all. It is actually your problem, and the speaker is merely describing it—knowing that the description is not the described. Let us share this problem together, which is: how can human beings, you and I, find a right relationship in all this turmoil, hatred, destruction, pollution, and among these terrible things which are going on in the world?

To find that out, it seems to me, one must examine what is taking place, see what actually "is". Not what we should like to think it should be, or try to change our relationship to a future concept, but actually observe what it is now. In observing the fact, the truth, the actuality of it, there is a possibility of changing it. As we said the other day, when there is a possibility then there is great energy. What dissipates energy is the idea that it is not possible to change.

So we must look at our relationship as it is actually now, every day; and in observing what it is, we shall discover how to bring about a change in that actuality. So we are describing what actually is, what is: each one lives in his own world, in his world of ambition, greed, fear, the desire to succeed and all the rest of it—you know—what is going on. If I am married, I have responsibilities, children, and all the rest of it. I go to the office, or some place of work, and we meet each other, husband and wife, boy and a girl, in bed. And that's what we call love, leading separate lives, isolated, building a wall of resistance round ourselves, pursuing a self-centred activity; each one is seeking security psychologically, each one is depending on the other for comfort, for pleasure, for companionship; because each one is so deeply lonely, each demands to be loved, to be cherished, each one is trying to dominate the other.

You can see this for yourself, if you observe yourself. Is there any kind of relationship at all? There is no relationship between two human beings, though they may have children, a house, actually they are not related. If they have a common project, that project sustains them, holds them together, but that's not relationship.

Realising all this, one sees that if there is no relationship between two human beings, then corruption begins—not in the outward structure of society, in the outer phenomenon of pollution, but inner pollution, corruption, destruction begins, when human beings have actually no relationship at all, as you haven't. You may hold the hand of another, kiss each other, sleep together, but actually, when you observe very closely, is there any relationship at all? To be related means not to be dependent on each other, not to escape from your loneliness through another, not to try to find comfort, companionship, through another. When you seek comfort through another, are dependent and all the rest of it, can there be any kind of relationship? Or are you then using each other?

We are not being cynical, but actually observing what is: that is not cynicism. So to find out what it actually means to be related to another, one must understand this question of loneliness, because most of us are terribly lonely; the older we grow the more lonely we become, especially in this country. Have you noticed the old people, what they are like? Have you noticed their escapes, their amusements? They have worked all their lives and they want to escape into some kind of entertainment.

Seeing this, can we find a way of living in which we don't use another?—psychologically, emotionally, not depend on another, not use another as a means of escape from our own tortures, from our own despairs, from our own loneliness.

To understand this is to understand what it means to be lonely. Have you ever been lonely? Do you know what it means?—that you have no relationship with another, are completely isolated. You may be with your family, in a crowd, or in the office, wherever you are, when this complete sense of utter loneliness with its despair suddenly comes upon you. Till you solve that completely, your relationship becomes a means of escape and therefore it leads to corruption, to misery. How is one to understand this loneliness, this sense of complete isolation? To understand it, one has to look at one's own life. Is not your every action a self-centred activity? You may occasionally be charitable, generous, do something without any motive—those are rare occasions. This despair can never be dissolved through escape, but by observing it.

So we have come back to this question, which is: how to observe? How to observe ourselves, so that in that observation there is no conflict at all? Because conflict is corruption, is waste of energy, it is the battle of our life, from the moment we are born till we die. Is it possible to live without a single moment of conflict? To do that, to find that out for ourselves, one has to learn how to observe our whole movement. There is observation which becomes harmonious, which is true, when the observer is not, but only observation. We went into that the other day.

When there is no relationship can there be love? We *talk* about it, and love, as we know it, is related to sex and pleasure, isn't it? Some of you say "No". When you say "No", then you must be without ambition, then there must be no competition, no division—as you and me, we and they. There must be no division of nationality, or the division brought about by belief, by knowledge. Then, only, can you say you love. But for most people love is related to sex and pleasure and all the travail that comes with it: jealousy, envy, antagonism, you know what happens between man and woman. When *that* relationship is not true, real, deep, completely harmonious, then how can you have peace in the world? How can there be an end to war?

So relationship is one of the most, or rather the most important thing in life. That means that one has to understand what love is. Surely, one comes upon it, strangely, without asking for it. When you find out for yourself what love is not, then you know what love is—not theoretically, not verbally—but when you realise actually what it is not, which is: not to have a mind that is competitive, ambitious, a mind that is striving, comparing, imitating; such a mind cannot possibly love.

So can you, living in this world, live completely without ambition, completely without ever comparing yourself with another? Because the moment you compare, then there is conflict, there is envy, there is the desire to achieve, to go beyond the other.

Can a mind and a heart that remembers the hurts, the insults, the things that have made it insensitive and dull—can such a mind and heart know what love is? Is love pleasure? And yet that is what we are pursuing, consciously or unconsciously. Our gods are the result of our pleasure. Our beliefs, our social structure, the morality of society—which is essentially immoral—is the result of our pursuit of pleasure. And when you say, "I love somebody", is it love? That means: no separation, no domination, no self-centred activity. To find out what it is, one must deny all this—deny it in the sense of seeing the falseness of it. When you once see something as false—which you have accepted as true, as natural, as human—then you can never go back to it; when you see a dangerous snake, or a dangerous animal, you never play with it, you never come near it. Similarly, when you actually see that love is none of these things, feel it, observe it, chew it, live with it, are totally committed to it, then you will know what love is, what compassion is—which means passion for everyone.

We have no passion; we have lust, we have pleasure. The root-meaning of the word passion is sorrow. We have all had sorrow of some kind or another, losing somebody, the sorrow of self-pity, the sorrow of the human race, both collective and personal. We know what sorrow is, the death of someone whom you consider you have loved. When we remain with that sorrow totally, without trying to rationalise it, without trying to escape from it in any form through words or through action, when you remain with it completely, without any movement of thought, then you will find, out of that sorrow comes passion. That passion has the quality of love, and love has no sorrow.

One has to understand this whole question of existence, the conflicts, the battles: you know the life that one leads, so empty, so meaningless. The intellectuals try to give it a meaning and we also want to find significance to life, because life has no meaning as it is lived. Has it? The constant struggle, the endless work, the misery, the suffering, the travail that one goes through in life, all that has actually no meaning—we go through it as a habit. But to find out what the significance is, one must also understand the significance of death; because living and dying go together, they are not two separate things.

So one must enquire what it means to die, because that is part of our living. Not something in the distant future, to be avoided, only to be faced when one is desperately ill, in old age or in an accident, or on a battlefield. As it is part of our daily life to live without a single breath of conflict, so it is part of our life to find out what it means to love. That is also part of our existence, and one must understand it.

How do we understand what death is? When you are dying, at the last moment, can you understand the way you have lived?—the strains, the emotional struggles, the ambitions, the drive; you are probably unconscious and that makes you incapable of clear perception. Then there is the deterioration of the mind in old age and all the rest of it. So one has to understand what death is *now*, not tomorrow. As you observe, thought does not want to think about it. It thinks about all the things it will do tomorrow—how to make new inventions, better bathrooms, all the things that thought can think about. But it does not want to think about death, because it does not know what it means.

Is the meaning of death to be found through the process of thought? Please do share this. When we share it, then we will begin to see the beauty of all this, but if you sit there and let the speaker go on, merely listening to his words, then we don't share together. Sharing together implies a certain quality of care, attention, affection, love. Death is a tremendous problem. The young people may say: why do you bother about it? But it is part of their life, as it is part of their life to understand celibacy. Don't just say, "Why do you talk about celibacy, that's for the old fogeys, that's for the stupid monks." What it means to be celibate has also been a problem for human beings, that also is part of life.

Can the mind be completely chaste? Not being able to find out how to live a chaste life, one takes vows of celibacy and goes through tortures. That is not celibacy. Celibacy is something entirely different. It is to have a mind that is free from all images, from all knowledge; which means understanding the whole process of pleasure and fear.

Similarly, one has to understand this thing called death. How do you proceed to understand something of which you are terribly frightened? Aren't we frightened of death? Or we say, "Thank God I'm going to die, I've had enough of this life with all the misery of it, the confusion, the shoddiness, the brutality, the mechanical things by which one is caught, thank God all this will end!" That is not an answer; nor is it to rationalise death, or to believe in some reincarnation, as the whole Asiatic world does. To find out what reincarnation means, which is to be born in a future existence, you must find out what you are now. If you believe in reincarnation, what are you now?—a lot of words, a lot of experience, of knowledge; you are conditioned by various cultures, you are all the identifications of your life, your furniture, your house, your bank account, your experiences of pleasure and pain. That's what you are, aren't you? The remembrance of the failures, the hopes, the despairs, all that you are now, and that is going to be born in the next life—a lovely idea, isn't it!

Or you think there is a permanent soul, a permanent entity. Is there anything permanent in you? The moment you say there is a permanent soul, a permanent entity, the entity is the result of your thinking, or the result of your hopes, because there is so much insecurity, everything is transient, in a flux, in a movement. So when you say there is something permanent, that permanency is the result of your thinking. And thought is of the past, thought is never free—it can invent anything it likes!

So if you believe in a future birth, then you must know that the future is conditioned by the way you live now, what you do now, what you think, what your acts are, your ethics. So what you are now, what you do now, matters tremendously. But those people who believe in a future birth don't give a pin about what happens now, it's just a matter of belief.

So, how do you find out what death means, when you are living with vitality, with energy, full of health? Not when you are unbalanced, or ill, not at the last moment, but now, knowing the organism must inevitably wear out, like every machinery. Unfortunately we use our machinery so disrespectfully, don't we? Knowing the physical organism comes to an end, have you ever thought about what it means to die? You can't think about it. Have you ever experimented to find out what it means to die psychologically, inwardly?—not how to find immortality, because eternity, that which is timeless, is *now*, not in some distant future. To enquire into that, one must understand the whole problem of time; not only chronological time, by the watch, but the time that thought has invented as a gradual process of change.

How does one find out about this strange thing that we all have to meet one day or another? Can you die psychologically today, die to everything that you have known? For instance: to die to your pleasure, to your attachment, your dependence, to end it without arguing, without rationalising, without trying to find ways and means of avoiding it. Do you know what it means to die, not physically, but psychologically, inwardly? Which means to put an end to that which has continuity; to put an end to your ambition, because that's what's going to happen when you die, isn't it? You can't carry it over and sit next to God! (*Laughter*) When you actually die, you have to end so many things without any argument. You can't say to death, "Let me finish my job, let me finish my book, all the things I have not done, let me heal the hurts which I have given others"—you have no time.

So can you find out how to live a life now, today, in which there is always an ending to everything that you began? Not in your office of course, but inwardly to end all the knowledge that you have gathered—knowledge being your experiences, your memories, your hurts, the comparative way of living, comparing yourself always with somebody else. To end all that every day, so that the next day your mind is fresh and young. Such a mind can never be hurt, and that is innocence.

One has to find out for oneself what it means to die; then there is no fear, therefore every day is a new day—and I really mean this, one *can* do this—so that your mind and your eyes see life as something totally new. That is eternity. That is the quality of the mind that has come upon this timeless state, because it has known what it means to die every day to everything it has collected during the day. Surely, in that there is love. Love is something totally new every day, but pleasure is not, pleasure has continuity. Love is always new and therefore it is its own eternity.

Do you want to ask any questions?

Questioner: Supposing, Sir, that through complete, objective, self-observation I find that I am greedy, sensual, selfish and all that. Then how can I know whether this kind of living is good or bad, unless I have already some preconceptions of the good? If I have these preconceptions, they can only derive from self-observation.

KRISHNAMURTI: Quite, Sir.

Questioner: I also find another difficulty. You seem to believe in sharing, but at the same time you say that two lovers, or husband and wife, cannot base their love, shouldn't

base their love, on comforting each other. I don't see any-
thing wrong in comforting each other—that is sharing.

KRISHNAMURTI: The gentleman says, "One must have a
concept of the good, otherwise, why should one give up all
this ambition, greed, envy and all the rest of it?" You can
have a formula or a concept of what is better, but can you
have a concept of what is good?

Questioner: Yes, I think so.

KRISHNAMURTI: Can thought produce what is good?

Questioner: No, I meant the conception of such good.

KRISHNAMURTI: Yes, Sir. The conception of good is the
product of thought; otherwise how can you conceive what
is good?

*Questioner: The conceptions can only be derived from
our self-observation.*

KRISHNAMURTI: I'm just pointing that out, Sir. Why
should you have a concept of the good at all?

*Questioner: Otherwise how do I know whether my life is
good or bad?*

KRISHNAMURTI: Just listen to the question. Don't we
know what conflict is? Do I have to have a concept of
non-conflict before I am aware of conflict? I know what
conflict is—the struggle, the pain. Don't I know that, without knowing a state when there is no conflict? When I
formulate what is good, I will formulate it according to
my conditioning, according to my way of thinking, feeling,
my particular idiosyncrasy and all the rest of my cultural
conditioning. Is the good to be projected by thought?—and
will thought then tell me what is good and bad in my life?
Or has goodness nothing whatsoever to do with thought,
or with formula? Where does goodness flower?—do tell
me. In a concept? In some idea, in some ideal that lies in
the future? A concept means a future, a tomorrow. It may
be very far away, or very close, but it is still in time. And
when you have a concept, projected by thought—thought
being the response of memory, the response of accumu-

lated knowledge depending on the culture in which you have lived—do you find that goodness in the future, created by thought? Or do you find it when you begin to understand conflict, pain and sorrow?

So in the understanding of "what is"—not by comparing "what is" with "what should be"—in that understanding flowers goodness. Surely, goodness has nothing whatsoever to do with thought—has it? Has love got anything to do with thought? Can you cultivate love by formulating it and saying, "My ideal of love is *that*"? Do you know what happens when you cultivate love? You are not loving. You think you will have love at some future date; in the meantime you are violent. So is goodness the product of thought? Is love the product of experience, of knowledge? What was the second question, Sir?

Questioner: The second question was about sharing.

KRISHNAMURTI: What do you share? What are we sharing now? We talked about death, we talked about love, about the necessity of total revolution, about complete psychological change, not to live in the old pattern of formulas, of struggle, pain, imitation, conformity and all the rest of those things man has lived for through millennia and has produced this marvellous, messy world! We have talked about death. How do you share that together?—share the understanding of it, not the verbal statement, not the description, not the explanations of it? What does sharing mean?—to share the understanding, to share the truth which comes with the understanding. And what does understanding mean? You tell me something which is serious, which is vital, which is relevant, important, and I listen to it completely, because it is vital to me. To listen vitally, my mind must be quiet, mustn't it? If I am chattering, if I am looking somewhere else, if I am comparing what you are saying with what I know, my mind is not quiet. It is only when my mind is quiet and listens completely, that there is the understanding of the truth of the thing. *That* we share together, otherwise we can't share; we can't share the words—we can only share the truth of something. You and I can only see the truth of something when the mind is totally committed to the observation.

To see the beauty of a sunset, the lovely hills, the shadows and the moonlight—how do you share it with a friend? By telling him, "Do look at that marvellous hill"?

You may say it, but is that sharing? When you actually share something with another, it means you must both have the same intensity, at the same time, at the same level. Otherwise you can't share, can you? You must both have a common interest, at the same level, with the same passion—otherwise how can you share something? You can share a piece of bread—but that's not what we are talking about.

To see together—which is sharing together—we must both of us see; not agree or disagree, but see together what actually is; not interpret it according to my conditioning or your conditioning, but see together what it is. And to see together one must be free to observe, one must be free to listen. That means to have no prejudice. Then only, with that quality of love, is there sharing.

Questioner: How can one quieten, or free the mind, from interruptions by the past?

KRISHNAMURTI: You cannot quieten the mind: full stop! Those are tricks. You can take a pill and made the mind quiet—*you* absolutely cannot make the mind quiet, because *you are the mind.* You can't say, "I will make my mind quiet". Therefore one has to understand what meditation is—actually, not what other people say it is. One has to find out whether the mind can ever be quiet; not: how to make the mind quiet. So one has to go into this whole question of knowledge, and whether the mind, the brain cells, which are loaded with all the past memories, can be absolutely quiet and come into function when necessary; and when it is not necessary, be completely and wholly quiet.

Questioner: Sir, when you speak of relationships, you speak always of a man and a woman or a girl and a boy. Will the same things you say about relationships also apply to a man and a man, or a woman and a woman?

KRISHNAMURTI: Homosexuality?

Questioner: If you wish to give it that name, Sir, yes.

KRISHNAMURTI: You see, when we are talking of love, whether it is of man and man, woman and woman, or man and woman, we are not talking of a particular kind

69

of relationship, we are talking about the whole movement, the whole sense of relationship, not a relationship with one, or two. Don't you know what it means to be related to the world?—when you feel you are the world. Not as an idea—that's appalling—but actually to feel that you are responsible, that you are committed to this responsibility. That is the only commitment; not to be committed through bombs, or committed to a particular activity, but to feel that you are the world and the world is you. Unless you change completely, radically, and bring about a total mutation in yourself, do what you will outwardly, there will be no peace for man. If you feel that in your blood, then your questions will be related entirely to the present and to bringing about a change in the present, not to some speculative ideals.

Questioner: The last time we were together, you were telling us that if someone has a painful experience and it is not fully faced, or is avoided, it goes into the unconscious as a fragment. How are we to free ourselves from these fragments of painful and fearful experiences, so that the past won't have a grip on us?

KRISHNAMURTI: Yes, Sir, that is conditioning. How does one free oneself from this conditioning? How do I free myself from my conditioning of the culture in which I was born? First, I must be aware that I am conditioned—not somebody telling me that I am conditioned. You understand the difference? If somebody tells me I am hungry, that's something different from actually being hungry. So I must be aware of my conditioning, which means, I must be aware of it not only superficially, but at the deeper levels. That is, I must be aware totally. To be so aware, means that I am not trying to go beyond the conditioning, not trying to be free of the conditioning. I must see it as it actually is, not bring in another element, such as: wanting to be free of it, because that is an escape from actuality. I must be aware. What does that mean? To be aware of my conditioning totally, not partially, means my mind must be highly sensitive, mustn't it? Otherwise I can't be aware. To be sensitive means to observe everything very, very closely —the colours, the quality of people, all the things around me. I must also be aware of what actually is without any choice. Can you do that?—not trying to interpret it, not trying to change it, not trying to go beyond it or trying to be free of it—just to be totally aware of it.

When you observe a tree, between you and the tree there is time and space, isn't there? And there is also the botanical knowledge about it, the distance between you and the tree—which is time—and the separation which comes through knowledge of the tree. To look at that tree without knowledge, without the time-quality, does not mean identifying yourself with the tree, but to observe the tree so attentively, that the boundaries of time don't come into it at all; the boundaries of time come in only when you have knowledge about the tree. Can you look at your wife, or your friend, or whatever it is without the image? The image is the past, which has been put together by thought, as nagging, bullying, dominating, as pleasure, companionship and all that. It is the image that separates; it is the image that creates distance and time. Look at that tree, or the flower, the cloud, or the wife or the husband, without the image!

If you can do that, then you can observe your conditioning totally; then you can look at it with a mind that is not spotted by the past, and therefore the mind itself is free of conditioning. To look at myself—as we generally do—I look as an observer looking at the observed: myself as the observed and the observer looking at it. The observer is the knowledge, is the past, is time, the accumulated experiences—he separates himself from the thing observed.

Now, to look without the observer! You do this when you are completely attentive. Do you know what it means to be attentive? Don't go to school to learn to be attentive! To be attentive means to listen without any interpretation, without any judgement—just to listen. When you are so listening there is no boundary, there is no "*you*" listening. There is only a state of listening. So when you observe your conditioning, the conditioning exists only in the observer, not in the observed. When you look without the observer, without the "*me*"—his fears, his anxieties and all the rest of it—then you will see, you enter into a totally different dimension.

NEW YORK CITY
24 APRIL 1971

71

3

RELIGIOUS EXPERIENCE. MEDITATION

Is there a religious experience? Search for truth; the meaning of search. "What is a religious mind?" "What is the quality of mind which is no longer experiencing?" Discipline; virtue; order. Meditation is not an escape. The function of knowledge and freedom from the known. "Meditation is to find out if there is a field not already contaminated by the known." "The first step is the last step."

Questions: *The analogy of dirt; awareness; consciousness; love; psychological time.*

KRISHNAMURTI: We said that we would talk over together a very complex problem, which is: is there a religious experience, and what are the implications of meditation? If one observes, it appears that throughout the world man has always been seeking something beyond his own death, beyond his own problems, something that will be enduring, true and timeless. He has called it God, he had given it many names; and most of us believe in something of that kind, without ever actually experiencing it.

Various religions have promised that if you believe in certain forms of rituals, dogmas, saviours, you might, if you lead a certain kind of life, come upon this strange thing, whatever name one likes to give to it. And those who have directly experienced it, have done it according to their conditioning, to their belief, to their environmental and cultural influences.

Apparently religion has lost its meaning, because there have been religious wars; religion does not answer all our problems, religions have separated peoples. They have brought about some kind of civilising influence, but they have not changed man radically. When one begins to enquire if there is such a thing as religious experience and what that experience is, why one calls it "religious", obviously one must first have a great deal of honesty. It is not to be honest according to a principle or a belief, or to some form of commitment, but to honestly see things exactly as they are, without any distortion, not only outwardly, but also inwardly: never to deceive oneself. For deception is quite easy if one craves for some kind of experience, call it religious or otherwise—if one takes a trip and so on. Then you are bound to be caught in some kind of illusion.

One has to find out for oneself, if one can, what religious experience is. One needs a great sense of humility and honesty, which means never to ask for experience, never to demand for oneself a reality or an achievement. So one has to look very closely at one's own desires, attachments and fears and understand them wholly, if one can, so that the mind is in no way distorted, so that there will be no illusion, no deception. And one has to ask also: what does it mean to experience?

I do not know if you have gone into that question at all. Most of us are bored with the usual experiences of every day. We are tired of them all, and the more one is sophisticated, intellectual, the more one wants to live only in the present—whatever that may mean—and invent a philosophy of the present. The word experience means to go through, to go right to the end and finish with it. But unfortunately for most of us, every experience leaves a scar, a memory, pleasant or unpleasant, and we want to retain only the pleasant ones. When we are asking for any kind of spiritual, religious, or transcendental experience, we must try to find out first of all whether there is such an experience, and also what experience itself means. If you experience something and you cannot recognise it, then that experience ceases to be. One of the essential meanings of experience is recognition. And when there is recognition, it has already been known, has already been experienced, otherwise you could not recognise it.

So when they talk about religious, spiritual, or transcendental experience—that word is so misused—you must already have known it, to be able to recognise that you are experiencing something other than an ordinary experience. It seems logical and true that the mind must be able to recognise the experience, and recognition implies something you have already known, therefore it is not new.

When you want experience in the religious field, you want it because you have not solved your problems, your daily anxieties, despairs, fears and sorrows, therefore you want something more. In that demand for more lies deception. That is fairly logical and true, I think. Not that logic is always true, but when one uses logic and reason healthily, sanely, one knows the limitations of reason. The demand for wider, deeper, more fundamental experiences only leads to a further extension of the path of the known. I think that is clear, and I hope we are communicating, sharing with each other.

Then also in this religious enquiry one is seeking to find out what truth is, if there is a reality, if there is such a thing as a state of mind that is beyond time. Search again implies a seeker—doesn't it? And what is he seeking? How will he know that what he has found in his search is true? Again, if he finds what is true—at least what he thinks is true—that depends on his conditioning, on his knowledge, on his past experiences; search then merely becomes a further projection of his own past hopes, fears and longings.

A mind that is enquiring—not seeking—must be totally free of these two, that is, of the demand for experience and the search for truth. One can see why, because when you are seeking, you go to various teachers, read various books, join various cults, follow various gurus and all the rest of it, like window-shopping. Such a search has no meaning whatsoever.

So when you are enquiring into this question, "What is a religious mind, and what is the quality of mind that is no longer experiencing anything at all?"—you must find out if the mind can be free from the demand for experience and can completely end all seeking. One has to investigate without any motive, without any purpose, the facts of time and if there is a timeless state. To enquire into that means to have no belief whatsoever, not to be committed to any religion, to any so-called spiritual organisation, not to follow any guru, and therefore to have no authority whatsoever—including that of the speaker especially. Because you are very easily influenced, you are terribly gullible, though you may be sophisticated, may know a great deal; but you are always eager, always wanting, and therefore are gullible.

So a mind that is enquiring into the question of what is religion, must be entirely free of any form of belief, any form of fear; because fear, as we explained the other day, is a distorting factor, bringing about violence and aggression. Therefore the mind that is enquiring into the quality of the religious state and movement, must be free

74

of this. That demands great honesty and a great sense of humility.

For most of us, vanity is one of the major impediments. Because we think we know, because we have read a great deal, because we have committed ourselves, have practised this or that system, followed some guru peddling his philosophy, we think we know, at least a little bit, and that's the beginning of vanity. When you are enquiring into such an extraordinary question, there must be the freedom of actually not knowing a thing about it. You really don't know, do you? You don't know what truth is, what God is—if there is such a thing—or what is a truly religious mind. You have read about it, people have talked about it for millennia, have built monasteries, but actually they are living on other people's knowledge, experience and propaganda. To find out, surely one must put aside all that completely, and therefore the enquiry into all this is a very serious matter. If you want to play with it, there are all kinds of so-called spiritual, religious entertainments, but they have no value whatsoever to a serious mind.

To enquire into what is a religious mind, we must be free of our conditioning, of our Christianity, of our Buddhism, with all the propaganda of thousands of years, so that the mind is really free to observe. That is very difficult because we are afraid to be alone, to stand alone. We want security, both outwardly and inwardly; therefore we depend on people, whether it is the priest, or the leader, or the guru who says: "I have experienced, that is why I know." One has to stand completely alone—not isolated. There is a vast difference between isolation and being completely alone, integral. Isolation is a state of mind in which relationship ceases, when in your daily life and activity you have actually built a wall around yourself, consciously or unconsciously, so as not to be hurt. That isolation obviously prevents every form of relationship. Aloneness implies a mind that does not depend on another psychologically, is not attached to any person; which does not mean that there is no love—love is not attachment. Aloneness implies a mind that is deeply, inwardly without any sense of fear and therefore without any sense of conflict.

If you go as far as that, then we can proceed to find out what discipline means. For most of us discipline is a form of drill, of repetition; either overcoming an obstacle, or resisting or suppressing, controlling, shaping, conforming—all that is implied in the word discipline. The root-meaning of that word is to learn; a mind that is willing to learn—not to conform—must be curious, must have great interest, and a mind that already knows, cannot possibly learn. So discipline means to learn why one controls, why one suppresses, why there is fear, why one conforms, compares, and is therefore in conflict. That very learning brings about order; not order according to a design or pattern, but in the very enquiry into the confusion, into the disorder, there is order. Most of us are confused for a dozen reasons, which we needn't go into for the moment. One has to learn about confusion, about the disorderly life one leads; not try to bring order into the confusion, or into the disorder, but to learn about it. Then, as you are learning, order comes into being.

Order is a living thing, not mechanical, and order surely is virtue. A mind that is confused, conforming, imitating, is not orderly—it is in conflict. And a mind that is in conflict is disorderly and therefore such a mind has no virtue. Out of this enquiry, out of learning, comes order, and order is virtue. Please observe it in yourself, see how disordered one is in one's life, so confused, so mechanical. In that state one tries to find a moral way of living, which will be orderly and sane. How can a mind that is confused, conforming, imitative, have any kind of order, any kind of virtue? The social morality, as you observe, is totally immoral; it may be respectable, but what is respectable is generally disorderly.

Order is necessary, because only out of order can there be a total action and action is life. But our action brings disorder; there is political action, religious action, business action, family action—they are fragmentary actions. And naturally such action is contradictory. You are a businessman and at home you are a kindly human being—at least you pretend to be; there is contradiction and therefore there is disorder. A mind that is in disorder cannot possibly understand what virtue is. And nowadays, when there is permissiveness of every kind, virtue and order are denied. The religious mind must have this order, not according to a pattern, or a design laid down by you or by another. But that order, that sense of moral recititude, comes only when you understand the disorder, the confusion, the mess that one lives in.

Now all this is to lay the foundation for meditation. If you don't lay the foundations, meditation then becomes an escape. You can play with that kind of meditation endlessly. And that is what most people are doing—leading ordinary, confused, messy lives and somehow finding a corner to bring about a quiet mind. And there are all these people who promise to give you a quiet mind, whatever that may mean.

So for a serious mind—and it is a very serious thing, not a game—one must have this freedom from all belief, from all commitments, because one is committed to the whole of life, not to one fragment of it. Most of us are committed to physical or political revolution, or to a religious activity, to some kind of religious, monastic life and so on. Those are all fragmentary commitments. We are talking of freedom, so that you can commit your whole being, your whole energy, vitality and passion to the whole of life, not to one part of it. Then we can proceed to find out what it means to meditate.

I don't know if you have gone into this at all. Probably some of you have played with it, have tried to control your thoughts, followed various systems, but that is not meditation. One has to dispose of the system one has been offered: Zen, Transcendental Meditation, the various things that have been brought over from India and Asia, in which people are caught. One has to go into this question of systems, of methods, and I hope you will; we are sharing this problem together.

When you have a system to follow, what happens to the mind? What do systems and methods imply—a guru? I don't know why they call themselves gurus—I can't find a strong enough word to deny that whole world of gurus, of their authority, because they think they know. A man who says "I know", such a man does not know. Or if a man says, "I have experienced truth", distrust him completely. These are the people who offer systems. A system implies practice, following, repetition, changing "what actually is" and therefore increasing your conflict. Systems make the mind mechanical, they don't give you freedom, they may promise freedom at the end, but freedom is at the beginning, not at the end. To enquire into the truth of any system, if you have no freedom at the beginning, then you are bound to end up with a system and therefore with a mind which is incapable of subtlety, swiftness and sensitivity. So one can dispose entirely of all systems.

What is important is not controlling thought, but understanding it, understanding the origin, the beginning of

77

thought, which is in yourself. That is, the brain stores up memories—you can observe this yourself, you don't have to read books about it. If it had not stored up memories it would not be able to think at all. That memory is the result of experience, of knowledge—yours, or of the community, of the family, of the race and so on. Thought springs from that storehouse of memory. So thought is never free, it is always old, there is no such thing as freedom of thought. Thought can never be free in itself, it can talk about freedom, but in itself it is the result of past memories, experiences and knowledge; therefore it is old. Yet one must have this accumulation of knowledge, otherwise one could not function, one could not speak to another, could not go home, and so on. Knowledge is essential.

In meditation one has to find out whether there is an end to knowledge and so to freedom from the known. If meditation is a continuation of knowledge, is the continuation of everything that man has accumulated, then there is no freedom. There is freedom only when there is an understanding of the function of knowledge and therefore the freedom from the known.

We are enquiring into the field of knowledge, where it has its function and where it becomes an impediment to further enquiry. While the brain cells continue to operate, they can only operate in the field of knowledge. That is the only thing the brain can do, to function in the field of experience, of knowledge in the field of time—which is the past. Meditation is to find out if there is a field which is not already contaminated by the known.

If I meditate and continue with what I have already learnt, with what I already know, then I am living in the past, within the field of my conditioning. In that there is no freedom. I may decorate the prison in which I live, I may do all kinds of things in that prison, but there is still a limitation, a barrier. So the mind has to find out whether the brain cells, which have developed through millennia, can be totally quiet, and respond to a dimension they do not know. Which means, can the mind be totally still?

This has been the problem of all religious people throughout the centuries; they realise that you must have a very quiet mind, because then only can you see. If you are chattering, if your mind is constantly in movement, rushing all over the place, obviously it cannot look, it cannot listen totally. So they say, "Control it, hold it, put it in a prison"; they have not found a way of bringing about a mind that is completely and utterly quiet. They say, "Don't yield to any desire, don't look at a woman, don't look at the beautiful hills, the trees and the beauty of the earth, because if you do, it might remind you of a woman, or a man. Therefore control, hold on, and concentrate." When you do all that, you are in conflict, and therefore there has to be more control, more subjugation. This has been going on for millennia, because they realise they must have a quiet mind. Now, how does the mind become quiet?—without effort, without control, without giving it a frontier? The moment you ask "how" you are introducing a system. Therefore there is no "how".

Can the mind become quiet? I don't know what you are going to do about it when you see the problem, when you see the necessity, the truth of having this delicate, subtle mind, which is absolutely quiet. How is it to happen? This is the problem of meditation, because only such a mind is a religious mind. It is only such a mind that sees the whole of life as a unit, as a unitary movement, not fragmented. Therefore such a mind acts totally, not fragmentarily, because it acts out of complete stillness.

The foundation is a life of complete relationship, a life that is orderly and therefore virtuous, a life that is extraordinarily simple inwardly, and therefore totally austere—the austerity of deep simplicity, which means that the mind is not in conflict. When you have laid that foundation, easily, without any effort—because the moment you introduce effort there is conflict—you see the truth of it. Therefore it is the perception of "what is" that brings about a radical change.

It is only the still mind that understands that in a quiet mind there is a movement that is totally different, that is of a different dimension, of a different quality. That can never be put into words, because it is indescribable. What can be described is what comes up to this point, the point when you have laid the foundation and seen the necessity, the truth, and the beauty of a still mind.

For most of us, beauty is in *something*, in a building, in a cloud, in the shape of a tree, in a beautiful face. Is beauty "out there", or is it a quality of mind that has no self-centred activity? Because like joy, the understanding of beauty is essential in meditation. Beauty is really the total abandonment of the "me", and the eyes that have abandoned the "me" can see the trees, the beauty of it all, and the loveliness of the cloud; that happens when there is no centre as the "me". It happens to each one of us, doesn't it?—when you see a lovely mountain, when you come upon it suddenly, there it is! Everything has been pushed aside except the majesty of that hill. That mountain, that tree, absorbs you completely.

It is like a child with a toy—the toy absorbs the child, and when the toy is destroyed the child is back again in whatever he is doing, in his mischief, in his crying. Likewise with us: when you see the mountain, or the single tree on a hilltop, it absorbs you. And we want to be absorbed by something, by an idea, by an activity, by a commitment, by a belief, or we want to be absorbed by another; which is like the child with a toy.

So beauty means sensitivity—a body that is sensitive, which means the right diet, the right way of living, and you have all this, if you have gone that far. I hope you will, or are doing it now; then the mind will inevitably and naturally, unknowingly, become quiet. You can't make the mind quiet, because *you* are the mischief-maker, you are yourself disturbed, anxious, confused—how can you make the mind quiet? But when you understand what quietness is, when you understand what confusion is, what sorrow is and whether sorrow can ever end, and when you understand pleasure, then out of that comes an extraordinarily quiet mind; you don't have to seek it. You must begin at the beginning and the first step is the last step, and this is meditation.

Questioner: When you make the analogy of the mountain, the hills, the beautiful sky—that's wrong for these people, that's not the analogy for them—the analogy is the dirt.

KRISHNAMURTI: Right, take that—the analogy of the dirty streets of New York, the analogy of squalor, poverty, the ghettos, the wars to which each one of us has contributed. You don't feel that way, because you have separated yourself, isolated yourself; therefore, having no relationship with another, you become corrupt and allow corruption to spread in the world. That's why this corruption, this pollution, these wars, this hatred, cannot be stopped by a political or religious system, or by any organisation. *You* have to change. Don't you see this? You have to cease completely to be what you are. Not through will—meditation is the emptying of the mind of will; then a totally different action takes place.

Questioner: If one can have the privilege of becoming totally aware, how can we then help those who are conditioned, who have a deep resentment in them?

KRISHNAMURTI: Why, if I may ask, do you use the word privilege? What is there sacred or privileged about being aware? That's a natural thing, isn't it, to be aware? If you are aware of your own conditioning, of the turmoil, the dirt, the squalor, the war, the hatred, if you are aware of all that, you will establish a relationship with another so complete, that you are related to every other human being in the world. You understand this? If I am related to somebody completely, totally—not as an idea or an image—then I am related to every human being in the world. Then I will see I will not hurt another—they are hurting themselves. Then go, preach, talk about it—not with the desire to help another, you understand?—that's the most terrible thing to say, "I want to help another". Who are you to help another?—including the speaker.

Sir, look, the beauty of the tree or the flower doesn't want to help you, it is there; it is for you to look at the squalor or at the beauty, and if you are incapable of looking at it, then find out why you have become so indifferent, so callous, so shallow and empty. If you find out that, then you are in a state where the waters of life flow, you don't have to do anything.

Questioner: What is the relationship between seeing things exactly as they are and consciousness?

KRISHNAMURTI: You only know consciousness by its content, and its content is what is happening in the world, of which you are a part. To empty all that is not to have no consciousness, but a totally different dimension. You cannot speculate about that dimension—leave that to the scientists, to the philosophers. What we can do is to find out whether it is possible to uncondition the mind by becoming aware, by becoming totally attentive.

Questioner: I don't know myself what love is or what truth is, or what God is, but you describe it as, "Love is God", instead of "Love is love". Can you explain why you say "Love is God"?

KRISHNAMURTI: I didn't say love is God.

Questioner: I read one of your books ...

KRISHNAMURTI: I'm sorry, don't read books! (*Laughter*) That word has been used so much, is so loaded by man's despairs and hopes. You have your God, the Communists have their gods. So find out, if I may suggest, what love is. You can only find out what love is, by knowing what it is not. Not knowing intellectually, but actually in life putting aside what it is not—jealousy, ambition and greed, all the division that goes on in life, the me and the you, we and they, the black and white. Unfortunately you won't do it because it needs energy, and energy comes only when you observe actually what is and don't run away from it. When you see actually what is, then in the observing of it, you have the energy to go beyond it. You cannot go beyond it if you are trying to escape from it, to translate it, or to overcome it. Just observe actually what is, then you have an abundance of energy, then you can find out what love is. Love is not pleasure, and to really find that out, inwardly, for yourself, do you know what that means? It means that there is no fear, that there is no attachment, no dependency, but a relationship in which there is no division.

Questioner: Could you talk about the role of the artist in society—does he serve a function beyond his own?

KRISHNAMURTI: Who is an artist? Someone who paints a picture, writes a poem, who wants to express himself through painting or through writing a book or a play? Why do we divide the artist from the rest of us?—or the intellectual from the rest of us? We have placed the intellectual at one level, the artist perhaps at a higher level, and the scientist at a still higher level. And then we say, "What is their role in society?" The question is not, what is their role, but what is *your* role in society; because you have created this mess. What is your role? Find out, Sir. That is, find out why you live within this world of squalor, hatred and misery; apparently it does not touch you.

Look, you have listened to these talks, shared some of

the things together, understood, let's hope, a great deal. Then you become a centre of right relationship and therefore it is your responsibility to change this terrible, corrupt, destructive society.

Questioner: Sir, could you go into psychological time?

KRISHNAMURTI: Time is old age, time is sorrow, time doesn't heed. There is chronological time by the watch. That must exist, otherwise you won't be able to catch your bus, cook a meal, and all the rest of it. But there is another kind of time, which we have accepted. That is, "Tomorrow I will be, tomorrow I will change, tomorrow I will become"; psychologically we have created time—tomorrow. Is there a tomorrow, psychologically? That question fills us with dread to ask seriously. Because we *want* tomorrow: "I shall have the pleasure of meeting you tomorrow, I am going to understand tomorrow, my life will be different tomorrow, I will realise enlightenment tomorrow." Therefore tomorrow becomes the most important thing in our life. You have had sex yesterday, all the pleasures, all the agonies—whatever it is—and you want it tomorrow, because you want that same pleasure repeated.

Put that question to yourself and find out the truth of it. "Is there a tomorrow at all?"—except in thought which projects tomorrow. So tomorrow is the invention of thought as time, and if there is no tomorrow psychologically, what happens in life today? Then there is a tremendous revolution, isn't there? Then your whole action undergoes a radical change, doesn't it? Then you are completely whole now, not projecting from the past, through the present, into the future.

That means to live, dying every day. Do it, and you will find out what it means to live completely today. Isn't that what love is? You don't say, "I will love tomorrow", do you? You love or you don't love. Love has no time, only sorrow has time—sorrow being thought, as in pleasure. So one has to find out for oneself what time is, and find out if there is a "no tomorrow". That is to live, then there is a life which is eternal, because eternity has no time.

NEW YORK CITY
25 APRIL 1971

83

AMERICA

III

Two Conversations:
J. Krishnamurti and Alain Naudé

THE CIRCUS OF MAN'S STRUGGLE

*Conversation between J. Krishnamurti
and Alain Naudé*

Naudé:[1] You speak about the whole of life. When we look about us there is so much disorder everywhere; it seems that people are so confused. In the world we see that there is war, ecological disorder, political and and social disorder, crime, and all the evils of industrialisation and over-population. And it seems that the more people try to solve these problems the more they augment. Then there is man himself, who is full of problems. He has not only the problems of the world about him, but is full of problems inwardly—loneliness, despair, jealousy, anger— all this we may call confusion. And presently he dies. Now we have always been told that there is something else, which has variously been called God, eternity, creation. And about this man knows nothing. He has tried to live for this, in relation to this; but it has again made problems. It seems from what you have said so many times that one must find a way of dealing with these three sets of problems, these three aspects of life at the same time, because these are the problems confronting man. Is there a way to ask the question properly so that it will answer these three sets of problems at the same time?

KRISHNAMURTI: First of all, Sir, why do we make this division? Or is there only one movement which must be taken on the wave itself? So first let's find out why we have divided this whole existence into the world outside of me, the world inside of me, and something beyond me. Does this division exist because of the chaos outwardly

[1] Alain Naudé, musician, for six years closely associated with Krishnamurti as his secretary and assistant, and (as he says) above all as his student. At present living in the U.S.A.

and are we only concerned with the outer chaos, and totally neglect the inner chaos? Not finding a solution for the outer, or for the inner, we then try to find a solution in a belief, in the divine?

Naudé: Yes.

KRISHNAMURTI: So in asking a question of this kind, are we dealing with the three things separately, or as a total movement?

Naudé: How can we make them into a unitary movement? How are they related? What is the action in man which will make them the same?

KRISHNAMURTI: I wouldn't come to that yet. I would ask: why has man divided the world, his whole existence into these three categories? Why?—and from there move. Now why have I, as a human being, divided the world outside of me from the world inside me, and from the world which I am trying to grasp—of which I know nothing—and to which I give all my despairing hope?

Naudé: Right.

KRISHNAMURTI: Now why do I do this? Tentatively we are asking: is it that we have not been able to solve the outer with its chaos, confusion, destruction, brutality, violence and all the horrors that are going on, and therefore we turn to the inner and hope thereby to solve the outer? And not being able to solve the inner chaos, the inner insufficiency, the inner brutality, violence and all the rest of it, not being able to solve anything there either, then we move away from both, the outer and the inner, to some other dimension.

Naudé: Yes, it is like that. That is what we do.

KRISHNAMURTI: That is what is happening all the time around us and in us.

Naudé: Yes. There are the problems outside which engender the problems inside. Not being able to deal with either, or both, we create the hope of some other, some third state, which we call God.

KRISHNAMURTI: Yes, an outside agency.

Naudé: An outside agency which will be the consolation, the final solution. But it is also a fact that there are things which are really outer problems: the roof leaks, the sky is full of pollution, the rivers are drying up, there are such problems. And there are wars—they are visible outer problems. There are also problems which we think to be inner problems, our secret and closed longings, fears and worries.

KRISHNAMURTI: Yes.

Naudé: There is the world, and there is man's reaction to it, man's living in it. And so there are these two entities— at least in a practical sort of way we can say there are. And so probably the trying to solve practical problems overflows into the inner state of man and engenders problems there.

KRISHNAMURTI: That means we are still keeping the outer and the inner as two separate movements.

Naudé: Yes, we are. We do.

KRISHNAMURTI: And I feel that is a totally wrong approach. The roof does leak and the world is over-populated, there is pollution, there are wars, there is every kind of mischief going on. And not being able to solve that we turn inward; not being able to solve the inward issues we turn to something outer, still further away from all this. Whereas if we could treat the whole of this existence as one unitary movement, then perhaps we would be able to solve all these problems intelligently and reasonably and in order.

Naudé: Yes. It seems that is what you speak about. Would you mind telling us how these three problems are really one thing?

KRISHNAMURTI: I am coming to that, I am coming to it. The world outside of me is created by me—not the trees not the clouds, the bees and the beauty of the landscape— but human existence in relationship, which is called society, *that* is created by you and by me. So the world is me and I am the world. I think that is the first thing that must be established: not as in intellectual or an abstract fact, but in actual feeling, in actual realisation. That is a fact, not a supposition, not an intellectual concept, but it is a fact that the world is me and I am the world. The world being the society in which I live, with its culture, morality, inequality, all the chaos that is going on in society, that is myself in action. And the culture is what I have created and what I am caught in. I think that is an irrevocable and an absolute fact.

Naudé: Yes. How is it that people don't see this enough? We have politicians, we have ecologists, we have economists, we have soldiers all trying to solve the outside problems simply as outer problems.

KRISHNAMURTI: Probably because of a lack of the right kind of education: specialisation, the desire to conquer and go to the moon and play golf there, and so on and so on! We always want to alter the outer hoping thereby to change the inner. "Create the right environment"—the communists have said it a hundred times—"then the human mind will change according to that."

Naudé: That is what they say. In fact, every great university, with all its departments, with all its specialists, one could almost say that these great universities are founded and built on the belief that the world can be changed by a certain amount of specialised knowledge in different departments.

KRISHNAMURTI: Yes. I think we miss this basic thing, which is: the world is me and I am the world. I think that feeling, not as an idea, that feeling brings a totally different way of looking at this whole problem.

Naudé: It is an enormous revolution. To see the problem as one problem, the problem of man and not the problem of his environment, that is an enormous step, which people will not take.

KRISHNAMURTI: People won't take any step. They are used to this outward organisation and disregard totally what is happening inwardly. So when one realises that the world is me and I am the world, then my action is not separative, is not the individual opposed to the community; nor the importance of the individual and his salvation. When one realises that the world is me and I am the world, then whatever action takes place, whatever change takes place, that will change the whole of the consciousness of man.

Naudé: Would you like to explain that?

KRISHNAMURTI: I, as a human being, realise that the world is me and I am the world: realise, feel deeply committed, am passionately aware of this fact.

Naudé: Yes, that my action is in fact the world; my behaviour is the only world there is, because the events in the world are behaviour. And behaviour is the inner. So the inner and the outer are one because the events of history, the events of life, are in fact this point of contact between the inner and the outer. It is in fact the behaviour of man.

KRISHNAMURTI: So the consciousness of the world is my consciousness.

Naudé: Yes.

KRISHNAMURTI: My consciousness *is* the world. Now the crisis is in this consciousness, not in organisation, not in bettering the roads—tearing down the hills to build more roads.

Naudé: Bigger tanks, intercontinental missiles.

KRISHNAMURTI: My consciousness is the world and the consciousness of the world is me. When there is a change in this consciousness it affects the whole consciousness of the world. I don't know if you see that?

Naudé: It is an extraordinary fact.

KRISHNAMURTI: It is a fact.

Naudé: It is consciousness that is in disorder; there is no disorder anywhere else.

91

KRISHNAMURTI: Obviously!

Naudé: Therefore the ills of the world are the ills of human consciousness, and the ills of human consciousness are my ills, my malady, my disorder.

KRISHNAMURTI: Now when I realise that my consciousness is the consciousness of the world, and the consciousness of the world is me, whatever change that takes place in me affects the whole of consciousness.

Naudé: To this people always say: that's all very well, I may change, but there will still be a war in Indo-China!

KRISHNAMURTI: Quite right, there will be.

Naudé: And ghettos and over-population.

KRISHNAMURTI: Of course, there will be. But if each one of us saw the truth of this, that the consciousness of the world is mine, and mine is the world's; and if each one of us felt the responsibility of that—the politician, the scientist, the engineer, the bureaucrat, the business man—if everybody felt that, what then? And it is our job to make them feel this; that is the function of the religious man, surely?

Naudé: This is an enormous thing.

KRISHNAMURTI: Wait, let me go on. So then it is one movement. It is not an individual movement and his salvation. It is the salvation, if you like to use that word, of the whole of man's consciousness.

Naudé: The wholeness, and the health of consciousness itself, which is one thing and in which is contained what appears to be the outer, and what appears to be the inner.

KRISHNAMURTI: That's right. Let's keep to that one point.

Naudé: So what you are speaking about is in fact that health, that sanity, and that wholeness of consciousness, which always has been in fact an indivisible entity.

KRISHNAMURTI: Yes, that's right. Now when the people who want to create a different kind of world, the educators, the writers, the organisers, when they realise the world as it is now is their responsibility, then the whole of the consciousness of man begins to change. Which is what is happening in another direction, only they are emphasising organisation, division; they are doing exactly the same thing.

Naudé: In a negative way.

KRISHNAMURTI: In a destructive way. So from that the question arises: can this human consciousness, which is me—which is the community, which is the society, which is the culture, which is all the horrors that are produced by me in the context of the society, in the culture which is me—can this consciousness undergo a radical change? That is the question. Not escape into the supposed divine, not escape. Because when we understand this change in consciousness the divine is there, you don't have to seek it.

Naudé: Would you please explain what this change in consciousness consists of?

KRISHNAMURTI: That's what we are going to talk about now.

Naudé: And then perhaps we can ask about the divine if it arises.

KRISHNAMURTI: (*Pause*) First of all, is there any possibility of a change in consciousness? Or is any change made consciously no change at all? To talk about a change in consciousness implies changing from this to that.

Naudé: And both this and that are within consciousness.

KRISHNAMURTI: That is what I want to establish first. That when we say there must be a change in consciousness, it is still within the field of consciousness.

Naudé: The way we see the trouble, and the way we see the solution, which we call change—that is all within the same area.

93

KRISHNAMURTI: All within the same area and therefore no change at all. That is, the content of consciousness is consciousness and the two are not separate. Let's be clear on that point too. Consciousness is made up of all the things that have been collected by man as experience, as knowledge, as misery, confusion, destruction, violence—all that is consciousness.

Naudé: Plus so-called solutions.

KRISHNAMURTI: God, no-God, various theories about God, all that is consciousness. When we talk about change in consciousness we are still changing the pieces from one corner to the other.

Naudé: Yes.

KRISHNAMURTI: Moving one quality into another corner of the field.

Naudé: Juggling with the contents of this huge box.

KRISHNAMURTI: Yes, juggling with the contents. And therefore ...

Naudé: We are changing variables in the same set of things.

KRISHNAMURTI: That's right. You have put it perfectly, better than I have. When we talk about changing, we are really thinking of juggling with the contents—right? Now that implies a juggler and the thing with which he is juggling. But it is still within the field of consciousness.

Naudé: There are two questions which arise. Are you saying that there is no consciousness at all outside of the content of consciousness? And secondly, that there is no entity at all to juggle, there is no entity called "me" outside of this content of consciousness?

KRISHNAMURTI: Obviously not.

Naudé: These are two big statements, Sir. Would you be kind enough to explain them?

94

KRISHNAMURTI: What is the first question?

Naudé: The first thing you are saying, if I have understood correctly, is: that this consciousness which we are discussing, which is all we are and all we have, and which we have seen is the problem itself, you are saying that this consciousness *is* its very content, and that there is nothing to be called consciousness outside of the content of consciousness?

KRISHNAMURTI: Absolutely right.

Naudé: Are you saying, outside of man's problems, outside of his misery, outside of his thinking, outside of the formulations of his mind, there is nothing at all we call consciousness?

KRISHNAMURTI: Absolutely right.

Naudé: This is a big statement. Would you explain this? We all think—and this has been postulated by Indian religions since the beginning of time—that there is a super-consciousness outside of this shell which is the consciousness we are talking about.

KRISHNAMURTI: To find out if there is something beyond this consciousness, I must understand the content of this consciousness. The mind must go beyond itself. Then I shall find out if there is something other than this or not. But to stipulate that there is has no meaning, it is just a speculation.

Naudé: So are you saying that what we commonly call consciousness, and what we are talking about, is the very content of this consciousness? The container and contained are an indivisible thing?

KRISHNAMURTI: That's right.

Naudé: And the second point you are making is: that there is no entity to decide, to will, and to juggle, when the contents to be juggled are absent.

KRISHNAMURTI: That is, my consciousness is the consciousness of the world, and the consciousness of the

95

world is me. This is a truth, not just my invention or dependent on your acceptance. It is an absolute truth. Also the content is consciousness: without the content there is no consciousness. Now when we want to change the content we are juggling.

Naudé: The content is juggling itself, because you have a third point, that there is nobody outside of this content to do any juggling at all.

KRISHNAMURTI: Quite right.

Naudé: So the juggler and the content are one, and the container and the content are one.

KRISHNAMURTI: The thinker who within this consciousness says that he must change, is consciousness trying to change. I think that is fairly clear.

Naudé: So that the world, the consciousness and the entity who supposedly will change it, are all the same entity, masquerading, as it were in three different roles.

KRISHNAMURTI: If that is so, then what is a human being to do to bring about a total emptying of the content of consciousness? How is this particular consciousness, which is me and the world with all its miseries, how is that to undergo complete change? How is the mind—which is consciousness, with all its content, with the accumulated knowledge of the past—how is that mind to empty itself of all its content?

Naudé: But people will say, hearing what you have said, understanding it imperfectly, they will say: can that consciousness be emptied, and when that consciousness is emptied, supposing this were possible, doesn't that reduce one to a state of considerable vagueness and inertia?

KRISHNAMURTI: On the contrary. To have come to this point requires a great deal of enquiry, a great deal of reason, logic, and with it comes intelligence.

Naudé: Because some people may think that the empty consciousness, which you speak about, is something like the consciousness of the child at birth.

KRISHNAMURTI: No, Sir, not at all. Let's go slowly at this, step by step. Let's begin again. My consciousness is the consciousness of the world. The world is me and the content of my consciousness is the content of the world. The content of consciousness is consciousness itself.

Naudé: And also that is the entity who says he is conscious.

KRISHNAMURTI: Now I am asking myself, realising I am that, what is then changed?

Naudé: What is changed which will solve these three sets of problems that are really one?

KRISHNAMURTI: What is implied by change? What is implied by revolution?—not physical revolution.

Naudé: We have gone beyond that.

KRISHNAMURTI: Physical revolution is the most absurd, primitive, unintelligent destruction.

Naudé: It is fragmentation in this consciousness.

KRISHNAMURTI: Yes.

Naudé: Are you asking what it is which will restore order to this consciousness?—an order which is whole.

KRISHNAMURTI: Can there be order within this consciousness?

Naudé: Is that the next step?

KRISHNAMURTI: That is what you are asking.

Naudé: Yes. Since we see that the disorder, which is the sorrow and the suffering, is the disorder in this indivisible consciousness, the next question must be: what are we going to do about it?

KRISHNAMURTI: Yes.

97

Naudé: And since there is no entity who can do something about it ...

KRISHNAMURTI: Wait, don't jump to that immediately.

Naudé: Because we have seen that the disorder is the entity.

KRISHNAMURTI: Do we realise that? No. Do we realise that the thinker is part of this consciousness and is not a separate entity outside this consciousness? Do we realise that the observer, seeing the content, examining, analysing, looking at it all, is the content itself? That the observer *is* the content?

Naudé: Yes.

KRISHNAMURTI: But stating a truth is one thing, the realisation of it is another.

Naudé: That's right. I think we do not fully understand that there is no entity separate from this thing we are trying to change.

KRISHNAMURTI: When we talk of change it seems to imply that there is an entity separate within the consciousness, who can bring about a transformation.

Naudé: We think that somehow we can step aside from the mess and look at it and juggle with it. We always tell ourselves, "Well, I'm still here to do something about it." And so we juggle more and more.

KRISHNAMURTI: More mess, more confusion.

Naudé: A change of decor and things get worse.

KRISHNAMURTI: The consciousness of the world is my consciousness. In that consciousness is all the content of human endeavour, human misery, human cruelty, mischief, all human activities are within that consciousness. Within that consciousness man has brought about this entity which says, "I am separate from my consciousness." The observer there says, "I am different from the thing observed." The thinker says, "My thoughts are different from me." First, is that so?

Naudé: We all believe that the two entities are different. We say to ourselves, "I must not be angry, I must not be sorrowful, I must improve, I must change myself." We are saying this either tacitly or consciously all the time.

KRISHNAMURTI: Because we think these two are separate. Now we are trying to point out that they are not separate, that they are one, because if there is no thought at all there is no thinker.

Naudé: That is right.

KRISHNAMURTI: If there is nothing observed there is no observer.

Naudé: There are a hundred observers and a hundred thinkers during the course of the day.

KRISHNAMURTI: I am just saying: is that so? I observe that red-tailed hawk flying by. I see it. When I observe that bird, am I observing with the image I have about that bird, or am I merely observing? Is there only mere observation? If there is an image, which is words, memory and all the rest of it, then there is an observer watching the bird go by. If there is only observation, then there is no observer.

Naudé: Would you explain why there is an observer when I look at the bird with an image?

KRISHNAMURTI: Because the observer is the past. The observer is the censor, is the accumulated knowledge, experience, memory; that is the observer, with that he observes the world. His accumulated knowledge is different from your accumulated knowledge.

Naudé: Are you saying that this total consciousness, which is the problem, is not different from the observer who is going to deal with it, and this would seem to bring us to a deadlock, because the thing we are trying to change is the person trying to change it? And the question is: what then?

KRISHNAMURTI: That is just it. If the observer is the observed, what is the nature of change in consciousness? That is what we are trying to find out. We realise that there must be a radical revolution in consciousness. How is this to take place? Is it to take place through the observer? When the observer is separate from the observed, then this change is merely juggling with the various contents of consciousness.

Naudé: That's right.

KRISHNAMURTI: Now let's go slowly. One realises that the observer is the observed, the thinker is the thought, that is a fact. Let's stop there a minute.

Naudé: Are you saying that the thinker is the totality of all these thoughts which create the confusion?

KRISHNAMURTI: The thinker is the thought, whether it is many, or one.

Naudé: But there is a difference, because the thinker thinks of himself as some sort of crystallised concrete entity. Even through this discussion, the thinker sees himself as the concrete enity to whom all these thoughts, all this confusion belongs.

KRISHNAMURTI: That concrete entity, as you say, is the result of thought.

Naudé: That concrete entity is ...

KRISHNAMURTI: ... put together by thought.

Naudé: Put together by his thoughts.

KRISHNAMURTI: By thought, not "his", by thought.

Naudé: Yes.

KRISHNAMURTI: And thought sees that there must be a change. This concrete entity, which is the result of thought, hopes to change the content.

Naudé: Itself.

KRISHNAMURTI: And so there is a battle between the observer and the observed. The battle consists of trying to control, change, shape, suppress, give a new shape, all that, that is the battle that goes on all the time in our life. But when the mind understands the truth that the observer, the experiencer, the thinker, is the thought, is the experience, is the observed, then what takes place?—knowing that there must be a radical change.

Naudé: That is a fact.

KRISHNAMURTI: And when the observer, who wants to change, realises he is part of what has to be changed?

Naudé: That he is in fact a thief pretending to be a policeman to catch himself.

KRISHNAMURTI: Right. So what takes place?

Naudé: You see, Sir, people don't believe this; they say, "By exercising will I have stopped smoking, by exercising will I have got up earlier, I have lost weight and I have learnt languages"; they say, "I am the master of my destiny, I can change"—everybody really believes this. Everybody believes that he is capable somehow of exercising will upon his own life, upon his own behaviour, and his own thinking.

KRISHNAMURTI: Which means, one has to understand the meaning of effort. What it is, why effort exists at all. Is that the way to bring about a transformation in consciousness? Through effort, through will?

Naudé: Yes.

KRISHNAMURTI: Which means what? Change through conflict. When there is the operation of will, it is a form of resistance; to overcome to suppress, to deny, to escape—all that is will in action. That means life is then a constant battle.

Naudé: Are you saying that simply one element in this consciousness is dominating another?

101

KRISHNAMURTI: Obviously. One fragment dominates another fragment.

Naudé: And that there is still conflict? There is still disorder by that very fact. Yes, this is clear.

KRISHNAMURTI: So, the central fact still remains. There must be a radical transformation in consciousness and of consciousness. Now, how is this to be brought about? That is the real question.

Naudé: Yes.

KRISHNAMURTI: We have approached it by thinking that one fragment is superior to the rest, to the other fragments within the field of consciousness.

Naudé: Indeed we have.

KRISHNAMURTI: Now that fragment which we call superior, intelligence, intellect, reason, logic, is the product of the many other fragments. One fragment has assumed authority over other fragments. But it is still a fragment and therefore there is a battle between it and the many other fragments. So is it possible to see that this fragmentation does not solve our problems?

Naudé: Because it causes the division and the conflict, which right from the start was our problem.

KRISHNAMURTI: That is, when there is division between man and woman there is conflict. When there is a division between Germany and England or Russia, there is conflict.

Naudé: And all this is division within consciousness itself. Also, the exercise of will upon consciousness is again a division within consciousness.

KRISHNAMURTI: So one has to be free of the idea that through will you can change the content. That is important to understand.

Naudé: Yes, that the exercise of will is simply the tyranny of one fragment over another.

KRISHNAMURTI: That's simple. One also realises that to be free of will is to be free of this fragmentation.

Naudé: But religions in the world have always called upon will to come in and do something.

KRISHNAMURTI: Yes. But we are denying the whole of that.

Naudé: Yes.

KRISHNAMURTI: So what is a mind to do, or not to do, when it sees will is not the way, when it sees that one fragment taking charge over another fragment is still fragmentation and therefore conflict?—and therefore still within the field of misery. Then what is such a mind to do?

Naudé: Yes, this is really the question.

KRISHNAMURTI: Now, for such a mind is there anything to do?

Naudé: When you say that, one says, "If there is nothing to do then the circus goes on."

KRISHNAMURTI: No, Sir. Look! The circus goes on only when there is the exercise of will.

Naudé: Are you saying that the circus that we have been discussing and trying to change, is in fact made up of will?

KRISHNAMURTI: My will against your will, and so on.

Naudé: My will against another part of me.

KRISHNAMURTI: And so on.

Naudé: My desire to smoke . . .

KRISHNAMURTI: That's just it. A mind which starts by saying, "I must change," realises that one fragment asserting it must change is still in conflict with another fragment, which is part of consciousness. It realises that. Therefore it also realises that will, to which man has become accustomed, which he takes for granted is the only way to bring about change ...

Naudé: ... is not the factor of change.

KRISHNAMURTI: Is not the factor of change. Therefore such a mind has come to quite a different height.

Naudé: It has cleared up a great deal.

KRISHNAMURTI: A vast quantity of rubbish.

Naudé: It has cleared up the division between the inner and the outer; the division between consciousness and its content. It has cleared up also the division between the conscious entity and the consciousness belonging to him and the various fragments. And it has cleared up the division between different fragments in that consciousness.

KRISHNAMURTI: So what has happened? What has happened to the mind that has seen all this? Not theoretically but actually felt it and says, "No more will in my life". Which means no more resistance in my life.

Naudé: This is so extraordinary it is like finding the sky at the bottom, one day. It is such a great change, it is difficult to say what the extent of that change is.

KRISHNAMURTI: It has already taken place! That is my point.

Naudé: You are saying that there is no more will, there is no more effort, there is no more division between the outside and the inside ...

KRISHNAMURTI: ... no more fragmentation within consciousness.

Naudé: No more fragmentation.

KRISHNAMURTI: That is very important to understand, Sir.

Naudé: No more observer separate from what he has observed.

KRISHNAMURTI: Which means what? No fragmentation within consciousness. Which means consciousness only exists when there is conflict between fragments.

Naudé: I am not sure that I have understood that. Consciousness is its fragments?

KRISHNAMURTI: Consciousness is its fragments and consciousness is the battle between the fragments.

Naudé: Are you saying that there are only fragments because they are in conflict, in battle? When they are not battling together they are not fragments, because they are not acting as parts. The acting of one part on another ceases. That is what it means when you say fragmentation. That is what fragmentation is.

KRISHNAMURTI: See what has taken place!

Naudé: The fragments disappear when they are not acting against each other.

KRISHNAMURTI: Naturally! When Pakistan and India ...

Naudé: ... are no longer fighting, there is no more Pakistan and India.

KRISHNAMURTI: Naturally.

Naudé: Are you saying that that is the change?

KRISHNAMURTI: Wait, I don't know yet. We'll go into it. A human mind has realised that the world is "me" and I am the world, my consciousness is the consciousness of the world, and the world's consciousness is me. The content of consciousness with all its miseries and so on is consciousness. And within that consciousness there are a thousand fragmentations. One fragment of those many fragments becomes the authority, the censor, the observer, the examiner, the thinker.

Naudé: The boss.

KRISHNAMURTI: The boss. And so he maintains fragmentation. See the importance of this! The moment he assumes the authority, he must maintain fragmentation.

Naudé: Yes, obviously. Because it is a part of consciousness acting on the rest of consciousness.

KRISHNAMURTI: Therefore he must maintain conflict. And conflict is consciousness.

Naudé: You have said that the fragments are consciousness; and are you now saying that the fragments are in fact the content?

KRISHNAMURTI: Of course.

Naudé: Fragments are conflict. There is no fragment without conflict?

KRISHNAMURTI: When is consciousness active?

Naudé: When it is in conflict.

KRISHNAMURTI: Obviously. Otherwise there is freedom, freedom to observe. So radical revolution in consciousness, and of consciousness, takes place when there is no conflict at all.

MALIBU, CALIFORNIA
27 MARCH 1971

2

ON GOOD AND EVIL

*Conversation between J. Krishnamurti
and Alain Naudé*

Naudé: Do good and evil really exist, or are they simply conditioned points of view? Is there such a thing as evil and if so what is it? Is there such a thing as sin? And is there such a thing as goodness? And what is it to be really and deeply good?

KRISHNAMURTI: I was thinking this morning on the same theme as your questions imply, whether there is an absolute good and absolute evil: as the Christian idea of sin and the Asiatic idea of Karma—as action which breeds more misery and more sorrow and yet out of that conflict of sorrow and pain a goodness is born. I was thinking about it the other day when I saw on the television some men killing baby seals. It is a terrible thing, I turned my head away quickly. Killing has always been wrong, not only human beings but animals. And religious people, not the people who believe in religion, but the really religious mind, has always shunned every form of killing. Of course, when you eat a vegetable you are killing—a vegetable—but that is the least form of killing and the simplest form of survival: I wouldn't call that killing. One has watched in India, in Europe, and in America the acceptance of killing in war, in organised murder, which war is. Also "killing" people with words, with a gesture, with a look, with contempt: this form of killing has also been decried by religious people. But in spite of it all, killing has been going on—killing, violence, brutality, arrogance, aggressiveness—all ultimately leading, in action or in thought, to hurting, to brutalising others. Also one has seen those ancient caves in North Africa and in the South of France where man is shown fighting animals, where perhaps fighting evil is understood. Or is it fighting as a form of amusement, to kill something, to overcome? So when one looks at all this, one asks if there is such a thing as evil in itself, totally devoid of the good; and what is the distance between evil and good. Is evil the diminution of good, slowly ending in evil? Or is good the diminution of evil, gradually becoming good? That is, through the time interval, moving from goodness to evil, and from evil to good?

Naudé: You mean are they two ends of the same stick?

KRISHNAMURTI: Two ends of the same stick—or are they two wholly separate things? So what is evil and what is good? The Christian world, the Inquisition, used to burn people for heresy, considering that was good.

Naudé: The Communists do the same.

KRISHNAMURTI: The Communists do it in their own way: for the good of the community, for the good of society, for the good of an economic well-being for the whole of man, and so on. In Asia too they have done all this kind of thing in various forms. But there has always been a group, until recently, where killing in any form was considered evil. Now all that is slowly disappearing, for economic and cultural reasons.

Naudé: You mean the group that avoids killing . . .

KRISHNAMURTI: . . . is gradually disappearing. So there it is. Now is there such a thing as absolute good, and absolute evil? Or is it a gradation: relative goodness and relative evil?

Naudé: And do they exist as facts outside of conditioned points of view? For instance, for the Frenchman during the war the invading German was evil; and similarly for the German, the German soldier was good, he represented protection. Now is there a good and an evil, absolutely? Or is it simply the result of a conditioned point of view?

KRISHNAMURTI: Is goodness dependent on the environment, on the culture, on economic conditions? And if it is, is it good? Can goodness flower as an environmental, cultural conditioning? And is evil also the result of environmental culture? Does it function within that frame, or does it function outside it? All these questions are implied when we ask: is there an absolute goodness and absolute evil?

Naudé: Right.

KRISHNAMURTI: First of all, what is goodness? Isn't the word "goodness" related to the word "God"? God being the highest form of the good, truth, excellence, and the capacity to express in relationship that quality of godliness, which is goodness; and anything opposite that is considered evil. If goodness is related to God, then evil is related to the devil. The devil being the ugly, the dark, the . . .

Naudé: . . . the twisted . . .

108

KRISHNAMURTI: . . . the distorted, the purposefully direct-ed harmful, such as the desire to hurt—all that is con-trary to the good; that is, the idea of God being good and the devil being the evil—right? Now I think we have more or less indicated what is good and what is evil. So we are asking if there is such a thing as absolute good and abso-lute, irrevocable evil.

Naudé: Evil as a fact, as a thing.

KRISHNAMURTI: Therefore let us first examine if there is absolute good. Not in the sense of goodness being related to God, or approximating itself to the idea of God, be-cause then that goodness becomes merely speculative. Be-cause God to most people is really a pretence of a belief in something—something excellent, noble.

Naudé: Felicity?

KRISHNAMURTI: Felicity and so on. Now what is good? I feel goodness is total order. Not only outwardly, but es-pecially inwardly. I think that order can be absolute, as in mathematics I believe there is complete order. And it is disorder that leads to chaos, to destruction, to anarchy, to the so-called evil.

Naudé: Yes.

KRISHNAMURTI: Whereas total order in one's being, order in the mind, order in one's heart, order in one's physical activities—the harmony between the three is goodness.

Naudé: The Greeks used to say that perfected man had at-tuned in total harmony his mind, his heart and his body.

KRISHNAMURTI: Quite. So we shall say for the moment that goodness is absolute order. And as most human beings live in disorder they contribute to every form of mischief, which ultimately leads to destruction, to brutal-ity, to violence, to various injuries, both psychic and physi-cal. For all that one word may be used: "evil". But I don't like that word "evil" because it is loaded with Christian meaning, with condemnation and prejudice.

Naudé: Conditioning.

KRISHNAMURTI: That's right. In India and in Asia the words "evil", "sin", are always loaded—as "goodness" is always loaded. So could we brush away all the accumulations around these words and look at it as though anew. That is: is there absolute order in oneself? Can this absolute order be brought about in oneself and therefore in the outer world? Because the world is me, and I am the world; my consciousness is the consciousness of the world, and the consciousness of the world is me. So when there is order within the human being then there is order in the world. Now can this order, right through, be absolute? Which means: order in the mind, in the heart and in the bodily activities. That is, complete harmony. How can this be brought about? That is one point.

Then the other point is: is order something to be copied according to a design? Is order pre-established by thought, by the intellect, and copied in action by the heart? Or in relationship? So is order a blueprint? How is this order to be brought about?

Naudé: Right.

KRISHNAMURTI: Order is virtue. And disorder is non-virtue, is harmful, is destructive, is impure—if we can use that word.

Naudé: One thinks of the Sanskrit word *"Adharma"*.

KRISHNAMURTI: *Adharma*, yes. So is order something put together according to a design drawn by knowledge, thought? Or is order outside the field of thought and knowledge? One feels there is absolute goodness, not as an emotional concept, but one knows, if one has gone into oneself deeply, that there is such a thing: complete, absolute, irrevocable goodness, or order. And this order is not a thing put together by thought; if it is, then it is according to a blueprint, but if it is imitated then the imitation leads to disorder, or to conformity. Conformity, imitation, and the denial of what is, is the beginning of disorder, leading ultimately to what may be called evil. So we are asking: is goodness, which is (as we said) order and virtue, is it the product of thought? Which means can it be cultivated by thought? Can virtue ever be cultivated? To cultivate implies to bring slowly into being, which means time.

110

Naudé: Mental synthesis.

KRISHNAMURTI: Yes. Now is virtue the result of time? And is order therefore a matter of evolution? And so is absolute order, absolute goodness, a matter of slow growth, cultivation, all involving time? As we said the other day, thought is the response of memory, knowledge, and experience, which is the past, which is stored up in the brain. In the brain cells themselves the past *is*. So does virtue lie in the past and is it therefore cultivatable, to be pushed forward? Or is virtue, order, only in the now? The now is not related to the past.

Naudé: You are saying that goodness is order and that order is not the product of thought; but order, if it exists at all, must exist in behaviour, behaviour in the world and in relationship. People always think that proper behaviour in relationship, in the world, must be planned, that order is always the result of planning. And quite often people get the idea, when they have listened to you, that awareness, the state of being you speak about in which there is no room for the action of thought, they get the feeling that this is a sort of disincarnate energy, which can have no action and no relationship to the world of men and events and behaviour. They think that therefore it has no real value, and not what you might call a temporal and historical significance.

KRISHNAMURTI: Right, Sir.

Naudé: You are saying that goodness is order and order is not planned.

KRISHNAMURTI: When we talk about order, don't we mean order in behaviour, in relationship, not an abstract order, not a goodness in heaven, but order, goodness in relationship and action in the now. When we talk about planning, obviously there must be planning at a certain level.

Naudé: Architecture.

KRISHNAMURTI: Architecture, building railways, going to the moon and so on, there must be a design, a planning, a very coordinated, intelligent operation taking place. We

111

are surely not mixing up the two: there must be planning, order, cooperation, the carrying out together of certain plans, a well laid-out city, a community—all that demands planning. We are talking of something entirely different. We are asking if there is absolute order in human behaviour, if there is absolute goodness, as order, in oneself and therefore in the world. And we said order is not planned, can never be planned. If it is planned, then the mind is seeking security, because the brain demands security; seeking security it will suppress, or destroy, or pervert what is and try to conform, imitate. This very imitation and conformity is disorder, from which all the mischief begins, the neuroses and various distortions of the mind and the heart. Planning implies knowledge.

Naudé: Thinking.

KRISHNAMURTI: Knowledge, thinking and ordering the thought as ideas. So we are asking: is virtue the outcome of planning? Obviously it is not. The moment your life is planned according to a pattern then you are not living, you are merely conforming to a certain standard and therefore that conformity leads to contradiction in oneself. The "what is" and the "what should be", that breeds contradiction and therefore conflict. That very conflict is the source of disorder. So order, virtue, goodness is in the moment of the now. And therefore it is free of the past. That freedom can be relative.

Naudé: How do you mean?

KRISHNAMURTI: One may be conditioned by the culture in which one lives, by the environment and so on. One either frees oneself totally from all the conditioning and therefore is absolutely free; or there may be partial unconditioning.

Naudé: Yes, get rid of one set of conditions . . .

KRISHNAMURTI: . . . and fall into another.

Naudé: Or just discard one set like Christianity and its taboos.

KRISHNAMURTI: So that slow discarding may appear orderly, but it is not; because the slow peeling off of conditioning may temporarily give the appearance of freedom, but is not absolute freedom.

Naudé: Are you saying that freedom is not the result of a particular operation with regard to one conditioning or another?

KRISHNAMURTI: That's right.

Naudé: You have said that freedom is at the beginning and not at the end. Is that what you mean?

KRISHNAMURTI: Yes, that's it. Freedom is now, not in the future. So freedom, order, or goodness, is now, which expresses itself in behaviour.

Naudé: Yes, else it has no meaning.

KRISHNAMURTI: Otherwise it has no meaning at all. Behaviour in relationship not only with a particular individual, who is close to you, but behaviour with everybody.

Naudé: In the absence of all those elements of the past which make most people behave, what will make us behave? This freedom seems to so many people such a disincarnate thing, such a bleak sky, such an immaterial thing. What is it in that freedom which will make us behave in the world of people and events with order?

KRISHNAMURTI: Sir, look. We said in the last conversation that I am the world and the world is me. We said the consciousness of the world is my consciousness. My consciousness is the world's consciousness. When you make a statement of that kind, either it is purely verbal and therefore has no meaning at all, or it is something actual, living, vital. when one realises that it is vital, in that realisation is compassion—real compassion, not for one or two, but compassion for everybody, for everything. Freedom is this compassion, which is not disincarnate as an idea.

Naudé: As a state of withdrawal.

113

KRISHNAMURTI: My relationship is only in the now, not in the past, because if my relationship is rooted in the past I am not related now. So freedom is compassion, and that comes when there is the real deep realisation that I am the world, the world is me. Freedom, compassion, order, virtue, goodness are one; and that is absolute. Now what relationship has non-goodness—which has been called evil, sin, original sin—what relationship has that with this marvellous sense of order?

Naudé: Which is not the product of thinking, of civilisation, of culture.

KRISHNAMURTI: What is the relationship between the two? There is none. So when we move away from this order—move away in the sense of misbehave—does one enter into the field of evil, if we can use that word? Or is evil something totally apart from the good?

Naudé: Whether deviation from the order of goodness is already an entry into the field of evil, or can these two not even touch at all?

KRISHNAMURTI: That's right. I may misbehave. I may tell a lie. I may consciously or unconsciously hurt another, but I can clear it. I can wipe it away by apologising, by saying "forgive me". It can be done immediately.

Naudé: It can be ended.

KRISHNAMURTI: So I am finding out something, which is: the non-ending of it, carrying it over in one's mind day after day, as hate, as a grudge . . .

Naudé: . . . guilt, fear . . .

KRISHNAMURTI: . . . does that nourish the evil? You follow?

Naudé: Yes.

KRISHNAMURTI: If I continue with it, keep within my mind the grudge which I bear against you, carry it on day after day, the grudge which involves hate, envy, jealousy, antagonism—all that is violence. So what is the relation-

114

ship of violence to evil and goodness? We are using the word "evil" very . . .

Naudé: . . . cautiously.

KRISHNAMURTI: Cautiously. Because I don't like that word at all. So what is the relationship between violence and goodness? Obviously none at all! But the violence which I have cultivated—whether it is the product of society, the product of the culture, the environment, or inherited from the animal—that violence, by becoming aware of it, can be wiped away.

Naudé: Yes.

KRISHNAMURTI: Not a gradual wiping away; wipe it away as you wipe out a clean . . .

Naudé: . . take a mark off the wall.

KRISHNAMURTI: Then you are always in that goodness.

Naudé: Are you saying that goodness is a wholly negative affair then?

KRISHNAMURTI: Yes, it must be.

Naudé: And in that way the negative is not related at all to the positive, because it is not the result of a gradual decline or accumulation of the positive. The negative exists when the positive is wholly absent.

KRISHNAMURTI: Yes; put it round the other way. The negation of the grudge, the negation of violence and the negation of the continuity of the violence, that negation of it is the good.

Naudé: Is the emptying.

KRISHNAMURTI: The emptying of violence is the richness of the good.

Naudé: Therefore the good is always intact.

KRISHNAMURTI: Yes, it is never broken up, not fragmented. Sir, wait! So is there such a thing as absolute evil? I don't know if you have ever considered this: I have seen in India little statues made of clay in which needles, or thorns, have been put; I have seen it very often. The image is supposed to represent a person whom you want to hurt. In India there are very long thorns, you have seen them, from bushes, and they are stuck into these clay statuettes.

Naudé: I didn't know they did that in India.

KRISHNAMURTI: I have seen it. Now *there* is a determined action to produce evil in another, to hurt another.

Naudé: An intent.

KRISHNAMURTI: The intent, the ugly, deep, hatred.

Naudé: Deliberate. This must be evil, Sir.

KRISHNAMURTI: What is its relationship to good—good being all that we have said? This is a real intent to hurt people.

Naudé: Organised disorder, one might say.

KRISHNAMURTI: Organised disorder, which is the organised disorder of a society that rejects the good. Because the society is me. I am the society; if I don't change, society cannot change. And here is the deliberate intention to hurt another, whether it is organised as war or not.

Naudé: In fact, organzied war is the group manifestation of the phenomenon you are speaking about in India, putting the thorns through the little statues.

KRISHNAMURTI: This is well known, this is as old as the hills. So I am saying this desire to hurt, consciously or unconsciously, and yielding to it, and giving it sustenance, is what? Would you call that evil?

Naudé: Of course.

116

KRISHNAMURTI: Then we shall have to say that will is evil.

Naudé: Aggression is evil. Violence is evil.

KRISHNAMURTI: Wait, see it! Will is evil, because I want to hurt you.

Naudé: Someone might say though: the will to do you good—is that will also evil?

KRISHNAMURTI: You cannot will to do good. Either you are good, or not good, you can't will goodness. Will being the concentration of thought as resistance.

Naudé: Yes, you said that goodness is the absence of a blueprint.

KRISHNAMURTI: So I am asking: is evil related to the good, or are the two things totally apart? And is there such a thing as absolute evil? There is absolute good, but absolute evil cannot exist. Right?

Naudé: Yes, because evil is always cumulative, it is always to some degree or another.

KRISHNAMURTI: Yes. So a man with the deep intention to hurt another—some incident, some accident, some affection or care, might change the whole thing. But to say that there is an absolute sin, absolute evil, is the most terrible thing to say. That is evil.

Naudé: The Christians have personified evil as Satan and as an almost immutable force, almost equal to the good, almost equal to God. The Christians have enthroned evil almost eternally.

KRISHNAMURTI: Look, Sir. You have seen those bushes in India, they have got long thorns, nearly two inches long.

Naudé: Yes.

KRISHNAMURTI: There are snakes which are poisonous, deadly poisonous, there are other things which are frighteningly cruel in nature, like the white shark, that appalling thing we saw the other day. Is that evil?

Naudé: No.

KRISHNAMURTI: No?

Naudé: No, Sir.

KRISHNAMURTI: It is protecting itself: the thorn is protecting itself against the animal so that the leaves are not eaten.

Naudé: Yes and so is the snake.

KRISHNAMURTI: So is the snake.

Naudé: And the shark is following its nature.

KRISHNAMURTI: So see what it means. Anything that is self-protective in the physical sense is not evil. But protecting oneself psychologically, resisting any movement, leads to disorder.

Naudé: If I may interrupt here. This is the argument which many people use about war. They say that building up an army and using it, for instance, in South East Asia is the kind of physical protection which the shark . . .

KRISHNAMURTI: That is too absurd an argument. The whole world is divided up for psychological reasons as "my country" and "your country", "my God" and "your God"—that and economic reasons are the cause of war, surely? But I am trying to get at something different. Nature is terrible in certain ways.

Naudé: Ruthless.

KRISHNAMURTI: We human beings looking at it say, "That's evil, how terrible".

Naudé: Lightning.

KRISHNAMURTI: Earthquakes which destroy a thousand people in a few seconds. So the moment we assert that there is absolute evil, that very assertion is the denial of the good. Goodness implies total abnegation of the self. Because the "me" is always separative. The "me", "my family", the self, the person, the ego, is the centre of disorder, because it is a divisive factor. The "me" is the mind, is thought. And we have never been able to move away from this egocentric activity. To move completely away from it is complete order, freedom, goodness. And to remain in the circle of self-centred movement breeds disorder; there is always conflict there. And we attribute this conflict to evil, to the devil, to bad karma, to environment, to society; but the society is me and I have built this society. So unless this "me" is totally transformed, I am always contributing to a major extent or to a minor extent, to disorder.

Order means behaviour in freedom. And freedom means love and not pleasure. When one observes all this one sees very clearly that there is a marvellous sense of absolute order.

MALIBU, CALIFORNIA
28 MARCH 1971

INDIA

IV

Two Conversations:
J. Krishnamurti and Swami Venkatesananda

1 The guru and search. Four schools of Yoga
scrutinised (Karma, Bhakti, Raja, Gnana Yoga)
2 Four "mahawakyas" from the Upanishads
discussed. Communication and the Bodhisattva
ideal. Vedanta and the ending of knowledge

1

J. KRISHNAMURTI AND
SWAMI VENKATESANANDA

The guru and search.
Four schools of Yoga scrutinised
(Karma, Bhakti, Raja and Gnana Yoga)

Swami Venkatesananda:[1] Krishnaji, I come as a humble speaker to a *guru,* not in the sense of hero-worship but in the literal sense which the word *guru* means, that is the remover of darkness, of ignorance. The word *"gu"* stands for the darkness of ignorance and *ru* stands for the remover, the dispeller. Hence *guru* is the light that dispels the darkness of ignorance and you are that light for me now. We sit in the tent here at Saanen listening to you and I cannot help visualising similar scenes; for instance, of the Buddha addressing the Bikshus, or of Vasishta instructing Rama in the royal court of Dasaratha. We have a few examples of these *gurus* in the Upanishads; first there was Varuna, *the guru.* He merely prods his disciple with the words "Tapasa Brahma . . . Tapo Brahmeti". "What is *Brahman?*—Don't ask me." Tapo Brahman, *tapas,* austerity or discipline—or as you yourself often say, "Find out"—is Brahman and the disciple must himself discover the truth, though by stages. Yajnyavalkya and Uddhalaka adopted a more direct approach. Yajnyavalkya instructing his wife Maitreyi, used the *neti-neti* method. You cannot describe *Brahman* positively, but when you eliminate everything else, it is there. As you said the other day, love cannot be described—"this is it"—but only by eliminating what is not love. Uddhalaka used several analogies to enable his disciples to see the truth and then nailed it with the famous expression *Tat-Twam-Asi.* Dakshinamurti instructed his disciples by silence and Chinmudra. It is said

[1] Swami Venkatesananda, scholar and teacher, asks to be identified only by his name.

123

that the Sanatkumaras went to him for instruction. Dakshinamurti just kept silent and showed the Chinmudra and the disciples looked at him and got enlightened. It is believed that one cannot realise the truth without the help of a *guru*. Obviously even those people who regularly come to Saanen are greatly helped in their quest. Now, what according to you is the role of a *guru*, a preceptor or an awakener?

KRISHNAJI: Sir, if you are using the word *guru* in the classical sense, which is the dispeller of darkness, of ignorance, can another, whatever he be, enlightened or stupid, really help to dispel this darkness in oneself? Suppose "A" is ignorant and you are his *guru*—guru in the accepted sense, one who dispels darkness and one who carries the burden for another, one who points out—can such a *guru* help another? Or rather can the *guru* dispel the darkness of another?—not theoretically but actually. Can you, if you are the *guru* of so and so, dispel his darkness, dispel the darkness for another? Knowing that he is unhappy, confused, has not enough brain matter, has not enough love, or sorrow, can you dispel that? Or has he to work tremendously on himself? You may point out, you may say, "Look, go through that door," but he has to do the work entirely from the beginning to the end. Therefore, you are not a *guru* in the accepted sense of that word, if you say that another cannot help.

Swamiji: It is just this: the "if" and "but". The door is there. I have to go through. But there is this ignorance of where the door is. You, by pointing out, remove that ignorance.

KRISHNAJI: But I have to walk there. Sir, you are the *guru* and you point out the door. You have finished your job.

Swamiji: So darkness of ignorance is removed.

KRISHNAJI: No, your job is finished and it is now for me to get up, walk, and see what is involved in walking. I have to do all that.

Swamiji: That is perfect.

KRISHNAJI: Therefore you do not dispel my darkness.

Swamiji: I am sorry, but I do not know how to get out of this room. I am ignorant of the existence of a door in a certain direction and the *guru* removes the darkness of that ignorance. And then I take the necessary steps to get out.

KRISHNAJI: Sir, let us be clear. Ignorance is lack of understanding, or the lack of understanding of oneself, not the big self or the little self. The door is the "me" through which I have to go. It is not outside of "me". It is not a factual door as that painted door. It is a door in me through which I have to go. You say, "Do that."

Swamiji: Exactly.

KRISHNAJI: Your function as the *guru* is then finished. You do not become important. I do not put garlands around your head. I have to do all the work. You have not dispelled the darkness of ignorance. You have, rather, pointed out to me that, "You are the door through which you yourself have to go."

Swamiji: But would you, Krishnaji, accept that the pointing out was necessary?

KRISHNAJI: Yes, of course. I point out, I do that. We all do that. I ask a man on the road, "Will you please tell me which is the way to Saanen", and he tells me; but I do not spend time and express devotion and say, "My God, you are the greatest of men." That is too childish!

Swamiji: Thank you, Sir. Closely related to what the *guru* is, there is the question of what discipline is, which you defined as learning. Vedanta classifies the seekers according to their qualifications, or maturity, and prescribes suitable methods of learning. The disciple with the keenest perception is given instruction in silence, or with a brief awakening word like *Tat-Twam-Asi*. He is called *Utta-madhikari*. The disciple with the mediocre ability is given more elaborate treatment; he is called *Madhyamadhikari*. The dull-witted is entertained with stories, rituals, etc., hoping for greater maturity; he is called *Adhamadhikari*. Perhaps you will comment on this?

KRISUKAJI: Yes, the top, the middle and bottom. That implies, Sir, that we have to find out what we mean by maturity.

Swamiji: May I explain that? You said the other day, "The whole world is burning, you must realise the seriousness of it." And that hit me like a bolt—even to grasp that truth. But there may be millions who just do not bother; they are not interested. Those we shall call the *Adhama*, the lowest. There are others like the Hippies and so on who play with it, who may be entertained with stories and who say, "We are unhappy," or who tell you, "We know society is a mess, we will take L.S.D.", and so on. And there may be others who respond to that idea, that the world is burning, and that immediately sparks them. We find them everywhere. How does one handle them?

KRISHNAJI: How to handle the people who are utterly immature, those who are partially mature, and those who consider themselves mature?

Swamiji: Correct.

KRISHNAJI: To do that, we have to understand what we mean by maturity. What do you think is maturity? Does it depend on age, time?

Swamiji: No.

KRISHNAJI: So we can remove that. Time, age is not an indication of maturity. Then there is the maturity of the very learned man, the man who is highly, intellectually capable.

Swamiji: No, he may twist and turn the words.

KRISHNAJI: So, we will eliminate that. Whom would you consider as a mature, ripe man?

Swamiji: The man who is able to observe.

KRISHNAJI: Wait. Obviously the man who goes to churches, to temples, to mosques is out; so is the intellectual, the religious and the emotional. We should say, if we eliminate all that, maturity consists of being not self-centred—not "me" first and everybody else second, or my emotions first. So maturity implies the absence of the "me".

Swamiji: Fragmentation, to use a better word.

KRISHNAJI: The "me" which creates the fragments. Now, how would you appeal to that man? And to the man who is half one and half the other, "me" and "not me", who plays with both? And the other one who is completely "me", who enjoys himself? How do you appeal to these three?

Swamiji: How do you awaken these three?—that is the trouble.

KRISHNAJI: Wait! The man who is completely "me", there is no awakening in him. He is not interested. He won't even listen to you. He will listen to you if you promise him something, heaven, hell, fear or more profit in the world, more money; but he will do it in order to gain. So the man who wishes to gain, achieve, is immature.

Swamiji: Quite right.

KRISHNAJI: Whether Nirvana, Heaven, Moksha, attainment, or enlightenment, he is immature. Now, what will you do with such a man?

Swamiji: Tell him stories.

KRISHNAJI: No, why should I tell him stories, befuddle him more by my stories or by your stories? Why not leave him alone? He would not listen.

Swamiji: It is cruel.

KRISHNAJI: Cruel on whose part? He won't listen to you. Let us be factual. You come to me. I am the total "me". I am not concerned with anything but "me", but you say "Look, you are making a mess of the world, you are creating such a misery for man", and I say, please go away. Put it any way you like; put it in stories, cover it with pills, sweet pills, but he is not going to change the "me". If he does, he comes to the middle—the "me" and

127

the "not me". This is called evolution. The man who is the lowest reaches the middle.

Swamiji: How?

KRISHNAJI: By knocking. Life forces him, teaches him. There is war, hatred; he is destroyed. Or he goes into a church. The church is a trap to him. It does not enlighten him, it does not say, "For God's sake break through," but it says it will give him what he wants—entertainment, whether Jesus entertainment, or Hindu entertainment, or Buddhist, or Muslim or whatever it is—it will give him entertainment, only in the name of God. So they keep him at the same level, with little modifications, a little bit of polish, better culture, better clothes, etc. That is what is happening. He probably makes up (as you said just now) eighty per cent of the world, more perhaps, ninety per cent.

Swamiji: What can you do?

KRISHNAJI: I won't add to it, I won't tell him stories, I won't entertain him; because there are others who are already entertaining him.

Swamiji: Thank you.

KRISHNAJI: Then there is the middle type, the "me" and the "not-me", who does social reforms, a little bit of good here and there, but always the "me" operating. Socially, politically, religiously, in every way, the "me" is operating. But a little more quietly, with a little more polish. Now to him you can talk a little bit, say, "Look, a social reform is all right in its place but it leads you nowhere," and so on. You can talk to him. Perhaps he will listen to you. The other one will not listen to you at all. This chap will listen to you, pay a little attention and perhaps say this is too serious, this requires too much work and slips back into his old pattern. We shall talk to him and leave him. What he wants to do is up to him. Now, there is the other one who is getting out of the "me", who is stepping out of the circle of the "me". There, you can talk to him. He will pay attention to you. So one talks to all the three, not distinguishing between those who are mature and those who are not mature. We will talk to all the three categories, the three types, and leave it to them.

Swamiji: The one who is not interested, he will walk out.

KRISHNAJI: He will walk out of the tent, he will walk out of the room. That is his affair. He goes to his church, football, entertainment or whatever it is. But the moment you say "you are immature and I will teach you more", he becomes ...

Swamiji: Boosted up.

KRISHNAJI: The seed of poison is already there. Sir, if the soil is right, the grain will take root. But to say, "You are mature, and you are immature", that is totally wrong. Who am I to tell somebody that he is immature? It is for him to find out.

Swamiji: But can a fool find out that he is a fool?

KRISHNAJI: If he is a fool he won't even listen to you. You see, Sir, we start out with the idea of wanting to help.

Swamiji: That is what we are basing our whole discussion upon.

KRISHNAJI: I think the approach of wanting to help is not valid, except in the medical world or in the technological world. If I am ill it is necessary to go to the doctor to be cured. Here, psychologically, if I am asleep, I won't listen to you. If I am half awake, I will listen to you according to my vacant state, according to my moods. Therefore, to the one man who says, "I really want to keep awake, keep psychologically awake", to him you can talk. So we talk to all of them.

Swamiji: Thank you. That clears up a big misunderstanding. When sitting alone, I reflected over what you had said earlier in the day. I cannot help the spontaneous feeling. "Ah, the Buddha said so, or Vasishtha said so", though immediately I endeavour to cut through the imagery of the words to find the meaning. You help us find the meaning, though perhaps that is not your intention. So did Vasishtha and the Buddha. People come here as they went to those great ones. Why? What is there in human nature that seeks, that gropes and grasps for a crutch? Again, not to help them may be a cruelty, but to spoon-feed them may be greater cruelty. What does one do?

KRISHNAJI: The question being, why do people need crutches?

Swamiji: Yes, and whether to help them or not.

KRISHNAJI: That is it: whether you should give them crutches to lean on. Two questions are involved. Why do people need crutches? And whether you are the person to give them the crutches?

Swamiji: Should one or should one not?

KRISHNAJI: Should one or should one not, and whether you are capable of giving them help?—those two questions are involved. Why do people want crutches, why do people want to depend on others, whether it is Jesus, Buddha, or ancient saints, why?

Swamiji: First of all, there is something that is seeking. The seeking itself seems to be good.

KRISHNAJI: Is it? Or is it their fear of not achieving something which the saints, the great people, have pointed out? Or the fear of going wrong, of not being happy, of not getting enlightenment, understanding, or whatever you call it?

Swamiji: May I quote a beautiful expression from the Bhagavadgita? Krishna said: four types of people come to me. The one who is in distress; he comes to me for the removal of distress. Then there is the one who is a curious man; he just wants to know what is this God, truth, and whether there is heaven and hell? The third one wants some money. He also comes to God and prays to get more money. And the Gyani, the wise man, also comes. All of them are good, because they are all, somehow or the other, seeking God. But of all these, I think the Gyani is the best one. So the seeking may be due to various reasons.

130

KRISHNAJI: Yes, Sir. There are these two questions. First of all, why do we seek? Then, why does humanity demand crutches? Now, why does one seek, why should one seek at all?

Swamiji: Why should one seek—because one finds something missing.

KRISHNAJI: Which means what? I am unhappy and I want happiness. That is a form of seeking. I do not know what enlightenment is. I have read about it in books and it appeals to me and I seek it. Also I seek a better job, because there is more money, more profit, more enjoyment and so on. In all these there is seeking, searching, wanting. I can understand the man wanting a better job, because society as it is constituted is so monstrously arranged, that it makes him seek more money, a better job. But psychologically, inwardly, what am I seeking? And when I do find it, in my search, how do I know that what I find is true?

Swamiji: Perhaps the seeking drops.

KRISHNAJI: Wait, Sir. How do I know? In my search, how do I know that this is the truth? How do I know? Can I ever say "This is the truth"? Therefore why should I seek it? So what makes me seek? What makes one seek is a much more fundamental question than the search, and saying, "This is the truth." If I say, "This is the truth", I must know it already. If I know it already, it is not truth. It is something dead, past, which tells me that is the truth. A dead thing cannot tell me what is truth.

So why do I seek? Because, deeply I am unhappy, deeply I am confused, deeply there is great sorrow in me and I want to find a way out of it. You come along as the *guru,* as an enlightened man, or as a professor and say, "Look, this is the way out." The basic reason for my search is to escape from this agony and I posit that I can escape sorrow, and that enlightenment is over there, or in myself. Can I escape from it? I cannot in the sense of avoiding it, resisting it, running away from it; it is there. Wherever I go, it is still there. So what I have to do is to find out in myself why sorrow has come into being, why I am suffering. Then, is that a search? No. When I want to find out why I am suffering, that is not searching. It is not even a quest. It is like going to a doctor and saying I have

131

a bad tummy, and he says you have eaten the wrong kind of food. So I will avoid wrong food. If the cause of my misery is in myself, not necessarily created by the environment in which I live, then I have to find out how to be free from it for myself. You may, as the *guru*, point out that that is the door, but as soon as you have pointed it out, your job is over. Then I have to work, then I have to find out what to do, how to live, how to think, how to feel this way of living in which there is no suffering.

Swamiji: Then to that extent the helping, the pointing out, is justified.

KRISHNAJI: Not justified, but you do it naturally.

Swamiji: Supposing the other man gets stuck somewhere, that as he proceeds, in going there he knocks against the table ...

KRISHNAJI: He must learn that the table is there. He must learn that when he is going towards the door there is an obstacle in the way. If he is enquiring, he will find out. But if you come along and say "There is the door, there is the table, don't knock against it", you are treating him just like a child, leading him to the door. There is no meaning to it.

Swamiji: So that much of help, the pointing out, is justified?

KRISHNAJI: Any decent man with a decent heart will say, Don't go there, there is a precipice. I once met a very well-known *guru* in India. He came to see me. There was a mattress on the floor and we said to him politely, please sit on the mattress—and he quietly sat on the mattress, assumed the position of the *guru*, put his stick in front of him and began to discuss—it was quite a performance he put up! And he said: human beings need a *guru* because we *gurus* know better than the layman; why should he go through all the danger alone? We will help him. It was impossible to discuss with him because he had assumed that he alone knew and everybody else was in ignorance. At the end of ten minutes he left. annoyed.

Swamiji: That is one of the things for which Krishnaji is famous in India!—Next, while you rightly point out the utter futility of blindly accepting dogmas, formulas, you will not ask for their summary rejection. While tradition can be a deadly block, it is perhaps worth understanding it and its origin; otherwise, in destroying one tradition an equally pernicious one might spring up.

KRISHNAJI: Quite right.

Swamiji: Hence may I offer a few traditional beliefs for your scrutiny so that we may discover where and how what you called "good intentions" veered towards hell— the shell that imprisons us? Each branch of Yoga prescribed its own disciplines in the firm conviction that if one pursued them in the right spirit one would end sorrow. I shall enumerate them for your comments.

First, Karma Yoga: it demanded Dharma, or a virtuous life, which was often extended to include the much abused Varnashrama Dharma. Krishna's dictum "Swadharme . . . Bhayavaha"—seems to have indicated that if a man voluntarily submitted himself to certain rules of conduct, his mind would be free to observe and learn with the help of certain Bavanas. Would you comment on this?—the concept of Dharma and rules and regulations: "do this", "that is right", "that is wrong. . . ."

KRISHNAJI: Which means really, lay down what is right conduct, and I voluntarily adopt it. There is a teacher who lays down what is righteous behaviour, and I come along and voluntarily, to use your word, take to it, accept it. Is there such a thing as voluntary acceptance? And should the teacher lay down what is right conduct, which means he has set the pattern, the mould, the conditioning? You follow the danger of it?—in his having laid down the conditioning which produces right behaviour, which will lead one to heaven.

Swamiji: That is one aspect of it. The other aspect in which I am more interested, is if that is accepted, then the psychological apparatus is free to observe.

KRISHNAJI: I understand. No, Sir. Why should I accept it? You are the teacher. You lay down the mode of conduct. How do I know that you are right? You may be wrong. And I won't accept your authority. Because I see the authority of the gurus, the authority of the priest, the authority of the Church—they have all failed. Therefore, with a new teacher laying down a new law, I would say, "For God's sake you are playing the same game; I do not accept it." And is there such a thing as voluntary acceptance—voluntary, free acceptance? Or am I already influenced, because you are a teacher, you are the great one, and you promise me a reward at the end of it, unconsciously or consciously, which leads me to "voluntarily": accept it? I do not accept it freely. If I am free, I do not accept it at all. I live righteously.

Swamiji: So righteousness must come from within?

KRISHNAJI: Obviously, what else, Sir? Look at what is going on in the study of behaviour. They say outward circumstances, environment, culture, produce certain types of behaviour. That is, if I live in a communist environment with its domination, with its threats, concentration camps, all that will make me behave in a certain way; I put on a mask, frightened, and I behave in a certain way. In society which is more or less free, where there are not so many rules, because nobody believes in rules, where everything is permitted, there I play.

Swamiji: Now, which one is more acceptable from the spiritual point of view?

KRISHNAJI: Neither. Because behaviour, virtue, is something which cannot be cultivated by me or by society. I have to find out how to live rightly. Virtue is something which is not an acceptance of patterns, or following a deadly pattern of routine. Goodness is not routine. Surely, if I am good because my teacher says I am good, it is meaningless. Therefore there is no such thing as voluntary acceptance of the righteous behaviour which is laid down by a guru, by a teacher.

Swamiji: One has to find it for oneself.

KRISHNAJI: Therefore I have to begin to enquire. I begin to look, to find out how to live. I can only live when there is no fear.

134

Swamiji: Perhaps I should have explained this. According to Sankara it is meant only for the lower.

KRISHNAJI: What is low and high? The mature and the immature? Sankara or XYZ says. "Lay down the rule for the low and for the high" and they do it. They read the books of Sankara, or some pundit reads it to them, and they say how marvellous it is and go back and live their own life. This is an obvious fact. You see it in Italy. They listen to the Pope—they listen earnestly for two or three minutes and then go on with their daily life; nobody cares, it does not make any difference. That is why I want to ask, why the so-called Sankaras, Gurus, lay down laws about what is behaviour.

Swamiij: Otherwise there would be chaos.

KRISHNAJI: There is chaos anyhow. There is terrible chaos. In India they have read Sankara and all the teachers for a thousand years. Look at them!

Swamiji: Perhaps, according to them, the alternative is impossible.

KRISHNAJI: What is the alternative? Confusion? And that is what they are living in. Why not understand the confusion in which they are living instead of Sankara? If they understand confusion, they can change it.

Swamiji: Perhaps that leads us on to this question of *Bhawana* where a bit of psychology is involved. Coming to the Sadhana of Karma Yoga, the Bhagavad Gita prescribes among other things a *Nimitta Bhawana*. *Bhawana* is undoubtedly *Being* and *Nimitta Bhawana* is being an egoless instrument in the hands of God or the Infinite Being. But it is also taken to mean an attitude or a feeling in the hope that it will help a beginner to observe himself and thus the *Bhawana* will fill his being. Perhaps it is indispensable for the people of little understanding; or will it permanently distract them by self-deception? How shall we make this work?

KRISHNAJI: What is the question you are asking, Sir?

Swamiji: There is the technique of *Bhawana*.

135

KRISHNAJI: That implies a system, a method, by the practice of which, you ultimately reach enlightenment. You practise in order to come to God or whatever it is. The moment you practise a method, what happens? I practise day after day the method laid down by you. What happens?

Swamiji: There is a famous saying, "As you think so you become".

KRISHNAJI: I think that by the practice of this method I will reach enlightenment. So what do I do? Every day I practise it. I become more and more mechanical.

Swamiji: But there is a feeling.

KRISHNAJI: The mechanical routine is going on with the feeling added, "I like it", "I don't like it", "it is a bore"— you know, there is a battle going on. So anything I practise, any discipline, any practice in the accepted sense of the word makes my mind more and more narrow, limited and dull, and you are promising at the end of it, heaven. I say it is like soldiers being trained day after day—drill, drill—till they are nothing but instruments of the commanding officer or sergeant. Give them a little initiative. So I am questioning the whole approach of system and method towards enlightenment. Even in factories a man who merely moves a button or pushes this or that does not produce as much as the man who is free to learn as he goes along.

Swamiji: Can you put that into *Bhawana*?

KRISHNAJI: Why not?

Swamiji: So it works?

KRISHNAJI: This is the only way. That is real *Bhawana*: Learn as you go along. Therefore keep awake. Learn as you go along, therefore be alert as you go along. If I take a walk and I have a system, a method of walking, that is all I am concerned with: I shall not see the birds, the trees, the marvellous light on the leaf, nothing. And why should I accept the teacher who gives me the method, the mode? He may be as peculiar as I am, and there are teachers who are very odd. So I reject all that.

Swamiji: The problem again is that of the beginner.

KRISHNAJI: Who is the beginner? The immature one?

Swamiji: Probably.

KRISHNAJI: Therefore you are giving him a toy to play with?

Swamiji: Some sort of opening.

KRISHNAJI: Yes a toy and he enjoys that and practises all day and his mind remains very small.

Swamiji: Perhaps that is your answer to this Bhakti Yoga question too. Again, somehow they wanted these people to break through.

KRISHNAJI: I am not at all sure, Sir.

Swamiji: I will discuss this Bhakti. Coming to Bhakti Yoga, the *Bhakta* is encouraged to worship God even in temples and images, feeling the Divine presence within. In quite a number of mantras, it is repeated again and again, "You are the All Pervading . . . you are the Omnipresent", etc. Krishna asks the devotees to see God in the objects of nature and then as the "All". At the same time through japa, or the repetition of mantra with the corresponding awareness of its significance, the devotee is asked to perceive that the divine presence outside is identical with the indwelling presence. Thus the individual realises his oneness with the collective. Is there anything fundamentally wrong with that system?

KRISHNAJI: Oh! Yes, Sir. The Communist block does not believe in God at all. The Communists have set the State above God. They are selfish, they are frightened, but there is no God, no mantras, etc. Another does not know the mantras, japa, repetition but he says, "I want to find out what truth is. I want to find out if there is a God at all. There may be no such thing." And the Gita and all of them assume that there is. They assume there is God. Who

137

are they to tell me there is or there is not, including Krishna or X, Y, Z? I say it may be your own conditioning; you are born in a particular climate and with a particular conditioning, with a particular attitude and you believe in that. And then you lay down rules. But if I reject all authority, including the Communists, including the Western and the Asiatic authorities, all authority, then where am I? Then I have to find out, because I am unhappy, I am miserable.

Swamiji: But I might be free from conditioning.

KRISHNAJI: That is my *business*—to be free. Otherwise I cannot learn. If I remain a Hindu for the rest of my life, I am finished. The Catholic remains a Catholic and the Communist is equally dead. But is it possible—that is really the question—to reject all conditioning which accepts authority? Can I really reject all authority and stand alone to find out? And I must be alone. Otherwise, if I am not alone in the deeper sense of that word, I am just repeating what Sankara, Buddha, or X, Y, Z said. What is the point of it, knowing very well that repetition is not the real? So, must not I—mature, or immature, or half mature—must not they all learn to stand alone? It is painful; they say, "My God, how can I stand alone?"—to be without the children, to be without God, to be without the Commissar? There is fear.

Swamiji: Do you think that every one can work out this?

KRISHNAJI: Why not, Sir? If you cannot, then you are caught in it. Then no amount of Gods, and mantras, and tricks will help you. They may cover it up. They may bottle it up. They may suppress it and put it in the refrigerator. But it is always there.

Swamiji: Now there is the other method, that of standing alone: Raja Yoga. The student here is again asked to cultivate certain virtuous qualities which, on the one hand, make of him a good citizen and on the other, remove possible psychological barriers. This *Sadhana*, which is mainly awareness of thought which includes memory imagination and sleep, seems to be close to your own teaching. *Asana* and *Pranayama* are auxiliaries, perhaps. And even the *Dhyana* of Yoga is not intended to bring

138

about self-realisation, which is admittedly not the end-product of a series of actions, Krishna clearly says that Yoga clarifies perception: *"Atma Shuddhaye"*. Do you approve of this approach? There is not much of help involved here; even Iswara is only *"Purusha Visheshaha"*. It is a sort of a *guru*, invisible in the indwelling process. Do you approve of this approach: there is this method of sitting in meditation and trying to delve deeper and deeper.

KRISHNAJI: Certainly. Then one has to go into the question of meditation.

Swamiji: And Patanjali defines meditation as, "The absence of all world idea or any extraneous idea." That is the *"Bhakti Sunyam"*.

KRISHNAJI: Look, Sir, I have not read anything. Now here I am: I know nothing. I only know that I am in sorrow and that I have got a fairly good mind. I have no authority—Sankara, Krishna, Patanjali, nobody—I am absolutely alone. I have got to face my life and I have got to be a good citizen—not according to the Communists, Capitalists, or Socialists—Good citizenship means behaviour, which is not one thing in the office and different at home. First, I want to find out how to be free of this sorrow. Then being free, I shall find out if there is such a thing as God or whatever it is. So how am I to learn to be free of this enormous burden? That is my first question. I can only understand it in relationship with another. I cannot sit by myself and dig into it because I may pervert it; my mind is too silly, prejudiced. So, I have to find out in relationship—with nature, with human beings—what is this fear, this sorrow; in relationship, because if I sit by myself I can deceive myself very easily. But by being awake in relationship, I can spot it immediately.

Swamiji: If you are alert.

KRISHNAJI: That is the point. If I am alert, watchful, I shall find out; and that does not take time.

Swamiji: But if one is not?

KRISHNAJI: Therefore, the problem is to be awake, to be aware, alert. Is there a method for it? Follow it, Sir. If

139

there is a method which will help me to be aware, I shall practise it; but is that awareness? Because in that is involved routine, acceptance of authority, repetition; that is gradually making my alertness dull. So I reject that: the practice of alertness. I say I can only understand sorrow in relationship and that understanding comes only through alertness. Therefore, I must be alert. I am alert because my demand is to end sorrow. If I am hungry, I want food and I go after food. In the same way, I discover the enormous burden of sorrow in me and I discover it through relationship—how I behave with you, how I talk to people. In that process of relationship, this thing is revealed.

Swamiji: In that relationship you are all the time self-aware, if I may put it that way.

KRISHNAJI: Yes, I am aware, alert, watching.

Swamiji: Is it so easy for an ordinary person?

KRISHNAJI: It is, if the man is serious and says, "I want to find out." The ordinary man, eighty to ninety per cent of them, is not really interested. But the man who is serious, he says, "I shall find out—I want to see if the mind can be free from sorrow." And it is only possible to discover it in relationship. I cannot invent sorrow. In relationship sorrow comes.

Swamiji: The sorrow is within.

KRISHNAJI: Naturally, Sir, it is a psychological phenomenon.

Swamiji: You would not want man to sit and meditate and sharpen?

KRISHNAJI: So let us come back to the question of meditation. What is meditation?—not according to what Patanjali and others say because they may be totally mistaken. And I might be mistaken when I say I know how to meditate. So one has oneself to find out, one has to ask, "What is meditation?" Is meditation sitting quiet, concentrating, controlling thoughts, watching?

140

Swamiji: Watching, perhaps.

KRISHNAJI: You can watch when you are walking.

Swamiji: It is difficult.

KRISHNAJI: You watch while eating, when you are listening to people, when somebody says something that hurts you, flatters you. That means, you have to be alert all the time—when you are exaggerating, when you are telling half-truths—you follow? To watch, you need a very quiet mind. That is meditation. The whole of that is meditation.

Swamiji: To me it looks as though Patanjali evolved an exercise for quietening the mind, not on the battlefield of life, but to start it when you are alone and then extend it to relationship.

KRISHNAJI: But if you escape from the battle . . .

Swamiji: For a little while . . .

KRISHNAJI: If you escape from the battle you have not understood the battle. The battle is you. How can you escape from yourself? You can take a drug, you can pretend that you have escaped, you can repeat mantras, japas and do all kinds of things, but the battle is going on. You say, "Get away quietly from it and then come back to it." That is a fragmentation. We are suggesting: "Look at the battle you are involved in; you are caught in it: you are *it*."

Swamiji: That leads us to the last discipline: *you are it.*

KRISHNAJI: You are the battle.

Swamiji: You are it, you are the battle, you are the fighter, you are away from it, you are with it—everything. That is perhaps what is implied in Gnana Yoga. According to Gnana Yoga, the seeker is asked to equip himself with the four means. *Viveka*, seeking the real and discarding the false; *Vairagya*, not seeking pleasure; *Shat Satsampath*, which meant in effect living a life conducive to the practice of this yoga; and *Mumukshutva*, a total dedication to the search of Truth. The disciple then ap-

141

proached a *guru* and his *Sadhana* consisted of *Sravana* (hearing), *Manana* (reflection) and *Niryudhyajna* (assimilation), which all of us do here. The *guru* adopted various means to enlighten the student, which usually implied the realisation of the All or the Whole Being. Sankara describes it thus: "The infinite alone is real, the world is unreal. The individual is non-different from the infinite, so there is no fragmentation there." Sankara said that the world is Maya by which he meant that the world-appearance is not the real, which one has to investigate and discover. Krishna describes it thus in the Gita: "The yogi is then aware that the action, the doer of the action, the instruments involved, and the object towards which the action is directed, are all one whole and thus fragmentation is overcome."

How do you react to this Gnana Yoga method? First there is this *Sadhana Chaturdhyaya*, for which the disciple prepares himself. Then he goes to the *guru* and sits and hears the Truth from the *guru* and reflects over it and assimilates the truth, till it becomes one with him; and the truth is usually said in terms of these formulas. But these formulas that we repeat are supposed to be realised. Has this perhaps some validity?

KRISHNAJI: Sir, if you have read none of these—Patanjali, Sankara, Chan Upanishads, Raja Yoga, Karma Yoga, Bhakti Yoga, Gnana Yoga, nothing—what would you do?

Swamiji: I shall have to find out.

KRISHNAJI: What would you do?

Swamiji: Struggle.

KRISHNAJI: Which you are doing anyhow. What would you do? Where would you start?—knowing nothing about what others have said, including what the Communist leaders have said—Marx, Engels, Lenin, Stalin. I am here, an ordinary human being. I have not read a thing. I want to know. Where am I to begin? I have to work—Karma Yoga—in a garden, as a cook, in a factory, an office, I have to work. And also there are the wife and children: I love them, I hate them, I am a sexual addict, because that is the only escape offered to me in life. Here I am. That is my map of life and I start from here. I cannot start from

142

over there; I start here and I ask myself what it is all about. I know nothing about God. You can invent, pretend: I have a horror of pretending. If I do not know, I do not know. I am not going to quote Sankara, Buddha, or anybody. So I say: this is where I start. Can I bring about order in my life?—order, not invented by me or by them, but order that is virtue. Can I bring it about? And to be virtuous there must be no battle, no conflict in me or outside. Therefore, there must be no aggressiveness, no violence, no hate, no animosity. I start from there. And I find out I am afraid. I must be free of fear. To be conscious of it is to be aware of all this, aware of where I am; from there I will move, I shall work. And then I find out I can be alone—not carry all the burdens of memory, of Sankaras, of Buddhas, Marx, Engels—you follow? I can be alone because I have understood order in my life; and I have understood order because I have denied disorder, because I have learnt about disorder. Disorder means conflict, acceptance of authority, complying, imitation, all that. That is disorder, the social morality is disorder. Out of that I will bring order in myself; not myself as a potty little human being in a backyard, but as a Human Being.

Swamiji: How do you explain it?

KRISHNAJI: It is a human being who is going through this hell. Every human being is going through this hell. So if I, as a human being, understand this, I have discovered something which all human beings can discover.

Swamiji: But how does one know that one is not deceiving oneself?

KRISHNAJI: Very simple. First, humility: I do not want to achieve anything.

Swamiji: I do not know if you have come across people who say, "I am the humblest person in the world."

KRISHNAJI: I know. That is all too silly. Not to desire achievement is not.

Swamiji: When one is in it, in the soup, how does one know?

KRISHNAJI: Of course you will know. When your desire says, "I must be like Mr. Smith who is the Prime Minister, the General, or the Executive Officer", then there is the beginning of arrogance, pride, achievement. I know when I want to be like the hero, when I want to become like the Buddha, when I want to reach enlightenment, when desire says, "Be something." Desire says in being something there is tremendous pleasure.

Swamiji: But have we still tackled the root of the problem in all this?

KRISHNAJI: Of course we have. "Me" is the root of the problem. Self-centredness is the root of the problem.

Swamiji: But what is it? What does it mean?

KRISHNAJI: Self-centredness? I am more important than you, my house, my property, my achievement, "me" first.

Swamiji: But the martyr may say, "I am nothing, I can be shot."

KRISHNAJI: Who?—they do not.

Swamiji: They may say they are completely unselfish, selfless.

KRISHNAJI: No, Sir. I am not interested in what somebody else says.

Swamiji: He may be bluffing himself.

KRISHNAJI: As long as I am quite clear in myself, I am not deceiving myself. I can deceive myself the moment I have a measure. When I compare myself with the man with a Rolls-Royce, or with the Buddha, I have a measure. Comparing myself with somebody is the beginning of illusion. When I do not compare, why should I move from there?

Swamiji: To be the Self?

KRISHNAJI: Whatever I am; which is: I am ugly, I am full of anger, deception, fear, this and that. I start from there and see if it is at all possible to be free of all this. My thinking about God is like thinking about climbing those hills, which I never will.

Swamiji: But even so you said something very interesting the other day: the individual and the collective are one. How does the individual realise that unity with the collective?

KRISHNAJI: But that is a fact. Here I am living in Gstaad; somebody is living in India, it is the same problem, the same anxiety, the same fear—only different expressions but the root of the thing is the same. That is one point. Second, the environment has produced this individuality and the individuality has created the environment. My greed has created this rotten society. My anger, my hatred, the fragmentation of my life has created the nation and all this mess. So I am the world, the world is me. Logically, intellectually, verbally, it is so.

Swamiji: But how does one feel it?

KRISHNAJI: That comes only when you change. When you change, you are no longer a national. You do not belong to anything.

Swamiji: Mentally I may say I am not a Hindu, or I am not an Indian.

KRISHNAJI: But, Sir, that is just a trick. You must feel it in your blood.

Swamiji: Please explain what that means.

KRISHNAJI: It means, Sir, when you see the danger of nationalism, you are out of it. When you see the danger of fragmentation, you no longer belong to the fragment. We do not see the danger of it. That is all.

SAANEN
JULY 1969

145

J. KRISHNAMURTI AND
SWAMI VENKATESANANDA

Four "mahavakyas" from the Upanishads discussed.
Communication and the Bodhisattva ideal.
Vedanta and the ending of knowledge.

Swami Venkatesananda: Krishnaji, we are sitting near
each other and enquiring, listening and learning. Even so
did the sage and the seeker, and that is the origin they say
of the Upanishads. These Upanishads contain what are
known as Mahavakyas, Great Sayings, which perhaps had
the same effect upon the seeker then as your words have
upon me now. May I beg of you to say what you think of
them are they still valid, or do they need revision or
renewal?

The Upanishads envisaged the Truth in the following
Mahavakyas:

  Prajnanam Brahma: "Consciousness is infinite, the absolute, the highest Truth."
  Aham Brahmasmi: "I am that infinite", or "I is that infinite"—because the "I" here does not refer to the ego.
  Tat Tvam-asi: "Thou art that".
  Ayam Atma Brahma: "The self is the infinite", or "the
  individual is the infinite."

These were the four Mahavakyas used by the ancient sage
to bring home the message to the student, and they were
also sitting just like us, face to face, the guru and the
disciple, the sage and the seeker.

KRISHNAJI: Yes, what is the question, Sir?

Swamiji: What do you think of them? Are these Mahavakyas valid now? Do they need a revision or a
renewal?

KRISHNAJI: These sayings, like, "I am that", "Tat Tvamasi" and "Ayam Atma Brahma"?

Swamiji: That is, "Consciousness is Brahman".

KRISHNAJI: Isn't there a danger, Sir, of repeating something not knowing what it means? "I am that." What does it actually mean?

Swamiji: "Thou are that."

KRISHNAJI: "Thou are that." What does that mean? One can say, "I am the river". The river that has got tremendous volume behind it, moving, restless, pushing on and on, through many countries. I can say, "I am that river." That would be equally valid as "I am Brahman."

Swamiji: Yes. Yes.

KRISHNAJI: Why do we say, "I am that"? And not "I am the river," nor "I am the poor man", the man that has no capacity, no intelligence, who is dull—this dullness brought about by heredity, by poverty, by degradation, all that! Why don't we say, "I am that also"? Why do we always attach ourselves to something which we suppose to be the highest?

Swamiji: "That", perhaps, only means that which is unconditioned.
YO VAI BHUMA TATSUKHAM[1]
That which is unconditioned.

KRISHNAJI: Unconditioned, yes.

Swamiji: So, since there is in us this urge to break through all conditioning, we look for the unconditioned.

KRISHNAJI: Can a conditioned mind, can a mind that is small, petty, narrow, living on superficial entertainments, can that know or conceive, or understand, or feel, or observe the unconditioned?

[1] 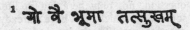 यो वै भूमा तत्सुखम्

147

Swamiji: No. But it can uncondition itself.

KRISHNAJI: That is all it can do.

Swamiji: Yes.

KRISHNAJI: Not say, "There is the unconditioned, I am going to think about it", or "I am that". My point is, why is it that we always associate ourselves with what we think is the highest? Not what we think is the lowest?

Swamiji: Perhaps in Brahman there is no division between the highest and the lowest, that which is unconditioned.

KRISHNAJI: That's the point. When you say, "I am that", or "Thou are that", there is a statement of a supposed fact. . . .

Swamiji: Yes.

KRISHNAJI: . . . which may not be a fact at all.

Swamiji: Perhaps I should explain here again that the sage who uttered the Mahawakyas was believed to have had a direct experience of it.

KRISHNAJI: Now, if he had the experience of it, could he convey it to another?

Swamiji: (Laughs)

KRISHNAJI: And the question also arises, can one actually experience something which is not experienceable? We use the word "experience" so easily—"realise", "experience", "attain", "self-realisation", all these things—can one actually experience the feeling of supreme ecstasy? Let's take that for the moment, that word. Can one experience it?

Swamiji: The infinite?

KRISHNAJI: Can one experience the infinite? This is really quite a fundamental question, not only here but in life. We can experience something which we have already known. I experience meeting you. That's an experience,

148

meeting you, or you meeting me, or my meeting X. And when I meet you next time I recognise you, don't I? I say, "Yes, I met him at Gstaad." So there is in experience the factor of recognition.

Swamiji: Yes. That is objective experience.

KRISHNAJI: If I hadn't met you, I should pass you by—you would pass me by. There is in all experiencing, isn't there, a factor of recognition?

Swamiji: Possibly.

KRISHNAJI: Otherwise it is not an experience. I meet you—is that an experience?

Swamiji: Objective experience.

KRISHNAJI: It can be an experience, can't it? I meet you for the first time. Then what takes place in that first meeting of two people. What takes place?

Swamiji: An impression, impression of like.

KRISHNAJI: An impression of like or dislike, such as, "He's a very intelligent man", or "He's a stupid man", or "He should be this or that". It is all based on my background of judgment, on my values, on my prejudices, likes and dislikes, on my bias, on my conditioning. That background meets you and judges you. The judgment, the evaluation, is what we call experience.

Swamiji: But isn't there, Krishnaji, another. . . ?

KRISHNAJI: Wait, Sir, let me finish this. Experience is after all the response to a challenge, isn't it? The reaction to a challenge. I meet you and I react. If I didn't react at all, with any sense of like, dislike, prejudice, what would take place?

Swamiji: Yes?

KRISHNAJI: What would happen in a relationship in which the one—you, perhaps—have no prejudice, no reaction; you are living in quite a different state and you meet me. Then what takes place?

Swamiji: Peace.

KRISHNAJI: I must recognise that peace in you, that quality in you, otherwise I just pass you by. So when we say, "Experience the highest", can the mind, which is conditioned, which is prejudiced, frightened, experience, the highest?

Swamiji: Obviously not.

KRISHNAJI: Obviously not. And the fear, the prejudice, the excitement, the stupidity is the entity that says, "I am going to experience the highest." When that stupidity, fear, anxiety, conditioning ceases, is there experiencing of the highest at all?

Swamiji: Experiencing of "that".

KRISHNAJI: No, I haven't made myself clear. If the entity—which is the fear, the anxiety, the guilt and all the rest of it—if that entity has dissolved itself, discarded the fear and so on, what is there to experience?

Swamiji: Now that beautiful question was actually put in just so many words. He asked the very same question:
VIJNATARAM ARE KENA VIJANIYAT[1]
"You are the knower, how can you know the knower?"
"You are the experiences!" But there is one suggestion that Vedanta gives and that is: we have so far been talking about an objective experience:
PAROKSANUBHUTI[2]
Isn't there another experience? Not my meeting X Y Z, but the feeling "I am", which is not because I encountered desire somewhere, or because I was confronted with some desire. I don't go and ask a doctor or somebody to certify that "I am". But there is this feeling, there is this knowl-

[1] विज्ञातारम् अरे केन विजानीयाद्

[2] परोक्षानुभूति

edge, "I am". This experience seems to be totally different from objective experience.

KRISHNAJI: Sir, what is the purpose of experience?

Swamiji: Exactly what you have been saying: to get rid of the fears, and get rid of all the complexes, all the conditioning. To see what I am, in truth, when I am *not* conditioned.

KRISHNAJI: No, Sir. I mean: I am dull.

Swamiji: Am I dull?

KRISHNAJI: I am dull; and because I see you, or X Y Z, who is very bright, very intelligent. . . ?

Swamiji: There is comparison.

KRISHNAJI: Comparison: through comparing, I find that I am very dull. And I say, "Yes, I am dull, what am I to do?", and just remain in my dullness. Life comes along, an incident takes place, which shakes me up. I wake up for a moment and struggle—struggle not to be dull, to be more intelligent, and so on. So experience generally has the significance of waking you up, giving you a challenge to which you have to respond. Either you respond to it adequately, or inadequately. If it is inadequate, the response then becomes a medium of pain, struggle, conflict. But if you respond to it adequately, that is fully, you are the challenge. You are the challenge, not the challenged, but you are that. Therefore you need no challenge at all, if you are adequately responding all the time to everything.

Swamiji: That is beautiful, but (*laughing*) how does one get there?

KRISHNAJI: Ah, wait, Sir. Just let us see the need for experience at all. I think it is really extraordinary, if you can go into it. Why do human beings demand not only objective experience, which one can understand—in going to the moon they have collected a lot of information, a lot of data . . .

Swamiji: . . . rocks . . .

151

KRISHNAJI: That kind of experience is perhaps necessary, because it furthers knowledge, knowledge of factual, objective things. Now apart from that kind of experience, is there any necessity for experience at all?

Swamiji: Subjectively?

KRISHNAJI: Yes. I don't like to use "subjective" and "objective". Is there the need of experience at all? We have said: experience is the response to a challenge. I challenge you, I ask, "Why?" You may respond to it, and say, "Yes, perfectly right, I am with you." "Why?" But the moment there is any kind of resistance to that question, "Why?", you are already responding inadequately. And therefore there is conflict between us, between the challenge and the response. Now, that's one thing. And there is a desire to experience, let's say God, something Supreme, the highest; or the highest happiness, the highest ecstasy, bliss, a sense of peace, whatever you like. Can the mind experience it at all?

Swamiji: No.

KRISHNAJI: Then what does experience it?

Swamiji: Do you want us to enquire what the mind is?

KRISHNAJI: No.

Swamiji: What the "I" is?"

KRISHNAJI: No! Why does the "I", me or you, demand experience?—that is my point—demand the experience of the highest, which promises happiness, or ecstasy, bliss or peace?

Swamiji: Obviously because in the present state we feel inadequate.

KRISHNAJI: That's all. That's all.

Swamiji: Correct.

KRISHNAJI: Being in a state in which there is no peace, we want to experience a state which is absolute, permanent, eternal peace.

Swamiji: It is not so much that I am restless, and there is a state of peace; I want to know what is this feeling, "I am restless". Is the "I" restless, or is the "I" dull? Am I dull, or is dullness only a condition which I can shake off?

KRISHNAJI: Now who is the entity that shakes it off?

Swamiji: Wakes up. The "I" wakes up.

KRISHNAJI: No, Sir. That's the difficulty. Let's finish this first. I am unhappy, miserable, laden with sorrow. And I want to experience something where there is no sorrow. That is my craving. I have an ideal, a goal, and by struggling towards it I will ultimately get that. That's my craving. I want to experience that and hold on to that experience. That is what human beings want—apart from all the clever sayings, clever talk.

Swamiji: Yes, yes; and that is perhaps the reason why another very great South Indian sage said (in Tamil):
ASAI ARUMIN ASAI ARUMIN
ISANODAYINUM ASAI ARUMIN[1]
It's very good really.

KRISHNAJI: What's that?

Swamiji: "Cut down all these cravings. Even the craving to be one with God, cut it down", he says.

KRISHNAJI: Yes, I understand. Now look, Sir. If I—if the mind—can free itself from this agony, then what is the need of asking for an experience of the Supreme? There won't be.

Swamiji: No. Certainly.

KRISHNAJI: It is no longer caught in its own conditioning. Therefore it is something else; it is living in a different dimension. Therefore the desire to experience the highest is *essentially* wrong.

[1] ஆசை அறுமின் ஆசை அறுமின்
ஈசனோடாயினும் ஆசை அறுமின்

153

Swamiji: If it is a desire.

KRISHNAJI: Whatever it is! How do I know the highest? Because the sages have talked of it? I don't accept the sage. They might be caught in illusion, they might be talking sense or nonsense. I don't know; I am not interested. I find that as long as the mind is in a state of fear, it wants to escape from it, and it projects an idea of the Supreme, and wants to experience that. But if it frees itself from its own agony, then it is altogether in a different state. It doesn't even ask for the experience because it is at a different level.

Swamiji: Quite, quite.

KRISHNAJI: Now, why do the sages, according to what you have said, say, "You must experience that, you must be that, you must realise that"?

Swamiji: They didn't say, "You must" . . .

KRISHNAJI: Put it any way you like. Why should they say all these things? Would it not be better to say, "Look here, my friends, get rid of your fear. Get rid of your beastly antagonism, get rid of your childishness, and when you have done that . . ."

Swamiji: . . . nothing more remains.

KRISHNAJI: Nothing more. You'll find out the beauty of it. You don't have to ask, then.

Swamiji: Fantastic, fantastic!

KRISHNAJI: You see, Sir, the other way is such a hypocritical state; it leads to hypocrisy. "I am seeking God", but I am all the time kicking people. (*Laughs*)

Swamiji: Yes, that could be hypocrisy.

KRISHNAJI: It is, it is.

Swamiji: That leads me on to the last and perhaps very impertinent question.

KRISHNAJI: No, Sir, there is no impertinence.

Swamiji: I am neither flattering you, nor insulting you, Krishnaji, when I say that it is a great experience to sit near you and talk to you like this. Your message is great, and you have been talking for over forty years of things you have considered very important to man. Now three questions. Do you think a man can communicate it to another man? Do you think that others can communicate it to still others? If so, how?

KRISHNAJI: Communicate what, Sir?

Swamiji: This message, that you have dedicated your life to. What would you call it?—You may call it a message.

KRISHNAJI: Yes, call it what you like, it doesn't matter. Am I—the person who is speaking, is he conveying a message, telling you a message?

Swamiji: No. You may call it an awakening, a questioning ...

KRISHNAJI: No, no. I am asking, Sir. Just look at it.

Swamiji: I guess we feel so, the listeners ...

KRISHNAJI: What is he saying? He says, "Look, look at yourself."

Swamiji: Exactly.

KRISHNAJI: Nothing more.

Swamiji: Nothing more is necessary.

KRISHNAJI: Nothing more is necessary. Look at yourself. Observe yourself. Go into yourself, because in this state as we are, we will create a monstrous world. You may go to the Moon, you may go further, to Venus, Mars and all the rest of it, but you will always carry yourself over there. Change yourself first! Change yourself—not first—change yourself. Therefore to change, look at yourself, go into yourself—observe, listen, learn. That's not a message. You can do it yourself if you want to.

Swamiji: But somebody has to tell . . .

KRISHNAJI: I *am* telling you. I say, "Look, look at this marvellous tree; look at this beautiful African flower."

Swamiji: Till you said that, I hadn't looked at it.

KRISHNAJI: Ah! Why?

Swamiji: (*Laughs*)

KRISHNAJI: Why? It is there, round you.

Swamiji: Yes.

KRISHNAJI: Why didn't you look?

Swamiji: There could be a thousand answers.

KRISHNAJI: No, no. I asked you to look at that flower. By my asking you to look at that flower, do you look at that flower?

Swamiji: I have the opportunity, yes.

KRISHNAJI: No. Do you really look at that flower because somebody asks you to look?

Swamiji: No.

KRISHNAJI: No, you can't. That's just it. I say to you, "You are hungry." Are you hungry because I say it?

Swamiji: No.

KRISHNAJI: You know when you are hungry, and yet you want somebody to tell you to look at the flower.

Swamiji: I may know when I am hungry, but it is the mother that tells me where the food is.

KRISHNAJI: No, no. We're not talking about where the food is, but we are saying "hunger". You know when you're hungry. But why should somebody tell you to look at a flower?

156

Swamiji: Because I am not hungry to look at the flower.

KRISHNAJI: Why not?

Swamiji: I am satisfied with something else.

KRISHNAJI: No. Why aren't you looking at that flower? I think first of all nature has no value at all for most of us. We say, "Well, I can see the tree any time I want to." That's one thing. Also, we are so concentrated upon our own worries, our own hopes, our own desires and experiences, that we shut ourselves in a cage of our own thinking; and we don't look beyond it. He says, "Don't do that. Look at everything and through looking at everything you'll discover your cage." That's all.

Swamiji: Isn't that a message?

KRISHNAJI: It is not a message in the sense . . .

Swamiji: No.

KRISHNAJI: It doesn't matter what you call it—call it a message. All right. I tell you that. You play with it, or take it very seriously. And it is very serious for you, you naturally tell it to somebody else. You don't have to say, "I am going to make propaganda about it . . ."

Swamiji: No, no.

KRISHNAJI: You will say, "Look at the beauty of those flowers."

Swamiji: Yes.

KRISHNAJI: You say that. And the person doesn't listen to you. And there it is—finished! So is propaganda necessary?

Swamiji: Propagation, Sir.

KRISHNAJI: Yes, propagation, that is the word—propagate.

Swamiji: Yes. We are talking about these forty years of talking ...

KRISHNAJI: ... more than forty years ...

Swamiji: Yes, millions of people have been talking for centuries, wasting their ...

KRISHNAJI: We have been talking, yes. We have been propagating ...

Swamiji: ... something which is extremely important, which I'm sure you consider is extremely important.

KRISHNAJI: Otherwise I wouldn't go on.

Swamiji: I have read some of the books you have published, but this experience of sitting and talking to you ...

KRISHNAJI: ... is different from reading a book.

Swamiji: Completely, completely, different!

KRISHNAJI: I agree.

Swamiji: Last night I read one and there was a little more meaning. How does one bring that about?

KRISHNAJI: You are a serious person, and the other person being serious there is a contact, there is a relationship, there is a coming together in seriousness. But in you're not serious, you will just say, "Well, it's very nice talking about all these things, but what's it all about?"—and walk off.

Swamiji:: Yes.

KRISHNAJI: Surely, Sir, with any kind of relationship that has meaning there must be a meeting at the same level, at the same time, with the same intensity, otherwise there is no communication, there is no relationship. And perhaps that's what takes place when we are sitting together here. Because one feels the urgency of something and the intensity of it, there is a relationship established which is quite different from reading a book.

Swamiji: A book has no life.

KRISHNAJI: Printed words have no life, but you can give life to the printed word if you are serious.

Swamiji: So how does it go on from there?

KRISHNAJI: From there you say, is it possible to convey to others this quality of urgency, this quality of intensity, and action which takes place now?

Swamiji: ... really now ...

KRISHNAJI: Yes, not tomorrow or yesterday.

Swamiji: Action, which means observation at the same level.

KRISHNAJI: And is always functioning—seeing and acting, seeing, acting, seeing, acting.

Swamiji: Yes.

KRISHNAJI: How is this to take place? First of all, Sir, most people, as we said yesterday, are not interested in all this. They play with it. There are very, very few really serious people. Ninety-five per cent say, "Well, if you are entertaining it's all right, but if you are not, you're not welcome"—entertainment, according to their idea of entertainment. Then what will you do? Knowing there are only very, very few people in the world who are really desperately serious, what will you do? You talk to them, and you talk to the people who want to be entertained. But you don't care whether they listen to you or don't listen.

Swamiji: Thank you. Thank you.

KRISHNAJI: I don't say, "To the people who need crutches, offer crutches!"

Swamiji: No.

KRISHNAJI: Nor to the people who want comfort, an avenue of escape, "Go away somewhere else ..."

Swamiji: ... to the Palace Hotel! ...

KRISHNAJI: I think, Sir, that is perhaps what has taken place in all these religions, all the so-called teachers. They have said, "I must help this man, that man, that other man."

Swamiji: Yes?

KRISHNAJI: The ignorant, the semi-ignorant, and the very intelligent. Each must have his particular form of food. They may have said that; I am not concerned. I just offer the flower, let them smell it, let them destroy it, let them cook it, let them tear it to pieces. I have nothing to do with it.

Swamiji: Well, they glorify that other attitude, the Bodhisattva ideal.

KRISHNAJI: Again, the Bodhisattva ideal—is it not an invention of our own, the desperate hope, desire for some kind of solace? The Matraiya Bodhisattva, the idea that He has relinquished the ultimate in life, enlightenment, and is waiting for all humanity ...

Swamiji: Thank you.

* * *

KRISHNAJI: What is Vedanta?

Swamiji: The word means, "The end of the Vedas" ... Not in the manner of "full stop".

KRISHNAJI: The end of all knowledge.

Swamiji: Quite right, quite right. Yes, the end of knowledge; where knowledge matters no more.

KRISHNAJI: Therefore, leave it.

Swamiji: Yes.

KRISHNAJI: Why proceed from there to describe what it is not?

Swamiji: As I've been sitting and listening to you, I've thought of another sage who is reported to have gone to another greater one. And he says, "Look my mind is restless; please tell me what must I do." And the older man says, "Give me a list of what you know already, so that I can proceed from there." He replies, "Oh, it will take a long time, because I have all the formulas, all the shastras, all of that." The sage answers, "But that's only a set of words. All those words are contained in the dictionary, it means nothing. Now what do you know?" He says, "That is what I know. I don't know anything else."

KRISHNAJI: Vedanta, as it says, means the end of knowledge

Swamiji: Yes, it's wonderful, I never heard it put that way before. "The end of knowledge."

KRISHNAJI: Freedom from knowledge.

Swamiji: Yes indeed.

KRISHNAJI: Then why have they not kept to that?

Swamiji: Their contention is that you have to pass through it in order to come out of it.

KRISHNAJI: Pass through what?

Swamiji: Through all this knowledge, all this muck, and then discard it.
PARIVEDYA LOKAN LOKAJITAN
BRAHMANO NIRVEDAMAYAT[1]
That is, "After examining all these things and finding that they are of no use to you, then you must step out of it."

KRISHNAJI: Then why must I acquire it? If Vedanta means the end of knowledge, which the word itself means, the ending of Vedas, which is knowledge—then why should I go through all the laborious process of acquiring knowledge, and then discarding it?

[1] 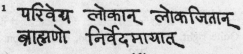 परिवेद्य लोकान् लोकजितान्
ब्राह्मणो निर्वेदमायात्

Swamiji: Otherwise you wouldn't be in Vedanta. The end of knowledge is, having acquired this knowledge, coming to the end of it.

KRISHNAJI: Why should I acquire it?

Swamiji: Well, so that it can be ended.

KRISHNAJI: No, no. Why should I acquire it? Why should not I, from the very beginning, see what knowledge is and discard it?

Swamiji: See what knowledge is?

KRISHNAJI: And discard, discard all that: never accumulate. Vedanta means the end of accumulating knowledge.

Swamiji: That's it. That's correct.

KRISHNAJI: Then why should I accumulate?

Swamiji: Pass through, perhaps.

KRISHNAJI: Pass through? Why should I? I know fire burns. I know when I am hungry, when I must eat. I know I mustn't hit you; I don't hit you. I don't go through the process of hitting you, acquiring the knowledge that I'll be hurt again. So each day I discard. I free myself from what I have learnt, every minute. So every minute is the end of knowledge.

Swamiji: Yes, right.

KRISHNAJI: Now you and I accept that, that is a fact, that's the only way to live—otherwise you can't live. Then why have they said, "You must go through all the knowledge, through all this?" Why don't they tell me, "Look my friend, as you live from day to day acquiring knowledge, end it each day"? Not "Vedanta says so and so".

Swamiji: No, no.

KRISHNAJI: *Live it!*

Swamiji: Quite right. Again this division, classification.

KRISHNAJI: That's just it. We are back again.

Swamiji: Back again.

KRISHNAJI: We're back again to a fragment—a fragmentation of life.

Swamiji: Yes. But I'm too dull, I can't get there; so I'd rather acquire all this . . .

KRISHNAJI: Yes, and then discard it.

Swamiji: In the religious or spiritual history of India, there have been sages who were born sages: the Ramana Maharishi, the Shuka Maharishi, etc. etc. Well, they were allowed to discard knowledge even before acquiring it. And in their cases of course, the usual argument was that they have done it all . . .

KRISHNAJI: In their past lives.

Swamiji: Past lives.

KRISHNAJI: No, Sir, apart from the acquiring of knowledge and the ending of knowledge, what does Vedanta say?

Swamiji: Vedanta describes the relationship between the individual and the Cosmic.

KRISHNAJI: The Eternal.

Swamiji: The Cosmic, or the Infinite, or whatever it is. It starts well:
ISAVASYAM IDAM SARVAM
YAT KIMCHA JAGATYAM JAGAT[1]
"Till the whole universe is pervaded by that one . . ."

KRISHNAJI: That one thing . . .

Swamiji: . . . and so on. And then it's mostly this, a dialogue between a master and his disciple.

[1] ईशावास्यमिदं सर्वं यत् किञ्च जगत्यां जगत्।

KRISHNAJI: Sir, isn't it extraordinary, there has always been in India this teacher and disciple, teacher and disciple?

Swamiji: Yes—Guru.

KRISHNAJI: But they never said, "You are the teacher as well as the pupil."

Swamiji: Occasionally they did.

KRISHNAJI: But always with hesitation, with apprehension. But why?—if the fact is, you are the teacher and you are the pupil. Otherwise you are lost, if you depend on anybody else. That's one fact. And also I would like to ask why, in songs, in Hindu literature, they have praised the beauty of nature, the trees, the flowers, the rivers, the birds. Why is it most people in India have no feeling for all that?

Swamiji: Because they are dead?

KRISHNAJI: Why? And yet they talk about the beauty, the literature, they quote Sanskrit, and Sanskrit itself is the most beautiful language.

Swamiji: They have no feeling for . . .

KRISHNAJI: And they have no feeling for the poor man.

Swamiji: Yes, that is the worst tragedy of all.

KRISHNAJI: Nor for the squalor, the dirt.

Swamiji: And heaven knows from where they got this idea because it is not found in any of the scriptures. That means we are repeating the scriptures without realising their meaning.

KRISHNAJI: That's it.

Swamiji: Krishna:

ISVARAH SARVABHUTANAM
HRIDDESSERJUNA TISTHATI[1]

"I am seated in the hearts of all beings." Nobody bothers about the hearts of all beings. What would you think is the cause? They repeat it daily, every morning they are asked to repeat a chapter of the Bhagavad Gita.

KRISHNAJI: Every morning they do Puja and the repetition of things.

Swamiji: Now why have they lost the meaning? Obviously great meaning was put into those words by the authors. We are even asked to repeat them every day in order that we might keep them ...

KRISHNAJI: Alive.

Swamiji: Keep them alive. When and how did I kill the spirit? How was it possible? How to prevent it?

KRISHNAJI: What do you think is the reason, Sir? No, you know India better.

Swamiji: I am shocked at it.

KRISHNAJI: Why do you think it happens? Is it over population?

Swamiji: No, overpopulation is a result, not the cause.

KRISHNAJI: Yes. Is it that they have accepted this tradition, this authority ...

Swamiji: But the tradition says something good.

KRISHNAJI: But they have accepted it. They never questioned it. Sir, I have seen M.A.s and B.A.s in India, who have passed degrees, are clever, brainy—but they wouldn't know how to put a flower on a table. They know nothing but memory, memory, the cultivation of memory. Isn't that one of the causes?

[1] ईश्वरः सर्वभूतानां हृद्देशेऽर्जुन तिष्ठति।

Swamiji: Perhaps. Mere memorising.

KRISHNAJI: Memorising everything.

Swamiji: Without thinking. Why does man refuse to think?

KRISHNAJI: Oh, that's different—indolence, fear, wanting always to tread in the traditional path so that he doesn't go wrong.

Swamiji: But we have discarded the tradition which they say didn't suit us.

KRISHNAJI: Of course. But we find a new tradition that suits us—we are safe.

Swamiji: We never felt that the healthy tradition is a good tradition to keep.

KRISHNAJI: Throw out all tradition! Let's find out, Sir, whether these teachers and gurus and sages, have really helped people. Has Marx really helped people?

Swamiji: No.

KRISHNAJI: They have imposed their ideas on them.

Swamiji: And others have used the same ideas . . .

KRISHNAJI: Therefore I question this whole thing, because they are really not concerned with people's happiness.

Swamiji: Though they say so.

KRISHNAJI: If the Marxists and all those Soviet leaders are really interested in the *people* then there would be no concentration camps. There would be freedom. There would be no repressive measures.

Swamii: But I suppose they think, we have to imprison the lunatics . . .

KRISHNAJI: That's it. The lunatic is a man who questions my authority.

Swamiji: Yesterday's ruler might be today's lunatic.

KRISHNAJI: That always happens, that's inevitable, that's why I'm asking, whether it's not important to make man, a human being, realise that he's solely responsible.

Swamiji: Each one.

KRISHNAJI: Absolutely! For he does, what he thinks, how he acts. Otherwise we end up in this memorising, and complete blindness.

Swamiji: That is your message. And how to nail it?

KRISHNAJI: By driving it in every day *(laughs)*. And driving it into oneself. Because man is so eager to put his responsibility on others. The army is the safest escape—you're told what to do. You don't have any responsibility. It's all been thought out, what you should do, how you should think, act, carry your gun, how you should shoot—and finished! They provide you with a meal, sleeping-quarters, and for sex you can go to the village. That's the end of it. And strangely they talk about Karma.

Swamiji: That is Karma. PRARABDHA KARMA[1]

KRISHNAJI: They insist on Karma.

Swamiji: That is Karma—I was a Brahmin, and I know what happened. We played with that Karma and then it came back on us.

KRISHNAJI: Playing havoc now in India.

Swamiji: We toyed with the idea of Karma and we said: it's your Karma, you must suffer. My Karma is good and so I'm divorced from it all; I'm the landlord. And now they have turned the tables.

KRISHNAJI: Quite.

[1] 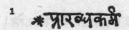 प्रारब्धकर्म

Swamiji: A vegetarian—she's a fanatical vegetarian—asked me, "Is pure vegetarianism necessary for yoga practice?" I said, "Not so important. Let's talk about something else." And she was horrified. She came back to me and said, "How can you say that? You can't say that vegetarianism is of secondary value. You must say it's of primary value." I replied, "Forgive me—I said something, but it doesn't matter." I then asked her,—"Do you believe in war, defence forces, defending your country and so on?" "Yes," she said, "otherwise how can we live—we have to." I replied, "If I call you a cannibal, how do you react to that? This man kills a small animal to sustain his life, but you are willing to kill people to sustain yours. Like a cannibal." She didn't like that—but I think she saw the point later.

KRISHNAJI: Good.

Swamiji: It's so fantastic. People don't want to think. And I suppose with you, Krishnaji, if you say the truth, you become very unpopular. A priest said:
APRIYASYA TU PATHYASYA VAKTA SROTA NA VIDYATE[1]
Very beautiful! "People love to hear pleasant things; pleasant to say and pleasant to hear."

SAANEN
26 JULY 1969

[1] अप्रियस्य तु भथ्यस्य वक्ता श्रोता न विद्यते।

168

INDIA

V

Three Talks in Madras

1

THE ART OF SEEING

To see, not partially but totally. "The act of seeing is the only truth." Of the vast mind only a fragment is used. The fragmentary influence of culture, tradition. "Living in a little corner of a distorted field." "You cannot understand through a fragment." Freedom from "the little corner". The beauty of seeing.

WE WERE SAYING the other day how very important it is to observe. It is quite an art to which one must give a great deal of attention. We only see very partially, we never see anything completely, with the totality of our mind, or with the fullness of our heart. And unless we learn this extraordinary art, it seems to me that we shall be functioning, living through a very small part of our mind, through a small segment of the brain. We never see anything completely, for various reasons, because we are so concerned with our own problems, or we are so conditioned, so heavily burdened with belief, with tradition, with the past, that this actually prevents us from seeing or listening. We never see a tree, we see the tree through the image that we have of it, the concept of that tree; but the concept, the knowledge, the experience, is entirely different from the actual tree. Here one is surrounded by a great many trees, fortunately, and if you look around you, as the speaker is going on with the subject of seeing, if you actually look at it, you will find how extraordinarily difficult it is to see it all, so that no image, no screen, comes between the seeing and the actual fact. Please do this, don't watch me—look at the tree, find out whether you can see it completely. By completely I mean with the totality of your mind and heart, not a fragment of it, because what we are going to go into this evening demands such observation, such seeing. Unless you actually do this (not theorise, intellectualise or bring up various issues which are irrelevant) I am afraid you will not

171

be able to follow closely what we are going to go over together.

We never see, or actually hear, what another is saying; we are either emotional, sentimental or very intellectual—which obviously prevents us from actually seeing the colour, the beauty of the light, the trees, the birds, and from listening to those crows; we never are in direct relationship with any of this. And I doubt very much if we are in relationship with anything, even with our own ideas, thoughts, motives, impressions; there is always the image which is observing, even when we observe ourselves.

So it is very important to understand that the act of seeing is the only truth; there is nothing else. If I know how to see a tree, or a bird, or a lovely face, or the smile of a child—there it is, I don't have to do anything more. But that seeing of the bird, of the leaf, listening to the noise of birds, becomes almost impossible because of the image that one has built, not only about nature but also about others. And these images actually prevent us from seeing and feeling; feeling being entirely different from sentimentality and emotion.

And, as we said, we see everything fragmentarily and we are trained from childhood to look, to observe, to learn, to live in a fragment. And there is the vast expanse of the mind which we never touch or know; that mind is vast, immeasurable, but we never touch it, we don't know the quality of it because we have never looked at anything completely, with the totality of our mind, of our heart, of our nerves, of our eyes, of our ears. To us the word, the concept is extraordinarily important, not the acts of seeing and doing. But having the concept, which is a belief, an idea—having this—conceptual living, prevents us from actually seeing, doing; and therefore we say we have problems of action, of what to do or not to do, and the conflict that arises between the act and the concept.

Do please observe what I am talking about, not merely hear the words of the speaker, but observe yourselves, using the speaker as a mirror in which you can see yourself. What the speaker has to say is of very little importance, and the speaker himself is of no importance whatsoever, but what you gather out of observing yourself is important. It is so because there must be a total revolution, a complete mutation in our minds, in our way of living, in our feeling, in the activities of our daily life. And to bring about such fundamental, deep revolution is only possible when we know how to look; because when you do look, you are not only looking with your eyes but you are also looking with your mind. I do not know if you have ever driven a car; if you have, you are not only visually aware of the approaching car, but your mind is far ahead watching the bend of the road, the side road, other cars coming and going. And this seeing is not only seeing through your eyes and nerves, but seeing with your heart, with your mind, and you cannot see completely in this way if you are living, functioning, thinking, acting within a fragment of the total mind.

Look what is happening in the world—we are being conditioned by society, by the culture in which we live, and that culture is the product of man—there is nothing holy, or divine, or eternal about culture. Culture, society, books, radios, all that we listen to and see, the many influences of which we are either conscious or unconscious, all these encourage us to live within a very small fragment of the vast field of the mind. You go through school, college, and learn a technique to earn a living; for the next forty or fifty years you spend your life, your time, your energy, your thought, in that specialised little field. And there is the vast field of the mind. Unless we bring about a radical change in this fragmentation there can be no revolution at all; there will be modifications, economic, social and so-called cultural but man will go on suffering, will go on in conflict, in war, in misery, in sorrow and in despair.

I do not know if you read some time ago how one of the Marshals of the Russian army reporting to the Polit Bureau, said that in the army they were training soldiers under hypnosis—you know what that means? You are put under hypnosis and taught how to kill, how to obey completely, function with complete independence, but within a pattern, under the authority of a superior. Now culture and society are doing exactly the same thing to each one of us. Culture and society have hypnotised you. Do please listen to this very carefully, it is not only being done in the army in Russia, but it is being done all over the world. When you read the Gita endlessly, or the Koran, or repeat some mantram, some endlessly repeated words, you are doing exactly the same thing. When you say, "I am a Hindu", "I am a Buddhist", "I am a Muslim", "I am a Catholic", the same pattern is being repeated, you have been mesmerised, hypnotised; and technology is doing exactly the same thing. You can be a clever lawyer, a first-class engineer, or an artist, or a great scientist, but always within a fragment of the whole. I do not know if you see this, not because I describe it, but actually see what is taking place. The Communists are doing it, the Capitalists are doing it, everybody, parents, schools, education, they are all shaping the mind to function within a certain pattern, a certain fragment. And we are always concerned with bringing about a change within the pattern, within the fragment.

So, how is one to realise this, not theoretically, not as a mere idea, but see the actuality of it—you understand, see the actual? The actual being what is everyday taking place and is spoken of in newspapers, by politicians, through culture and tradition, in the family, making you call yourselves Indians, or whatever you think you are. Then when you see, you must question yourself (I am sure you would if you saw it), and that is why it is very important to understand how you see. If you really saw it, then the question would be, "How can the total mind act?" (I do not mean the fragment, not the conditioned mind, nor the educated, sophisticated mind, the mind that is afraid, the mind that says, "there is God" or "there is no God", "there is my family, your family, my nation, your nation".) Then you will ask, "How can this totality of the mind be, how can it function completely, even while learning a technique?" Though it has to learn a technique and to live in relationship with others, in our present disordered society—bearing that in mind, one must ask this question, which is a fundamental one: "How can this totality of the mind be made completely sensitive, so that even the fragment becomes sensitive?" I don't know if you have understood my question, we shall come to it in another way.

At present we are not sensitive; there are spots in this field that are sensitive, sensitive when our particular personality, our particular idiosyncracy, or our particular pleasures are denied—then there is a battle. We are sensitive in fragments, in spots, but we are not sensitive completely; so the question is, "How can the fragment, which is part of the total, which is being made dull every day by repetition, how can that part also be made sensitive as well as the total?" Is this question fairly clear? Do tell me.

Perhaps this is a new question to you, probably you have never asked yourself about it. Because we are all sat-

174

isfied to live with as little trouble and conflict as possible, in that little part of that field which is our life, appraising the marvellous culture of that little part as opposed to other cultures, Western, ancient or any other. We are not even aware what the implications of this are—of living in a tiny fragment, a corner of a very vast field. We don't see for ourselves how deeply we are concerned with the little part, and we are trying to find answers to the problem within the fragment, within that little corner of this vast life. We ask ourselves, how can the mind (which is now half asleep in this vast field, because we are only concerned with the little part), how can we become totally aware of this whole thing, become completely sensitive?

Now, first of all there is no method. Because any method, system, repetition or habit, is essentially part of the corner of that field. (Are we travelling together, taking a journey together, or are you falling behind?) The first thing is to see the actual fact of the little corner and what its demands are. Then we can put the question, "How can we make the whole field completely sensitive?" because in that lies the only true revolution. When there is total sensitivity of the whole of the mind, then we will act differently; our thinking, feeling, will be wholly of a different dimension. But there is no method. Don't say, "How am I to arrive, achieve, become sensitive?"—you can't go to college to become sensitive, you can't read books or be told what to do to become sensitive. This is what you have been doing within that corner of the field, and it has made you more and more insensitive, which can be seen in your daily life, with its callousness, brutality, and violence. (I do not know if you have seen the pictures in magazines of the American and Vietnamese soldiers being wounded. You may see it and say, "I am so sorry", but it has not happened to you, not to your family, not to your son.) So we become callous because we are functioning, living, acting, within the small petty little corner of a distorted field.

There is no method. Please do realise this, because when you realise it, you are free of the enormous weight of all authority, and so free of the past. I don't know if you see this. The past is implicit in our culture, which we think is so wonderful (the tradition, the beliefs, the memories, the obedience to it), and all that is put aside completely, forever, when you realise there is no method of any kind to bring freedom from the "little corner". But you have to learn all about the little corner. Then you are free of the burden which makes you insensitive. Soldiers are trained to kill, practise day after day, day after day, ruthlessly, so that they have no human feeling left at all. And that is the type of thing which is being done to each one of us every day, all the time, by newspapers, by political leaders, by the gurus, by the Pope, by the bishops, everywhere, all over the world.

Now, as there is no method, what is one to do? Method implies practice, dependence, your method, my method, his path and another's path, my guru who knows a little better, this guru who is phoney, that guru who is not (but all gurus are phoney, you can take that for granted right from the beginning, whether they are Tibetan Lamas or Catholics, or Hindus)—all of them are phoney because they are still functioning in a very small part of a field that has been spat on and trodden upon and destroyed.

What is one to do? You understand my question now? The problem is this: we don't know the depth and the immensity of the mind. You can read about it, you can read the modern psychologists, or the ancient teachers who have talked about it—distrust them because it is you yourself who have to find out, not according to somebody else. We don't know it—the mind—you don't know it, so you cannot have any concept about it. You understand what we are saying? You can't have any ideas, any opinions, any knowledge about it. So you are free from any supposition, from any theology.

So once again, what is one to do? All that one has to do is to see. See the corner, the little house that one has built in a corner of a vast, an immeasurable field; and living there, fighting, quarrelling, improving (you know all that is going on there), *see it*. And that is why is is very important to understand what it means to see, because the moment here is conflict you belong to that isolated corner. Where there is seeing there is no conflict. That is why one has to learn from the very beginning—no, not the beginning, but *now*—to see. Not tomorrow, because there is no tomorrow—it is only search for pleasure, or fear, or pain that invents "tomorrow". Actually there is no tomorrow psychologically, but the brain, the mind, has invented time; but we shall go into this later.

So what one has to do is to see. You cannot see, if you

are not sensitive, and you are not sensitive if you have an image between you and the thing seen. Do you understand? So seeing is the act of love. You know what makes the total mind sensitive?—only love. You can learn a technique and yet love; but if you have technique and no love you are going to destroy the world. Do watch it in yourselves, Sirs, do go into it in your own minds and hearts and you will see it for yourselves. Seeing, observing, listening, these are the greatest acts, because you cannot see if you are looking out from that little corner, you cannot see what is happening in the world, the despair, the anxiety, the aching loneliness, the tears of the mothers, wives, lovers, of those people who have been killed. But you have to see all this, not emotionally, nor sentimentally, not saying, "Well! I am against war" or, "I am for war", as that sentimentality and emotionalism are the most destructive things—they avoid facts and so avoid what is. So, the seeing is all important. The seeing is the understanding; you cannot understand through the mind, through the intellect, or understand through a fragment. There is understanding only when the mind is completely quiet, which means when there is no image.

Seeing destroys all barriers. Look, Sirs, as long as there is separation between you and the tree, between you and me, and between you and your neighbour (that "neighbour" being a thousand miles away or next door), there must be conflict. Separation means conflict, that is very simple. And we have lived in conflict, we are used to conflict and to separation. You see India as a unit—geographical, political, economical, social, cultural, and the same goes for Europe, and America, and Russia: separate units, each against the other, and all this separation is bound to breed war. This doesn't mean that we must all agree, or if we disagree that I am doing battle with you; there is no disagreement whatsoever, or agreement, when you see something as it is. It is only when you have opinions about what you see, that there is disagreement and that there is separation. When you and I see that it is the moon, then there is no disagreement, it is the moon. But if you *think* it is something, and I think it is something else, then there must be division and hence conflict. So in seeing a tree, when you actually *see* it, there is no division between you and the tree, there is no observer seeing the tree.

We were talking one day to a very learned doctor, who had taken a drug called L.S.D., a minute dosage, and there were two doctors beside him with a tape recorder registering what he was saying. After a few seconds he saw the flowers on the table in front of him, and between those flowers and himself there was no space. It doesn't mean he identified himself with those flowers, but there was no space, which means that there was no observer. We are not advocating that you should take L.S.D., because it has its own deleterious effects; and also when you take such things you become a slave to them. But there is a much simpler, more direct, more natural way, which is to observe for yourself a tree, a flower, the face of a person; to look at any one of them, and so look that the space between you and them is non-existent. And you can only look that way when there is love—that word which has been so misused.

We will not go into the question of love for the time being, but when you have this sense of real observation, real seeing, then that seeing brings with it this extraordinary elimination of time and space which comes about when there is love. And you cannot have love without recognising beauty. You may talk about beauty, write, design, but if you have no love nothing is beautiful. Being without love means that you are not totally sensitive. And because you are not totally sensitive you are degenerating. This country is degenerating. Don't say, "Aren't other countries degenerating too?"—of course they are, but you are degenerating, though technically you may be an extraordinarily good engineer, a marvellous lawyer, technician, know how to run computers; but you are degenerating because you are not sensitive to the whole process of living.

Our fundamental problem then is—not how to stop wars, not which god is better than another god, not which political system or economic system is better, not which party is worth voting for (they are all crooked anyhow), but the most fundamental problem for the human being, whether he is in America, India, Russia, or anywhere else, is this question of freedom from "the little corner". And that little corner is ourselves, that little corner is your shoddy little mind. We have made that little corner, because our own little minds are fragmented and therefore incapable of being sensitive to the whole; we want that little part to be made safe, peaceful, quiet, satisfying, pleasurable, thereby avoiding all pain, because, fundamentally, we are seeking pleasure. And if you have examined pleasure, your own pleasure, have observed it, watched it, gone into it, you will see that where there is pleasure, there is pain. You cannot have one without the other; and we are always demanding more pleasure and therefore inviting more pain. And on that we have built this part, which we call human life. Seeing is to be intimately in contact with it and you cannot be intimately, actually in contact with it if you have concepts, beliefs, dogmas, or opinions.

So what is important is not to learn but to see and to listen. Listen to the birds, listen to your wife's voice, however irritating, beautiful or ugly, listen to it and listen to your own voice however beautiful, ugly, or impatient it may be. Then out of this listening you will find that all separation between the observer and the observed comes to an end. Therefore no conflict exists and you observe so carefully that the very observation is discipline; you don't have to impose discipline. And that is the beauty, Sirs (if you only realise it), that is the beauty of seeing. If you can see, you have nothing else to do, because in that seeing there is all discipline, all virtue, which is attention. And in that seeing there is all beauty, and with beauty there is love. Then when there is love you have nothing more to do. Then where you *are*, you have heaven; then all seeking comes to an end.

MADRAS
3 JANUARY 1968

FREEDOM

To share a free mind. "If we could come upon this, it is really a mysterious flower." Why has man not got this thing? Fear. "Living" is not living. Words taken for substance. Wastage of energy. "The mature mind has no comparison . . . no measure." The validity of "the life that you lead every day . . . without understanding it you will never understand love, beauty, or death." Through negation, that thing which alone is the positive comes into being.

IT WOULD BE rather interesting and worth while if we could share together a mind that is not tortured, that is fundamentally free, that has no barriers, that sees things as they are, that sees that an interval of time separates man from nature and from other human beings, that sees the meaning of dreadful, frightening time and space, that knows what is really the quality of love. If we could share this—not intellectually, not in a most cunning, elaborate, philosophical, metaphysical way, but actually partake of it, if we could do that I think all our problems would end. But this sharing is not with another, one must have it first. Then when you have it you have it in abundance. And when there is this abundance the one and the many are the same, like a tree that is full of leaves of which one leaf is perfect and is part of the whole tree.

If we could, this evening, share this quality, not with the speaker, but by having it and then sharing it. Then the question of sharing it would no longer arise. It is like a flower full of scent which doesn't share, but is always there for any passer-by to delight in. And whether anyone is very near in the garden, or very far away, it is all the same to the flower, because it is full of that perfume, and so it is sharing with everything. If one could come upon this, it is really a mysterious flower. It only seems mysterious because we are so full of emotion and sentiment, and sentiment, in that emotional sense, has very little meaning;

one can have sympathy, be generous, be very kind, gentle and extremely polite but the quality of which I have been speaking is entirely different from all this. And don't you wonder (not in abstract terms, nor according to something to be gained by a system, by a philosophy or by following some guru), don't you wonder why it is that human beings lack this thing? They beget children, they enjoy sex, tenderness, a quality of sharing something together in companionship, in friendship, in fellowship, but this thing—why is it that we haven't got it? For, when it is, then all problems whatever they may be, come to an end. And haven't you wondered lazily, on occasion, when you were walking by yourself in a filthy street, or sitting in a bus, or when you were on a holiday by the seaside, or in a wood with a lot of birds, trees, streams and wild animals, hasn't it ever come upon you to ask—why is it that man, who has lived for millions of years, why is it that he hasn't got this thing, this extraordinarily unfading flower?

If you have asked this question, even out of casual curiosity, you must have had an inkling, an intimation, a hint. But, probably, you have not asked it. We live such a monotonous, dull, sloppy life within the field of our own problems and anxieties that we have never even asked this question. And if we were to ask this question of ourselves (as we are going to do now, sitting under this tree on a quiet evening, with the noise of the crows), I wonder what would be our reply. What would each one of us honestly give as a direct answer, without equivocation or cunning, what would be the answer if you put this question to yourself? Why do we go through all this excruciating torture, with so many problem, with mutlitudinous fears piling up, yet this one thing seems to go by, seems to have no place at all. And if you were to ask why, why one has not found this quality, I wonder what would be your answer? Your answer would be according to your own intensity in asking that question, and its urgency. But we are neither intense nor urgent and we are not urgent or intense because we haven't got the energy. To look at anything, a bird, a crow sitting on a branch preening itself, to look at it with all your being, with all your eyes, ears, nerves, mind and heart, to look at it completely, requires energy, but not the shoddy energy of a dissipated mind that has struggled, that has tortured itself, that is full of innumerable burdens. And most minds, ninety-nine point nine per cent recurring of minds have this terrible burden, this tortured existence. And so they have no energy, energy being passion. And you can't find any truth without passion. That word "passion" is derived from the Latin word for suffering which again derives from Greek and so on; from this "suffering" the whole of Christendom worships sorrow, not passion. And they have given "passion" a special significance. I don't know what significance you give to it, the feeling of complete passion, with a fury behind it, with total energy, that passion in which there is no hidden want.

And if we were to ask, not just with curiosity but with all the passion we have, then what would be the answer? But probably you are afraid of passion, because for most people passion is lust, passion that is derived from sex and all that. Or it may come from the passion that is felt through identification with the country to which we belong, or passion for some mean little god, made by the hand or by the mind; and so to us, passion is rather a frightening thing because if we have such a passion, we do not know where it will take us. And so we are very careful to canalise it, to build a hedge around it through philosophical concepts, ideals, so that energy, which is demanded in order to solve this extraordinary question (and it is quite extraordinary if you put it to yourself honestly, directly), why we human beings, who live in families with children, surrounded by all the turmoil and violence of the world, why, when there is one thing that could cover all this, why it is that we haven't got it? I wonder, is it because we really don't want to find out? Because to find out anything there must be freedom, to find out what I think, what I feel, what are my motives, to find out, not merely to analyse intellectually, but to find out, there must be freedom to look. To look at that tree you must be free from worry, from anxiety, from guilt. To look you must be free from knowledge; freedom is a quality of mind that cannot be got through renunciation nor sacrifice. Are you following all this, or am I talking to the winds and the trees? Freedom is a quality of mind that is essential for seeing. It is not freedom *from* something. If you are free *from* something that is not freedom, it is only a reaction. If you smoke and you give up smoking, and you say, "I am free", you are really not free although you may be free *from* that particular habit. Freedom concerns the whole habit-forming machinery, and to understand this whole problem of habit-forming one must be free to look at its mechanism. Perhaps we are afraid of that freedom too; and therefore we put freedom far away from us, in some heaven.

So fear is perhaps the reason why we have not the energy of that passion to find out for ourselves why that quality of love is lacking in us. We have everything else, greed, envy, superstition, fear, the ugliness of a shoddy little life, the routine of going to an office every day for the next forty, fifty years—not that one shouldn't go to an office, one has to, unfortunately, but it becomes a routine, and that routine, that going to the office, doing the same thing day after day, day after day, for forty years, shapes the mind, makes it dull, stupid, or clever in only one direction.

It may be, probably it is, that each one of us is so frightened of life, because without understanding this whole process of living, we can never possibly understand what it is not to live. You understand? What we call living, the daily boredom, the daily struggle, the daily conflict within oneself and outside of oneself, the hidden demands, the hidden wants, the ambitions, the cruelties, and the enormous burden of conscious or unconscious sorrow—that is what we call living—don't we? We may try to escape from it, go to the temple, or the club, follow a new guru, or become a hippy or take to drink, or join some society which promises us something—anything to escape. In fear lies the major problem of what we call living (fear of not being, fear of being attached, with all the great pain it brings—how to be detached—whether there is physical, emotional, psychological, security—the fear of that—the fear of the unknown, fear of tomorrow, the fear of your wife leaving you, the fear of having no belief and being isolated, lonely, in despair at every moment, deep down), this is what we call living, a battle, a tortured existence with barren thoughts. We live like this because that is our life, with occasional moments of sanity, occasional moments of clarity to which we cling furiously.

Please, Sirs, don't merely listen to words and don't be carried away by them; explanations, definitions, descriptions, are not the fact. The fact is your life, the fact is whether you are aware of it, and you cannot be aware of it through the speaker's words, which merely describe your condition and if you are caught up in the description, in the words, then you are certainly lost forever. And that is what we are—we are lost, we are forlorn because we

183

have accepted words, words, words. So don't please, I beg of you, be caught in words, but watch yourself, watch your life, your daily life which you call living, which consists of going to the office, passing examinations, getting a job, not having a job, fear, family and social pressure, tradition, the torture of not arriving, the uncertainty of life, the utter deep boredom of life that has no meaning whatsoever. You may give significance to life, you can invent as philosophers and theoreticians do, as religious people do—invent the significance of life, that is their job. But this is feeding on words when you need substance; you are fed with words, and you are satisfied with words. So to understand this living we have to look at it: to come intimately into contact with it, not have the space and time interval between yourself and it. You don't have this time-space interval when you have deep physical pain, you act, you don't theorise, you don't quarrel about whether there is Atman or no Atman, soul or no soul, you don't begin to quote the Gita, the Upanishads, the Koran, or the Bible or some saint. Then you are face to face with actual life. Life is that movement which is active, the doing, the thinking, the feeling, the fears, the guilt, the despair—that is life. And one has to be intimately in contact with it. And one cannot be intensely, passionately, vitally, in contact, if there is fear.

Fear is what makes us believe, whether our belief is in the ideological community of the Communist, or the theocratical idea of a clergyman or a priest. All these things are born out of fear; obviously all gods, all, are the outcome of our agony; and when we worship them we are worshipping our agony, our loneliness, despair, misery and sorrow. Do please listen to all this—it is your life, not my life. You have to face this and so you have to understand fear. And you cannot understand fear if you don't understand life. You have to understand the jealousy that you have, the envy—envy and jealousy which are merely the indications of fear. And you can understand totally (not intellectually, there is no such thing as understanding intellectually, there is only understanding totally), you can understand totally and it is like looking at that sunset with your mind, with your heart, with your eyes, with your nerves; it is then you understand. And to understand jealousy, envy, ambition, cruelty, violence (to understand them and give your complete attention at the moment anything happens, at the moment you feel envious, angry, jealous or full of hate, or feel dishonest in yourself), then, if you understand that, you will understand fear. But you can't take fear as an abstraction. After all fear exists in relation to something. Are you not afraid of your neighbour, of the government, of your wife, or your husband, afraid of death, and so on? You have to observe, not fear, but enquire as to what has brought this about.

Now we are going to examine what living is, to which we cling so desperately, the living of our daily, monotonous, tragic life—the life of the bourgeois, the mediocre, the down-trodden—because we are all down-trodden by society, by culture, by religions, by priests, by leaders, by saints, and unless you understand this you will never understand fear; so we are going to understand this living and also that enormous source of fear, which is called death. And to understand it you have to have tremendous energy, passion. You know how we waste our energy (I don't mean through sex, that is a very small affair, don't make that into something unnecessarily tremendous), but one must enquire directly, not according to Shankara or any of those people, who have invented their own particular form of escape from life.

To find out what living is, we must not only have energy but also the quality of passion that is sustained, and intellect cannot possibly sustain passion. And to have that passion one has to enquire into the wastage of energy. One can see that it is a waste of energy to follow anybody—you understand?—to have a leader, to have a guru, because when you follow you are imitating, you are copying, you are obeying, you are establishing authority and your energy is therefore diffused. Do observe this; please do so. Don't go back to your gurus, to your societies, to your authorities, drop them like hot potatoes. You can also see how you waste your energy when there is compromise. You know what compromise is? There is compromise only when there is comparison. And we, from childhood, are trained to compare between what we are and what the head of the class in our school is; compare ourselves with what we were yesterday, noble or ignoble, with the happiness that we felt yesterday, that came upon us without warning, suddenly it came, the delight of looking at a tree, at flowers, at the face of a lovely woman, a child or a man, and then we compare what is today with what was yesterday. This comparison, this measurement, is the beginning of compromise. Do please look at this for yourself. Find out the truth of it, that the moment you have a measure, which is comparison, you are already compromising with what is. When you say that man is an I.C.S., he earns so much, he is the head of this or that, you are comparing, judging, placing people as important, not as human beings, but according to their degrees, their qualities, their earning capacity, their job, their Ph.D.s and the whole lot of alphabets after their names; and so you are comparing, comparing yourself with another, whether "the other" is a saint, a hero, a god, an idea, or an ideology—comparing, measuring—and all this breeds compromise which is a tremendous wastage of energy. This is not a question of when you are sexual and the tradition behind that. So, one sees how this is a waste of energy and the energy is wasted when you indulge in ideation, in theories: whether there is a soul or no soul, whether there is an Atman, or no Atman—isn't it a waste of time, a waste of energy? When you read or listen to some saint endlessly, or some sannyasi, making commentaries on the Gita, or the Upanishads—just think of it!—the absurdity of it!—the childishness of it! Somebody explains some book which in itself is dead, written by some dead poet, giving to it a tremendous significance. All this shows that immaturity is essentially a waste of energy.

The immature mind compares itself with what is and what should be, but it is only the immature mind that compares. The mature mind has no comparison, the mature mind has no measure. I don't know if you have ever looked into yourself and watched how you compare yourself with another, saying, "He is so beautiful, so intelligent, so clever, so prominent; and I am nobody, I would like to be like him." Or, "She is so beautiful, has a good figure, has a nice mind, intelligent, bright, better." We think and function in this comparative, measuring world. And if you have ever questioned and observed maybe you have said, "No more comparison, no more comparison with anybody, not with the most beautiful actress." You know that beauty is not in the actress, beauty is something total, not in the face, in the figure, in the smile, but where there is a quality of total comprehension, the totality of one's being; when that is what looks, there is beauty. Do watch it in yourself, please, try it, or rather do it—when you use the word "try", you know how such a mind is the most deplorable, foolish mind; when it says, "I am doing my best, I am trying", this indicates a mind that is essentially bourgeois, capable of measuring, which is doing better every day; so, find out for yourself whether you can live, not theoretically but actually, without comparison, measure, never using the words "better" or "more". See what happens. It is only such a mature mind that is not wasting energy, only such a mind can live a very simple life, I mean a life of real simplicity, not the so-called simplicity of the man who has one meal, or one loincloth—that's exhibitionism—but the mind that has no measure and is therefore not wasting energy.

So to come to the point. We are wasting energy and you need this energy to understand this monstrous way of living. And we must understand it, that is the only thing we have, no gods, Bibles, Gitas, or ideals; what you have is this thing—the daily torture, the daily anxiety. And to understand it, be in contact with it, is to have no space between yourself as the observer and the thing as despair, and for this you must have tremendous, driving energy. To have that energy, it cannot be dissipated—when this occurs you will understand what living is. Then there is no fear of life, of the movement of life. You know what a movement is? A movement has no end and no beginning, and therefore the movement in itself is the beauty, the glory. Are you following this?

So life is this movement and to understand it there must be freedom, there must be energy. And to understand death is to understand something which is closely related to life. You know, beauty (not in pictures, not in a person, not in the tree or in the cloud or in the sunset) beauty cannot be divorced from love. And where there is love and beauty there is life and also there is death. You cannot separate one from the other. The moment you separate there is conflict, there is no relationship. So we have looked, not in great detail or widely, perhaps, but we have looked at life.

Now let us consider, go into, this question of death. Have you asked why you are frightened of death? Apparently most people are. Some don't want even to know about it, or if they do, they want to glorify it. Or some invent a theory, a belief, an escape—an escape such as resurrection, or reincarnation. The majority of the people who live in the East believe in reincarnation—you all do, probably. That is, a permanent entity, or a collective memory, is reborn again in the next life—isn't it? That is what you all believe; to have a better opportunity, to live

187

more fully, to perfect yourself, because this life is so short, this life can't give you all the experience, all the joy, all the knowledge, therefore—let's have a next life! You want a next life where you will have time and space to perfect yourself, so you have that belief. This is escape from the fact—we are not concerned with whether there is or there is not reincarnation, or whether there is continuity or no continuity. That requires quite a different analysis. We can see briefly how that which has continuity is that which has been, that which has been yesterday will continue today, through today to tomorrow. And such a continuity is within time and space. This is not intellectual, you can observe it very simply for yourself. And we are frightened of this thing called death. We are not only frightened of living but we are also frightened of this unknown thing. Are we frightened of the unknown, or frightened of the known, of losing the known? That is, the family, your experiences, your daily monotonous existence—the known—the house, the garden, the smile to which you are accustomed, the food which you have eaten for thirty years, the same food, the same climate, the same books, the same tradition—you are frightened of losing that, aren't you? How can you be frightened of something you don't know?

So thought is frightened not only of losing the known but also thought is frightened of something which it calls death, unknown. As we said, fear cannot be got rid of, but it can be understood only when the things that produce the fear, like death, are understood. Now man throughout time has pushed death far away; the ancient Egyptians for instance lived to die. Death is something in the distance, that time-space interval between life and that which we call death. Thought, which has divided this, divided the living from the dying, thought keeps it apart. Do go into it, Sirs, it is very simple if you do so. Thought keeps it separate because thought has said, "I don't know what the future is"; I can have a lot of theories if I believe in reincarnation, it means I must behave, work, act, now—if I believe that. What you do now matters when you die—but you don't believe that way. You believe in reincarnation as an idea, a comforting idea, but rather vague, so you don't care what you do now. You really don't believe in karma although you talk a great deal about it. If you really, actually, vitally, believed in it, as you believe in earning money, in sexual experience, then every word, every gesture, every movement of your being would matter, because you are going to pay for it in the next life. So that belief would bring tremendous discipline—but you don't believe, it is an escape, you are frightened because you don't want to let go.

And what are you letting go? Look at it. When you say, "I am afraid to let go"—what are you afraid of? Letting go what? Do look at it very closely. Your family, your mother, your wife, your child? Were you ever in relation with them? Or were you related to an idea, to an image? And when you say, "I am afraid to let go, to be detached"—what are you thinking of being detached from? Memories? Surely memories, memories of sexual pleasure, memories of your becoming a big man, or a little man climbing up the ladder, memories of your character, memories of your friendship—just memories. And you are afraid to let those memories go. However pleasant or unpleasant they may be, what are memories? They have no substance whatsoever. So you are frightened of letting go something which has no value at all, memory being that which has continuity, the bundle of memories, a unit, a centre.

So when one understands living, that is, when one understands jealousy, anxiety, guilt and despair and when one is beyond and above them, then life and death are very close together. Then living is dying. You know if you live according to memories, traditions, and what you "should be", you are not living. But if you put away all that, which means dying to all that you know—freedom from the known—this is death, and then you are living. You are living, not in some fantastic world of concepts but actually living, not according to the Vedas, the Upanishads which have no validity; what has validity is the life that you lead every day, that is the only life you have, and without understanding it, you will never understand either love, beauty, or death.

We come back to that original thing, which is: why there is not this flame in our heart. Because if you have examined very closely what has been said (not verbally, intellectually, but examined it in your own mind, in your own heart), then you will know why you haven't got it. If you know why you haven't got it, if you feel it and live with it, if you are passionate in your search for why you haven't got it, then you will find that you have it. Through complete negation, that thing which alone is the positive, which is love, comes into being. Like humility, you cannot cultivate love. Humility comes into being when there is total ending of conceit, vanity, but then you will never know what is to be humble. For a man who knows what it is to have humility is a vain man. In the same way when you give your mind and your heart, your nerves, your eyes, your whole being to find out the way of life, to see what actually "is" and go beyond it, and deny completely, totally, the life that is lived now, in that very denial of the ugly, brutal, in its complete denial, the other comes into being. But you will never *know* it either. A man who knows that he is silent, or knows that he loves, doesn't know what love is, nor what silence is.

MADRAS
10 JANUARY 1968

3

THE SACRED

Ploughing, never sowing. Ideation. Sensitivity lacking in daily life. Attention and intelligence. Disorder in ourselves and the world: our responsibility. The question of seeing. Images and direct contact. The sacred. "When you have that love you can put away all your sacred books."

ONE CAN GO on endlessly reading, discussing, piling up words upon words, without ever doing anything about it. It is like a man that is always ploughing, never sowing, and therefore never reaping. Most of us are in that position. And words, ideas, theories, have become much more important than actual living, which is acting, doing. I do not know if you have ever wondered why, throughout the world, ideas, formulas, concepts, have tremendous significance, not only scientifically but also theologically. I wonder why? Is it an escape from actuality, from daily, monotonous life? Or, is it that we think ideas and theories will help us to live more—will give us greater vision, greater depth to life? Because we say that without ideas, without having a significance, an objective in life, life is very shallow, empty and has no meaning at all. That may be one of the reasons. Or, is it because we find living, the daily grind, the routine, the boredom, lacking in a quality of sensitivity that we hope to derive from ideation?

Life as we live it is obviously very brutal, and makes us insensitive, dull, heavy, stupid, and so we may hope through ideas, through ideational mentation, to bring about a certain quality of sensitivity. Because we notice that our life inevitably is a repetitive affair (sex, office, eating, the endless chatter about things that really don't matter, the constant friction in relationship), all this does make for crudeness, for brutality, for hardness. And being aware of that (perhaps not consciously but deep down), one may think that ideas, ideals, theories about God, the hereafter, may give a quality of refinement, may perhaps bring to this dull, aching life, a meaning, a significance, a purpose; perhaps we think it may polish our minds, give them sharpness, give them a quality that the ordinary daily worker in the field or in the factory does not have. So perhaps that is one of the reasons why we indulge in this peculiar game. But even when we are sharpened and quickened intellectually by argument, by discussion, by reading, this does not actually bring about that quality of sensitivity. And you know all those people who are erudite, who read, who theorise, who can discuss brilliantly, are extraordinarily dull people.

So I think sensitivity, which destroys mediocrity, is very important to understand. Because most of us are becoming, I am afraid, more and more mediocre. We are not using that word in any derogative sense at all, but merely observing the fact of mediocrity in the sense of being average, fairly well educated, earning a livelihood and perhaps capable of clever discussion; but this leaves us still bourgeois, mediocre, not only in our attitudes but in our activities. And maturity does not bring about a mutation, a change, a revolution in mediocrity (this can be observed very clearly), although one may have an old body, mediocrity in different forms continues.

Perhaps we could go into this question of sensitivity (not mere physical refinement, which is obviously necessary), but into the question of sensitivity, the highest form of sensitivity which is the highest intelligence; without being sensitive you are not intelligent. To listen to that crow, to be aware of it, to feel its movement, to have no space between that and yourself (which doesn't mean identity with the crow, as this would be too absurd), but that quality of a mind that is highly sharpened, attentive, in which the observer, which is the centre, the censor, with his accumulated memories and tradition, *is not*. It is after all a question of constant habit, the way we think, the food that we eat, the way we choose our friends, who obviously are our friends because they don't contradict, they don't disturb us too much. So life becomes not only repetitive but also habitual, routine. So sensitivity needs attention.

You know concentration is a most deadly thing. You accept it, do you? I am saying, the speaker is saying something totally contradictory to what you all feel is necessary. So don't accept it, nor deny it, but look at it. Feel your way into what is true and what is false. What the speaker is saying may be utterly stupid and nonsensical, or it may be true. But to accept or to deny makes you remain as you are, dull, heavy, habit-ridden, insensitive. But in what we are going to say in a moment and even now, do not accept or compare with what you already know or what you have been told or read, but listen in order to find out for yourself what is true. And to give attention, to listen, you have to give your *total* attention. You cannot give your total attention if you are merely learning to concentrate, or if you are trying to concentrate on a few words, or on the meaning of words, or what you have already heard. But give your attention, and this means listening without any barrier, without any interference or comparison, or condemnation; that is giving total attention; then you will find out for yourself what is true or false without being told. But this is one of the most difficult things to do—to give attention. Attention does not demand any quality of will or desire. We function within the pattern of desire, which is will. That is, we say, "I will pay attention, I will try to listen without the barriers, without all the screens between the speaker and myself." But the exercise of will is not attention.

Will is the most destructive thing that man has cultivated. Do you again accept that? To accept, or to deny, is not to find the truth of it; but to find the truth of it you have to give attention to it, to what the speaker is saying. Will is, after all, the culmination of desire—I want something, I desire something, I want it and I pursue it. The desire may be a very thin thread, but it is strengthened by constant repetition, and this becomes the will—"I will" and "I will not". And on that assertive level (which can also be negative), we function, we operate and we approach life. "I will succeed, I will become, I will be noble"—all very strong desires. And we are now saying that to be attentive has nothing whatsoever to do with desire or will.

Then, how is one to be attentive? Please follow this. Knowing one is not attentive (knowing one has a certain amount of concentration, which is an exercise of will which excludes and resists, knowing that any form of effort, which again is will, is not attention), how is one to attend? Because if you can give total attention to everything that you do (and you therefore do very little), what you do, you do completely with your heart, with your mind, with your nerves, with *everything* you have. And how is this attention to come about, naturally, without any effort, with no exercise of the will, without using attention as a means to something else? I hope you are following all this. You know, you are going to find it awfully difficult if you don't follow this step by step, as you are probably not used to it; you are used to being told what to do, which you do repetitively, and you think you have understood it. But what we are trying to say is something entirely different.

This attention then comes about naturally, easily, when you know you are inattentive—right? When you are aware that you are inattentive, not giving attention, being aware of that fact is being attentive, and you have nothing else to do. Do you understand? Through negation you come to the positive, but not through the pursuit of the positive. When you do things without this action you do things in a state of inattention, and to be aware of action in a state of inattention, is attention. This makes the mind very subtle, makes the mind tremendously alert, because then there is no wastage of energy. Whereas the exercise of will is wastage of energy, just as concentration is.

We said that this attention is necessary—don't say, "Define what you mean by attention", you might just as well look it up in a dictionary. We are not going to define it, what we are trying to do is, by denying what is not, to come upon it by yourself. We are saying, this attention is necessary for sensitivity, which is intelligence at the deeper level. Again, these words are difficult because there is no measurement—when you say, "deeper", "more", you are

193

comparing, and comparison is a waste of energy. So, if that is understood, we can use words to convey a meaning which is not comparative but actual.

This sensitivity implies intelligence and we need great intelligence to live, to live our daily life, because it is only intelligence that can possibly bring about a total revolution in our psyche, in the very core of our being. And such a mutation is necessary, because man has lived for millions of years in agony, in despair, always battling with himself and with the world. He has invented a peace which is not peace at all; such peace is between two wars, between two conflicts. And as society is getting more and more complex, disorderly, competitive, there must be radical change, not in society, but in the human being who has created society. The human being, as he is, is a very disorderly person, he is very confused; he believes, he doesn't believe, he has theories and so on and so on; he lives in a state of contradiction. And he has built a society, a culture which is contradictory, with its rich and its poor. There is disorder, not only in our life, but also outwardly in society. And order is completely necessary. You know what is happening in the world—here in India—look at it! What is happening? Colleges are closed, a whole generation of young people is without education; they will be destroyed by politicians quarrelling over some silly division of language. Then there is the Vietnamese war in which human beings are being destroyed for an idea. There are the racial riots in America, terribly destructive things. And in China there is civil war; in Russia, tyranny, suppression of freedom, at best slow liberalisation—there is division between nationalities, separation due to religions, all of which indicate complete disorder. And this disorder is brought about by each of us; *we* are responsible. Do please see the responsibility of it. The older generation has made a mess of the world, you have made a terrible mess of the world with your pujas, your gurus, with your gods, with your nationalities, because you are only concerned with earning a livelihood and cultivating part of the brain, the rest you neglect, you discard. Each human being is responsible for this disorder within himself and in the society in which he lives; Communism and other forms of tyranny are not going to bring order, on the contrary they are going to bring about more disorder, because man needs to be free.

So there is disorder. And order is necessary, otherwise

there can be no peace at all. And it is only in peace, in quietness, in beauty, that goodness can flower. Order is virtue, not the cultivated virtue of a cunning mind. Order is virtue, and order is a living thing, just as virtue is a living thing. So virtue cannot be practised as things are. We are going to go into this, listen to it. You cannot practise it any more than you can practise humility, or have a method to find out what love is.

So order in this sense has the same pattern as mathematics; in the highest mathematics is the highest order, absolute order. And that absolute order, one must have it in oneself. And as virtue cannot be cultivated, put together, so order cannot be engendered, put together by the mind; but what the mind can do is to find out what disorder is. You are following this? You know what is disorder—living in the way we live is total disorder. As things are, each man is out for himself, there is no co-operation, there is no love, there is complete callousness as to what happens in Vietnam or in China, or at your next door neighbour's. Be aware of this disorder, and out of the understanding of this disorder understand how it has come about, the cause of it, so that when you understand the causes, the forces that are at work bringing about this disorder, understand it truly, not merely intellectually; then out of that understanding will come order. Now let us try to understand disorder, which is our daily life, understand it, not intellectually or verbally, but observe it, how one has been separated from others by being a Hindu, a Muslim, a Christian (the Christian with his god, with his ideals and the Hindu with his ideals, the Muslim with his own ideals peculiar to him, and so on), observe it, come closely into contact with it, do not have prejudices, otherwise you cannot come directly into contact with another human being.

So, out of disorder comes order, and it comes about naturally, freely, easily, with great beauty and vitality, when you are directly in contact with disorder in yourself. You are not in contact with this disorder directly, with yourself, if you do not know how to look at yourself. How to see yourself (we have gone into this question of seeing), how to look at a tree, a flower—because as we said the other day, the act of seeing is the act of love? The act of seeing is action. We will go into this a little bit because this is really very important.

When you give your attention completely, that is, with

your mind, with your eyes, with your heart, with your nerves—when you give complete attention, you will find there is no centre at all, there is no observer and therefore there is no division between the observed and the observer, and you eradicate conflict totally, this conflict brought about by separation, by division. It only seems difficult because you are not used to this way of looking at life. It is really quite simple. It is really very simple if you know how to look at a tree, if you know how to see anew the tree, your wife, your husband, your neighbour, if you look anew at the sky with its stars, with its silent depth—look, see and listen, then you have solved the whole problem of understanding, because then there is no "understanding" at all, then there is only a state of mind that has no division, and therefore no conflict.

To come upon this naturally, easily, fully, there must be attention. This attention can only come about easily when you know how to look, how to listen—how to look at a tree, or your wife, or your neighbour, or at the stars, or even at your boss, without any image. The image is, after all, the past—the past, which has been accumulated through experience, pleasant or unpleasant; and with that image you look at your wife, your children, your neighbour, the world; you look with that image at nature. So what is in contact is your memory, the image which has been put together by memory. And that image looks and therefore there is no direct contact. You know when you have pain there is no image, there is only pain, and therefore there is immediate action. You may postpone going to the doctor, but action is involved. In the same way when you look and listen, you know the beauty of immediate action in which there is no conflict whatsoever. That is why it is important to know the art of looking, which is very simple—to look with complete attention, with your heart and with your mind. And attention means love, because you cannot look at that sky and be extraordinarily sensitive if there is a division between yourself and the beauty of that sunset.

This order can only come about when we see, that is actually come into contact with disorder, which is in ourselves, which is us. We are not *in* disorder—"we" is a state of disorder. Now when you look at yourself without any image about yourself, actually at what you are (not what Shankara, Buddha, Freud, Jung, or X Y Z says, because then you are looking at yourself according to their image),

you look at the disorder in yourself, the anger, the brutality, the violence, the stupidity, the indifference, the callousness, the constant drive of ambition with its peculiar
cruelty—if you can be aware of that without any image,
without any word, and look at it, then you are directly in
contact with it. And when there is direct contact there is
immediate action. There is immediate action when you
have intense pain, and when there is great danger there is
instant action. And this instant action is life, not the thing
that we have hitherto called life, which is a battlefield, an
agony in that battlefield, despair, hidden wants and so on;
that is what we have called life. Please do observe this in
yourself. Use the speaker as a mirror in which you can see
yourself now. What the speaker is saying is merely exposing yourself to yourself. And therefore look at this,
listen to it and become completely in contact with it, be
totally with it, and, if you are, you will see that there is
immediate action.

The past is then destroyed. You know the past is the
unconscious. You know what the unconscious is? Don't go
back to Freud, Jung or all the rest of those people, but
look at it for yourself and find out, not through empiri-
cism, but actually observe it. The past in you is your tradition, the books that you have read, the racial inheritance
as the Hindu, Buddhist, Muslim, Christian, and all the rest
of it, and the culture in which you have lived, the temples,
the beliefs that have been handed down from generation
to generation. This constitutes the propaganda to which
you have been subjected, your propaganda; you are slaves
to the propaganda of five thousand years. And the Christian is a slave to propaganda of two thousand years. He
believes in Jesus Christ and you believe in Krishna, or
whatever you do believe in, as the Communist believes in
something else. We are the result of propaganda. Do you
realise what it means?—words, the influence of others; so
there is nothing whatsoever original. And to find out the
origin of anything we must have order. Order that can
only come about when there is the cessation of total
disorder in oneself. Because all of us, at least those who
are even a little serious and thoughtful and earnest, must
have asked whether there is anything sacred at all, anything holy. Of course the answer is that the temple, the
mosque, or the church is not holy, is not sacred, nor the
images therein.

I do not know if you have experimented with yourself.

Take a piece of stick, put it on the mantelpiece and every day put a flower in front of it—give it a flower—put in front of it a flower and repeat some words—"Coca-cola", "Amen", "Om", it doesn't matter what word—any word you like—listen, don't laugh it off—do it and you will find out. If you do it, after a month you will see how holy it has become. You have identified yourself with that stick, with that piece of stone or with that piece of idea and you have made it into something sacred, holy. But it is not. You have given it a sense of holiness out of your fear, out of the constant habit of this tradition, giving yourself over surrendering yourself to something, which you consider holy. The image in the temple is no more holy than a piece of rock by the roadside. So it is very important to find out what is really sacred, what is really holy, if there is such a thing at all.

You know, man has spoken of this throughout the centuries, seeking something that is imperishable, that is not created by the mind, that is holy in itself, something that is never touched by the past. Man is always seeking that. And man, seeking that, not finding it, has invented religion, organised belief. A serious man has to find out, not through some rock, temple or idea, but he has to find what is really, truly, everlastingly sacred. If you cannot find it, you will always be cruel, you will always be in conflict. And if you will, this evening, listen, perhaps you may come upon it, not through the speaker, not through his words, not through his statements, but you may come upon it when there is discipline through the understanding of disorder. When you watch, see what is disorder; the very seeing of disorder demands attention. Please do follow this. You know, for most of us, discipline is a drill, as it is for the soldier, drill, drill from morning until night so that there is nothing but slavery to a habit. And that is what we call discipline; suppression, control—that is deadly, that is not discipline at all. Discipline is a living thing, it has its own beauty, its own freedom. And this discipline comes naturally, when you know how to look at a tree, how to look at the face of your wife, your husband, when you can see the beauty of a tree or a sunset. To see, to look at that sky, the glow of it, the beauty of the leaves against that glow, the orange colour, the depth of that colour, the swiftness of that colour—*see* it! To see it you must give your whole attention to it. And to give your whole attention has its own discipline, you don't want any other discipline. So that thing, that attention is a living thing, moving and vital.

This attention itself is virtue. You need no other ethical standard, no morality (anyhow you have no morality, except on the one hand the morality that the society which you have built tells you, and on the other hand what you want to do, and neither has anything whatsoever to do with virtue). Virtue is beauty and beauty is love, and without love you have no virtue and therefore no order. So again, if you have *done* it now, as the speaker is talking about it, looking at that sky with your whole being, that very act of looking has its own discipline and therefore its own virtue, its own order. Then the mind reaches the highest point of absolute order and therefore because it is absolutely orderly, *it* itself becomes the sacred. I do not know if you understand this. You know, when you love the tree, the bird, the light on the water, when you love your neighbour, your wife, your husband, without jealousy, that love that has never been touched by hate, when there is that love, that love itself is sacred, you have no other thing that can be more so.

So there is that sacred thing, not in the things that man has put together, but which comes into being when man cuts himself off entirely from the past, which is memory. This does not mean that man becomes absent-minded, he must have memory in a certain direction, but that memory will be found to be part of this whole state in which there is no relation with the past. And that cessation of the past can only be when you see things as they are and come directly in contact with them—as with that marvellous sunset. Then out of this order, discipline, virtue, there comes into being love. Love is tremendously passionate and therefore it acts immediately. It has no time interval between the seeing and the doing. And when you have that love you can put away all your sacred books, all your gods. And you *have* to put away your sacred books, your gods, your everyday ambitions, to come upon that love. That is the only sacred thing there is. And to come upon it, goodness must flower. Goodness—you understand, Sirs?—goodness can only flower in freedom, not in tradition. The world needs change, you need tremendous revolution in yourself; the world needs this tremendous revolution (not economic, Communist, bloody revolution that man has tried throughout history, that has only led him to more misery). But we do need fundamental, psychological, revolution, and this revolution *is* order. And order is peace; and this order, with its virtue and peace, can only come about when you come directly into contact with disorder in your daily life. Then out of that blossoms goodness and then there will be no seeking any more. For that which *is,* is sacred.

MADRAS
14 JANUARY 1968

INDIA

VI

Four Dialogues in Madras

1

CONFLICT

Images: are we aware that we see through images? Concepts; the gap between concepts and daily living; resulting conflict. "To get illumination you must be able to look." "To live without conflict, but not to go to sleep."

KRISHNAMURTI: I think that these should not really be called "discussions", but rather conversations between two people or between many of us—conversations about serious matters in which most of us are not merely interested but seriously concerned with deep intention to understand the problems involved. And so the conversations become not only objective but also very intimate. It is like two people talking things over together amicably, easily—exposing themselves to each other. Otherwise I do not see the point of such conversations. What we are trying to do, aren't we, is to understand (not intellectually or verbally or theoretically but actually) what are the imperative necessities in life, and in what way one can resolve the deep fundamental problems that every human being is concerned with. So is that very clear—that we are conversing together as two friends making themselves known to each other, not merely dialectically giving their opinions, but actually investigating, thinking over their problems together? Now if that is clear, what shall we talk about together?

Questioner: *The other day you were talking about the observer and the observed, and resolving the conflict between . . .*

KRISHNAMURTI: Is that what you want to discuss? Please Sir, let us all find out what each one of us wants to discuss and then put it all together and see what happens.

Questioner: Why do you say that studying Indian culture and art and Indian philosophies is violence?

Questioner: What are the steps to take to uncondition ourselves?

Questioner: The mind produces images, but what is seen by the mind is not true.

KRISHNAMURT: Is that what we are all concerned about in our daily life? Sirs, are we reducing, this morning, this gathering to a mere intellectual, verbal exchange of ideas?

Questioner: What is meant by clear thinking?

Questioner: What is the "actual" . . .

Questioner: Do you suggest that violence and non-violence are two extremes?

Questioner: Can we not guide our lives by certain principles?

KRISHNAMURTI: Haven't we got enough questions? What do you think, Sirs, is the most important question of all these?

Questioner: What is it to pay attention?

KRISHNAMURTI: Sirs, what do you think is the most important thing to discuss? Can we take this question of observation and thinking? Shall we? That is—what is it to observe, to listen, and who is it that listens, who is it that thinks? We shall relate it to daily living and not to some abstract concepts, because this country—like every other country in the world—functions at the conceptual level, except technologically. What do we mean by *seeing*? What do *you* think?

Questioner: Observing a little more attentively.

KRISHNAMURTI: Why do you say "a little more"? Sir, when we use the words "I see a tree", "I see you", "I see or understand what you are saying"—what do we mean by

204

the word "seeing"? Let us go slowly if you do not mind—step by step. When you see a tree, what do you mean by that?

Questioner: We only look superficially.

KRISHNAMURTI: What do you mean by "superficially" looking at it? When you see a tree, what do you mean by "seeing"? Do please stick to that one word.

Questioner: Catching a glimpse of it.

KRISHNAMURTI: First of all, Sirs, have you looked at a tree? If you have looked, what do you see through your "seeing" eyes, the image of the tree or the tree?

Questioner: The image of the tree.

KRISHNAMURTI: Do be careful, please, Sirs. Do you see the image in the sense of the mental construction or the concept of that tree, or do you actually see the tree?

Questioner: The physical existence of the tree.

KRISHNAMURTI: Do you actually see that? Sirs, there is a tree ... You must be able to see a tree or a leaf out of that window as I see it. When you see it what do you actually see? Do you see only the image of that tree or do you actually see the tree itself, without the image?

Questioner: We see the tree itself.

Questioner: We come to understand it.

KRISHNAMURTI: Before we come to understand it, when I say "I see a tree" do I actually see the tree or the image I have about that tree? When you look at your wife or your husband, do you see her or him or the image you have about him or her? (*Pause*) When you look at your wife you see her through your memories, through your experience of her and her ways, and through those images you see her. And do we do the same with regard to the tree?

Questioner: When I look at a tree I just see a tree.

205

KRISHNAMURTI: Ah, you are not a botanist, you are a lawyer and therefore you look at that tree actually as a tree, but if you were a botanist, if you were really interested in the tree, how it grows, what it is like, the aliveness, the quality of it, then you would have images, you would have pictures, you would compare it with other trees, and so on. You are looking at it aren't you, with a comparative look, with botanical knowledge, seeing whether you like it or not, whether it gives shade or not, whether it is beautiful or not, and so on and so on. So, when you have all those images, associations, memories with regard to that tree, are you then actually looking at that tree? Are you directly looking at that tree or have you a screen between that tree and the visual perception of it?

Questioner: I tell myself what kind of a tree it is.

KRISHNAMURTI: As a symbol. So you do not actually look at that tree. But this is simple, isn't it?

Questioner: A tree is a tree.

KRISHNAMURTI: The "tree", Sirs, I see is rather difficult. Let us look at it differently. Do you look at your wife or your husband through the image you have built about her or him? Or your friend? You have created an impression, and the impression has left an image, an idea, a memory, isn't that so?

Questioner: My impressions of my wife have accumulated . . .

KRISHNAMURTI: Yes, they have solidified, thickened, grown solid. So when you look at your wife or husband you are looking at him or her through the image you have built. Right. This is simple, isn't it? This is what we are all doing. Now, are we really looking at her or at the symbol, the memories?—is this the screen through which we look?

Questioner: How can we prevent that?

KRISHNAMURTI: It is not a question of *preventing*. Let us see first what is actually taking place.

Questioner: When you look for the first time at a woman or a man you have no previous impression.

KRISHNAMURTI: Naturally not.

Questioner: Are we not then looking at the woman or the man?

KRISHNAMURTI: Of course you are. Why do you make it into such an abstraction? What actually takes place in daily life? You are married, or you live with a person, there is sex, pleasure, pain, insults, annoyance, boredom, indifference, nagging, bullying, domination, obeying and all the rest of it—all that has created an image in you about the other person and through that image you look at each other. Right? So are we looking at the woman or at the man, or are the images looking at each other?

Questioner: The image is the person.

KRISHNAMURTI: No, no. There is a vast difference between them. Is there not a difference?

Questioner: We don't know any other way.

KRISHNAMURTI: That is the only method of seeing you know.

Questioner: We alter our impressions . . .

KRISHNAMURTI: It is all part of that image, Sir—adding and subtracting. Look, Sir. Have you an image of the speaker? You *have* an image of the speaker and the image is based on his reputation, on what he has said previously, on what he condemns or what he approves, and so on. You have built an image. And through that image you listen or look. Right? That image either increases or decreases according to your pleasure or pain. And that image is obviously interpreting what the speaker is saying.

Questioner: We feel a strong impulse to come to your talks . . .

KRISHNAMURTI: No, no, Sir. You may like my "blue eyes" or something! All that is included, Sir. The stimulation, the inspiration, the drive—you can add lots of things to that image!

Questioner: We don't know of any other way of looking.

KRISHNAMURTI: We are going to find out, Sir. We not only look at people or trees in that way, but also we look at concepts, don't we—at the Communist ideology, the Socialist ideology, and so on. We look at everything through concepts. Right? Concepts, beliefs, ideas, knowledge or experience, or what appeals to us. Communism appeals to one person and does not appeal to the other; one person believes in God and another does not believe in God. These are all concepts, Utopias, and on that level we live. Now, are they of any value? Being on an abstract level, conceptual; have they any value? Have they any significance in daily life? Life means living: living means relationship; relationship means contact; contact means cooperation. Have concepts of any kind of significance, in that sense, in relationship? But the only relationship we *have* is conceptual. Right?

Questioner: Then we have to find a right relationship.

KRISHNAMURTI: No, it is not a question of right relationship, Sir. We are just examining. Do please understand this, Sirs. Let us go into it slowly. Don't let us jump. We live in concepts, our life is conceptual. We know what we mean by "conceptual" so we do not have to analyse that word. And so there is an *actual* daily living and a conceptual living. Or, is all living conceptual? Do I live according to my concepts? One person believes, let us suppose, that one must be non-violent.

Questioner: I have not met anyone who actually believes in violence.

KRISHNAMURTI: All right, Sir. My question is: Is all living conceptual?

Questioner: The building of a concept is due to habit and becomes a habit.

KRISHNAMURTI: Perhaps we shall be able to come to that question later, if we can tackle this problem first. Our question is: Is all my living conceptual?

Questioner: Is there no such thing as spontaneous living?

KRISHNAMURTI: There is conceptual living and spontaneous living, but do I know what spontaneous living is when I am so conditioned, when I have inherited so many traditions?—is there any spontaneity left? Whether you have one concept or a dozen, it is still a question of concepts. Please Sirs, do hold to this for a minute. Is all life, all living, all relationship merely conceptual?

Questioner: How can that be?

KRISHNAMURTI: Have you not an idea, Sir, that you should live *this* way and not *that* way? Therefore when you say "I must do this and I must not do that"—it is conceptual. So, is all living conceptual or is there a difference between non-conceptual living and conceptual living —and hence a conflict between the two?

Questioner: I would say that we have a concept, but after experience the concept is modified.

KRISHNAMURTI: Yes Sir, concepts are modified, obviously—modified, changed a little; but is conceptual living different from daily living or . . .

Questioner: It is different.

KRISHNAMURTI: Wait Sir, wait Sir! I want to analyse this a little more. Is conceptual living different from daily living, or is there a gap between the two? I say there is a gap. What is this gap? Why should there be a gap?

Questioner: (Inaudible)

KRISHNAMURTI: That's it. My concept is different from the actuality that is taking place now. Right? So there is an interval, a gap between what *is*, and what *should be,* or the concept. I am still sticking to the word "concept".

209

Questioner: When you talk about "the actuality", that, to me, is the concept.

KRISHNAMURTI: No sir. When you have toothache it is not a concept. When I have toothache it is not a concept. It is an actuality. When I am hungry, it is not a concept. When I have sexual desire, it is not a concept. But the next moment I say "No, I must not" or "I must", "It is evil", or "It is good". So there is a division between the actual, and what *is,* and the conceptual. So there is a duality. Right?

Questioner: If I am hungry it is not just a concept.

KRISHNAMURTI: That is what we are saying, Sir. The primary urges, hunger, sex and so on, are actual, but we also have concepts about them. Concepts of class division, and so on. So, we are trying to find out why this gap exists and if it is possible to live without this gap, to live only with what *is.* Right? That is what we are trying to find out.

Questioner: Animals just eat when they are hungry.

KRISHNAMURTI: But you and I are not animals. We may be at moments, but actually, now, we are not animals. So do not let us go back to animals, babies and previous generations; let us stick to *ourselves.* So there is the actual moment of living and the ideational, conceptual, non-factual living. Right Sirs? I *believe* in something, but that belief has nothing to do with the actuality, though the actuality may have produced the belief; the actual is not related to that belief. "I believe in universal brotherhood." God knows who can believe it, but I say, "I believe in universal brotherhood"—but *actually* I am competing with you. So the actuality of competition with you is entirely different from the conceptual.

Questioner: (Inaudible)

KRISHNAMURTI: We have made it fairly clear up to now. The actual is, *"what is"*—the factual. There is hunger in this country, poverty, over-population, corruption, inefficiency, brutality, and all the rest of it. That is the *fact,* but the ideation is that we should not be that. Right? In our daily life the "actual", the "what is", the "factual" is something entirely different from the real fact; it is the conceptual. Right?

Questioner: But what you call the actual is just another concept, surely.

KRISHNAMURTI: No. I am hungry—that is not a concept, I *am* hungry. It is not born out of a memory of yesterday's hunger. If it is born out of yesterday's hunger it is not actual. Take sex—you do not mind my talking about sex do you? We all ... but never mind. *(Laughter)* The sexual urge may or may not be there, but it is stimulated into being by the image which is fictional, not actual. So I am asking why do we have the conceptual at all?

Questioner: Perhaps it is ...

KRISHNAMURTI: No, no, Sir. Don't just answer me but find out if you have a concept at all. Why do I have a concept at all?

Questioner: There are some things like anger which are psychological ...

KRISHNAMURTI: All that is related, Sir. When I am angry, when there is irritation—it is a *fact*. It is there. But the moment I say, "It must not be there" it becomes conceptual. If you say "Well, the Indian starvation can only be solved by a particular political party," then it is conceptual—then you are not dealing with the fact. The Communist, the Socialist, the Congressman—whatever the parties are, they all think they will solve the problem of starvation if you follow their method—which is sheer nonsense, of course. Starvation is the *fact* and the conceptual is the idea, the method, the system. So I am asking myself, why do I have concepts at all? (Don't answer me, Sirs. Ask yourself that question.) Why do you believe in the Masters, the Gurus, in God, in the perfect state? Why?

Questioner: I wonder if ...

KRISHNAMURTI: Listen to what the first gentleman says. He says that by having a concept I reform myself. Everybody thinks that, not only you. By having an ideal, a goal, a principle, a hero, and so on, you think you will be

211

helped to improve yourself. Now, what does this do actually, does it improve you or does it create conflict, conflict between what is and what should be?

Questioner: We are afraid, and therefore we retreat into these concepts.

KRISHNAMURTI: All right. Now, can we live without concepts? Please let us go on, step by step. Can you live without a belief—follow this slowly—without a concept, without hope or despair?

Questioner: Surely we must have some beliefs ...

KRISHNAMURTI: Go into it, find out. Find out why you have concepts, first. Is it because you are afraid?

Questioner: One has to battle with others for the primary needs of life.

KRISHNAMURTI: You say one has to battle.

Questioner: (Inaudible)

KRISHNAMURTI: You haven't answered the other gentleman's question. You have no respect for each other in this questioning! Let us find out what the other chap wants. You know there are two theories about this, one concerns "the survival of the fittest", which implies everlasting battle, wars, the superior race, the perfect concept, and so on. Then there is the other, that through violence there can be no change at all—in the most fundamental sense of that word. I do not know why you have any belief about this, one way or the other. The actual fact is that to survive at all in the world you have to battle, either very cunningly, cleverly, brutally or very subtly exploiting people in a nice gentle way. That is the fact. And why do we have a concept about it or about anything else?

Questioner: (Inaudible)

KRISHNAMURTI: (Wait, wait Sir. Go slowly. You are much too quick. Go slowly.) First there is, as one observes in one's daily life, the non-conceptual and the conceptual, and I ask myself—and I hope you are asking

212

yourself too—why do I have concepts at all—belief that Communism or Capitalism is the most wonderful way of life? Why? Or the concept that there is God or there is no God. Why do we have concepts at all, including concepts of Rama and Sita?

Questioner: Without concepts we would be in a state of vacuum.

KRISHNAMURTI: Have you found that out? Is that a fact? Is that so? You are really not being very serious in going into this question. You have to be very precise and very clear, and not just jump from one concept to another. You are not answering the question. Why do you have, if you do have, any concept at all? You want to escape from the actual, from the "what is", don't you? (That is what that gentleman says, Sir ... Let us understand that question first. "To escape from what is.") Why do you want to escape from what is? You would not want to escape from what is if it were pleasurable. You only want to escape from what is when it is painful.

Questioner: We do not exactly know "what is", and we are trying to understand.

KRISHNAMURTI: Don't you know what is? And what do you mean by *trying*? Don't you have stomach-ache? Don't you get angry? Aren't you frightened, aren't you miserable, aren't you confused? Those are actual facts, Sir, there is nothing that requires you "to try" about them. Do consider all this, Sirs. If it were only a case of pleasure we would not have concepts at all. We would just say "Give me everything that will give me pleasure and don't bother about anything else." But if it is painful we want to escape from what *is*, into a concept. This is our daily life, Sirs. There is nothing to argue about. So your Gods, your beliefs, your ideals, principles are an escape from the daily misery, daily fears, daily anxieties. So, to understand something, cannot we ask: "Are concepts necessary?" You understand, Sir? I am afraid, and I see the absurdity of escaping from that into something which is a concept, a belief in the Masters, in God, in the Hereafter, into leading a perfect life—you know, all that stuff. Why can't I *look* at that fear? Why do I have to have concepts at all? And do not concepts prevent me from looking at that fear? Right

213

Sirs? So concepts are a barrier; they act as a barrier which prevents you from looking.

Questioner: Please clarify what you have said.

KRISHNAMURTI: Clarify what?

Questioner: Please make a clearer analysis.

KRISHNAMURTI: A clearer analysis? Perhaps you would do it yourself, Sir.

Questioner: You do it better than I.

KRISHNAMURTI: What does it matter, who does it better or worse? What is important is whether we understand this thing clearly. It is fairly simple, Sirs. My life is very dull. I live in a shoddy little house with an ugly little wife and I am miserable, anxious, and I want satisfaction, I want happiness, I want a glimpse, a moment of inexpressible bliss, and so I escape to something which I can call X. That is the whole principle, isn't it? That does not need further explanation, does it? And I live *there*, in an ideological world, a world which I have conceived, or inherited, or been told about. And thinking and living in that abstraction gives me a great delight. It is an escape from the actual daily boredom of life. Right? Then I say to myself, "Why do I have to escape?" Why can't I live and understand this terrible boredom? Why do I waste my energies in escaping? . . .

Questioner: You are conceiving a different form of existence from anything we know.

KRISHNAMURTI: I am not conceiving *anything*. I say, *look*. And I am looking at this fact that I have escaped, that I am escap*ing*, and I see how absurd it is. I have to deal with what *is*, and to deal with what is I need energy. Therefore I will not escape. Escape is a waste of energy. So, I will have nothing whatsoever to do with beliefs, Gods, concepts. I will have no concept at all. (Of course not, Sir, of course not.) If you burn your finger, and the pain creates a concept that you must never put your finger in the fire, then that concept has value, doesn't it? You have also had wars, thousands of wars. Why haven't you

214

learnt from that not to have any more wars? (Come off it, Sir. You know very well what I mean.) We don't have to analyse all this every step as we go along. I burn my finger, and I say to myself I must be careful hereafter. Or, you tread on my toe, both metaphorically and physically, and I get angry physically, and I boil inwardly. I have learnt something from that, and I say, "I must not", or "I must". (It is the same thing. Avoid, build a resistance. I understand those things very clearly. They are necessary.)

Questioner: When someone makes me angry I remember it and when I meet him next time I am ready for him.

KRISHNAMURTI: That's it, Sir! That's just it! Can I meet him without the concept next time? He might have changed, but if I meet him with my concept, that he has trodden on my toe, I have no relationship with him. Therefore, is it possible, though you have had some sort of experience, is it possible to be without the concept? So we must come back to the question—"Is it possible to live in this world without any concept?"

Questioner: I don't think so.

KRISHNAMURTI: Do not let us say it is possible or it is not possible. Let us find out. You have separated yourselves from others, Sirs, as Hindus. This is a concept. (Yes, you are! My God, you are). Would you marry your daughter to a Muslim? Let us be clear. I am taking an instance, Sir. You hurt me, and that hurt remains in my memory. I try to avoid you if I can. But unfortunately as you live in the same house or the same street I have to meet you every day. And I have an image, the crystallised image, thickened memory, which is meeting you every day. Hence there is a battle going on between us two. And so I say to myself, is it possible to live without that image, so that I really meet you? You might have changed or your might not have changed, but I will not have the image. Can I not find out how to live without the image, so that my mind is not cluttered up with images? Do you follow, Sirs. So that my mind is free, free to look, to enjoy, to live.

Questioner: That's an idea.

KRISHNAMURTI: Oh no! To *you* it is an idea, but not to me. I say, "He has hurt me, but why should I carry on that burden?"

Questioner: I just take care next time.

KRISHNAMURTI: Yes, but I won't keep on repeating, "I must be careful", which only thickens the memory. I say that is not way to live, but I only say so for me, not for you. I don't want that image and to be carrying it with me all the time. That is not freedom. You may have changed, and also I like to be *without* an image. Not as an idea, but it is an actual fact that I do not want it. It is absurd for me to have an image about anybody. So let us come back to the other things.

Questioner: If I meet a good man, is it not a good thing to have a memory, an impression that he is a good man?

KRISHNAMURTI: A bad impression or a good impression is still an impression. There is no "good image" and "bad image". (*Inaudible remark*) (For bad eyesight you must go to a better occulist.) This division between the conceptual and the actual breeds conflict. And a man who wants to investigate and go beyond the actual must have all his energy. That energy cannot be wasted through conflict. So I say to myself—and I am not telling *you* what to do—I say to myself, "It is absurd to live with concepts at all." I will deal with facts, with what is, all the time, and will never be immersed in the concept. So then I am faced with the question, "How do I look at the fact, at what is?" I am not concerned with the conceptual at all. I am only concerned in the observation of actually *what is*. Right?

Questioner: (Inaudible)

KRISHNAMURTI: (Yes, but you take things as they come with a series of habits. Habits of which you may be conscious or unconscious ... Sirs, we keep going away from the main issue.) So the question is, "Can I live with what is, without creating conflict?" Do you follow? I am angry. That is a fact. I am jealous. I like and dislike. That is a

216

fact. Can I live with that, with what is, without making a problem, a conflict out of it?

Questioner: It is not a very happy thought for me! I am at a loss . . . (inaudible)

KRISHNAMURTI: The gentleman says he is at a loss because he is at a certain level and his wife, children and neighbour are at another level—higher or inferior. And so, he says, there is no co-operation. I carry on and they carry on. That is what we are all doing, Sir. So then, what? . . . You see, we will not come to the central issue, which is, "Can I live, without conflict, with what is?" And not go to sleep, because conflict, apparently does keep one half-awake. I am asking, "Is it possible to live with what is, without conflict, and to go beyond it?" I am jealous. That is a fact. I see that in my life. I am jealous of my wife, jealous of the man who has more, more of worldly goods and of intellect: I am envious. I know how envy comes. It comes through comparison—but I do not have to analyse how envy arises. Now can I live with that, understand it, not have concepts about it? So that after looking at it, so that by understanding it, studying its structure and nature I have really understood it and so can go beyond it, so that envy never touches the mind again? You see, you are not interested in it. You really are not interested in it, are you?

Questioner: Yes we are. If we were not interested we would not be here, but we are not in contact with you.

KRISHNAMURTI: Why? Why are you not in contact with the speaker and what he is saying? He has questioned very clearly, whether it is possible to live without concepts? And he took the example of envy. We know the nature and the structure of envy. Now can you live with it, and go beyond it, without conflict? So why are you not in contact with what the speaker is saying? If you are not in contact (not you, not you personally Sir), it may be because you *like* envy. *(Inaudible)* Look, Sirs—what happens? I am envious. That envy arises through measurement. I have little and you have more, or I am dull and you are very clever. I have a low position and you have a high position, you have a car and I have no car. So, through comparison, through measurement this envy arises. Right? Is not that clear? So, can I live without measurement? This is *not* a concept.

Questioner: It is a question of reconciling ourselves to the fact that there is inequality.

KRISHNAMURTI: You are not reconciling, Sir. I am asking you a question and you are talking about a reconciliation between black and white. Then you only produce grey. (*Laughter*) I am asking quite a different question. Do *please* listen, Sir. Can you live your daily life at the office, at home, without any measurement, without any comparison? No? Why do you have comparison? Because you have been conditioned from childhood to compare. Follow this, Sirs. It has become a habit, and you keep on repeating that habit. And though that habit creates misery, confusion and all the rest of it, you don't care. You carry on with the habit. Now, what will make you aware of the nature of this habit of comparison? Somebody forcing you to be aware of the habit? If the Government were to say, "You must not be envious", you would then find other ways of being envious, more subtle ones. Religions have tried this, but you have overcome all religions. So by forcing you to be non-envious you will revolt against it, and the revolt is violence. You understand, Sirs? If I force you into a corner and say, "You must do this", then you will kick me. But if you become aware of the habit you have cultivated for forty, twenty or ten years of comparing yourself with another, then what takes place? You see, you are not interested in this. I have lost you. Because you are not interested in breaking down your habits. The Communist has his habits, and the non-Communist has his habits, and those two are going to battle with each other. That is what is going on in the world. You have *your* habit in believing in something, and I have no habit in belief. So, what is our relationship? None at all!

So we come back to a very simple thing, and God knows why you sit here and listen. Is this becoming a habit?

Questioner: We hope so.

KRISHNAMURTI: You hope it will become a habit!

Questioner: We hope to get illumination.

KRISHNAMURTI: You won't. Sir, to get illumination you must have a clear mind, you must be able to *look*.

Questioner: You said . . . (inaudible)

KRISHNAMURTI: No Sir, I did not say that. I did not say that. I will not go back through all that again—it is useless. You see you will not face the actuality, the "what is"! You want to live in concepts, and I do *not* want to live in concepts. For Heaven's sake: love is not a concept. And because you have no love, you live in concepts. (And you all shake your heads and agree and go on with your habits.) So why do you listen, why do you come here, because when we talk about these real things you are off—away at some tangent! Unfortunately, or fortunately, the speaker has talked for forty-two years. And when it comes to the point—which is to live without envy—you are not there!

Questioner: The truth is we don't want to be disturbed.

KRISHNAMURTI: Then don't be disturbed. Go away! Why do you come? You are not going to get any "poonyum" out of this, poonyum being merit. Here is a fundamental issue, and please do listen. It is a fundamental issue—to live without conflict, but not go to sleep. To live without the concept requires extraordinary intelligence and a great deal of energy. And I say that when you live in concepts you are wasting energy. And you say, "Oh, that's a very nice idea", and you still live there in concepts. You say, "I am a Communist, I believe in God, I don't believe in God and so on." And so I say to myself, "What is wrong?"

Questioner: There is an urge to know more.

KRISHNAMURTI: Then pick up an encyclopaedia or a dictionary and you will know more. To know more truly, means to know more about oneself. Otherwise there is only ignorance. You may be technologically brilliant, but if you do not know about *yourself* you are an ignorant person. Here I am, and I say, "I *must* know why I live in concepts. I want to analyse it, to understand it." Not that I must or must not live in concepts, but I want to know *why*. And when I *look* I know why. Because my life is so shoddy, mediocre, petty, and to escape from that I go off into concepts—and I have lovely concepts, immense concepts, concepts invented by Lenin, or Trotsky or Nehru or Gandhi, it does not matter who. I escape into those but I am still angry, I am still envious, I am still bored. So, why should I live in concepts at all? So I say, "I won't, because it is stupid." I will *not* do it! But you don't say that.

Questioner: Do we understand the meaning of the word?

KRISHNAMURTI: I'm afraid we do not understand about *anything*. So we will have to re-start. Too bad!

Questioner: It is something which needs going into and we must think about it.

KRISHNAMURTI: Really! If I hit you, you will *know* about that! If you are insulted, or have pain, you do not say you will think about it. This is all so obvious, but you quote a platitude and think you have understood it. So we lose contact with each other when we are *not* talking about concepts. When we talk about concepts, we are in contact. When we talked about God (if I was foolish enough to talk about God), then we were both in contact. But when you come down to an actual *fact*—of greed, envy—then we lost contact. Do you know, Sirs, what is happening in the world? The world being India also. How India is degenerating, don't you know it? Not only here, but in the world. And probably you cannot do anything about it. At least, there can be a few who will keep the light burning. That is all. But that is up to you, Sirs.

MADRAS
2 JANUARY 1968

2

THE PURSUIT OF PLEASURE

*Self-interest and self-dedication. Demand for satisfaction. Levels
of gratification. Has psychological gratification any meaning?
"A whirlpool of mischief and misery inwardly." Aggression.
Pursuit of pleasure. "There are no roots of heaven in pleasure—
there are only roots of indifference and pain." Watching is its
own discipline.*

KRISHNAMURTI: What shall we talk over together this
morning? (*Pause*).

*Questioner: May we pursue what we talked about last time
we met here, with regard to concepts? Can we live without
concepts, beliefs?*

KRISHNAMURTI: Do you think that before we can go into
that or any other question it is important to question, to
question critically, not only someone else, but, what is
much more important, to be critically *self*-aware. It seems
to me much more important to question one's own motives, one's attitudes, beliefs, ways of life, habits, traditions, the way one thinks and why one thinks in that way.
Because I do not see how we can have sanity if we are not
aware of our own reasoning or non-reasoning, if we are
not aware of our own emotional attitudes and our narrow
or wide beliefs. I do not see how we can bring about any
kind of sanity in our lives (sanity being a way of living
which is fairly healthy) unless we are critically aware of
what we are talking about, and therefore questioning everything, not accepting a *thing* about ourselves or others. I
think if we could start from that—which does not mean
that we must be sceptical about everything as this would
be another form of insanity. But if we can question, then I
think what we shall discover, talking it over together this
morning, will have some value.

221

Questioner: Can we continue with what you have just said?

Questioner: Will you take up the subject of space and time?

Questioner: Will you explain about the doctor who took L.S.D. and destroyed a space within himself, in terms of the observer and the observed?

Questioner: Could we discuss envy, and its activities?

KRISHNAMURTI: Sir, if I may ask you a question—What is your deep, fundamental, lasting interest in life?

Questioner: (Inaudible)

KRISHNAMURTI: Is *that* your deep fundamental interest, Sir? Rather feeble isn't it? If you skipped all these double, indirect, oblique questions which are beside the point and if you dealt with one question directly and honestly, would you know what is your fundamental, lasting, total interest?

Questioner: To be free.

Questioner: We want to be happy.

Questioner: I am really interested in myself . . .

KRISHNAMURTI: . . . as most of us are, interested in my progress, interested in my job, interested in my little family, getting a better position, more prestige, more power, dominating others, and so on and so on. I think it would be logical, would it not, to admit to yourselves that that is what most of us are interested in—me first, and everyone else second.

Questioner: And that is very wrong.

KRISHNAMURTI: I do not think it is wrong. What is there wrong about it? You see, Sir, that is what we are doing all the time. Now let us take that fact. Most of us are interested, in the little corner in which we live, not only outwardly but inwardly. We are interested in it, but we never decently, honestly, admit that to ourselves. If we do, we

222

are rather ashamed of it and so we add such comments as; "I do not think it is right", "It is wrong", "It does not help mankind", and all that blaa. So there it is. One is interested in *oneself* fundamentally and one thinks it is wrong (for various reasons, ideologically, traditionally, and so on). The actual daily fact is that one is interested in oneself, and you think it is *wrong*. But what you *think* is irrelevant, it has no validity at all. Why introduce that factor? Why say "It is wrong"? That is an *idea*, is it not?—it is a concept. What *is* is the fact, which is that one is interested in oneself.

Questioner: I don't know if it's all right to ask a question.

KRISHNAMURTI: Quite right. Go ahead, Sir.

Questioner: When I do something for others I feel more satisfied. I see that to be so self-concerned is not satisfactory, but to work in a school or to help another is more satisfactory than to think about oneself, which is not quite so satisfying.

KRISHNAMURTI: What is the difference? You want satisfaction—which is self-concern. Follow this out, Sir, for yourself. If you are seeking satisfaction in helping others and therefore that gives greater satisfaction, you are still concerned about yourself, about what will give you greater satisfaction. Why bring any ideological concept into it? One wants freedom because it is much more satisfying and to live a petty little life is not so satisfactory. So why have this double thinking? Why say one is satisfactory and the other is not. You understand, Sir? Why not say—I really want *satisfaction*, whether it is in sex, in freedom, or helping others, in becoming a great saint, or politician, or engineer, or lawyer. It is all the same process, is it not? Satisfaction in many ways, both subtle and obvious, that is what we want. Right? When we say we want freedom we want it because we think perhaps it may be terribly satisfying; and the ultimate satisfaction, of course, is this peculiar idea of self-realisation.

Questioner: So we must get rid of this search for satisfaction.

223

KRISHNAMURTI: Ah, no Sir. Wait Sir. To get rid of satisfaction is not freedom. Freedom is something entirely different; not something to be had *from* something. If I get rid of or free myself from satisfaction, I am freeing myself from it because I seek a much greater satisfaction. No? So why not find out why we want satisfaction? Not that "we should not", that is only a concept, a formula, and hence there is contradiction, and therefore conflict. So let us take this one thing. Most of us want, desire, search for, crave for satisfaction. Right?

Questioner: I don't think so.

KRISHNAMURTI: You don't think so. Why not, Sir?

Questioner: I am not interested specially in satisfaction, but I would like to know why I am dissatisfied.

KRISHNAMURTI: (Oh! my lord!) How do you know that you are dissatisfied. Because you have known satisfaction! (*Laughter*) Don't laugh Sirs, for goodness sake, don't laugh. This is not a clever weaving of argument, please. Why am I dissatisfied? Because I am married and that does not give me satisfaction; because I go to the temple and that does not give me satisfaction; (follow all this.) I go to meetings and that means nothing; I look at trees and feel nothing; and so gradually I am dissatisfied with everything I see, or have or have felt. Which means, what? I am seeking a satisfaction in which there is no satisfaction in which there is no dissatisfaction at all! No? This is not a clever statement; it is obvious, isn't it? No, Sir? Look, each one of us is seeking satisfaction although he is dissatisfied. Right? Now, why do we seek satisfaction?—Not that it is right or it is wrong, but what is the mechanism of this search? (*Long pause.*) Do you expect me to analyse it for you?

Questioner: In some spheres we have to seek satisfaction to live.

KRISHNAMURTI: Yes Sir, of course there are basic necessities; but wait, Sir, before we come to that, can we find out why we seek satisfaction? Go into it, Sir. What is satisfaction?

224

Questioner: I think we need some of that awareness of which you speak in order to distinguish for ourselves what will give us permanent happiness.

KRISHNAMURTI: Don't just use words, but think it out a little bit, just think it out. I do not know anything about awareness—out it goes, if I may suggest it. We are not discussing that, Sir, nor are we talking about the permanent or the impermanent. We want to find out why we human beings are always seeking satisfaction.

Questioner: (The audience suggested many reasons but they were almost inaudible.) We seek satisfaction because we want to change.

KRISHNAMURTI: Wait a minute, Sirs, just a minute, Sir. Food satisfies you, doesn't it—having a good meal? Why? Because I'm hungry, and it is good to get rid of the empty feeling. Move a little higher, up to sex. Very satisfying, apparently. You are all silent! Then, having a position in which you can dominate others, that is also very satisfying, isn't it? You feel powerful, you feel you are in a position to order others to do things, and so that is very satisfactory. One seeks different ways of finding gratification—through food, sex, position, through various virtues, and so on. Why? One can understand when you want food that you feel gratified when you eat it, but why move to another level for satisfaction; and is there such a thing? I feel satisfied with food, I want varieties of food, and, if I have the money and appetite for it I get it. I also want a good position in society, a respected position, which is very gratifying because there I am secure, with a big house, a policeman at the gate, and all the rest of it. After that, I want some more of it—a bigger house and two more policemen, and so on. Now, what is this craving for gratification? You understand, Sirs, the craving, what is it? I have a craving for food and I eat it—if I can get it. But the craving for position—let us take that one thing. Most of us want position—as the best engineer, or the best lawyer, or the President of some society, or this or that. Why? Apart from the money it gives, apart from the comfort, why this craving?

Questioner: I want to show to others what I can do.

225

KRISHNAMURTI: Which is, to make the neighbours feel envious!

Questioner: (Several interjections. Inaudible)

KRISHNAMURTI: (Is that it? Wait Sir—you have not heard that other gentleman, Sir.) If you had not your position you would be nobody. Strip the Pope of his robes, or the Sanyasi of his tamasha and he would be nobody. Is that it? So are we afraid of being nobody, and that is why we want position? To be considered a great scholar, a philosopher, a teacher? If you find yourself in that position it is very gratifying—to have your name printed in the newspaper, and people coming to you and all the rest of it. Is that why we do all this? That is, inwardly we are just ordinary people with aching sorrows, conflict, fighting in the family, bitterness, anxiety and fear which is there constantly. And to have an outward position where I am regarded as a terribly respectable citizen, that is *very* satisfactory. Right? Why do I want this outward position, I ask, and you say "I want it because in my daily life I am just a sorry little human being." Right? Is that it? (*Long pause.*)

Questioner: (Several inaudible suggestions.)

KRISHNAMURTI: What is actually taking place? We have come to a certain point, Sir, let us pursue it; this point is that one finds that one wants a position which will be gratifying because inwardly one is . . . just a shoddy little man. But to have a policeman at the gate gives me tremendous importance. Right? This is obvious, isn't it? We don't have to go into all that, do we?

Questioner: We have to expose ourselves, Sir.

KRISHNAMURTI: I am exposing you now! You may not want to be exposed but that is the fact!—I am a sorry little entity inside, with all sorts of dogmas, beliefs in God, rituals and all that—a whirlpool of mischief and misery inwardly, and outwardly I want the policeman at the gate! Now why do I have this craving for outward position? You understand? Why?

Questioner: (Inaudible)

KRISHNAMURTI: No Sir. Please go into it. Why do we want? What is the reason? Don't reduce it to the word "selfishness", Sir.

Questioner: (Long inaudible contribution.)

KRISHNAMURTI: Sir, Sir. Look, Sir! Don't you have a craving for position, for power, for prestige, to be recognised as a great man, have fame, notoriety, and so on? Have you not got this desire?

Questioner: (Inaudible remark.)

KRISHNAMURTI: You see how you are escaping from this! Have you not got this desire, Sir?

Questioner: Yes.

KRISHNAMURTI: At last! Now why? Go into it, Sir. Why? Why do you crave for a position? Don't say it is due to circumstances, that I have been put in that position by society, that I have been conditioned that way.

Questioner: I desire position in the same way as when I am hungry I want food.

KRISHNAMURTI: Oh no, Sir! Oh no! You see we can't face this thing at all!

Questioner: Further suggestions. (Inaudible)

KRISHNAMURTI: Do let us be serious. Throwing in all these words is so silly. You are not really thinking at all. Sir, here is a very simple question. Everybody throughout the world wants a position—whether in society, in the family, or to sit next to God, "on the right-hand of the Father". Everybody wants a position. There is a craving for it. Why?

Questioner: (Inaudible)

KRISHNAMURTI: No Sir! Don't throw out words. Analyse it, Sir, don't just answer! Why do you want it?

Questioner: It is natural.

KRISHNAMURTI: It is natural? Oh Sir! You say one thing and then go on to another. Have you ever noticed animals, Sir? You've got a chicken yard; have you ever noticed that there is always one chicken pecking another? There is an order of pecking. So we have perhaps inherited this thing—to dominate, to be aggressive, to seek a position is a form of aggression. No? Of course it is. I mean the saint who seeks a position with regard to his saintliness is as aggressive as the chicken pecking in the yard! I don't know if you follow all this. You don't. Perhaps we have inherited this aggressive urge to dominate, that is, to have a position. Right? And what does this involve, this aggression, to have a position in society (a position which must be recognised by others, otherwise it is no position at all)? I must always sit on the platform. Why? (*Pause*) Do please go on with it, Sirs. I am doing all the work. Why do you have this aggression? (*Audience suggests something.*) No Sir. It is not a question of something lacking. Oh, how are we going to discuss with a group of people who never want to go into anything.

Questioner: (Inaudible)

KRISHNAMURTI: That is one of the reasons, Sir. But, let us look at this, Sir. There is aggression. Right? When I want a position in society, which is recognised by society, it is a form of aggression. Now, why am I aggressive?

Questioner: (Inaudible)

KRISHNAMURTI: You see, you do not apply it to yourself. You do not find out, in yourself, why you are aggressive. Forget the "position in society" we have analysed that now. Why are we aggressive?

Questioner: To reach what we want, what we aim at.

KRISHNAMURTI: And what do you aim at? (We have said that, Sir. We have moved away from that.) The question now is, why are we aggressive? Please go into it, Sir. The politician is aggressive, the big shots are aggressive, whether in business or in religion they are aggressive—why?

Questioner: Aggressiveness arises from fear.

KRISHNAMURTI: Is that so? Maybe! Find out for yourself, Sir. You are aggressive in the family. Why? In the office, in the bus, and so on. Why are you aggressive? Don't explain it, Sir. Just find out why you *are*.

Questioner: Why am I afraid to be nothing?

KRISHNAMURTI: Look! As the gentleman said just now, fear may be the cause of this aggression because society is so constructed that a citizen who has a position of respect is treated with great courtesy, whereas a man who has no position at all is kicked around—sent into the army and to Vietnam, to be killed. So why are we aggressive? Is it because we are frightened of being nobodies? Don't answer it, Sirs, go into it! Go into it in yourselves? Or, we are frightened because it has become a habit. Seeking a position has become a habit. We are not really frightened, but it has become a habit. I don't know if you are following this. If it is fear that makes us aggressive, that is one thing. But it may be the momentum of society that is making you aggressive. You know Sirs, they have made an experiment, putting rats, thousands of rats, in a very small room. And when they are there they lose all sense of proportion. The mother who is about to have babies, the mother rat, does not care, because the pressure of space, absence of space, the fact of so many rats living together makes them crazy. Follow this. In the same way, if people live in a very, very crowded city and have no space, it makes them also very aggressive, makes them violent. Animals do need space to hunt in; they have territorial rights, like the birds. They establish their territory and they will hunt any other animal that comes into that territory. So they have territorial rights, and sexual rights—all animals have this. And sexual rights do not have such a great importance as territorial rights. Right? Of course some of you may know all about this. So we may be aggressive because we have not enough space around us physically. Are you following all this? And this may be one of the reasons why we are aggressive. A family living in a small room, or a small house with ten of you in it, you explode, get angry about nothing. So man must have space, and because he has not enough physical space, that may be one of the reasons for aggression. And also one may be aggressive because one is frightened. Now to which category do you belong? Are you aggressive because you are frightened?

Questioner: (Suggestion inaudible.)

KRISHNAMURTI: So, you are saying, guarantee my physical security and then I will not be aggressive. But is there such a thing as guaranteed security in life? And so that may be the basic reason why we are frightened—knowing that there is no such lasting security. In Vietnam there is no security. You may have a little security here but where there is war there is no security and, when an earthquake comes, it destroys everything—and so on. So, go into this yourselves, Sirs, and find out whether your aggression is born of fear, or of the fact that you are enclosed tightly, both outwardly and inwardly. Inwardly you have no freedom—intellectually you are *not* free, you repeat what others have said. Technological inventions, society, the community, all that is felt constantly as a pressure on you which you are not capable of meeting and therefore you explode, you feel frustrated. Now, which is it—to which category do you belong? Find out, Sirs, (*Long pause.*) If you are frightened, and therefore you are aggressive, how are you going to deal with fear? And if you are free of fear will you lose the pleasure of being aggressive? And knowing that you will lose the pleasure of being aggressive, you do not mind being afraid. Right? Do you follow this? (*Pause.*) Fear is unpleasant and aggressiveness is more pleasant. Right? And so I do not mind being a little bit afraid because aggressiveness with its pleasure balances fear.

Questioner: I am aware of the difficulties of the situation.

KRISHNAMURTI: Ah, I don't know what you are aware of, Sir. Go into it. I am just asking you. So you may prefer to be aggressive, but at the same time be afraid. So you really don't mind being afraid or being aggressive.

Questioner: (Inaudible)

KRISHNAMURTI: Sirs, this is a very difficult question because each one will interpret aggressiveness in his own way. But if we could face this question of fear and see if we can understand fear and see whether there is a possibility of being free from fear, then when that is gone through, then would there be aggressiveness—your kind, my kind, his kind or her kind? You follow Sir? So let us take that one thing. Is fear causing aggressiveness? Obviously it is. I am afraid of not having any belief and therefore I am aggressive about the belief I have. So fear has produced aggressiveness with regard to belief! That is simple. Right? (Are you all having an early-morning sleep, or what!) So, is it possible to be free of fear? (At last!) One only puts that question when one really wants to be free of fear. Is it possible to live without fear? It is a very complex problem. It is not a matter of saying, "Yes, we must live without fear" and make a lot of platitudes about it. But can one live without fear? What does it *mean*? Physically, what does it mean? We will go step by step. What does it mean physically to live without fear? Is it possible, in this society as it is constructed, in a culture of this kind, whether the culture is Communist or the present culture, or an ancient culture, is it possible to live in a society without fear?

Questioner: It is not possible.

KRISHNAMURTI: Why? Most extraordinary, Sirs! When one comes to basic questions you are all very silent.

Questioner: I'm only thinking of what would happen to my life.

KRISHNAMURTI: Are you afraid that if you had lasting security in a stable society, you would have no fear. (*Inaudible*) (Yes Sir. That is understood, Sir.) So, you will not be afraid if you can have a guarantee that the life, the daily existence you are used to will not be disturbed from the pattern you are used to. Right? And on that basis we build a society. Obviously. That is what the Communists have done. So you say it is not possible to live in a society without fear. Is that so? No?

Questioner: I think it must be possible but I don't know how to do it.

KRISHNAMURTI: Ah! If you think it must be possible, that is only a concept. The fact is that one is afraid to live in a society as it is, without fear. Right?

Questioner: (Inaudible)

231

KRISHNAMURTI: (We are doing that, Sir. That is what we are discussing, Sir.) One of our fears is that to live in a society one has to be aggressive. Let us for the moment accept that—that to live in a society of any kind, Communist, Capitalist, or Hindu or Moslem you have to be aggressive and therefore frightened in order to survive at all. Leave it there. Now at what other level of our existence are we afraid? I can understand that I am afraid that I may not have enough food for tomorrow and therefore I lay up stores for a month or for two days and I am going to guard it and to see that nobody steals it. And I'm afraid that the Government will come along and do something or other, and so I am afraid. I can understand that. Now are we only aggressive there, at that level. Are we only afraid at that level?

Questioner: *Inwardly we are also the same.*

KRISHNAMURTI: What do we mean by "inwardly"? What does that mean, Sir?

Questioner: *(Inaudible. Several comments.)*

KRISHNAMURTI: So there is fear at another level. It is suggested that there is fear in relationship, and therefore we are aggressive in relationship. Now why are we afraid in relationship? (I don't know what "truthful" means, Sir.) Why are we afraid in relationship? Are you afraid of your wife, or your husband, or your neighbour, or your boss? I know it's a rather awful thing to admit that you are afraid of your wife! One is afraid in every kind of relationship. Why?

Questioner: *(inaudible)*

KRISHNAMURTI: Why am I afraid? Please do be simple about it because it becomes very complex presently and if we are not simple at the beginning we shall not understand *anything*. Why am I afraid of my wife or my neighbour, or my boss (which is relationship)—why?

Questioner: *(Several comments, inaudible.)*

KRISHNAMURTI: My dear chap you're not married! So leave it for the moment. Your calamity will come presently!

Questioner: There is fear in relationship because "he" or "she" or "my boss" can withhold something from me. (Further comment inaudible.)

KRISHNAMURTI: How are you going to discuss this when you won't go step by step! Don't jump, don't conclude. Are you afraid of your neighbour, of your boss? *Fear*— you know. He might take away your job. He might not give you a raise, he might not encourage you. And also you are maybe afraid of your wife because she dominates, she nags, she bullies, she is not pretty. So one is afraid. Why? Because one yearns for continuity. Let us go slower than that. I am sorry to insist on going very slowly, step by step. I am afraid of my wife, why? I am afraid because—it is very simple—she bullies me and I don't like to be bullied. I am fairly sensitive and she is aggressive, and I'm tied to her through ceremony, through marriage, through children. And so I am frightened. She dominates me and I don't like it. Right Sirs? I am frightened for that reason, because I am fairly sensitive and I like to do things differently. I like to look at trees, I like to play with the children, I like to go to the office late, or do this or that, and she bullies me, and I don't like to be bullied. So I have the beginning of fear of her. Right? And also, if I retaliate and say "Don't bully me" she will withhold her sexual pleasure, my pleasure with her. So I am frightened of that. Right Sirs? Still you are all very silent about this! You are an extraordinary generation! I am frightened because she wants to pick a quarrel with me, and so on. So what shall I do? I am frightened and I am supposed to be related to her. She dominates me, she bullies me, and she orders me about, she has contempt for me. And, if I am a strong man, I have contempt for *her*. You know! So what shall I do? I am frightened. Do I acknowledge that fact, or do I cover it up and say "It's my karma", "It's my conditioning", you know—you complain against society and your environment.

Questioner: I suppose one has to suffer in silence.

KRISHNAMURTI: Suffer in silence! You do that anyhow.

Questioner: Divorce her!

KRISHNAMURTI: Divorce is rather expensive and takes too long, so what will you do?

Questioner: Put up with it.

KRISHNAMURTI: Now what takes place? Follow it, Sirs. What takes place? You are frightened and you put up with it. So what is happening to you? You are frightened and you get used to this fear. You get used to the bullying, used to the environment, so gradually you become duller and duller. Gradually you lose all sensitivity. You don't look at trees which you looked at before, you never smile. So gradually you become dull. That is exactly what has happened with you gentlemen and ladies. Because you have got used to it. You have got used to this rotten society, to the filthy streets. You look neither at the filthy streets nor at the lovely sky of an evening. So, fear (your not having understood it) reduces you to dullness. What will you do, Sirs! Don't just say "Yes, you're perfectly right". The doctor has diagnosed your disease and he asks what you are going to do? You have got used to the Upanishads, the Gita, the dirt, the squalor, the bullying of the wife, the bullying of the politicians, you have become totally insensitive, dull. You may cleverly give lectures, and read and quote and all that, but inwardly you are dull. So what will you do? *(Pause)* No answer?

Questioner: Get rid of it all.

KRISHNAMURTI: How? With a lovely gesture?

Questioner: Get rid of the relationship.

KRISHNAMURTI: Walk out on her, and on the children? And fall into another trap? So what will you *do*, Sir?

Questioner: Find out why she bullies me.

KRISHNAMURTI: She won't tell me. She has her own miseries. She has God knows what problems. She is unsatisfied, perhaps, sexually. Perhaps she is ill—Oh, a dozen things there may be. You know, she feels she must have a rest, have a holiday, have some time without her husband, away from him, take a holiday. So I can't find out from her why she bullies me. I have to deal with myself, first. Gosh. You people are so ... So, what shall I do?

Questioner: Resist her.

KRISHNAMURTI: I can't do that.

Questioner: Try to reconcile.

KRISHNAMURTI: Oh my God! She keeps to her character and I keep to mine. So what shall I do?

Questioner: You become indifferent.

KRISHNAMURTI: That is what you have already done. You are completely indifferent to *everything*—to the trees, to the beauty, to the rain, to the clouds, to the dirt, to the wife, to the children. You are completely indifferent.

Questioner: Maybe we have to doubt everything that we have accepted up to now.

KRISHNAMURTI: Look Sir, it's a much more serious problem than just this verbal exchange. Because you have become indifferent, callous—through fear, through bullying by the Gods, the Upanishads, the Gita, by the politican, by the wife. You have become dull, haven't you? So how do you awaken to this dullness and throw it out? You understand my question? I have been made dull by my wife, by the repetitions of the blasted sacred books, by the society in which I live, I have become completely indifferent. I don't care what happens to me or what happens to others. I have become callous, hard. I recognise that. That is a fact. You may not recognise it. You may say, "Well I may have little spots here and there which are fairly sensitive". Those little spots have no value at all, when the major field is dull. So, what shall I do? I recognise that as a fact. And the question is not how to get rid of it! I don't condemn it. I say, "That is a fact." So what shall I do? Well, Sirs. What shall I do.

Questioner: I feel helpless.

235

KRISHNAMURTI: Then you cannot do anything, and then you have the whole state of India as it is! Now *I* want to do something; I really do. You, your Gods, your religious books, society, the culture in which you have grown up, all these have made me incredibly callous and indifferent. So what shall I do? Well, Sirs. What shall I do?

Questioner: Break with the whole thing.

KRISHNAMURTI: Break? I'm afraid to break, am I not? First of all, am I conscious, am I aware that I am indifferent? Are you, Sirs? (What a generation you are!) (*Long pause.*) All right, Sirs, I will go through it. I have become callous, and I see the reasons for this in my wife, my family, over-population, the enormous weight of ten thousand years of traditions, the endless rituals, the squalor inside the house and outside the house, and so on. I see the reasons why the mind has been made dull, through education and so on. That's a fact. Now what shall I do? First of all, I do not want to live that way. Right? I cannot live that way. It is worse than an animal. (Oh! you are not interested.)

Questioner: Please go on.

KRISHNAMURTI: So first I see the cause, and the effect, and I see it is impossible to live that way. Now what makes me say, "It is impossible to live that way"? Please follow all this. (Sirs, please don't cough.) This requires great attention. What makes me say, "I must *not* live that way"? (*Long pause.*) I am insensitive. If it is painful and I want to change, then I am changing because I think something else will give me greater pleasure. (Oh! you don't see all this!) I want to change because I see that a mind that is so dull is really not existing and there must be change. If I change because it is painful—follow this, please—if I change because it is painful then I am pursuing pleasure. Right? And the pursuit of pleasure has been the cause of this indifference. This indifference has been caused because I have sought pleasure—pleasure in the family, in the Gods, in the Upanishads, Koran, Bible, in the Establishment. And all that has reduced me to this—*indifference*. The origin of the movement was pleasure, and if I revolt against this it will again be the pursuit of pleasure!

236

Are you following all this? I have realised something! I have realised that if I change with a motive of pleasure I shall be back in the same circle. Please, Sirs, do understand this—with your hearts, not with your silly little minds. Understand this with your hearts—that when you have started to seek pleasure you must end up in catastrophe, which is dullness. If you break away from that dullness because you want a different kind of pleasure then you are back in the same circle. So I say, "Look what I'm doing!" So I have to be very watchful of pleasure. I'm not going to deny it, because if I deny it I am seeking another, greater pleasure. So I see that pleasure reduces the mind to habits which bring about complete dullness. I hang up that picture on the wall because it has given me great pleasure. I have looked at it in the museum or in the gallery and I say, "What a lovely picture that is!" I buy it, if I have the money, and hang it up in my room. I look at it every day—and say "How nice". Then I get used to it. You understand? So the pleasure of looking at it every day has brought about a habit which now prevents me from looking. I don't know if you see this. Like sex! So habit, getting used to something, is the beginning of indifference. Are you following all this? You get used to the squalor of the next village as you pass it every day. The little boys and the little girls making messes on the road—the dirt, the squalor, the filth. You get used to it, and then you *have* got used to it. In the same way you have got used to the beauty of a tree, you simply do not see it any more. So, I have discovered that where I pursue pleasure there must be, deeply in it, the root of indifference. Oh! do please see this! There are no roots of heaven in pleasure, there are only roots of indifference and pain.

So what shall I do if I see that very clearly? Pleasure is such an enticing thing! You understand? I look at the tree it is a great delight. To see a dark cloud full of rain and a rainbow, and this seems a tremendous thing. That is a pleasure, that is a delight, that is a tremendous enjoyment. Why can't I leave it there. You understand? Why do I have to say, "I must store it up"? (I don't know if you are following all this.) Then when I see the next day the dark cloud, full of rain, and the leaves dancing in the wind, the memory of yesterday spoils the sight of it. I have become dull. So what shall I do? I cannot deny pleasure, but this does not mean I indulge in pleasure. So I understand now that pleasure inevitably breeds indifference. I see it. I see it

237

as a fact as I see the microphone—not as an idea, not as a theory, not as a concept, but as an actual fact. Right? So now I am watching the operation of pleasure. You follow? The process of pleasure is what I am watching. As, "I like you" and "I do not like someone else", which is again in the same pattern. All my judgments are based on likes and dislikes. I like you because you are respectable. I do not like you because you are *not* respectable. You are a Muslim, or a Hindu, or you have sexual perversions and I prefer the other perversions—and so on. You follow? Like and dislike. So I watch it. And like and dislike is again a habit, which I have cultivated through pleasure. The mind now is watching the whole movement of pleasure, and you cannot watch it if you condemn it. Are you following this? So what has happened to my mind? Watch it, Sir. What has happened to my mind? (Oh! you just throw out *words*. You don't know what you are saying.) (That's right, Sir.) It has become much more sensitive. Right? Therefore much more intelligent. Now that intelligence is operating—not *my* intelligence or *your* intelligence, just intelligence. I do not know if you are following this. Before, there was indifference and I did not care. The mind did not care two pins whether I lived like a pig or not. And I realised I must change. And I see that to change to a greater pleasure is to come back to the same filth. So the mind has realised something, seen something. Not because somebody has spoken of it—but it has seen something very clearly—that where there is the pursuit of pleasure, this must inevitably breed indifference. So the mind has sharpened. And it is watching pleasure in every movement. And you can only watch anything freely, without reservation, condemnation, or judgment. So the mind is watching. And it says "What is wrong with me why can't I look at a tree, why can't I see the beautiful face of a child or a woman?" I can't shut my eyes—blindly go running away to the Himalayas. It is *there*. Right? So what shall I do? Not look? Turn my head when I pass a woman? (Which the Sanyasis do, they know all the old tricks and all that.) So what shall I do? So I look. You understand? I look. I look at that tree, the beauty of the branch, the beauty of the curve of the tree. I look at a beautiful face, well proportioned, the smile, the eyes. I look. Follow this. When I *look*, there is no pleasure. Have you noticed it? Have you got it? Have you understood what we are talking about? When I look, where is there room for pleasure? I don't look with fear, saying "My God!

238

Am I caught in the trap of pleasure!" But I look, whether it is at the tree, the rainbow, the fly, or a beautiful woman, or the man. I look. In that look there is no pleasure. The pleasure only arises when thought comes in.

Now without understanding this whole process—the saints, the ugly, immature human beings called saints, the Rishis, the writers, they have condemned this. *Don't* look, they say. And so—*look*. And when you see very clearly there is neither pleasure nor displeasure. It is there. The beauty of the face, the walk, the dress, the beauty of the tree. A second later thought comes in and says, "That was a beautiful woman". And all the imagery, sex, intimations, thrills, begin. Are you following all this, Sirs, and what are you going to do about it? What happens? Thought comes in, and what is important now is not pleasure, because that is understood, there is nothing to it. Look what has happened. The mind has become extraordinarily sensitive, and therefore highly disciplined, highly disciplined but not through an imposed discipline. By watching that I am callous, indifferent—watching it, and watching it—the mind has become sensitive. Watching *is* the discipline. I wonder if you have got this! In this kind of discipline there is no suppression; there is no suppression in the discipline that is necessary in order to *see*. So the mind has become highly sensitive, highly disciplined, and therefore austere—not the austerity in regard to clothes and food, all that is too immature and childish. And the mind now says it is watching pleasure and it sees that the continuity of pleasure is created by thought. Right? So I have entered into a totally different dimension. You understand? A dimension in which I have to work very hard and which nobody is going to tell me about. I can tell you, but you have to work for yourself. So I say—"Why does thought come into this *at all*?" I look at that tree, I look at a woman, I see that man going by in a rich car, a nice car, driven by a chauffeur, and I say "All right". But why does thought come in? Why? (*Long pause*) (*Audience makes a suggestion.*) No Sir, no Sir. I haven't learnt the art of *looking*. Do listen to this. I haven't learnt it. When I said "I see indifference, callousness" I had not really seen it. Seeing it—not changing callousness, but just to see it. So now I am asking myself, "Why does thought come into the picture at all?" Why can't I just look at that tree, or that woman, or that car? Why? Why does thought come into this?

239

Questioner: Memory comes as a barrier.

KRISHNAMURTI: Ask *yourself* the question, Sir, and don't just say "Memory comes as a barrier". You have just heard somebody else say that. You heard *me* say that a dozen times, and you repeat and throw back those words at me. They have no meaning to me any more. I am asking quite a different question. I am asking why thought comes into it at all. (*Suggestions from audience.*) Ask yourself, Sir, and find out the answer. Why this constant interference of thought? You understand Sir? It is very interesting if you go into it for yourself. At present you cannot look at *anything* without thought, without an image, without a symbol. Why? (*Long pause*) Do you want *me* to answer it? The gentleman sits very comfortably and says "Yes". "Please answer it, will you?" And it's not going to make a pennyworth of difference to him. (That's right, and it has become a habit. For the last fifty years, doing whatever you have done.) If it is a habit, then what shall I do? Do I see the habit as an idea or *actually* as habit—Do you see the difference? If you do then you must find out.

MADRAS
5 JANUARY 1968

3

TIME, SPACE AND THE CENTRE

The ideal, the concept, and "what is". Need to understand suffering: pain, loneliness, fear, envy. The ego-centre. The space and time of the centre. Is it possible not to have an ego-centre and yet live in this world? "We live within the prison of our own thinking." To see the structure of the centre. To look without the centre.

KRISHNAMURTI: What shall we consider together this morning?

240

Questioner: What is psychological memory, and how is it imprinted on the brain?

Questioner: Will you go into the subject of pleasure and thought?

Questioner: What is the concept of life, and of this world?

KRISHNAMURTI: Do you want to discuss that? "What is the concept of life and of this world?" And also, what is the thinker, and thought ... What do you say, Sirs, I don't mind what we discuss.

Questioner: Can we continue talking about thought? The last talk ended with the problem of time and space.

Questioner: Could we talk a little more, explain more, about time, space and the centre, which we were talking about the other day?

Questioner: Why is it we want to discuss something from "the other day"? That is over.

KRISHNAMURTI: Perhaps if we discuss this question of a concept of life, and living, we shall come upon the question of time, space, and the centre. I think that all the other questions will be included in that. What is the concept of life? What do we mean by concept, the word? To conceive, to imagine, to bring out. A conceptual world is a world of ideas, formulas, a world of theories, a world of imaginative ideological formation. That is what we mean, don't we, when we talk about concepts? A conceptual world, an ideological world. First of all, what is its place in our relations with others, in the context of living? What is the relation between the conceptual world, which we have more or less described or verbally explained, what is the relationship between that, and actual daily living? Is there any relationship at all? I have toothache; that is an obvious fact. And the concept of not having toothache is an unreality. The fact is, I have it. The other is a fictitious thing, an idea. Now what relationship has the reality, the "what is", the actual daily living, to the formula, the concept? Has it any relationship? You believe, at least some of you, the Hindus, believe that there is the Atman.

241

(We are on a touchy subject.) That there is something permanent. That is an idea, a theory, a concept, is it not? No? Shankara or the Vedantas or some bird said that there is this Atman, or whatever it is, the spiritual entity. That is just an idea, isn't it?

Questioner: Much more than that.

KRISHNAMURTI: Much more?

Questioner: (Inaudible)

KRISHNAMURTI: It is said that there is some permanent thing ...

Questioner: (Inaudible)

KRISHNAMURTI: (I do not assume, Sir.) There is this theory, Sir, the concept that there is a permanent state, a reality within each one, God, or whatever you like to call it. The Christians, the Muslims all say so, and different people use different words. Here you use a series of words. Now, is that not a concept which has no reality whatsoever?

Questioner: Now it is a concept, but in the course of time we hope to discover that thing for ourselves.

KRISHNAMURTI: When you postulate that there *is* a certain thing, a something, then you will inevitably discover it! Psychologically, the process is very simple. But why state anything at all?

Questioner: I am in love with the most beautiful woman in the world, but I have never seen her. Although I have not seen her it is a fact that she is beautiful.

KRISHNAMURTI: Oh, come off it, Sir. It's not a bit like that. This will lead to cuckoodom. We have ideologies, concepts—the ideal of perfect man, the ideal of what should be, how the liberated person should act, think, feel, live and so on. But these are concepts, aren't they?

Questioner: Surely what you call "what is" is also a concept!

242

KRISHNAMURTI: Is it? When you have actual toothache, is that a concept: when you are actually miserable because you have no job, no food, is that a concept? When someone dies whom you love and you are in great sorrow, is that a concept?

Questioner: (Inaudible)

KRISHNAMURTI: What! A toothache is unreal? Where do you all live? When death comes in old age, or through an accident you break a leg, or whatever it is—is that theoretical, problematical? Is it a concept? Sir, we are dealing now with concepts. A concept of life. Why do you want concepts?

Questioner: To qualify life.

KRISHNAMURTI: Why should I qualify life? I *live*, I suffer.

Questioner: (Inaudible)

KRISHNAMURTI: That's just it. "How do you go about it, to conceive life?" Why do you want to conceive life; about what things *should be* like? What is the reality about life, you ask. The reality of life is there, it is misery. There is pain, there is pleasure, there is despair, there is agony.

Questioner: They are only apparent.

KRISHNAMURTI: What do you mean, "only apparent"? Oh, you mean it is an illusion! You mean that there is nothing like pleasure, pain, war? That this is a lovely world? (*Laughter*). When they take away your job you say there is no such thing, do you! When you have no food, you say that that is an illusion, do you? No? Then what are you talking about? You say it is not real? What *do* you mean?

You say a concept is a means to an end? Really this is a most extraordinary world. What are we all talking about! We very carefully analysed the word "concept", what it means. Right? The gentleman says many people need the concept. Well keep it, Sir, keep it.

Questioner: I did not say that. I said many people need to understand the word "concept".

243

KRISHNAMURTI: We explained it just now. So let us get on with it. We asked what relationship the concept has with daily living. Daily living is the daily grind of going to the office, the daily grind of the torture of loneliness, misery and so on. What relationship has *that*, which is the actual, which is what *is*, which is what is going on every day in our lives, what has *that* to do with the concept?

Questioner: Can I say something?

KRISHNAMURTI: Delighted, Sir. You take the field.

Questioner: (Long speech. Inaudible.)

KRISHNAMURTI: Ah! He says if we really understood the concept, life would be different, and he quoted some other gentleman, I do not know whom. Why should I understand concepts? When I am full of misery, when I have no food, when my son has died, when I am deaf, dumb, stupid—what has the concept got to do with all that? Concept being the word, the idea, the theory. What has that to do with my aching loneliness?

Questioner: (Inaudible)

KRISHNAMURTI: What Sir, what Sir! I think we must get on with it, otherwise we shall get nowhere. We are unwilling to face facts and we spin around with a lot of words. Reality is not a concept; reality is my daily life. Right? The reality is that I am in torture, and pain is not a theory, is not a concept, it is an actual process in life. So I say to myself—why do I have concepts about pain? It is such a waste to have concepts about pain. So I do not want concepts, I want to understand pain. Right?

The problem then is—what is pain? There is physical pain, such as toothache, stomach-ache, headache, and disease, and also there is pain at a different level, at the psychological level. Now, how am I to be free of *that*? Free of inward pain. I can go to a doctor to be cured of physical pain. But there is psychological pain in the sense that I suffer. What do I suffer? What does one have pain about, Sir?

Questioner: Loneliness and fear.

At Rishi Valley   January 1970

Krishnamurti talking to students at Rajghat School
December 1969

Talking at Rishi Valley School   January 1970

View of Rishi Valley

View of Saanen and Gstaad, Switzerland

Outside the Conference Tent at Saanen   July 1968

Talking to students and staff at Brockwood Park   October 1972

View of Brockwood Park, Hampshire, England

With students at Brockwood Park   October 1972

Krishnamurti

At Saanen   Summer 1968

Krishnamurti   Saanen Summer 1968

Talking at Brockwood   October 1972

Krishnamurti   June 1972

Talking to students and staff at Brockwood Park   October 1972

KRISHNAMURTI: Right! Loneliness and fear. And I want to be free of it, because this loneliness and fear are always a burden, they darken my thinking, my outlook, my vision, my way of acting. So, my problem is how to be free from fear, not from any theory; that has gone overboard. I do not accept any theory about anything. So, how do I get rid of fear? Will a concept help me to get rid of fear? It is what you were saying earlier, Sir; but will having a concept about fear help me to get rid of that fear? You say "Yes," you say "it is a scientific thought", "it is a basis for reality", it is a "logical conclusion". Do take a simple example, Sir, and work it out for yourself. Don't introduce scientific, logical and biological facts. There is fear; will a concept of no-fear help you get rid of fear? Sir, don't theorise about it. You have fear, haven't you? No? Don't just throw words about. You have fear, don't you? Will a concept help you to get rid of that fear? Do think it out, Sir; go into it. Don't go back into some theory, Sir. Do please stick to one thing. There is fear. You are afraid of your wife; you are afraid of death, afraid you might lose your job. Will any theory, concept, help you to get rid of those fears? You can escape from them. If you are afraid of death you can escape from that fear by believing in reincarnation, but fear is still there. You don't want to die, though you may believe in all kinds of stuff, the fact is that fear is still there. Concepts do not help to get rid of fear.

Questioner: They may gradually help us to be free.

KRISHNAMURTI: Gradually? By that time you will be dead. Sirs, don't theorise, for God's sake. These useless brains that theorise!

Questioner: Is it not escaping also to try and get rid of fear?

KRISHNAMURTI: Oh, how childish we are! You can escape from your wife, but your wife is still at home.

Questioner: You can change your way of life.

KRISHNAMURTI: Sirs, do please let us be simple about this, you know what fear is, don't you? You know what violence is, don't you? Will a theory of non-violence help

245

you to get rid of violence? Take that one simple fact. You are violent; that is a reality. In your daily life you are violent, and will that violence be understood through a concept the concept of non-violence? (*Long pause.*)

Questioner: (Inaudible long speech.)

KRISHNAMURTI: What are you saying, Sir! We are speaking English! Do you understand English, Sir? We are talking about violence. Have you ever been violent, Sir?

Questioner: Sometimes.

KRISHNAMURTI: Good. Now did you get rid of violence by a concept?

Questioner: Seeing that one is violent one tells oneself to be calm.

KRISHNAMURTI: I wonder if we are talking the same language. I give it up! You go on, Sir.

Questioner: (Continues inaudible statement.)

KRISHNAMURTI: All right, Sir. You win.

Questioner: (Further inaudible speech.)

KRISHNAMURTI: Thank God, Sir, you don't rule the world. You are losing time. You are wasting time. You are living in a world which is so unreal.

Questioner: (Continues to harangue. Inaudible.)

KRISHNAMURTI: That is what we are saying, Sir. Face the fact itself. And you can only face the fact if you have no theories about the fact. Right? And apparently you gentlemen of the older generation do not want to face the fact. You like to live in a world of concepts. Please live there, Sirs. Now let us proceed. The question is, is it possible for the mind to be free of fear? Now what is fear? We feel afraid. (We are coming back to your question, Sir.) (Not *your* question, Sir. You want to live in a world of theories; live there. I am answering this other gentleman.) You ask who is the entity or the being that says "I am afraid"?

246

You have been jealous, haven't you, envious? And who is the person who says "I am envious"?

Questioner: The ego. There is a sense of the ego.

KRISHNAMURTI: Now who is the ego? Sir, do analyse it. You know what analysis is? Go into it, step by step. Who is it? Think it out Sir, and don't quote Shankara, Buddha or X Y Z! When you say "I am afraid", who is the "I"?

Questioner: (Several inaudible suggestions.)

KRISHNAMURTI: Don't quote. *Do* think it out, Sirs.

Questioner: Is it not thought that conceives of itself as being permanent at the moment it is envious?

KRISHNAMURTI: Now, what is that moment when that thought regards itself as permanent? I am envious. I am conscious that I am envious. Now who is the entity, that thought which says "I am envious"?

Questioner: (Inaudible)

KRISHNAMURTI: Oh please, Sir! You do not analyse it; you just make a statement! Do go into it, Sir. You say that at that moment, when that thought makes the statement "I am jealous", that thought, for the time being, thinks itself permanent. Right? Now, why does that thought think it is permanent? Is it not that the thought has recognised a similar feeling which it has had before? Go slowly, step by step. I am envious. You know what envy is—I become aware that I am envious, now I am asking—"Who is the entity that has become aware? And how does that entity or that thought know that it is 'envy'?" That thought knows that it is envy because he has felt envy. The memory of previous envy comes up and the person who feels it says, "Here it is again." Right? Here is the envy which I have had before. Otherwise you would think of it quite differently. Because thought was able to recognise the feeling, it was able to call it "envy". It had experienced the same feeling before. So it says ("it" being thought) . . . (*Interruption from audience.*) Sirs, I know it is very complex so we must go slowly step by step. (Sirs, would you mind getting the coughing over—all of you at

247

once.) (*Laughter*) This is a very difficult question to go into and unless you give it your full attention you cannot understand its very intricate and subtle nature. We say— first of all there is envy; one becomes conscious of that envy; then thought says, "I have had that feeling before." Otherwise you would not be able to recognise that feeling which you have called "envy". What one has had as an experience before is given permanency, continuity through recognition of what is taking place now. So, thought has continuity because thought is the response of memory. Right? That thought, which is the outcome of yesterday's memory says, "Here it is again; it is envy". By calling it "envy" and recognising it, it has given it greater vitality. Thought is the response of the bundle of memories which constitute tradition, knowledge, experience and so on, and that thought recognises the feeling which it has now, "envy". So, thought *is* the *centre*, or the memory *is* the centre! Right? (*Pause*) Sirs, your centre says "It is *my* house, I live there, it belongs to me legally" and so on. You have certain memories, pleasurable and painful memories. The whole bundle of them is the centre, isn't it? The centre being violence, ignorance, ambition and greed—it has pain, despair and so on. That centre creates space around itself. Does it not? No? (*Interruption*). (Go slowly, Sirs . . . An interval? . . . Ah, the gentleman wants me to repeat what I have said. Sorry, Sir, I cannot repeat it, I cannot remember what I said.)

We will put it differently. There is this microphone. Round it there is space. That is the centre, and it has space around it, and it exists *in* space; as this room has space within it. But also this room has space outside it. So the centre has a little space in itself, and also it has space outside it. (I am not talking of creation. Just listen quietly.) Please observe this, Sir, please go into it, please observe it completely, not merely intellectually. It is more fun if you actually go into it. But if you theorise about it then the discussion can go on indefinitely and it leads nowhere. Here is the centre, and the centre is a bundle of memories. (It is so fascinating, Sirs. Please go into it.) The centre is a bundle of memories, a bundle of traditions, and the centre has been brought about by tension, through pressure, through influence. The centre is the result of time, within the field of culture—Hindu culture, Muslim culture, and so on. So that is the centre. Now that centre, because it is a centre, has space outside it, obviously. And because of the movement, it has space in itself. If it had no movement it would have no space. It would be non-existent. Anything that is capable of movement must have space. So there is space, outside the centre and in it. And the centre is always seeking wider space, to move more widely. To put it differently, the centre *is* consciousness. That is, the centre has the borders which it recognises as "the me". As long as there is a centre, it must have a circumference. Of course. And it tries to extend the area of the circumference—by drugs, which is now called the "psychedelic expansion of the mind"—through meditation, through various forms of will, and so on. It tries to extend the space it is aware of as consciousness, to make it grow wider and wider and wider. But, as long as it is a centre its space must always be limited. Right? So as long as there is a centre, space must always be confined—like a prisoner living in a prison. He has freedom to walk in the yard but he is always a prisoner. He may get a larger yard, he may get a better building, more comfortable rooms, with bathrooms and all the rest of it, but he is still limited. As long as there is a centre, there must be the limitation of space, and therefore the centre can never be free! It is like a prisoner saying "I am free", within the prison walls. He is not free. Many people may realise unconsciously that there is no such thing as freedom within the field of consciousness, with a centre, and therefore they ask whether it is possible to extend consciousness, expand consciousness—by literature, by music, by art, by drugs, by various processes. But as long as there is a centre, the observer, the thinker, the watcher, whatever he does will be within the prison walls. Right Sir? Please don't say "Yes". Because there is distance between the border and the centre, time comes in, because he wants to go beyond it, transcend it, push it further away. I don't know if you follow this? Sir, we are not dealing with theories, but if you do this actually inside yourself you will see the beauty of this thing.

Questioner: Would you go into the tendency to expand.

KRISHNAMURTI: You know what it means, to expand. A rubber band, you can stretch it, but if you stretch it beyond a certain point it, breaks. (Yes Sir. It will break beyond a certain point). I feel, living in Madras in a little house, that there is no space there. With my family, with my worries, with my office, my traditions—it is too deadly petty, and I want to break through it. There again is the desire to expand. And when society presses me in, drives me into a certain corner, I explode—which is again a revolt in order to expand. And when one lives in a small flat in a very crowded street and there is no open country to breathe in and no opportunity to go there, I become violent. The animals do this. They have territorial rights because they want space in which to hunt, and they prevent anyone else coming into that area. Right, Sir? So, *everything* demands expansion—trade, insects, animals and human beings, they all must have space. Not only outwardly, but inwardly. And the centre says, "I can expand by taking a drug." But you don't have to take a drug to have an experience of this kind of expansion. I don't have to take a drink to know what drunkenness is! I know what drunkenness is, I see it! I don't have to take a drink!

Questioner: (Inaudible)

KRISHNAMURTI: No Sir, please Sir, don't bring in other things. This is very complex Sir. If you go slowly into it, you will understand it. The centre, being the prisoner of its own limitation, wants expansion. It seeks expansion through identification—with God, with an idea, with an ideal, with a formula, with a concept. Please follow this, Sir! And it thinks it can live differently, at a different level, though it is living in a miserable prison. So concepts become extraordinarily important to a prisoner, because he knows he cannot escape. And the centre being thought—we examined that—then thought tries to expand by identification with *something*—with the nation, with the family, with the group, with culture—you know, expand, expand. But it is still living in prison! As long as there is a centre there is no freedom: right? (Don't agree Sir. For you all it is just a theory, and one theory is as good as another.) So, see what it does! It invents *time* as a means of escape. I will *gradually* escape from this prison. Right? I will practise, I will meditate, I will do this and won't do that. Gradually, tomorrow, tomorrow, next life, the future. It has not only created space which is limited, but also it has created time! And it has become a slave to a space and a time of its own. Ah! Do you see this, Sirs?

Questioner: How does memory . . . (inaudible)

KRISHNAMURTI: It is very simple, Sir. You asked that question before. It is very simple if you look at it for yourself. Somebody hits you, insults you, and you have a memory of that. I hit you, and you are hurt, you are insulted, you are made *little* and you dislike it, and that remains in your brain, in your consciousness, the memory of me insulting you or flattering you. So the memory remains and the next time you meet me you say to yourself, "That man insulted me", "That man flattered me". *The memory* responds when you meet me again. That's all, it's very simple. Don't waste time on it.

Questioner: Where are we, after these discussions and talks?

KRISHNAMURTI: I'm afraid I cannot tell you. If you understand what is being said and *live it* then you will be in a totally different world. But if you don't live it, daily, then you will just be living as you are. That's all.

So first the problem is that as long as there is a centre, and we know what we mean by "the centre", there must be time and limited space. That is a fact, as you can observe it in your daily life. You are bound to your house, to your family, to your wife, and then to the community, to society, and then to your culture and so on and so on. So this whole thing is the centre—the culture, the family, the nation—that has created a boundary, which is consciousness, which is always limited. And it tries to expand the boundary, to widen the walls, but the whole is still within the prison. So that is the first thing, that is what is taking place actually, in our daily life. Then the question arises (please listen, don't answer theoretically because that has no value), is it possible not to have a centre and live in the world? That is the real problem. Is it possible not to have a centre and yet live completely, fully, in this world? What do you say?

Questioner: One could be just a point.

KRISHNAMURTI: But a point is still a centre! No, Madame, don't answer this question. If you just answer it means you have not gone into it.

Questioner: (Inaudible)

251

KRISHNAMURTI: That's it. I knew you'd say that, Sir; but you are still within the circumference. You don't ... You keep on ... Sir, have you ever been to prison? Not you, Sir, personally. Have you just visited a prison? If you have visited a prison you will have seen that they are expanding the walls. Bigger rooms, bigger prisons, more and more. But you are still within a prison. And we are like that. We live within the prison of our own thinking. With our misery, our culture, saying "I'm a Brahmin, a non-Brahmin, I hate this, I like this and I do not like that, I love this and not that", and so on. We live within this prison, I may expand it a little bit but it's still a prison. So this question arises (please don't answer, because this is a very fundamental question, which you cannot possibly answer glibly by a few words) you have to find out in life, in daily living. So we are asking; "Is it possible to live in this world, completely doing your job, doing *everything* with tremendous vitality, without a centre, knowing what the centre is, and knowing that to live in this world you need memory?" You see this, Sir? You need memory to go to the office, to function there. If you are a merchant you need a memory to cheat others or not, whatever you do. You need memory, and yet to be free of the memory which creates the centre. See the difficulty? ... So what will you do? (*Interjection.*) Sir, please don't answer, you're back to theories. When I've got a toothache, stomach-ache, or I'm hungry and I come to your house, what do you give me? Theories? Or chase me out? Here is a tremendous problem. It is not for India alone. It's a problem round the world, a problem of every human being.

Now, is there a method to get rid of the centre? You follow? A method? Is there? Method belongs to time, obviously, and therefore a method is no good, whether it is the method of Shankara, Buddha, your pet Guru, or no Guru, or you invent it. Time has no value and yet, if you are not free from that centre you are *not* free. Therefore you must always suffer. So a man who says, "Is there an ending to sorrow?" must find the answer to this—not in a book, not in some theory. One must find, *see* it. Right? So if there is no method, no system, no leader, no guru, no saviour—all introducing time—then, what will happen, what will you do? To have come to this point, what has happened to your mind? What has happened to your mind which has investigated this, very carefully, not jumped to conclusions, nor theories, nor saying "It is marvellous"; but when it has *done* this, *actually*, step by step, has come to this point, put this question, what has happened to such a mind?

Questioner: (Inaudible)

KRISHNAMURTI: *Oh no. Please Sir.* What has happened to your mind, if you have done this? No, no. It is *something* that has happened to it. No you're only guessing, Sir. Don't guess. It's not a guessing game. Your mind has become highly active, hasn't it? Because to analyse so carefully, never missing a point, logically, step by step, you have to exercise your brain, you have to exercise logic, you have to exercise discipline. So the mind has become extraordinarily sensitive, hasn't it? The mind, by observing what it is doing, what it has done, which is building up the centre, by merely observing, the mind has become extraordinarily alert. Right? You have done nothing to make it alert, but by merely watching the movement of thought, step by step, it has become extraordinarily clear. So, being clear, it puts the question, "How is the centre to disappear?" When it has put that question it is already seeing the whole structure of the centre. Seeing, actually visually, as I see that tree, I also see this.

Questioner: What is the entity which sees the action?

KRISHNAMURTI: Sir, I said the mind ... You go back to something, Sir, I'm awfully sorry but we can't go back. It is no good going back to something which you have not actually *lived* as we went along. You are inactive but think you have become active by putting a question like, "Who is the entity that sees?" But you haven't actually understood, observed, how the centre is formed—through memory, through tradition, through the culture one lives in, including religion and all the rest of it. The centre has been formed through economic pressures, and so on. That centre creates space, consciousness, and it tries to expand. That centre is saying to *itself* (nobody else is asking it) "I realise I am living in a prison, and obviously to be free from pain, sorrow, there must be no centre." It *sees* this. The centre itself sees it—not somebody else above or below telling the centre. So the center says, seeing itself, "Is it possible for me not to be?" (*Long pause.*) That means that we have to go back to this question of *seeing*. Unless you understand that, you can't come to it.

Questioner: (Inaudible suggestion.)

KRISHNAMURTI: Ah, no, no, no. *Seeing*, without emotionalism, sentimentality, like and dislike. Which does not mean that you see something without feeling.

Questioner: (Inaudible interjection.)

KRISHNAMURTI: That is what you all do, Sir. You see that dirt on the road every day—and I have been here for the last twenty or thirty years, and I see that squalor every day. Of course you see it, without feeling. If you felt, you would *do* something about it. If you felt the rottenness of the corruption in this country you would do something. But you don't. If you saw the inefficiency of the Government, if you saw all the linguistic divisions which are destroying this country, if you felt it, if you were passionate about it, you would do something. You don't. Which means you don't see it at all.

Questioner: (Inaudible interjection.)

KRISHNAMURTI: Ah, no, no. "You see the bigger life"—what's the "bigger life"? You see how you want to twist everything to something else! You can't look at anything in a straight way, simple, honestly. So, unless you do it, we can sit here and discuss until Doomsday. What is *seeing*, is it this, is it that? But if you really saw the tree, without space and time, and therefore without the centre, then, when there is no centre and you look at the tree, there is vast space, immeasurable space. But first, one must learn, or watch, or hear *how to look*. But you won't do it. You won't begin the very complex thing called life, very simply. Your simplicity is to put on a loin cloth and travel third class and do so-called meditation, or whatever you do. But that is not simplicity. Simplicity is to look at things as they *are*—to look. To look at the tree, without the centre.

MADRAS
9 JANUARY 1968

4

A FUNDAMENTAL QUESTION

What is clear thinking in relation to daily living? Meeting the present with the past. How to live with memory and technological knowledge and yet be free of the past? Double life: temple, office. How to live without fragmentation?—to answer from a concept is further fragmentation. Silence before the immensity of a fundamental question. "Can you live so completely that there is only the active present now?"

KRISHNAMURTI: What shall we talk over this morning together?

Questioner: Is not love a method?

Questioner: Am I right in assuming, Sir, that time and space are one of our problems?

Questioner: What is the relation between memory and thought?

Questioner: We must have memory in order to function in daily existence, technological developments and so on, but is memory not also an impediment?

KRISHNAMURTI: I don't know if you have heard the previous questions—I had better repeat them. First, has love a method?

Questioner: Is not love a method?

KRISHNAMURTI: Is not love a method?—a lovely idea isn't it? What was the other?

Questioner: The relation between thought and memory.

KRISHNAMURTI: And your question, Madame, was—memory is necessary in daily existence, in technological development and so on, but is not memory also an impediment? Any more things that you want to throw in?

Questioner: We want to be aware of every thought, feeling and action, but thought, feeling and action go on being coloured and then are suppressed when the mind is silent. How can that take place?

KRISHNAMURTI: Is that really what you are all interested in?

Questioner: We have disorder in our daily life—how are we to go about bringing order?

KRISHNAMURTI: We have disorder in daily life, how are we to set about bringing order? Is that right, Sir?

Questioner: Or do we have to wait for a change to come of its own accord?

Questioner: What is clear thinking?

KRISHNAMURTI: All right. Let's take that up—shall we? And we can answer your questions and bring them all in. Is that all right?

What is clear thinking? Shall we discuss that? And relate it, if we can, to our daily living. What is clear thinking? Is thinking ever clear? We had better not go too quickly. First of all, let's find out what we mean by clarity, and what we mean by thinking. What do we mean by clarity? Clear—when you look through the water on a lake and see the bottom of that lake you see everything very clearly, the pebbles, the fish, the ripples on the water and so on. And you see very clearly, in bright light, the shade of the tree, the leaf, the branch, the flower—what do we mean by clarity?

Questioner: A direct impression.

KRISHNAMURTI: Oh! no. A definite outlined impression, is that it?

Questioner: Complete understanding.

KRISHNAMURTI: Clarity means complete understanding. We haven't come to that level yet. We are talking about what we mean by the word "clear"?

Questioner: Free of any obstruction.

Questioner: To see things as they are, actually see things as they are.

Questioner: To see without space.

Questioner: Sir, sometimes we don't get clarity if we look at the moon and a cloud at the same time we see the moon moving and not the clouds.

KRISHNAMURTI: Sir, we are talking about a word, the meaning of that word, its semantics.

Questioner: More details.

Questioner: I think it has something to do with light, Sir, seeing.

KRISHNAMURTI: Sir, would you mind just waiting a minute to examine this before we say anything else. What do we mean by the word "clear"? I see you clearly. I see the trees, the stars of an evening, very clearly.

Questioner: Without obstruction.

KRISHNAMURTI: Without obstruction. When the eye can see everything very, very clearly. The seeing—that is what we mean, when there is no obstruction, no barrier, no screen, no fog, and if your eyes are short-sighted you put on glasses to see more clearly into the distance and so on. Clarity—right—is that clear? I think we are clear as to the meaning of that word.

Then what do we mean by thinking?

Questioner: Reasoning.

KRISHNAMURTI: Thinking Sir, what does it mean?

Questioner: (Inaudible)

KRISHNAMURTI: Sir, look. The speaker is asking you a question. What is thinking?
(Interruption from audience)

KRISHNAMURTI: The speaker is asking you a question what is thinking?
(More interruptions)

KRISHNAMURTI: The speaker is asking you: what is thinking? And you don't even give space and time to find out what thinking is. A question is being put to you, it is a challenge to you. And you bubble over! You don't say, "Now how am I to find out what thinking is? How does thinking take place? What is the origin or the beginning of thinking?" It is a challenge and you have to respond to it. And to respond to it you have to (if you want to respond to it adequately) you have to examine what thinking is, how it happens. The speaker asks you—what is thinking? And what does the mind do when it receives this challenge? Do you search?

Questioner: What we are doing now.

KRISHNAMURTI: Do listen for a minute. You will have your chance, Sir. Give the poor speaker a chance. When that question is put to you what is the operation that your mind goes through? Where do you find the answer to that question?

Questioner: Mind.

KRISHNAMURTI: Sir, watch it, think it out, go into it. I ask you where you live or what your name is—your response is immediate, isn't it? Why is it immediate? Because you have repeated your name umpteen times, thousands of times, and you know where you live. So between the questioning and the answer, there is no time interval—right? It is immediate. I ask you what is the distance between Madras and Delhi or New York, and there is a hesitation—right? So you look into memory, into what you have learnt or what you have read and you say, "Well the distance is so many miles". So you have taken time between the question and the answer, there is a lag of time—right, Sirs?

Now what happens when there is the question, "What is thinking?" How do you find that out?

Questioner: It takes one's mind to bring all the answers.

KRISHNAMURTI: What do you do, Sir?

Questioner: (Inaudible)

KRISHNAMURTI: You probe into the memory and what do you get out of it? What is the answer?

Questioner: We study it a little more and more and then try to gather these extracts together.

KRISHNAMURTI: Sir look, I am asking you now, this morning, don't wait until the day after tomorrow until you and I have gone, or are dead, but I am asking you now—what is thinking? And you—either you find out or you don't know—right? Which is it?

Questioner: It is the process of a mind giving an answer.

KRISHNAMURTI: What do you mean by the process of the mind?

Questioner: Sir, what are you aiming at?—I don't understand.

KRISHNAMURTI: What am I aiming at? Just a minute Sir, you have asked a question. What am I aiming at? What I am aiming at is very simple. I want to know, when that question is put, "What is thinking?", I want to find out what it is. (*Interruptions from audience.*) Sir, give the other fellow a chance, don't answer so readily. I want to find out what thinking is—how does it come about, what is the beginning of it? Right? It is very simple, Sir. Now what is it, how does it come about? That is, you asked me a question—say, "What is thinking?"—and I really don't know—right? Or I do know, I know the whole process of it—how it operates, how it begins, what is its mechanism—right? No?

Questioner: One feels how it operates but I am unable to explain.

KRISHNAMURTI: One feels how it operates but one is not capable of explanation. Look, take a very simple thing, Sir. I ask you what your name is. You hear the words and then what happens?

Questioner: You really just answer.
(Various comments—inaudible.)

KRISHNAMURTI: You reply, don't you? Say your name is so and so. What has taken place there?

Questioner: I have referred to my memory and my memory responds.

KRISHNAMURTI: That's right, Sir, that's all. The question—to that question your memory responds and replies—right? Now I ask you—what is thinking?—and why doesn't your memory respond?

Questioner: Because . . . (inaudible).

KRISHNAMURTI: It may be, Sir, go into it, find out—why don't you reply what thinking is? Whether you know or you don't know. If you know, you will say, if you don't know you will say, "Sorry I don't know". Which is it?

Questioner: I don't know.

KRISHNAMURTI: The gentleman doesn't know. We are trying to answer the question, "What is clear thinking?" We more or less understood the meaning of the words clarity, clearness, clear. And we are finding it rather difficult to find out what thinking is. We say it is the response of memory to a challenge—right? And that response comes from accumulated memories, knowledge, experience. This is simple, Sir. You learn a language after having heard it from childhood, you can repeat it because you have stored up the words, the meaning of that word, the word in relation to the thing and so on, and you can speak because you have stored up the vocabulary, words, the structure and so on. Memory responds and the response of memory is thinking. Now what is the origin of thinking, the beginning of thinking? We know that after accumulating memory we respond and the response is thought. Now I want to find out also—that is, in order to find out what clear thinking is—I want to find out what is the beginning of memory? Or is that too difficult, too abstract?

Questioner: It is our conditioning.

KRISHNAMURTI: No, I am afraid I am going too fast. Sorry. All right, Sirs. I won't go into it. What is thinking—we know now! So when you respond, when thought is the response of memory and memory is the past (the accumulated experience, knowledge, tradition, and so on) that response is what we call thinking, whether it be logical, illogical, balanced, unbalanced, sane, healthy, it is still thinking. Now, please follow the next thing, can thought be clear?

Questioner: No, it is always conditioned.

KRISHNAMURTI: No, do please find out. Can thought be clear?

Questioner: (Inaudible)

KRISHNAMURTI: You see you are just supposing. You live on abstraction and that is why you cannot be practical. You live on concepts, ideas and theories and when you move out of that field you are completely lost: when you have to answer something directly, of yourself, you muddle along. We asked, "Can thinking, which is the outcome of memory (memory is always the past, there is no living memory) can thinking, which is of the past, ever be clear?" This is a very interesting question, Sirs. Can the past produce clear action? Because action is thought—right?

Questioner: Yes, that is a fact.

KRISHNAMURTI: Sirs, have we understood the question? We have more or less analysed the word "clear", and we have more or less analysed what thinking is. So the next thing we are asking is, can thinking (which is the outcome of a long past, which is not living, and is therefore always old) can that thing which is old, the past, ever be clear? You understand, Sir? If I do anything out of tradition, (which is the past, however noble, ignoble, or stupid)—if I do anything out of tradition, can that action be clear?

261

Questioner: It cannot because memory and tradition belong to the past ...

KRISHNAMURTI: I am asking, Sir, can action born out of the past, the doing, which is always in the present, the doing, not "having done" or "I will do", but the actual doing—can it ever be clear.

Questioner: The word action and the word clear have nothing to do with each other. "Clear" applies to seeing everything ...

KRISHNAMURTI: All right. Can that action be fresh, new, direct, as direct as when you meet fire and you move away. So I am asking, "When we live and function in the shadow of the past, is there any clarity?" Leave action out because that disturbs you—I know why it disturbs you—because you are never used to acting, you are used to conceptual thinking. And when you are faced with action, you get confused, because your life is confused, and that's your affair.

So, when you act from the past, from tradition, is it action, is it something living?

Questioner: Why should there be any difference between clarity and action?

KRISHNAMURTI: Oh! we can discuss this *ad nauseam*. But I am just asking, Sir. You are all tradition-ridden, aren't you?—traditionalists. You say this or that is sacred, or repeat some sloka, or, if you don't do any of that, you have your own tradition, your own experience, which you go on repeating. Now does this repetition bring understanding, clarity, freshness, newness?

Questioner: It is an aid to understanding the present situation.

KRISHNAMURTI: Is the past an aid to understanding the present?

Questioner: Things break down.

KRISHNAMURTI: Wait Sir, wait Sir. Look at it. Does the past help you to understand the present?

262

Questioner: The past is . . .

KRISHNAMURTI: Just listen, Sir, what she has said. You have had thousands and thousands of wars, does it help you to prevent all wars? You have had class division—Brahmin and non-Brahmin and all the hate involved—does the past help you now to be free of all caste?

Questioner: It should.

KRISHNAMURTI: It should—then we are lost! When you say, "It should" it is an idea, it is not an action. You will still be a Brahmin, you will still be superstitious, you will still be violent.

Questioner: People don't want to be free of the past.

KRISHNAMURTI: It doesn't matter if you are free or not—don't be free of it, live in your misery. But if you want to understand this thing called clear thinking and going beyond it, you have to face certain things. If you say "Well, I don't want to change my traditions" . . .

Questioner: Can you not help us to at least make a . . . ?

KRISHNAMURTI: We are doing that, Sir, we are doing that. Look Sir, if the past is a help, if tradition is a help, if culture is a help, to live now, fully, clearly, happily, sanely and flower in goodness, the past then has a value—but has it? Do you, with all your tradition, live happily?

Questioner: The past is like looking through smoked glass.

KRISHNAMURTI: That's right. So the past doesn't really help you.

Questioner: A little bit.

KRISHNAMURTI: Don't say "No", because you are only speaking of another idea; unless you *do* it, cut yourself from the past, you can't say "Yes, it is no good".

Questioner: We have the chance to understand you because we have listened to you for years. A child has no such chance.

KRISHNAMURTI: "We have the chance to understand you because we have listened to you for forty years—a child hasn't—and all the rest of it!" Why do you bother to listen to the speaker at all? Even for a day or, worse, for forty years? How tragic it all is! I don't know where you people live.

And so let's get back. When I am always looking over my shoulder to the past, I can never see anything clearly in the present, obviously. I need two eyes to look, but if I am looking over my shoulder all the time, I can't see the present. What I need to do is to look at the present, and I am not capable of looking at the present because I am burdened with the past, with my tradition. Tradition says to me "It is terrible to have a divorced wife"; or my respectability says to me. "That person is terrible because he is not moral", (whatever that may mean). We all do this. So what happens to my affection, to my kindliness towards that person? My prejudice, which is tradition, prevents me from being kind or affectionate to that person.

The past may help in the field of technology, but it does not help in the field of life. I know this is theory now and you will repeat that *ad nauseam* and think you have understood it. So the question arises: as thought is of the past and I have to live completely in the present to understand the present, how is the past to be put aside and yet be useful? That is what your question was. You understood my question? I have to live, to live in this world, and I need technological knowledge to go to the office—you know all that is involved in it, science, bureaucracy; this is the case if you are a professor or even if you are a labourer. And I see also—I have understood something this morning—that to live completely, fully, the past must not interfere; so I say to myself, "How is this possible? How is it possible for me to live in the technological world most efficiently, logically, with more and more technology, and yet live at another level, or even at the same level, without the interference of the past?" In the technological field I must have the past, in the other field of life—no past. Do we see this?

Questioner: Yes, now we have an understanding.

KRISHNAMURTI: Ah, good! And I ask myself (don't laugh, Sir)—now I ask myself how this is possible.

Questioner: Is a double life possible?

KRISHNAMURTI: No, you see, what you are leading is a "double life". You go to the temple, put on ashes; you know the set-up, ringing of bells and all the jingles. And at the same time you live at the technological level. You are leading a double life, and you say, "Is it possible?" Of course it is possible because you are leading it. We are not talking about a double life. Examine the complexity of this problem, that one has to have technological knowledge and that there must also be freedom from knowledge, from the past. Now, how is this possible? The double life which you are leading now is in existence, and therefore you are making a hideous mess of life, you go to the temple and at the same time run a machine. You put on ashes, or whatever you do, and go to the office. It is a form of insanity. Now, how is this possible? Have you understood my question, Sirs? *You* tell me how it is possible. Do you say it is not a double life?

Questioner: To use the technological knowledge only when it is necessary and not in other ways.

KRISHNAMURTI: But you have to use such knowledge all the time—to go to your office, to go to your home, to follow the road, when you look at a tree, when you do the bureaucratic job, and so on; this mental operation is functioning all the time. People don't see this. You can't divide it, can you? Go slow, go slow. You can't divide life into technological life and non-technological life. That is what you have done and therefore you are leading a double life. So we are asking, "Is it possible to live so completely that the part is included in the whole?" Right? Are you getting it? Now we lead a double life, the part, we keep it separate, going to the office, learning a technology, all that, and going to church or the temple and ringing bells. So you have divided life and therefore there is conflict in your life between the two. And we are asking for quite a different thing, to live so that there is no division at all. I don't know if you see this?

Questioner: You want us to . . .

KRISHNAMURTI: No, no, I don't want you to do anything.

265

Questioner: (Inaudible)

KRISHNAMURTI: Oh no, Sir. You are not meeting the question—please understand what the speaker is trying to convey. Don't go back to something he has said about psychological memory and all the rest of it. That is a set of words you have learnt. Find out what the speaker is trying to explain *now*. Can I live a life in which there is no division at all (sex, God, technology, getting angry)—you follow? A life in which there is no division, no fragments?

Questioner: The moment there is an end to these things . . .

KRISHNAMURTI: Sir—please Sir, don't just throw out words. Now to continue: How am I, who live in fragments, many fragments not just two (my whole life as I live it is a fragmentary existence, which is a result of the past, which is the result of my saying, "This is right, that is wrong", "This is sacred, that is not sacred" or "Technology and all that doesn't really matter, one has to earn, but going to some temple is endlessly important")—how can I live without fragmentation? You understand the question, Sir, now?

How? (Not "according to what method", because the moment you have introduced method you have introduced fragmentation). "How am I to do it?" is the question, but you say immediately, "Tell me the method" and "the method" means: a method which you practise as opposed to something else and therefore the whole thing is back where we started. So there is no method. But the question of "How" is merely asking, finding out, not searching for a method. Now, how is it possible so to live that there is no fragmentation at all? You understand my question, Sir? That means no fragmentation at all at any level of my being, of my existence.

Questioner: What is being, Sir?

KRISHNAMURTI: What is being?—I am sorry we are not discussing that, Sir. You see you are not even paying attention. You pick up a word like "being" or a phrase like "what is the purpose of life", and off you go. But that is not what we are talking about. Look, Sir, how am I to live so there is no fragmentation at all? I don't say, "Well, I'll go and meditate"—which becomes another fragmentation, or "I must not be angry", "I must be this or that"; these sentences all involve fragmentation. Can I live without any fragments, without being torn apart? Right, Sir? Have you understood the question?

Now who is going to answer you? Will you go back to memory? What the Gita said, what the Upanishads said, what Freud said, or somebody else said? If you went back and tried to find out what they said about living without fragmentation, then that would be another fragment, wouldn't it?

Questioner: What of those who don't seek their aid?

KRISHNAMURTI: If you do not seek their aid, then where are you? How do you find this out? How do you find out how to live so that there is no fragmentation at all? Oh, Sirs, you don't see the beauty of this.

Questioner: By integration.

KRISHNAMURTI: I knew you'd give that answer. (*Laughter*) The questioner says, "By integration"—integrating with what? Integrating all the fragments together? Or putting all the pieces together? And who is the entity that is putting all the pieces together? Is it the Higher Atman or the Cosmos or God or the Soul or Jesus Christ or Krishna? All that is fragmentation—you follow? So you have this challenge, and how do you respond to it, that is of the first importance—you understand? You are challenged, how do you respond to it?

Questioner: You work it out in life so that you become harmonious.

KRISHNAMURTI: Ah, lovely! When? (*Laughter*).

Questioner: Every day.

KRISHNAMURTI: There is no day, every day.

Questioner: Every morning.

KRISHNAMURTI: Now, look what you are doing. You are just adjusting yourself to the challenge. You are not answering it. (*Laughter*) How do you answer this, Sir?

267

Questioner: It is not a question of answering at all be-cause we are trying to meet you with the word.

KRISHNAMURTI: Find out, Sir, what you are doing. Find out. Here is a challenge and you can't go back to any books—right? You can't go back to your authority, the Gita and all that rubbish. So what will you do? You see I can go on explaining, Sir, but you will just accept it, as you have accepted so many things, and carry on. So let's look at it.

Here is a new challenge. The challenge being that I have lived in a fragments all my life (the past, the present and the future, God and the devil, evil and good, hap-piness and unhappiness, ambition and no ambition, vi-olence and non-violence, hate, love and jealousy) these are all fragments; all my life I have lived that way.

Questioner: (Inaudible)

KRISHNAMURTI: We have been through all that, Sir. Give the speakers two minutes, will you kindly?

Now, what is the answer? I have lived a fragmentary, destructive, broken life and now I have to live—now the challenge put to me has been: "Can I live without any fragmentation?" That is my challenge. Now how do I re-spond to it? I respond to it by saying, "I really don't know"—right? I really don't know. I don't pretend to know. I don't pretend to say "Yes, here is the answer". When a challenge is put to you, a new challenge, the in-stinctive response—I do not mean instinctive—the *right* response is humility: "I don't know." Right? But you don't say that. Can you honestly say you don't know? You can, good. Then what do you mean by that feeling, "I don't know"?

Questioner: (Inaudible)

KRISHNAMURTI: Don't answer it too quickly, find out. Use your brain cells.

Questioner: The recognition of fact, Sir.

KRISHNAMURTI: I have recognised the fact, otherwise I wouldn't even answer it.

Questioner: I have no means of finding out. I do not know and I don't know the means of finding out.

KRISHNAMURTI: Now wait. I don't know—right? Now what is the state of the mind—please follow it, listen quietly—what is the state of the mind that says "I really don't know"?

Questioner: Lack of . . . ?

KRISHNAMURTI: Oh, there we are! You people are so dull.

Questioner: I do not know.
(Various comments—inaudible.)

KRISHNAMURTI: Oh, you are so immature, like children in a class! This is a very serious question we are asking and you just throw in a lot of words, you haven't even the humility to listen and find out for yourselves.

Questioner: It is not easy, I don't know.

KRISHNAMURTI: When we say, when you say, as that gentleman said just now, he doesn't know, what is the state of mind that has replied "I don't know"?

Questioner: Waiting.

KRISHNAMURTI: You are—Sir, how old are you?

Questioner: (Inaudible)

KRISHNAMURTI: Oh, Sir. When I say "I don't know", I really don't know. But am I waiting to find out, or waiting for somebody to tell me—right? I am waiting. Therefore when I say "I don't know", it isn't an actual fact that I don't know, because I hope that somebody is going to tell me, or that I'll find out. Do you follow this? Right. Then you are waiting, aren't you? Why are you waiting? Who is going to tell you? Your memory? If your memory is going to tell you, you are back again in the same old rut. So what are you waiting for? So you say "I won't wait"—you follow, Sir?—there is no waiting. There is no "in the meantime"—you follow this? I wonder if you do. So when you say "I don't know", it means nobody knows—right?

Because if anybody tells me, he will tell me out of fragmentation—no? So I don't know, therefore there is no waiting, there is no answer—right? So I know. Then I find out what is the state of the mind that says "I don't know"—are you following it? It is *not* waiting, *not* expecting an answer, *not* looking to some memory, authority, it ceases—all that has stopped. Right? So the mind—follow it step by step—so the mind is silent in the face of a new challenge. It is silent because it can't answer the new challenge. I don't know if you are meeting this; right, Sirs? (No. No. You don't understand?)

You know when you see a marvellous mountain, the beauty, the height of it, the dignity, the purity of it, it forces you to be silent, doesn't it?—this may last a second but the very grandeur of it makes you silent. And a second later all the reactions begin. Now if you see the challenge in the same way—but you don't because your mind is chattering—so you don't see the importance or the magnitude of this question, which is: can I live (living meaning *now*, not tomorrow or yesterday, or a second after, or a second before) can I live without fragmentation? It is an immense question—right? Why aren't you silent?

Questioner: Because I want to live without fragmentation.

KRISHNAMURTI: Ah—which means what?

Questioner: I want to be out of it.

KRISHNAMURTI: Which means what? Go into it. You don't see the immensity of the question. All that you want to do is to get into another state, therefore you don't see the magnitude of the question. Why don't you? Pursue it. You do see it, when you see a marvellous mountain, sparkling with snow in the clear blue sky with great, deep shadows, and absolute silence. Why don't you see this in the same way? Because you want to live in the old way. You are not concerned with seeing the full meaning of that question, but you say, "For God's sake tell me quickly how to get there".

Questioner: I am already seeking the solution of how to get there.

KRISHNAMURTI: That's right. So you are more concerned with the solution than with the question. Which means what?

Questioner: I won't get it.

KRISHNAMURTI: No. Which means what? Look at it, look at it, don't answer it yet—which means what?

Questioner: (Inaudible)

KRISHNAMURTI: No, Madame, stick to it.

Questioner: (Inaudible)

KRISHNAMURTI: You have understood the question? You don't see the magnitude of this question because you want to reach it, get it, you are greedy. So your greed is preventing you from seeing the immensity of it. So what is important? (Follow it step by step.) Not the immensity but your greed. Why are you greedy—about something which you don't understand at all? (You don't mind, Sir, my pursuing what your daughter says like that?)

Questioner: Satisfaction!

KRISHNAMURTI: Now, see why. Why are you greedy, when you haven't even understood what is involved in it? So you say, "How stupid of me to be greedy about something when I don't know what it means"—right? So what I have to do is not, not to be greedy, but to find out the implications, the beauty, the truth, the loveliness of that thing. Why don't you do that, instead of saying "I must get it"?

So you respond to a new question, a new challenge, invariably from the old. Greed is from the old. Therefore is it possible to cut off the past entirely? You understand? It is the past that is fragmentary, that is bringing about fragmentation, breaking up life. So my question is: is it possible to be free of the past totally, so that I can live technologically? I don't know if you follow this? Can I be free from the past, can I be free from being a Hindu, Buddhist, Muslim, Christian, or anything else? Not "can I be"; I must be. It is stupid for me to belong to any caste, to any religion, to any group. Out it goes. There is no time to think about it as you suggested. Out it has gone—you follow? So it is possible to cut the past completely; if you can do it in one direction you can do it totally. Right? (Oh, no, you don't see.)

So, can you, from this moment, be free completely of your nationality, of your tradition, of your culture, of your past? If you can't, you live in fragmentation, and therefore everlastingly life becomes a battlefield. And nobody is going to help you in this. No guru, no Communist nobody is going to help you do it. And in your heart of hearts you know this jolly well. Well, Sirs? So thought is always old—right? Discover this for yourselves, don't repeat after me—discover it. And you see what an extraordinary thing you have discovered. So if you discover this—that thought is really old—then all the past—the Shankaras, the Buddhas, the Christ, the whole past is gone. No? But you don't discover it. You won't make the effort to discover it; you don't want to discover it.

Questioner: No Sir, there is the fear of being lost.

KRISHNAMURTI: Well, be lost, you are lost anyhow!

Questioner: Not completely lost.

KRISHNAMURTI: But you are lost, Sirs. What are you talking about? You are terribly lost. It is only a lost man that is everlastingly in conflict. You are lost, but you don't recognise that you are lost. So thought is always old; then, what is it—that is too difficult to go into now—I'll just put it forward and you will see for yourselves—what is it then that sees something new? You understand, Sirs? Thought is always old—follow it carefully—when the Adi Shankara, that old bird, said something, his thought was already old—do you understand? Therefore what he said was never new, he repeated in his own coinage of words something which he had heard, and you repeat it after him. So thought is never new and can never be new, and living now, every day, is something which is the active present; it is always active, in the present. Therefore when you try to understand activity in the present, with the past, which is thought, then you don't understand it at all; then there is fragmentation, and life becomes a conflict. So can you live so *completely* that there is only the active present now? And you cannot live that way if you haven't understood and thereby cut yourself off completely from the past, because you yourself are the past. You see you will unfortunately go on just listening—if I happen to come next year you will repeat the same old stuff.

Questioner: Sir, if we are not in the past, but in the present, does that not also become the past and the future—how are we to know that we are right,

KRISHNAMURTI: You don't have to be sure you are right—be wrong! Why are you frightened about being right or wrong? But your question has no validity at all because you are just talking, you are just theorising. You are saying, "If this happens, that would happen". But if you put it into action then you would know there is no such thing as "going wrong".

Questioner: Sir, when we go back home we see our children and the past comes in.

Questioner: Shankara may go.

KRISHNAMURTI: I hope it has gone. Shankara may go but the children remain. (*Laughter*) Are the children the past? They are in one sense. And as they are living human beings, can you educate them to live completely, in the way we are talking about?

Questioner: Right Sir, you have answered it, sorry.

KRISHNAMURTI: That means I have to help them to be intelligent, I have to help them to be sensitive, because sensitivity, highest sensitivity is the highest intelligence. Therefore if there are no schools around you, you have to help them at home to be sensitive, to look at the trees, to look at the flowers, to listen to the birds, to plant a tree if you have a little yard—or if you have no yard to have a tree in a pot and to look at it, to cherish it, to water it, not to tear its leaves. And as the schools do not want them to be sensitive, educated, intelligent (schools only exist to pass exams and get a job) you have to help them at home, to help them to discuss with you, why you go to a temple, why you do this ceremony, why you read the Bible, the Gita—you follow?—so that they are questioning you all the time, so that neither you nor anyone else becomes an

273

authority. But I am afraid you won't do any of this because the climate, the food, the tradition is too much for you, so you slip back and lead a monstrously ugly life. But I think, if you have the energy, the drive, the passion, that is the only way to live.

MADRAS
12 JANUARY 1968

EUROPE

VII

Seven Talks in Saanen, Switzerland

1

WHAT IS YOUR OVER-RIDING INTEREST?

Passion and intensity needed. The inner and outer; can they be divided?

Questions: *Pleasure and interest; God; children and education; many different interests; the meaning of demonstrations; of love, truth and order.*

WHAT IS YOUR primary interest, your deep, abiding intention? I think one should discover that for oneself. You must find that out and relate it to all the activities of daily life.

One may be deeply concerned with the world as it is, with the violence, the appalling chaos, the political divisions, and the corruption—which is death, not only outwardly but also inwardly. In discovering one's deep interest for oneself, one will be able to find out one's relationship with another, according to that interest. If that interest is vague, superficial, depending on surroundings and the wind that blows in any direction, then our activities, both outwardly and inwardly, will be rather casual, without any significance. During these talks and discussions, could you find out what is your major interest, whether you are really concerned with the world and your place in the world, with your relationship to another human being, your relationships politically, economically, socially and religiously? What is your deep, major interest in life? Is it acquiring money, prestige, security? Please listen to this carefully. If that is your real, vital, sustained interest, then you must see the consequences of such an interest. Or is your interest, considering the world and your relationship with it, not only to change yourself but also to change the world about you? Then you must also see the implications of this. Or is it that you want to establish a personal relationship with another so completely, so wholly, that there is no conflict: then also you must realise the consequences of this. Perhaps your interest is something more difficult:

trying to find out what is the place of thought, as the measurable and the immeasurable. To discover in which direction our interest lies, we must be willing to dedicate ourselves completely to it, and not just play with it, casually accepting or rejecting it according to circumstances, according to environmental influences and our own likes and dislikes. If we are prepared to go into this completely, then we can establish a relationship between ourselves—a relationship with the world, with our neighbour and with our intimate friend.

That is what we intend to do during these weeks, to find out where our major capacity and interest lies, and whether that interest is isolated, or is related to all human beings. If it is isolated and you are seeking your own particular enjoyment your own particular salvation, your own particular safety, a good position in the world, then in talking this over together, we shall be able to find out whether such an interest has any validity, whether it has any significance at all. But your interest, your deep purpose may be to find out how to live a totally different life. Seeing things as they are, the violence, the brutality, the enmity and hatred, the corruption and the utter chaos, your aim may be to find out whether the human mind, your mind, the mind of each one of us, is capable of completely changing, so that, as a human being, you not only bring about a radical revolution in yourself but also outwardly—although the outward revolution and the inward revolution are not separate.

We are not talking of physical revolution: violence, bombs, killing people in the name of peace. That is no revolution at all; it is merely childish destruction.

I do not know if you have observed the violence all over the world. The younger generation were at first giving flowers to everybody, living in a world of "beauty" and imagination; when that did not work, they took to drugs, they became violent, and we are now living in a world of complete violence. You can see this in India, in the Middle East, in America.

As we grow older our capacities are dulled, the world is too much for us. Therefore, it behoves each one of us to find out our purpose, our intention, our major interest. Once we have discovered this we can discuss it, then we can take a journey together, providing that your interest and the speaker's are the same, because the speaker knows exactly his intention, his drive, his interest, and if your interest is something quite different, then our relationship becomes difficult. If, however, your interest is to understand this world in which we live as human beings—not as technicians—then we can establish a relationship and together we can talk things over—together we can take a journey. Otherwise these talks and discussions will have very little meaning.

Please bear this in mind, although you are here for a holiday amongst the mountains, the hills and the streams, and the tourist entertainments, in spite of all that, we have an opportunity of sitting together for a whole hour. You know, that is quite interesting, to sit together for an hour and talk over our problems without any pretence, without any hypocrisy, and without assuming some ridiculous façade. To have a whole hour together is really extraordinary, because so rarely do we sit and discuss serious matters with anybody for a whole hour. You may go to the office for a whole day, but it has far greater meaning to spend sixty minutes or more together in order to investigate, to seriously examine our human problems hesitantly, tentatively and with great affection, without trying to impose one opinion upon another; because we are not dealing with opinions, ideas, or theories.

We are concerned with establishing a relationship between one another, and that can only be done if we know our mutual interests, and how deep those interests lie, and what energy we have to resolve the major problems of our life. Our life is not different from the rest of the world: we are the world. I don't think any of us realise, deeply and continuously, that we are the world and the world is us. This must be deeply rooted within us. We have made this social structure, this violence, according to our desires, according to our ambition, greed and envy, and if we would change society we must first change ourselves; that seems such a simple, radical approach to the whole problem. But we think that by changing the outer structure of society, by throwing bombs, making political divisions and the like, we shall by some miracle all become perfect human beings; I am afraid that never works. And to realise that we are the world, not as a verbal statement or a theory, but to actually feel it in our hearts, is very difficult, because our education, our culture, has laid emphasis on our being separate from the world; that as individuals we have a responsibility to ourselves and not to the rest of the world, that as individuals we are free to do as we like, within reason. But we are not individuals at all; we are the result of the culture in which we live. An individual means an entity who is not fragmented, who is whole; we are not that. We are broken up, fragmented, in a state of contradiction within ourselves, therefore we are not individuals. So, seeing all this, what is our major interest in life?

You must give yourself time to think it over. Let us sit together quietly and find out. Is it that you have so many problems, economic, social, the problem of personal relationship and you would like to solve them all wholly and completely? Is it that you have sexual problems which you have not been able to solve, so the solving of that becomes your major interest? Is it that you want to live peacefully in a world that is noisy, corrupt and violent? Or does your interest lie in the direction of social reform and to that you are dedicated? And if you are, then what is your relationship to that society? Or are you interested in finding out the limitations of thought? Thought is limited, however logical, however capable it may be; thought is also inventive and experimental, producing marvellous things technologically, but it is still limited. Do you want to find out if there is something more, something beyond thought—the measurable and the immeasurable? You have to look at all these problems.

Questioner: I don't understand what you mean when you say, "We are the world" and "The world is us".

KRISHNAMURTI: Is that your major problem? Don't bother about what I say. What is *your* problem, what is *your* major interest, and have you the energy, the capacity, the intensity, to solve that problem? It is really very important for you to find out. Don't concern yourself with what the speaker says; that is irrelevant. But find out for yourself what your interest is and see how much energy, passion and vitality you are prepared to give pursuing that interest; because if you have no passion, no intensity to pursue that interest then—if I may point out—corruption has set in and where there is corruption, there is death.

Then from which end shall we begin? Can this total movement of living, this whole human existence be split up in this way? Don't agree or disagree, just listen. Do you first of all establish a physical relationship of order, giving social and economic security, and after laying the foundations, build a complete house and then move from there to the other, or is it one total unitary movement, indivisible, non-fragmented, wherever you begin, because the two are related, the two are inseparable.

We want complete physical order, and we must have order in our life inwardly as well as outwardly. We must have order, not military order, not the order of the older generation nor the order of the younger generation—the permissive society is disorder, it is corruption and decay; and the so-called order of the older people is really disorder, with its wars, its violence, its division and snobbery—it is also corruption. So, seeing both the permissive disorder of the young and the "ordered" disorder of the old, observing both, one realises that there must be a different kind of order. And that order must assure physical security for everybody, not just for a few rich people, or for those who are well placed and have capacity. There must be physical security for everybody.

As you know, over six million people from the East have crossed the border into India. Do you realise what that means, not only for the refugees but also for the country that itself is already impoverished? How can you establish order there? And the young people have created total disorder with the so-called permissive society. They say the older generation have created disorder and they want to have nothing to do with it; they want a different way of living, so they do just as they like. But that too is disorder; both are disorder. I wish you could see this!

One realises that there must be physical order, physical security, for every human being in the world. This has always been the dream of the revolutionaries, of the idealists and the philosophers; they believed that through physical revolution they could achieve this ambition. But it has never succeeded. There have been so many revolutions and it has never happened. Look at the Communists with their divisions, their armies and the totalitarian state, and look at all the horrors that go on in the rest of the world; there is no order anywhere.

One realises that there must be physical order. Now does that order depend on the administration of the law, on the authority of society according to its culture and environment? Or does it depend entirely on the human being, on each one of us, the way we live, the way we think, the way we act in our relationships with one another? So, let's begin there. That is, living as a human being in a destructive, chaotic, violent world, how am I, or

281

how are you, going to bring about order? Does that order depend on you or on the politician? Does that order depend on you, or on the priest, or on the philosopher, or on an utopian ideal?

If you depend on the priest, on the politician, on a theory, on a belief, or on an ideal, see what takes place! You are then conforming to a pattern set by the politician, by the theorist, by an utopian ideal; hence there is a conflict between what you are and what you think should be. And that conflict is part of this violence, this disorder. So you can perceive that order in society can be brought about only by you and by nobody else? We are responsible for that order by our conduct, by our thoughts, by our way of life—the whole of it. And is that your real, deep, abiding interest, to discover what that order is? One must live when the world is in confusion and chaos, with its suffering and destruction—and to understand this confusion, one must live in total, complete order. If you are interested, if you are prepared to give your energy, your capacity, your passion to finding out what that order is, then we can go into it, then we can share this thing together; you won't be just an outsider looking in, because it's your problem and you must put your teeth into it! If that is your real, deep interest, then you must be passionate. I'm not talking about lust, about physical passion or sexual passion. I'm talking of that passion which comes when there is deep interest.

Say, for instance, one is deeply interested in finding out if sorrow can ever end (deeply interested, not superficially because it brings a reward, but because you really want to find out)—sorrow, the grief, the pain, the anxiety, the fear, which we all feel. If that sorrow can ever come to an end, then you will find that only then comes real passion, real intensity. So, is it your intention to discover for yourselves whether, living in this world, whether it is possible to bring about such order within yourselves?—because you are the world, and the world is you.

Questioner: You said you must have passion, but earlier on you stated that as we grow older our passion is dulled: so what are we to do?

KRISHNAMURTI: Do our passions become dull as we grow older? Perhaps our physical passions do, because our glands are not working so efficiently, but we are not talking about the passion of the young or of the old and the dissipation of that passion. We are talking about having an interest, a vital interest, a major issue with which you, as a human being, are concerned—not a gift, a technique, a capacity. If you have such a deep interest and you live with it, then out of that comes passion. And that passion doesn't disappear just because you have grey hair.

Questioner: What happens when you have this deep interest, but also you have the desire for pleasure?

KRISHNAMURTI: You have pleasure on the one hand and a vital, abiding interest on the other. Please just listen to it! Is there a contradiction between pleasure and a vital interest? If I am vitally interested in bringing about order within myself and in the world around me, then that becomes my most profound pleasure. I may have a nice car, I may look at a girl, or at the hills and all the rest of it; but they are all passing, trivial things which will in no way contradict my vital interest which is my pleasure. You see, we divide pleasure in ourselves; we say it would be nice to have a lovely car or listen to beautiful music. There is great delight in listening to music; it may quieten and pacify your nerves by its rhythm and quality of sound; it may carry you away to distant places, far away, and in that there is great pleasure. But that pleasure does not detract from your vital interest; on the contrary. When you have a tremendous interest in something, then that very interest becomes the major pleasure in your life; and all other pleasures become secondary and trivial; in that there is no contradiction. But when we are not sure of our major interest in life, then we are pulled in different directions by various pleasures and objects; and then there is a contradiction.

So one has to find out, and I hope you will find out during these coming weeks, what is your major interest in which passion and pleasure exist.

Questioner: Do you not think that this order can only come about by going to God the place he should hold in our lives? All the chaos that exists in the world today is because we live without the idea of God?

KRISHNAMURTI: To bring about this order in our lives, should we give first place to God? If we have no knowledge of God, no feeling for God, no understanding of that thing called God, then order becomes mechanical, superficial, and changeable. God is the most important thing, the questioner says, and then out of that will come order. Now, we are trying to investigate; we are not going to deny or to assert; we are trying to find out, to enquire. Our main difficulty is that we all interpret, or imagine what God is, according to our own culture, according to our own background, our fears, our pleasures, our sense of security and so on. Surely that is obvious. And if we don't know this ultimate reality and have no knowledge of it, can that bring about order? We are enquiring, trying to find out. Or must you have physical order first, which is measurable, and then having established that order, find out the immeasurable, in which order is something entirely different?

This has been the point of view of all the religious people throughout the world: concern yourselves with God and then you will have perfect order. And each religion, each sect, translates what God is according to its own beliefs and, brought up in that belief, we accept that interpretation. But if you really want to find out if there is such a thing as God, something that cannot possibly be put into words, something which is unnameable, if that really is the major interest in your life, then that very interest does bring about order. To find that reality, one must live differently: there must be austerity without harshness; there must be love. And love cannot exist if there is fear, or the mind is pursuing pleasure. So, to find that reality one must understand oneself, the structure and the nature of the self; and the structure and the nature of oneself is measurable by thought. It is measurable in the sense that thought can perceive its own activities, thought can see what it has created, what it has denied, what it has accepted; and when one realises the limitations of thought, then perhaps one can go into that which lies beyond thought.

Questioner: The problem of the parent is what to teach our children.

KRISHNAMURTI: First of all, what is our relationship with our children? Please bear in mind that we are investigating together. If you are the father, you go to the office and come home late in the evening. If you are the mother, you have your own ambitions and drives, your own loneliness and miseries, your own worries about being loved or not being loved; the children have to be looked after and there is the cooking and the washing-up; and if there is not enough money, you also probably go off to earn a living. Then what is your relationship with your children? Have you any relationship?

We are investigating, we are enquiring. I am not saying you don't have any relationship. Then, as they grow up you hand them over to a school where they are taught how to read and write; there they form gangs with other children who are also imitating and conforming and who are equally lost. You have the problem not only of your own children but also of other children who are bullying gangsters. Then what is your relationship with your child? You have children and you want to educate them rightly. Now, if that is really your deep, vital interest, you have to find out what is the meaning of education. Is it merely for children to acquire a particular kind of technological knowledge, so that they can earn a livelihood in a world that is becoming more and more competitive, because there are more and more people and therefore less and less jobs? You must face all this.

The world is divided by nationalities, with their sovereign governments, their armies and their navies, and all the butchery that goes with them. And if you are only concerned with the development of technological knowledge, then see the consequences of all that; the mind becomes more and more mechanical and you neglect the whole field of life. When the children grow up, if they are lucky they are sent to a university, where they are shaped more and more, forced to conform and put in a cage. Is that your interest? Is that your responsibility? And because they don't want to be put into a cage, they are in revolt. Please, see all this. And when that revolt proves to be ineffective, there is violence.

How are you, as a parent, going to educate your children to be different? Can you form a new kind of educational system, or can you, with the help of others, start a school which will be totally different? To do that you must have money and a group of people who are really dedicated. If you are a parent, is it not your responsibility to see that such schools *are* created? So you must work for it; you know, life isn't a plaything. Now, is this your deep, vital interest or, as a parent, are you only concerned with your own ambitions, greed, envy, with your position at the office, getting higher pay, a larger house, a bigger car and so on? You have to look at all this. Therefore, where does education begin? Does it start at school or with you? That means, are you, as a parent, as a human being, re-educating yourself all the time?

Questioner: Is there any meaning in education, or will our children finish up just like us?

KRISHNAMURTI: I was told that Socrates complained about the youth of his day. He said that they had no manners and no respect for their elders, that they were becoming permissive, and all the rest of it; and that was in Athens in the fourth century B.C. And we are still complaining about our children. So we are asking: does the education of children consist in training them to be like us, like other monkeys, or should education include not only technological instruction but also a deep understanding of the whole neglected field of life? The whole of life, not just one fragment of it, because the way we live we neglect all that, we are concerned only with one fragment; therefore there is chaos and violence in the world.

Questioner: Are you saying that we should only have one main interest? Should we not be interested in many things, in war, in pollution, and so on? Surely you have to be aware of these things, haven't you?

KRISHNAMURTI: Sir, when there is a major interest in your life, then you are aware of everything. When you are interested in order, it is not only order in yourself but order in the world. You don't want wars; you feel for those people because they have no order. You know what is happening, therefore, you are very concerned with pollution, poverty and war.

Wars are created by nationalities, by governments, by politicians, by dividing religion into sects and all the rest of it. In observing all that, I want order, not only order in myself, but in the world. And in wanting order, I have to find order in everything around me, which means I must work for order, be dedicated to order, be passionate about order. That means I have no nationality, do you follow, Sir? Disorder is violence, therefore I must find out how to end completely all violence within myself.

Questioner: Do you believe in demonstrations?

KRISHNAMURTI: You go up and down the street with a group of people demonstrating against the war in Vietnam. Do you want to end the war in Vietnam or do you want to end all wars? Can you demonstrate to end all wars or can you only demonstrate to end a particular war? Do think about this, give your heart to it. I can demonstrate against a particular war, but when I am concerned with the ending of all wars, not only outwardly but in myself, how can I demonstrate with a group of people? Do you also want to end all wars as I do? Do you understand? It means no nationally, no frontiers, no linguistic differences, no religious divisions—all that. No, Sir, you can't demonstrate, you have to live it. And when you live it, that in itself is a demonstration.

Questioner: Do not love and truth bring about order?

KRISHNAMURTI: But do you know what love is, Sir? Do you know what truth is? Can you love if you are jealous, greedy, ambitious? And is truth something fixed, static, or is it living, vital, moving, without any path to it. You have to find all this out for yourself.

SAANEN
18 July 1971

2

ORDER

The mind only knows disorder. The state of "not-knowing". The "self" is part of the culture, which is disorder.

Questions: *Is the mind capable of looking? Analysis; the guru: relationship with Krishnamurti; can you look at yourself?*

WE WERE TALKING about order. In a world that is so utterly confused and divided, in a world that is so violent and brutal, one would have thought that our main interest in life would be to bring about this order; not only in ourselves but also outwardly.

Order is not habit; habit becomes automatic and loses all its vitality when human beings merely become orderly in the mechanical sense. Order, as we were saying, covers not only our own particular life but also all the life about us, outwardly, in the world, and deeply inwardly. Now, being aware of this disorder, this confusion, how is one to bring about order in oneself without any conflict and without it becoming merely habitual, a routine, mechanical and neurotic? One has observed those people who are very orderly; they have a certain rigidity, they have no pliability; they are not quick and have become rather hard, self-centred, because they are following a particular pattern which they consider to be order; and gradually that becomes a neurotic state. So being aware that this kind of order (which is disorder) becomes mechanical and leads to neurosis, nevertheless one realises that one must have order in one's life. Then how is this to come about? That is what we are going to consider together this morning.

One must have physical order. It is essential to have a well-disciplined, sensitive, alert body, because that reacts on the mind. And how is one to have a highly sensitive organism that doesn't become rigid, hard, forced into a particular pattern or design—which the mind thinks is orderly and so forces the body to conform to. This is one of the problems.

Then there must be order in the whole totality of the mind, of the brain. The mind is the capacity to understand, the ability to observe logically, sanely, to function totally, all round, not fragmentarily, not to be caught in contradictory desires, purposes and intentions. How is this whole quality of mind to have total order, psychosomatic order without conformity, without the enforcement of a thought-up discipline?

See our difficulty first, what is involved in all this. One has to have order; this is absolutely essential. We are going to investigate together what we mean by that order. There is the order of the older generation, which is really total disorder as one observes its activities throughout the world, in business, in religion, in the economic field, amongst nations and everywhere else; there is total disorder.

In reaction to that there is the permissive society, the younger generation, who do quite the opposite to the older generation, which is also disorder—isn't it? A reaction is disorder. And how is the mind, with all its subtleties of thought, with all the images thought has built, the images that it has built about another, and the images about itself, the images of the "what is" and the "what should be" (therefore living in a state of contradiction), how is such a mind to have complete, total order within itself, so that there is no fragmentation, no reaction to a pattern and no contradiction of the opposites out of which arises violence? Now, seeing all this, how is the mind, your mind, to have complete, total order in action and in thought, in every movement both psychologically and physiologically?

The religious people have said that you can only have order through belief in a higher life, through belief in God, belief in something outside, and that you must conform, adjust, imitate according to that belief; that through discipline you must force your whole nature and change the structure of the psyche, as well as your physiological state. They have said all this. And there is a group of behaviourists who say that environment forces you to behave; if you don't behave properly then it destroys you. And people live that way, according to their own particular belief, whether it be the Communist belief, some religious belief or a sociological, economic belief.

In spite of this division in the world, the contradiction in ourselves as well as in society, and the counter culture against the existing culture, they all say that there must be order in the world; the military say it and so do the priests. And is order mechanical? Can order be brought about through discipline? Can order be brought about through conformity, imitation and control? Or, is there an order that has nothing whatever to do with control, with discipline as we know it, that has nothing whatever to do with conformity, with adjustment and so on?

Let us look at this whole idea of control and find out whether it does bring order (which doesn't mean we are talking against control). We are trying to understand; and if we understand, we may discover something entirely different. I hope you are following all this and that you are as interested in it and as passionate about it as I am. It is utterly useless to listen casually to some theoretical idea; we are not discussing theories or hypotheses; we are observing actually what is going on, seeing what is false. The very perception of seeing what is false is the truth. Do you understand?

289

Now what is implied in control? All our culture, all our education and the upbringing of our children is based on that; and in ourselves there is this urge to control. Now what is implied in that? We have never asked ourselves why we should control at all? Now, let us go into this question. Control implies, does it not, a controller and the thing to be controlled. Please give your attention to this. I am angry and I must control my anger; and where there is control, there is conflict; "I must" and "I must not". And conflict obviously distorts the mind. A mind is healthy when it has no conflict at all; then it can function without any friction and such a mind is a sane, clear mind, but control denies that, because in control there is conflict and contradiction, there is the desire to imitate and to conform to a pattern—the thing you think you ought to do. Is this clear?

So control is not order. This is very important to understand. One can never have order through control, because order implies functioning clearly, seeing wholly, without any distortion; but where there is conflict, there must be distortion. Control also implies suppression, conformity, adjustment and the division between the observer and the observed. We are going to find out what it is to act or bring about order without control. Not that we are denying the whole structure of control, but we are seeing the falseness of it and, therefore, out of that comes the truth of order. Are we following each other, not verbally but actually doing it as we go along, because we are trying to create an entirely different world, a different culture, to bring about a human being who lives without friction? It is only such a mind which is capable of living without distortion that knows what love is. And control in any form does breed distortion, conflict and an unhealthy mind.

The old culture has said that you must discipline, and this discipline begins with children at home, then in schools and colleges and all the way through life. Now that word "discipline" means to learn; it does not mean drilling, conforming, suppressing and so on. And a mind that is learning all the time, is actually in a state of order, but the mind that is not learning, which says "I have learnt", such a mind brings disorder. The mind itself resists being drilled, becoming mechanical, conforming and suppressing, which is all implied by discipline. And yet we said there must be order. How is this order to come into being without discipline in the accepted sense of that word?

Seeing the problem, which is very complex, what is your answer? If you are exercising your mind, if you are really deeply interested in this question of order, not only inwardly in yourself but also outwardly, what is your response to it? How do you find an answer to this urge for order, which does not depend on control, on discipline, on conformity and that totally denies all authority—which is freedom, isn't it? If there is any form of authority, then in the acceptance of that authority there is conformity, there is a following; and that breeds contradiction and therefore disorder.

So, no control, in the usual meaning of that word "discipline", and a total denial of the whole structure and nature of authority, which negates freedom. And yet there must be order; see the complications of it. There is the authority of law, of the policeman, the civil authority that one must abide by; but there must be freedom from the authority of the elders with their beliefs, and the authority of one's own demands, experience, knowledge; because all that denies freedom.

Seeing the actual state of the world as it is, observing our culture, social, economic and religious, our educational system and the family relationship, we see that they are all based on this authority. And it has caused utter confusion, great suffering, wars and the fragmentation of the world, as well as the division of man. Observing this, how is one to bring about order? That is your problem—you understand? How will you answer that question if you are really deeply, passionately, interested in trying to bring order to your life, as well as outwardly? What will your answer be? Will you turn to books, to the priests, to the philosophers, to the gurus, to the latest person who says, "I am enlightened, come and I'll tell you all about it?" To whom will you turn—to find out how to live a life that is totally orderly, denying all conformity, all authority, all discipline and control? You have to answer this question. We are coming to the problem afresh, that is, afresh in the sense that we don't know how to bring order out of this chaos. If you say, order should be this or that, then you are reacting to "what is", you are stating something which is in opposition to "what is", a reaction that has no validity whatever. So we are approaching the problem anew; we have so far only examined the actual fact of what is going on in the world and in ourselves, *the actual fact*. Now, we are going to find out together what order is. You are not accepting anything the speaker says, be quite sure about this, because if you do, then our relationship changes entirely. But if we are examining together, being totally interested in this issue, which is, that realising the state of confusion in the world, and seeing the disorder in ourselves, in all our lives, how tawdry they are, realising the actual fact of this, then we need intensity and passion to discover what is order.

We are going to find out, first of all, what it means to learn by observing "what is" and learning from that. Learning means the active present of that verb to learn, which is a constant movement of learning, not having learnt and then applying that knowledge, which is something quite different from learning all the time. Do you see the difference? We are learning together; we are not storing up knowledge and then acting according to that knowledge; in that there is contradiction and therefore control, whereas a mind that is constantly learning has no authority, no contradiction, no control, no discipline, but the very learning itself demands order. Please observe yourself. Are you in a state of learning—or waiting to be told what order is? Do watch yourself. If you are waiting to find out from another what order is, then you are dependent on that person, or on that book, or on that priest, or on that structure and so on. So we are learning together. Is that your state of mind, that you have understood control and all its implications, understood the full significance of discipline and also you are completely aware of what authority entails? If you have understood, then you are free; otherwise you cannot learn. Learning means a mind that is curious, that doesn't know, that is eager to find out, interested. Is your mind like that, interested? Are you saying I don't know what order is but I am going to find out? Are you very curious, passionate and deeply interested, is your mind like that and, therefore, willing to learn, not from another but to learn for yourself by the act of observation? Control and authority, which to you mean discipline, prevent observation. Do you see this? A mind can only learn when it is free, when it doesn't know, otherwise you cannot learn.

So, is your mind free to observe the world and observe yourself? You cannot observe if you are saying "This is right" and "This is wrong", "I must control", "I must suppress", "I must obey", "I must disobey"—you follow? And, if you are saying that I must live a permissive life, then you are not free to learn; if you are conforming, you are not free to learn. Are you conforming when you have long hair? Am I conforming because I put on a shirt and trousers? Please find out. Conformity is not merely to a national pattern, to a particular structure of a society or to a belief, but there is conformity in little things. And such a mind is incapable of learning, because behind this conformity there is this enormous sense of fear; the young have it as well as the old and that is why they conform. If all that is going on, you are not free to learn.

And there must be order, something living and beautiful, not a mechanical thing—the order of the universe, the order that exists in mathematics, the order that exists in nature, in the relationship between various animals, an order that human beings have totally denied, because in ourselves we are in disorder, which means that we are fragmentary, contradictory, frightened and all the rest of it.

Now, I am asking myself, and you are asking yourself, whether the mind is capable of learning, because it doesn't know what order is. It knows reaction to disorder, but the mind must discover whether it is actually capable of learning without reaction and can therefore be free to observe. In other words, is your mind aware of the problem of control, of discipline, of authority and the constant response of reaction—are you aware of that whole structure? Are you aware of all this in yourself as you live from day to day? Or are you only aware when it is pointed out to you? Please see the difference. If you are aware of this whole problem of confusion, discipline, control and suppression, which is conformity, because you have been observing, living, and watching, then it is your own; the other is second-hand. Now which is it?

For most of us, it is second-hand, because we are second-hand people, aren't we? All our knowledge is second-hand, our traditions are second-hand; there may perhaps be a few activities that are totally our own and not of another. So, are we aware that it is our own direct perception, and not second-hand knowledge learnt from another? Now, if it is learnt from another, one has to discard that totally, hasn't one? You have to discard all that has been said just now by the speaker about the implications of control, discipline, authority and so on; then you become aware that what has been pointed out to you must be totally rejected in order to learn. If you have rejected what others, including the speaker, have said, then you are actually learning, aren't you?

Now, let's find out together what order means. How do you find out what order is when you don't know anything about it? You can only do this by enquiring into the state of the mind that is trying to find out what order is. I only know what disorder is, I am completely familiar with it, the whole culture of disorder in this present society; I know it very well. But I don't know what order is; I can imagine what order is; I can theorise about it, but theories, imagination, speculation are not order; therefore I discard all that. So, I really don't know what order is.

My mind knows what disorder is, how it has come into being, through the culture and the conditioning of that culture and of the human beings; I am aware of all that which is total disorder. Now, I really don't know what order is, so what is the state of the mind that says I don't know?" What is the state of your mind that says, "I really don't know?" Is that state of mind waiting for an answer, waiting to be told, expecting to find order? If it is waiting, expecting to be told, then it is not the state which we are talking about, the state of not knowing. The state of "not knowing" is not waiting to be told, it is not expecting an answer; it is terribly alive, active, but it does not know; it knows what is disorder and therefore rejects it completely. When such a mind says, "I do not know", then it is totally free. It has denied the disorder and because it is free, it has found order. Do you understand this? It is really marvellous if you go into it for yourself.

I don't know what order is and I am not waiting for anybody to tell me. And because of my mind has denied everything that is disorder, totally, without holding back a thing, has emptied the cupboard completely, it is free; so it is capable of learning. And when the mind is totally free, which means non-fragmented, then it is in a state of order. Have you understood this?

Now, is your mind in total order, otherwise don't go any further. Nobody, no teacher, no guru, no saviour, no philosopher, can teach you what order is: in denying totally all authority, you are free from fear, and therefore you can find out what order is. Now, are you aware of your mind, of yourself, of your life—not the holiday life sitting here for an hour listening to a talk—but aware of your daily life, of your family life, of your relationship with each other? And in that life are you aware of the daily routine, the monotony, the boredom of going to the office? Are you aware of the quarrels, of the brutalities, of the nagging and the violence, of everything which is the result of a culture that is total disorder, which is your life? You can't pick and choose out of that disorder what you think is order. Are you aware that your life is disorderly and if you haven't got the interest, the passion, the intensity, the flame to find order, then you will pick and choose what you think is order out of the disorder. Can you observe yourself with great honesty, without any sense of hypocrisy or double talk, know for yourself that your life is disorderly, and can you put all that aside to find out what order is? You know, putting aside disorder is not so very difficult; we dramatise it, make much of it. But when you see something very dangerous, a precipice, a wild animal, or a man with a gun, you avoid it instantly, don't you? There is no arguing, no hesitation, no temporising, there is no immediate action. In the same way, when you see the danger of disorder, there is instant action which is the total denial of the whole culture which has brought about disorder, which is yourself.

Questioner: Is not the problem how *to look?*

KRISHNAMURTI: We have been asking, "Is one free to look?" You don't want to look, do you? Do you really want to look at all the things that you value, that you cherish, the beliefs which you think are important and which are surrounded by a great deal of confusion? Are you capable of looking at all that? Come on, Sirs, it is not my problem. Are you capable of looking at yourself without any distortion? Have you ever looked at yourself, without one image looking at a lot of other images?

Questioner: Aren't we conforming to a certain pattern now? You speak for an hour and then we ask questions. Isn't that a pattern too?

KRISHNAMURTI: Is this a pattern? You can make anything into a pattern; sitting on a chair is a pattern, sitting on the ground becomes a pattern. But is this a pattern? If it is, then let us break it up. You see, I am asking a question which is: have you ever looked at yourself? I am not talking about looking at your face in the mirror. But do you know what it means to look at yourself actually as

295

you really are? Does that frighten you? You are frightened because you have an image about yourself, haven't you? You think: I am better than that, I am more noble than that; or how dreadfully ugly, how old I am, how decrepit, how diseased, how silly I am. All that prevents you from looking, doesn't it? I just want to see myself as I am. I don't want to pick and choose out of what I see; I just want to look. Does that take a great deal of courage? My interest, my passion to observe what I actually am makes me look, not my fear of finding out what I am. I don't know if you are meeting this point. I am vitally, tremendously interested in seeing what I am, whatever it is—are you? In my relationships, I want to see whether I lie or tell the truth, or whether I am frightened; I want to see if I am greedy or ambitious, I want to watch all the subtle movements that creep in and out of my life.

Now, how do I look at myself? Is my mind capable of looking at itself? Does that mean one thought separating itself to look at other thoughts? The one thought that has separated itself from the other thought then says: this is right, this is wrong, this is good, this is bad, this I shall keep, this I won't keep, how frightened I am, how ugly— you follow? Now, is that looking? When one thought separates itself from the other thoughts, is such a thought capable of looking? Or can you look at yourself only when there is no fragmentation of thought?

Have you ever looked at yourself—the way you behave, why you behave like that, how you walk, how you talk, how you listen? Are you aware of what your body is doing, watching your nervous reactions like the twitching of your fingers? Are you aware of yourself, your thoughts, your feelings, of your inner motives, your inner drives and urges—are you completely aware of all this, not correcting it, but observing, watching, looking?

Questioner: It is very difficult not to analyse.

KRISHNAMURTI: When you are analysing, you are not looking.

Questioner: I know.

KRISHNAMURTI: You don't know otherwise you wouldn't analyse. Look, I want to see what is in the cupboard of my mind, what is stored up there; I want to read all the things it contains because the content of the mind *is* the mind. I want to see what I am during the waking hours, walking, talking, making gestures, when I am at the office, when I am angry, in the fleeting moments of pleasure and sex, and the delight of seeing the hills, the streams, the trees, the birds and the clouds. But I also want to see myself when I am asleep, be aware of what is going on. Don't you want to see yourself, awake and asleep? You think you do. Do you know what it means to learn about yourself? It means hard work, daily observation, watching, watching, watching, but not self-centred watching, just watching, like you watch a bird, or the movement of a cloud; you can't change the movement of the cloud, so just watch in the same way.

And the next question is: can the mind be watchful of what it is doing when it is asleep? We haven't time to go into that now, perhaps another day.

Questioner: I would like to examine the relationship between you and us. You say you are not a guru, but you talk and we listen; we ask questions and you answer them, so could we look at this relationship?

KRISHNAMURTI: Are we taking a journey together? Or are you merely following? It is for you to tell me, not for me to tell you. What is it you are doing? Are we journeying together or are you being led—which is it? If you are being led, if you are following, there is no relationship, because the speaker says, "Don't follow." He is neither your authority nor your guru; if you insist on following, if you insist on listening in order to learn what he is saying, then there is no relationship. But if you say, "I want to learn," we are taking a journey together into the extraordinary world in which we live, and that world is "me" and I want to penetrate into that "me," I want to learn; then we are together, then we have a relationship.

Questioner: But is it really together if you sit up there and we are down here?

KRISHNAMURTI: I happen to sit on the platform because it is more convenient, because you can see me and I can see you. It is of no account whether you are sitting up here or down there—we are taking a journey together into a world in which there is neither height nor depth; it is that world which we are trying to understand.

So I come back to my question which is: have you ever looked at yourself? Have you ever looked at yourself for any length of time, as you look at yourself in a mirror when you are shaving, or brushing your hair, or when you make-up? Have you ever spent ten minutes, as you do at a mirror, watching yourself, without any choice, without any sense of judgment or evaluation, just watching yourself? That is the main issue.

SAANEN
20 JULY 1971

3

CAN WE UNDERSTAND OURSELVES?

The problem of self-knowledge is the problem of looking. To look without fragmentation, without the "me". Analysis, dreams and sleep. The problem of the "observer" and of time. "When you look at yourself without the eyes of time, who is there to look?"

Questions: *Are some images necessary? Is evaluation vitiated by our state of confusion? Conflict.*

MOST OF US live a very superficial life and are content to lead such a life, meeting all our problems superficially and thereby increasing them, because our problems are extraordinarily complex, very subtle and need deep penetration and understanding. Most of us like to treat our problems at a superficial level according to the old tradition, or we try to adjust ourselves to a modern tendency, so we never resolve totally and completely any of our problems, such as war, conflict, violence and so on. We also tend to look only on the surface, not knowing how to penetrate deeply within ourselves; either we observe ourselves with a certain disgust, with a certain foregone conclusion, or we look at ourselves hoping to change what we see.

I think it is important, that we should understand ourselves totally, completely, because as we said the other

298

day, we are the world and the world is us. This is an absolute fact; it is not merely a verbal statement or a theory, but something that one feels deeply, with all the agony of it, the suffering, the pain, the brutality, the fragmentation, the division of nationalities and religions. And one can never solve any of these problems without really understanding oneself, because the world is oneself; and if I understand myself there is a living at a totally different dimension. Is it possible for each one of us to understand ourselves, not only at the superficial level of our minds, but also to penetrate the deep levels of our being? That is what we are going to talk over together this morning; when we say we are going to talk it over together, it doesn't mean that I talk and you listen—we are going to share it together.

How is one to look at oneself? Is it possible to look at oneself completely without the division of the conscious and the deeper layers of consciousness, of which we are perhaps completely unaware? Is it possible to observe, see the whole movement of the "me", the self, the "what I am", with a non-analytical mind, so that in the very observation itself there is instantly a total understanding? That is what we are going to investigate; it is a very important problem, to discover whether one can go beyond oneself and find reality, to come upon something that is not measurable by the mind, to live without any illusion. This has been the major aim of every religion throughout the world; and in the process of this search to go beyond oneself, they have been caught in various myths, the Christian myth, the Hindu myth, the whole culture of myths which is unnecessary and totally irrelevant.

Now is it possible to look at ourselves non-analytically and therefore observe without the "me" observing? I want to understand myself and I know the "me" is very complex; it is a living thing, not something dead; it is a living, vital, moving thing, it is not just an accumulation of memories, experiences, and knowledge. It is a living thing as society is a living thing, because we have created it. Now, is it possible to look without the observer looking at the thing called the observed? If there is the observer looking, then he must look through fragmentation, through division and where there is division, both in myself and outwardly, there must be conflict. Outwardly, the national conflicts, the religious conflicts, the economic conflicts, and inwardly there is this vast field, not only superficially but a wide area about which we know almost nothing. So, if in looking there is this division as the "I" and the "not I", as the observer and the observed, as the thinker and the thought, as the experiencer and the experience, then there must be conflict.

One asks whether it is possible—I am not saying it is, or it is not; we are going to find out for ourselves—to observe oneself without this division. And to find that out, we hope to come to that state of perception which is without division, but not through analysis—when there is a division between the analyser and the thing analysed. In observing myself, there is the actual fact of this division. When I observe myself I say, "This is good, This is bad", "This is right, this is wrong", "This has value, this has no value", "This has relevancy and that has not". Therefore, when I look at myself, the observer is conditioned by the culture in which he has lived; so the observer is the memory, the observer is the entity that is conditioned —the "me". According to that conditioned background of the "me", I judge, I evaluate; I observe myself according to that culture, and according to my conditioning I hope to bring about a change in the observed. This is what we are doing all the time: hoping to change what is observed through analysis, through control, through reformation and so on. That is a fact.

And I want to find out why this division exists, so I begin to analyse to discover the cause. The analysis is not only to find the cause, but one also hopes to go beyond it. I am angry, greedy, envious, brutal, violent, neurotic, or whatever it is, and I begin to analyse the cause of this neurotic state.

Analysis is part of our culture because we have been trained from childhood to analyse, hoping that in this way we shall solve all our problems. Volumes have been written on it; the psychologists hope to find the cause of neurosis, understand it and go beyond.

Now what is involved in analysis? It implies time, doesn't it? I need a great deal of time to analyse myself. I must very carefully examine every reaction, every incident, every thought and trace it to its source; all that takes time. Meanwhile other incidents are going on, other happenings, other reactions, which I am incapable of immediately understanding. That is one point: it takes time.

And analysis also implies that everything that is analysed must be final and complete, and if it is not (which it can't be), then that finding is incorrect, and with this faulty analysis I proceed to examine the next experience, the next incident, the next bit of the puzzle. So, all the time I am working from a false premise, consequently my judgments and evaluations are wrong and I am increasing the margin of error. Analysis, by its very nature, implies an analyser and the person or thing analysed, whether the analyser is the analyst, the psychologist, or you yourself; and the analyser in his examination nourishes and sustains the division, and therefore increases the conflict. Analysis implies all these things: time, evaluation of every experience and of every thought completely (which is not possible), and the division between the observer and the observed that increases conflict.

Now I can analyse my surface mind, its superficial daily activity, but how am I to understand, to investigate the much deeper layers, because I want to understand myself totally, right through? I don't want to leave any corner or dark spot unexamined; I want to analyse everything, so that nothing remains which the mind has not completely understood. If there is a corner that has not been examined, then that corner distorts all thought, all action. But analysis implies the postponement of action. When I am analysing myself, I am not acting; I am waiting until my analysis is over, then perhaps I shall act rightly; therefore analysis is the denial of action. Action means now, not tomorrow. Seeing all this, how can the mind understand its deep, hidden layers completely? All this is implied in understanding myself.

Can understanding come through dreams? That is, is it possible during sleep for dreams to reveal the deep layers of the unconscious, or the thing that is hidden? The specialists say that you must dream and that if you do not, it indicates a certain kind of neurosis. They also say that dreams help you to understand all the activities of the hidden mind. So one must enquire into the meaning of dreams and whether we should dream at all. Or are dreams merely in a symbolic form the continuation of our daily life?

During the day the mind is occupied with all the trivialities of daily life—office work, domesticity, the quarrels and the irritations of relationship, image fighting image, and so on. Then, just before you go to sleep, there is a taking stock of everything that has happened throughout the day. Doesn't this happen to you just before you fall asleep? You relive everything: "You should have done this, you ought to have said that or said it differently"; you go over the whole period of the day, all your thoughts, all your activities, how you were angry, jealous and all the rest of it.

Now, why does the mind do this? Why does it take stock of the day's happenings and events? Is it not because the mind wants to establish order? The mind goes over the day's activities because it wants to bring everything into order; otherwise when you fall asleep, the brain goes on working and tries to bring order in itself, because the brain can only function normally, healthily, in complete order. So if there is no order during the day, the brain tries to establish order while the body is quiet, is asleep, and the establishment of that order is part of the dreams. Do you accept all that the speaker is saying?

Audience: No.

KRISHNAMURTI: No? I am delighted. (*Laughter.*) Don't agree or disagree. Find out for yourself, not according to some philosopher, to some analyst, or psychologist, but find out for yourself. As long as there is disorder in your daily life, the brain must establish order otherwise it cannot function healthily, normally, and efficiently. And when there is disorder, dreams are necessary to bring about order either deep down or at a superficial level.

Examining all this one asks is it necessary to dream at all because it is very important not to dream; it is very important to have a mind that is completely quiet when you are asleep, then the whole mind, the whole brain, the whole body can rejuvenate itself. But if the brain goes on working, working while you are asleep, then it becomes exhausted, therefore neurotic, overstrained and all the rest of it. So is it possible not to dream at all?

I am asking all these questions because I want to understand myself: It is part of understanding myself. We are not merely investigating dreams, assessing the importance or non-importance of dreaming. Unless there is a deep understanding of oneself, all action becomes superficial and contradictory and creates more and more problems.

The old tradition says that to understand myself I must analyse, introspect; but I see the falseness of all this. I reject it because it is false although most of the psychologists say the opposite. And in observing oneself one asks: why does one dream at all and is it possible for the whole mind to be completely quiet when one is asleep? I am not asking this question, you are. I am only suggesting it to you; *you* have to find out. Now, how are you going to find out?

I realise that when the organism is quiet, completely still, the body is able to gather energy and is capable of functioning more efficiently. When the body has no rest, is driven from morning until night without a pause, it soon wears out, breaks down; but if the body can rest for ten or twenty minutes during the day, then it has more energy. The mind is very active, watching, observing, criticising, evaluating, struggling and all the rest of it. And when it goes to sleep, the same momentum is kept going. So I am asking myself whether during sleep the mind can be absolutely quiet. Just see the beauty of the question, not the answer yet. Unless the body is extraordinarily still, without any movement without any gestures or nervous twitches, and all the things that one does, unless it is absolutely quiet (not forced to be quiet) and relaxed, it cannot recuperate, it cannot gather energy.

Therefore I want to find out whether the mind can be absolutely quiet during the night when it is asleep; and I see it can only be quiet if every incident, every happening during the day is understood instantly, not carried over. If I carry over a problem from one day to the next, the mind is continuously engaged; but if the mind can solve the problem immediately, today, then it is finished. Is it possible for the mind each day to be so totally aware that problems no longer exist? By the evening, you have a clear, clean slate. If you do this, not just play with it, actually work at it, you will find that when the brain needs rest, it becomes very quiet, completely still; even ten minutes rest is enough. And if you pursue this very deeply, you will find that dreams become totally unnecessary because there is nothing to dream about; you are not concerned with your future, whether you are going to be a great doctor, a great scientist, or a brilliant writer, or whether you are going to reach enlightenment the day after tomorrow; you are not concerned with the future at all. I am afraid you don't see the beauty of all this! The mind is no longer projecting anything in time.

Now, having stated all that, can the mind, which is really the observer (not only the visual observer, the eyes and so on), can the mind observe without division? You understand the question? Can the mind observe without the division between the observer and the observed, because there is only the observed, not the observer.

Let us examine what the observer is. Surely the observer is the past, be it the past of a few seconds ago, of yesterday, or of many, many years, living as a conditioned entity in a particular culture. The observer is the sum total of past experiences. The observer is also knowledge. The observer is within the field of time. When he says I will be "that", he has projected "that" from his past knowledge—whether it be pleasure, pain, suffering, fear, delight, and so on—he says I must become that. The past therefore is going through the present, which is modified and which he calls the future, but it is really a projection of the past: so the observer is the past. You live in the past, don't you? Just think of it. You are the past, you live in the past and that is your life. Past memories, past delights, past remembrances, the things that gave you pleasure and displeasure, the failures, the disappointments, the lack of fulfillment and the misery, everything is in the past. And through the eyes of the observer you judge the present, which is living, moving, not a static, dead thing.

When I look at myself, I am looking with the eyes of the past; so I condemn, judge, evaluate, "This is right", "This is wrong", good or bad according to my particular culture and tradition, according to the knowledge and experience which I have gathered. Therefore it prevents observation of the living thing, which is the "me". And that "me" may not be "me" at all, because I only know the "me" as the past. When the Muslim says that he is a Muslim, he is the past, conditioned by the culture in which he has been brought up; it is the same with the Catholic or the Communist.

So when we talk about living, we are talking about living in the past; and there is conflict between the past and the present, because I am conditioned. I cannot meet the living present unless I break down my conditioning, and my conditioning is deliberately brought about by my parents, my grandparents, to keep me in the narrow line of their belief, of their tradition, to continue with their mischief and their misery. We are doing that all the time; we live in the past, not only through our conditioning, through the culture in which we have lived, but also through every experience, incident and happening in our life. I see a beautiful sunset and I think how marvellous it is with the light, the shadows, the rays of the sun on the distant hills, and it has already been stored up as memory and tomorrow I say I must look at the sunset again and see its beauty. Then I struggle to find it, and when I can't, I go to a museum and the whole circus begins.

Now, can I look at myself with eyes that have never been touched by time? Time involves analysis, time involves holding on to the past, time involves this whole process of dreaming, recollecting, gathering the past and holding it, all that. Can I look at myself without the eyes of time? Put that question to yourself. Don't say you can or cannot. You don't know. And when you look at yourself without the eyes of time, what or who is there to look? Don't answer me, please. Do you understand my question? I have looked at myself with the quality, the nature and the structure of time, the past. I have looked at myself through the eyes of the past; I have no other eyes to look. I have looked at myself as a Catholic, or something else, which is the past, so my eyes are incapable of looking at "what is" without time, which is the past.

Now I am asking a question, which is: can the eyes observe without the past?

Let me put it differently. I have an image of myself, created and imposed upon me by the culture in which I have lived; I also have my own particular image of myself, what I should be and what I am not. In fact, we have a great many images; I have an image about you, about my wife, my children, my political leader, my priest, and so on; so I have dozens of images. Don't you have them?

Questioner: Yes.

KRISHNAMURTI: Now, how can you look without an image, because if you look with an image, it is obviously a distortion? You were angry with me yesterday, so I have created an image about you, that you are no longer my friend, that you are ugly and all the rest of it. If I look at you with that image next time I meet you, that image will distort my perception. That image is of the past, as are all my images, and I dare not get rid of any of those images because I don't know what it would be like to look without an image, so I cling to images. The mind depends on an image for its survival. I wonder if you are following all this. So can the mind observe without any image, without the image of the tree, cloud, hills, without the image of my wife, my children, my husband? Can the mind be without any image in relationship?

It is the image that brings conflict in relationship. I cannot get on with my wife because she has bullied me; that image has been built up, day after day, and it prevents any kind of relationship; we may sleep together but that is irrelevant; so there is conflict. Can the mind look, observe without any image what has been put together by time? That means, can the mind observe without any image? Can it observe without the observer, which is the past, which is the "me"? Can I look at you without the interference of the conditioned entity, which is the "me"?

What do you say? "Impossible!" How do you know it is impossible? The moment you say it is not possible, then you have blocked yourself and if you say it is possible, it is also blocking you; but if you say let's find out, let's examine, let's go into it, then you will discover that the mind *can* observe without the eyes of time. And when it so observes, then what is there to be observed?

I started out learning about myself; I have explored all the possibilities of analysis, and I see that the observer is the past. The observer is much more complex; one can go much deeper into it. I see that the observer is the past, and the mind lives in the past because the brain has evolved through time which is the past. And in the past there is security—my house, my wife, my belief, my status, my position, my fame, my shoddy little self; in that there is great safety and security. So I am asking if the mind can observe without any of that, and if it can, what is there to see except the hills, the flowers, the colours, the people— you follow? Is there anything in me to be observed? Therefore, the mind is totally free.

You may ask what is the point of the mind being free. The point is that such a mind has no conflict, such a mind is completely quiet and peaceful, not violent, and it is only this quality of mind that can create a new culture, a new culture not a counter culture to the old, something totally different in which we shall have no conflict at all. One has discovered all this, not as a theory, not as a verbal statement, but one has seen this actual fact within oneself, that the mind can observe totally without the eyes of the past; then the mind is something completely new, completely different.

Questioner: I think we all see the danger of these images but surely, at certain times, some images are necessary. For instance, if somebody rushes at you with a knife, the image you have will help to save your life. How can we choose between useful and useless images?

KRISHNAMURTI: We all live with images, the questioner says, and some are useful, necessary and protective; others are not. The image of a tiger when you are in the jungle is protective, but the image that you have about your wife, your husband, or whatever it is, that image destroys relationship. The questioner asks, how is one to choose between which images to keep, and which to discard.

First of all, why do you choose at all? Listen to my question, please. Why do we choose? What is the structure, the nature of choice? I only choose, don't I, when I am uncertain. When there is uncertainty, when there is confusion. If there is no clarity then I choose, I say that I don't know what to do, perhaps I will do this or that. When you see something very clearly, is there any need to choose? Surely, it is only the confused mind that chooses. And we have made choice one of the most important things in life. We talk about freedom to choose, to choose this or that, to choose our political party, our politicians. So I ask myself, why do I choose at all? I choose between two coloured materials, but that is not what we are talking about. We are talking about choice which is the outcome of uncertainty, of confusion, where there is no clarity; then I have to choose, but a mind that is very clear has no choice. Now, is your mind confused? (I am coming to the question, Sir.) Obviously your mind is confused, otherwise you wouldn't all be sitting here. And out of that confusion you choose and increase the confusion.

You have so many images, some are protective, others are not necessary. Is there any choice? Listen carefully. Is choice necessary there at all? I have many, many images about everything, as well as opinions, judgments and evaluations; the more opinions I have, the more I think my mind is clear. And from all these images I try to decide which are important and relevant and which are not. Now why do I have to choose? It is because I am uncertain which images to keep and which to discard. I choose when I do not know which images to discard. Now who is the entity that is choosing? Knowledge, surely, and knowledge is the past—the past, which has created all these images, chooses which it shall keep and which it shall discard. So you are choosing according to the past and therefore your choice invariably must be confused; therefore, don't choose! Wait! See it! If you don't choose, then what happens? You won't obviously be run over by the bus. But it is the very choice, the choosing, that sustains the images.

Questioner: You mentioned that we are all confused otherwise we wouldn't be here.

KRISHNAMURTI: That's partly it, Sir.

Questioner: If I am confused how can I possibly listen to you without evaluating everything that you say?

KRISHNAMURTI: That's just it. That's what we are afraid of. The questioner says that if I am confused, which I am, how can I possibly listen to you clearly—right? But you are not listening, are you?

Questioner: Sometimes.

KRISHNAMURTI: Sometimes? We are not talking about "sometimes", we are asking: are you listening now? You know, when you listen with attention, with affection, with care, are you confused? It is only when you are not listening and you want to listen that confusion arises. At the actual moment of listening where is the confusion? And when you remember the moment when you listened so completely, you say to yourself, "I wish to goodness I could be like that again". And this produces conflict. See what has happened. When you say: how am I to get back to that state of listening, the memory of that state of listening remains and the actual fact has gone, so your memory then says I must listen more carefully; so there is a contradiction. Whereas if you listen completely, entirely, wholly, at the actual moment of listening there is no confusion and that moment is enough. Don't try to get back to it. Pick it up again ten minutes later, but during those ten minutes be aware that you have been inattentive.

Questioner: Will this new culture that is emerging from the still mind be peaceful.

KRISHNAMURTI: I don't know, Sir, that is a supposition.

Questioner: I haven't finished it . . .

KRISHNAMURTI: Oh! I beg your pardon.

Questioner: Well, if . . .

KRISHNAMURTI: Not if!

Questioner: If I were peaceful, would I be in conflict with the present structure of society?

KRISHNAMURTI: What do we mean by, "In conflict with the present structure"? Go on, investigate, Sir; don't wait for me to do it.

Questioner: Conflict through competition.

KRISHNAMURTI: Competition? I want to establish myself, my ideas, my beliefs and so on. That is exactly what they are doing, isn't it?

Questioner: If somebody says to you take this gun and shoot somebody, then you are in conflict.

KRISHNAMURTI: If somebody asks me to take a gun and shoot somebody I won't. What is the question?

Questioner: If I say I won't, then you are in conflict.

KRISHNAMURTI: Certainly not.

Questioner: They will say you are.

KRISHNAMURTI: All right, they put me in prison, but I am not in conflict with them. If the drug culture says you must take drugs and I say that I won't, are they in conflict, or am I? I am not; they are. What is the point of all this?

Questioner: There are two sides to conflict.

KRISHNAMURTI: No. There are not two sides, I don't want to have conflict. As a human being, I have investigated this whole business of conflict, outwardly and inwardly, and I have gone into it very thoroughly and let us suppose that I have completely eliminated all sense of violence within me. Now, if you are in conflict, what am I to do? You ask me to take a gun and shoot somebody and when I refuse, you get angry, you become violent, you beat me. That is your problem, not my problem.

Questioner: You say he is in conflict with me, but I am not in conflict with him.

KRISHNAMURTI: But I am not in conflict. Why should I shoot anybody? Look, Sir, you are not offering me a gun—here, now—are you? Then why does the problem arise? You see, the problem arises because we are beginning to speculate. "What will you do if you are peaceful?" First find out how to live peacefully and then ask the question.

Questioner: Does conflict come from imagination?

KRISHNAMURTI: When two people quarrel, does it come from imagination? Look at the question. I am attached, dependent on you, I depend on you emotionally, psychologically, physically, sexually and economically; I depend on you totally. And then one beautiful morning you tell me to go, because you like somebody else, so there is conflict—right? Is that imagination? It is a fact. And when you turn against me I am lost, because I depend on you for companionship and for so many other things; that is not imagination; it is an actual fact.

Then I begin to find out why I am dependent on you; I want to find out because it is part of self-knowledge. Aren't you all dependent on somebody? Psychologically, inwardly? Can you stand completely alone—inwardly, you understand? Outwardly you can't stand alone because you need the milkman, the postman, the bus driver and so on. But inwardly you can be completely alone, not dependent on anybody. So I have to find out why I am outwardly dependent.

I am lonely and I don't know how to go beyond this loneliness. I am frightened of it deep down and I am incapable of resolving this terrible thing called loneliness. Don't you know all this? Therefore not knowing how to resolve it, I attach myself to people, to ideas, to groups, to activities, to demonstrations, to climbing the mountains and all the rest of it. If only I could resolve totally this problem of loneliness so that it doesn't exist at all. How am I to be beyond this loneliness which man has inwardly fought at all times? He feels lonely, empty, insufficient, incomplete and he says there is God, there is this, there is that; he projects an outside agency. How can the mind free itself from this terrible burden of what it calls loneliness? Have you ever realised what horrors we commit out of this feeling of loneliness? We will go into this next time.

SAANEN
22 JULY 1971

4

LONELINESS

Preoccupation with oneself. Relationship. Action in relationship and daily life. Images isolate: the understanding of image-building. "Self-concern is my major image." Relationship without conflict means love.

Questions: *Can the self have unmotivated passion? Images; drugs and stimulants.*

MOST OF US realise, when we dare look at it, that we are terribly lonely, isolated human beings. Whether we are consciously or unconsciously aware of it, we want to escape from it, because we do not know what lies behind and beyond it; being frightened, we run away from it through attachment, through activity and every form of religious or worldly entertainment. This is fairly obvious when one observes it in oneself. We isolate ourselves by our everyday activities, by our attitude and our way of thinking; although we may have an intimate relationship with somebody, we are always thinking about ourselves. The result of this is more isolation, more loneliness, a greater dependence on outward things, greater attachments and the resultant suffering which arises from it. I do not know if you are aware of all this.

Perhaps we are sitting here, we could become aware of this thing called loneliness and of the isolation, dependency and suffering it brings. This is going on in ourselves all the time. If one is observant one can see that our whole activity is self-centred. We are thinking about ourselves endlessly: about our health, that we must meditate, that we must change; we want a better job with more money, a better relationship. "I want to attain enlightenment"; "I must achieve something in this life—"me" and "my life", my worries, my problems.

This eternal preoccupation with oneself is going on all the time; we are devoted to ourselves. That is an obvious fact. And whether we go to an office or to a factory, do social work or are concerned with the welfare of the world, our self-concern motivates all our activities; it is always "me" first. This self preoccupation which operates in daily life and relationship does bring about isolation. This again is fairly obvious, and if one goes into it very deeply one discovers that this isolation is an awareness of being completely alone, cut off, not having a relationship with anybody or anything. You may be amongst a crowd, or sitting with a friend, when suddenly this sense of utter isolation, of being completely cut off from everybody comes upon you. I do not know if you have noticed this or if it is something you have never experienced. When we become aware of this loneliness, then we try to escape by being occupied through domestic strife, or various forms of entertainment, by trying to meditate, and so on.

Surely, all this indicates that the mind, whether it is shallow or deep, superficial or merely caught in technological knowledge, must cut itself off from every form of relationship if it is constantly occupied with itself. Relationship is the most important thing in life, because if you don't have a right relationship with the one, you cannot possibly have it with any other human being. You can imagine that you will have a better relationship with another, but it is merely at the verbal level and therefore illusory. If you understand that relationship between two human beings is the same as relationship with the rest of the world, then isolation, loneliness, has quite a different meaning.

So what is relationship? We are trying to find out why human beings are so desperately lonely. Not having love, but wanting to be loved they cut themselves off, physically and psychologically and thereby become neurotic. Most people are neurotic, slightly unbalanced, caught in some particular idiosyncrasy. It seems, if you examine it closely, that all this arises from the utter lack of relationship. So before we can understand how to bring an end to this loneliness and suffering, to this ache and anxiety of human existence, we must first of all go into this question of relationship—what it means to be related.

Are we related at all with another? Thought asserts that we are related, but actually we may not be, even though one human being may have an intimate, a sexual relationship with another. Unless one deeply understands the truth about relationship, it appears that human beings must inevitably end in sorrow, in confusion and in conflict. They may accept various forms of belief, or do social work, but all that has no value, unless they have established between themselves a relationship in which there is no conflict whatever. Is that possible? Can you and I be related? Perhaps you could have a very good relationship with me, because soon I am going away and then it is finished. Can there be a relationship between two human beings if each one is occupied with himself?—if each one is concerned with his own ambitions and worries, his opposition in the world and all the absurdity that human beings go through? When a human being is caught in that net, can he have any relationship with another?

Please, follow all this. Can there be any relationship between a man and a woman when one is a Catholic and the other is a Protestant, when one is a Hindu and the other is a Buddhist?

What then is relationship? It seems to me that it is one of the most important things in life, because living is relationship. If there is no relationship, there is no living at all; then life merely becomes a series of conflicts, ending in separation or divorce, in loneliness, with all the fears, anxieties, problems of attachment, and all the things that are involved in this sense of being completely isolated. I am sure you know all this. One observes how extraordinarily vital relationship is in life, and how very few human beings have broken down the barrier that exists between themselves and another. To break down this barrier with all its implications—not just the physical barrier—one has to go deeply into this question of action.

What is action? Action is not future or past action, but *acting*. Is it the result of a conclusion and acting according to that conclusion? Or is it based on some belief and acting according to the belief. Is it based on some experience and acting according to that experience or knowledge? If it is, then action is always in the past, our relationship is always in the past, never in the present.

If I have a relationship with another—and relationship obviously is action—throughout the days, weeks or years of that relationship I have built an image and I act according to that image, and the other acts according to the image which he has; so the relationship is not between *us* but between these two images. Please do observe your own minds, your own activity in relationship, and you will soon find out the truth and validity of this statement. Our relationship is based on images, and how can there be a relationship with another, if it is merely the relationship of these images?

I am concerned with having a relationship in which there is no conflict whatsoever, in which I am not using or exploiting another, either sexually, for reasons of pleasure, or for the sake of companionship. I see very clearly that conflict destroys any form of relationship, so I must resolve that conflict at the very centre, not at the periphery. And I can only put an end to conflict by understanding action, not only in relationship but in daily life. I want to find out if all my activities are isolating, in the sense that I have built a wall round myself; the wall being myself concerned with myself, with my future, my happiness, my health, my God, with my belief, my success, my misery—you follow? Or is it that relationship has nothing whatsoever to do with me or myself? Myself is the centre, and all the activities that are concerned with my happiness, my satisfaction, my glory must isolate. Where there is isolation there must be attachment and dependency when there is uncertainty in that attachment and dependency; then there is suffering, and suffering implies isolation in any relationship. I see all this very clearly, not verbally but actually—it is a fact.

For many years I have built images about myself and about another; I have isolated myself through my activities, through my beliefs and so on. So my first question is—how am I to be free of these images?—the images of my God, my conditioning, that I must achieve fame or enlightenment (which is the same thing), that I must achieve success and so I am afraid of being a failure. I have so many images about myself and about you. How am I to be free of them? Can I end the building of images through the analytical process? Obviously not.

Then what am I to do? It is a problem and I must end it, not carry it over to the next day. If I do not end it today, then the problem creates disorder, a disturbance, and the brain needs order to function healthily, normally, not neurotically. I must establish order now, during the day, otherwise the mind worries about it, has dreams and is incapable of being fresh the next morning; so I must end this problem.

How am I to prevent this building of images? By not creating a super-image—obviously. I have many images and not being able to be free of them the mind unfortunately invents a super-image, the higher self, the Atman; or it introduces some outside agency, either spiritual or the "Big Brother" of the communist world. So without creating a higher, nobler image, there must be the ending of all the images which I have created. I see that if I have one single image, there is no possibility of any relationship, because images separate and where there is separation there must be conflict, not only nationally but between human beings; that is clear. Then how am I to be rid of every image which I have gathered, so that the mind is completely free, fresh and young, so that it can observe anew the whole movement of life?

First of all, I must find out non-analytically how the images come into being. That is, I must learn to observe. Is observation based on analysis? I observe, I see—is that the result of analysis, or practice, of time? Or is it an act outside of time? Man has always tried to go beyond time by various tricks and they have all failed. Suspecting that perhaps he is incapable of getting rid of these innumerable images, he has created a super-image, and to that image he has become a slave, therefore he is not free. Whether that super-image is the soul, the higher self, the State or anything else, it is still not freedom: it is another image. Therefore I am vitally interested in ending all images, because only then is there a possibility of having a relationship with another; my concern is to find out if it is at all possible to end the images *instantly*, not chase one image after another. That will obviously lead nowhere.

So I must find out if I can break the mechanism of the mind which builds images and at the same time go into the question of what it is to be aware; because that may solve my problem, which is the ending of all images. That gives freedom, and when there is freedom then only is there a possibility of having a true relationship in which every form of conflict has come to an end.

What does this awareness mean? It implies an attention in which there is no choice whatsoever. I can't choose one image instead of the other, then there is no ending of that image. So I must find out what it is to be aware, in which there is no choice at all, but only pure observation, pure seeing.

Now, what is seeing? How do I look at a tree, or a mountain, at the hills, the moon, the flowing waters? There is not only visual observation, but also the mind has an image about the tree, the cloud and the river. That river has a name; it makes a sound which is pleasant or unpleasant. I am always observing, am aware of things, in terms of like and dislike, in terms of comparison. Is it possible to observe, to listen to that river without any choice, any resistance and attachment, without any verbalisation? Please do this as we are talking—it is your morning-exercise!

Can I listen to that river without any sense of the past? Can I observe these various images without any choice?— which means without condemning any one of them, or being attached to them, but just observe without any preference. You can't do it, can you? Why not? Is it because my mind has become used to prejudices and preferences? Is it because it is lazy and has not sufficient energy? Or is it that my mind does not really want to be free of images and wants to hold on to one particular image? So it means that the mind refuses to see the fact that all existence is relationship, and when there is conflict in that relationship, then life becomes a misery and loneliness and confusion follow. Does the mind see the truth non-verbally, that where there is conflict there is no relationship?

How can one be free of the images that one has? First of all I must find out how these images come into being, what is the mechanism that creates them. You can see that at the moment of actual relationship, that is when you are talking, when there are arguments, when there are insults and brutality, if you are not completely attentive at that moment, then the mechanism of building an image starts. That is, when the mind is not completely attentive at the moment of action, then the mechanism of building images is set in motion. When you say something to me which I do not like—or which I like—if at that moment I am not completely attentive, then the mechanism starts. If I am attentive, aware, then there is no building of images. When the mind is fully awake at that actual moment, not distracted, not frightened, not rejecting what is being said, then there is no possibility of building an image. Try this—do it during the day.

So I have found how to prevent the building of images; but what happens to all the images that I have gathered? You are following the problem? Apparently this is not your problem, because if it were the real, deep, vital problem in your life, you would have solved it for yourself instead of sitting here waiting for me to find the answer for you. Now, what happens to all the images which you have collected? Do you know you have many images hidden away in the cupboard of your mind? Can you resolve them all, bit by bit, or would that take an infinite time? While you are dissolving one image, you are already creating others, so there is no ending to the gradual process of getting rid of one image after another. So you have discovered a truth, which is, that you cannot get rid of the images one by one; therefore the mind that really sees the truth of this is totally aware when it is creating an image. In that attention all the other images go away. I wonder if you see this.

Images, then, are formed when the mind is not attentive; and most of our minds are inattentive. Occasionally we give attention, but for the rest of the time we are inattentive. When you are aware of one image attentively, and you are also attentively aware of the whole mechanism of the building of images and how it operates, then in that attention the building of all images comes to an end; whether they be of the past, the present or of the future. What matters is the state of attention, not how many images you have. Do, please, try and understand this, because it is most important. If you can really grasp this, then you have understood completely all the machinery of the mind.

Most of us, unfortunately, have not been able to solve our problems; we don't know how to deal with them, so we live with them, they become our habit and they are like impenetrable armour. If you have a problem which has not been resolved, you have no energy; the energy that you have is taken up by the problem; if you have no energy, that too becomes a habit. So if you are at all serious, if you really want to live a life in which there is no conflict whatsoever, then you have to find out how to end a human problem instantly, immediately; which means that you give complete attention to the problem and that you are not seeking an answer to it. Because if you are trying to find an answer, then you are looking beyond the

317

problem, whereas if you remain with the problem and are completely attentive, then in the problem itself—not beyond it—is the answer.

Let me put it differently. We all know what suffering is, both physical and psychological, that is inwardly. One can deal with physical pain by various remedies and also by not allowing the memory of that pain to remain. If you are aware of the pain, and in that very awareness you see the memory of the past, then the pain disappears; therefore you have energy to meet the next pain, when it comes. We all have suffered psychologically in various ways, either with great intensity or to a lesser degree—we have all had suffering of one kind or another. When we suffer, instinctively we want to run away from it—through religion, through entertainment, reading books, through anything to get away from the suffering.

Now if the mind is attentive and does not move away from suffering at all, then you will see that out of total attention comes not only energy—which means passion—but also that suffering comes to an end. In the same way, all images can end instantly when there is no preference for any image; this is very important. When you have no preference, you have no prejudice. Then you are attentive, then you can look. In that observation there is not only the understanding of the building of images, but also the ending of all images.

So I see the importance of relationships, and there *can* be a relationship without any conflict, which means love. Love is not an image; it not a pleasure; it is not desire. Love is not something that can be cultivated; it is not dependent on memory. Can I live a daily life without any kind of self-concern, because the self-concern is my major image? Can I live without that major image? Then action does not bring loneliness, isolation and suffering.

Questioner: When one looks within and seems to experience a deep unmotivated passion to understand, with a bit of candour one finds that this feeling is actually a wish to experience reality. Can the self, which is all we know, have this unmotivated passion and see the essential difference between these two feelings?

KRISHNAMURTI: First of all, what is the self, the "me"? Surely, that "me" is the result of our education, of our conflicts, of our culture, of our relationship with the rest of the world; that "me" is the result of the propaganda which we have been subjected to for five thousand years. It is that "me" which is attached to our furniture, our wives or husbands and so on. It is that "me" which says "I want to be happy. I must be successful, I have achieved". It is that "me" which says I am a Christian, a communist or a Hindu. There are all those terrible divisions—the "me" is all that, isn't it?

Can that "me" which is isolated, which by its very structure and nature is limited and therefore creates division, can that "me" have any passion at all? Obviously not. It can have the passion of pleasure, which is something quite different from the passion we are talking about. Only with the ending of the "me" is there passion; it is only a mind that is free from all prejudices, opinions, judgments and all conditioning, that can have passion, energy and intensity, because it is able to see "what is". You agree and say "Yes". Is that merely a verbal statement, or have you really seen the truth of it and are free?

Questioner: Do these images we have waste our energy?

KRISHNAMURTI: It is obvious, isn't it? If I have an image about myself and that is in opposition to your image, there must be conflict, therefore it must waste energy, isn't that so?

Questioner: Can a person who is free from problems have a relationship with someone who is full of problems? (Laughter).

KRISHNAMURTI: Well, you have answered it, haven't you? If you are really free of problems—not just in your imagination—but actually free of every problem that human beings have, such as sorrow, fear, death, love and pleasure, can I have a relationship with you if I have problems? Obviously I can't. Please listen to this: you have no problems and I have problems, then what do I do? Either I shun you, avoid you, or I begin to worship you. I put you on a pedestal and say, "What an extraordinary man you are, because you have no problems." I begin to listen to whatever you say in the hope that you will be able to resolve my problems. And that means I am going to destroy you with my problems. First

319

I pushed you away; now I accept you, worship you, which means I will kill you with my problems.

Questioner: Is there any hope for us? (Laughter).

KRISHNAMURTI: It all depends on you! If you are really serious, if you are deeply interested in resolving your problems completely, then you will have the intensity and vitality to resolve them, but it is no use if you play with them one day and the next day forget about them.

Questioner: What can we do to prevent others from taking drugs?

KRISHNAMURTI: Do you take drugs?

Questioner: No, but I drink coffee and alcohol. Isn't that the same?

KRISHNAMURTI: We drink coffee, we take alcohol, we smoke, and some take drugs. Why do you take them? Coffee and tea are stimulants, aren't they? I don't take them myself, but I know about them. Physiologically you may need some form of stimulant; some people do. Are alcohol and tobacco the same as taking drugs? Go on, answer it.

Questioner: Yes.

KRISHNAMURTI: You say taking alcohol is the same as taking drugs.

(General disagreement.)

KRISHNAMURTI: Don't take sides, please. One says, "No", somebody else says "Yes". Then where are we? I am simply asking why you take any of these things at all. Do you need a stimulant, do you need something to pep you up, to encourage you? Please answer this question. Do you need constant stimulation and entertainment, must you have tea, tobacco, drugs and all the rest of it? Why do you need them?

Questioner: To escape.

KRISHNAMURTI: To escape, to take the easy way out. You drink a glass of wine and you are happy, it is done quickly!

Questioner: Yes.

KRISHNAMURTI: So you need stimulants in various forms. Are you being stimulated now by the speaker?

Questioner: Yes. (Laughter).

KRISHNAMURTI: Please pay a little attention. You say "No" and this gentleman says "Yes". Please investigate. Are you being stimulated at this moment? If you are, then the speaker is just as good as a drug. Then you depend on the speaker as you are dependent on tea, coffee, alcohol or drugs, whatever it is. I am asking why you depend, not whether it is right or wrong, whether you should or should not. Why do you depend on any of these stimulants?

Questioner: We can see what action it has on us, but we don't need to be dependent on it.

KRISHNAMURTI: But you *are* dependent! When the effect wears off you need more stimulants, which means you are dependent. I may take LSD one morning and get a kick out of it, and when it lets me down I need some more; the day after tomorrow I am dependent on it. Now I am asking why the human mind depends—why does it depend on sex, on drugs, on alcohol, on any form of outward stimulation? This is psychological, isn't it? There is a physiological need for tea and coffee because we eat wrongly, we live wrongly, because we overindulge and so on. But why do we want to be stimulated psychologically? Is it because we are so poor in ourselves? Is it because we have not the brain, not the capacity to be something entirely different, that we depend on stimulants?

Questioner: Doesn't alcohol destroy the brain as well as drugs?

KRISHNAMURTI: Alcohol may do it gradually, it may take a number of years, but drugs are very dangerous because they affect future generations, your children. So if you say, "I don't care what happens to my grandson, I am going to take drugs", then that is the end of the argument. But I am asking: what happens to your mind when you depend on *anything*, whatever it is, whether it's tea, coffee, sex, drugs or nationalism?

Questioner: I lose my freedom.

KRISHNAMURTI: You say these things, but you don't live it, do you? When you depend on anything it destroys freedom, doesn't it? It makes you a slave—to alcohol, for instance: you must have your drink, your dry Martini or whatever it is. So gradually your mind becomes dull through dependency. It was established a long time ago in India, that any man who is really religious will never touch any of these things. But you don't care; you say, "I need stimulation."

I once met a man who took LSD and he said that when he went to a museum after taking it, he could see all the colours more brightly, everything stood out more vividly, more sharply, there was great beauty. He may see the lovely light of a sunset more brilliantly, but his mind is gradually being destroyed and after a year or two he becomes just a useless entity. If you think it is worth it, that's up to you. But if you don't, then have nothing whatever to do with it.

SAANEN
25 JULY 1971

5

THOUGHT AND THE IMMEASURABLE

Can thought solve our problems? The function of thought. The field of thought and its projections. Can the mind enter into the immeasurable? What is the factor of illusion? Physical and mental fear and escapes. The mind that is constantly learning.

Questions: *Can one observe without judgment and evaluation? Is perception seeing something totally? Can words be used to describe a non-verbal state?*

SOME OF US feel that the world is so chaotic that if it had been organised by a madman it could not be worse than it is at this present moment. Many feel that there must be environmental, economic and political changes to stop wars, the pollution of the air, and to end the material inequality of the very rich and the very poor. Many consider that these things must be changed first, that if there is an environmental, peripheral transformation, then man will be capable of dealing with himself more reasonably and wisely.

I think the problem goes much deeper, is more complex, and that merely to change things outwardly will have little effect. Having observed the events in the world, the permissive society of the young and the terrible hypocrisy of the older generation, an educated and mature mind is fully aware that the problem is profound and that it demands a totally different way of dealing with it.

One also observes that most believe that all human endeavour can be achieved by thought, whether outwardly going to the moon, or inwardly transforming one's mind and heart. We have given tremendous importance to the functioning of thought. Thought, whether it be logical and objective, or irrational and neurotic, has always played an extraordinarily important role throughout the ages. Thought is measure; and in bringing about order and change in society thought has shown itself very limited. It has apparently not succeeded—it may have done so superficially but not fundamentally. The whole machinery of thinking is responsible for the present condition of the world; there is no denying that. We think that thought can change not only the outward events and happenings—the pollution, the violence and all the rest of it—but that also by careful and skilful usage it can transform human conditioning, the human way of action and our mode of living.

It is obvious that organised thought is necessary; that it requires organised thought, applied objectively and sanely, to change the environment with its pollution and to overcome poverty. The whole technological world in which we live is based on thought with its measurement; and thought can only function when there is space. Thought creates its own space, as time, the distance from here to there. On that the whole modern world is built.

Measurement, with its space, which is the very nature of thinking, is obviously limited, because thought is conditioned. Thought is the response of memory, which is the past; the response of thought when challenged in the past. And thought apparently has not put an end to wars; on

323

the contrary, thought has created wars, it has bred division—religious, economic, social and so on. Thought in itself is also the cause of fragmentation.

So one asks: what is the function of thought which is the response of knowledge? Knowledge is always rooted in the past and out of that thought projects the future, which is really a modification of the activities of the present. So through its knowledge, thought can project the future, what the world "should be"; but apparently the "should be" is never realised. Every philosopher, every so-called religious teacher, has projected a world of the future based upon knowledge of the past; he has projected its opposite, or something which is a response to the past. So thought has never united man. In fact, thought has divided man, because it can only function in knowledge and knowledge is measurable. So thought can never bring about a true relationship between people.

Therefore, I am asking: what is the function of knowledge, which is the known, the past? What is the function of the response to that past, which is thought, in daily life? Have you ever put that question to yourself? One lives and acts by thought; all our calculations, our relationships, our behaviour, are based on thought, on knowledge. That knowledge is more or less measurable; and knowledge is always in the field of the known. So can you and I realise the importance of knowledge yet see its limitations and go beyond it? This is what I want to find out.

I see that if you are always functioning in the field of knowledge, you will always be a prisoner; you will always be limited within either expansive or narrow borders which are measurable. Therefore the mind will be held within the frontiers of knowledge. I am asking myself whether that knowledge which is experience, gathered in the last few days or through many centuries, can free man so that he can function wholly, differently, so that he is not always living in the past, which is knowledge. This question has been put differently by many serious people, specially in the religious world; the scholars, the pundits and gurus who have talked with me have always asked whether man can go beyond time. Action in the field of knowledge is measurable, so unless man is free of that field, he will always be a slave. He may do all kinds of things within that field, but he will always live within the limitations which are time, measure and knowledge.

Please put this question to yourself. Must man always

324

be bound to the past? If he is, then he cannot ever be free; he will always be conditioned. He may project an idea of freedom, of heaven, and escape from the actual fact of time by projecting a belief, a concept, or escape into an illusion—but it is still an illusion.

So I want to find out if man can be free of time and yet still function in this world. Obviously there is chronological time—today, tomorrow, next year and so on. If there were no chronological time I should miss my train, so I realise that there must be time in order to function, but that time is always measurable. The action of time, which is knowledge, is absolutely necessary. But if that is the only way in which I can live and function then I am entirely bound, I am a slave. My mind observes, looks, enquires and wants to find out if it can ever free itself from the shackles of time. The mind rebels against the idea of being a slave to time; being caught in this trap, it rebels against the idea of living in a culture which is based on thought, time and knowledge.

Now the mind wants to find out whether it is possible to go beyond time. Can it enter into the immeasurable—which has its own space—and live in that world, free of time and yet function with time, with knowledge, and all the technological achievements which thought has brought about? This is a very important question.

Can the mind enquire into the quality and nature of the immeasurable?—knowing that any projection by thought, any form of illusion, is still within the field of time, hence of knowledge. Therefore the mind must be entirely free from any movement which might create illusion. It is very easy to imagine one is in a timeless world, to have all kinds of illusions and think one has caught God by the right hand. What is it that creates a fragmentary, neurotic mind which breeds deception and illusion? What makes for such a state, and what is the factor of illusion?

One has to go into this question very carefully. First, you have to be watchful never to deceive yourself under any circumstances, never to be a hypocrite and have double standards—the private standard and the public standard; saying one thing and doing another; thinking one thing and saying something else. That requires tremendous honesty, which means I must find out what is the factor in the mind which brings about this deception and hypocrisy, this double-talk, the various illusions and neurotic distortions; unless the mind is free of any distortion, it cannot possibly enquire into the immeasurable.

What do you think is the cause of illusions?—the illusion of grandeur, the illusion that you have achieved reality and reached enlightenment. One must see for oneself very clearly, without analysis, where distortion takes place; distortion is hypocrisy, it is the use of imagination where it has no place at all. Imagination may be in a place when you are painting a picture, writing a poem or a book, but if imagination says "That exists", then you are caught. So I must not only find out the factor of illusion and distortion, but be completely free of it.

I wonder if you have ever asked yourself whether the mind can be completely free of this distorting factor which governs our every action. The factor of distortion is thought; thought cultivates fear, as thought cultivates pleasure. Thought says, "I must enter into that timeless state because it promises freedom." It wants to achieve, it wants to gain, it wants a greater experience. When thought, which is knowledge, functions rationally, objectively, sanely, it is not a distorting factor. The major factors of distortion are fear and the demand for pleasure through gratification, so the mind must be completely free of fear. Can it? Don't say "Yes" or "No", you do not know. Let's investigate—please, see the importance of this. The factor of distortion is fear, it is the demand for pleasure, gratification, enjoyment—not the pleasure itself, but the *demand* for pleasure. All our moral and religious structure is based on this. So I am asking myself whether the human mind can be completely free of fear. If it cannot be free of fear then distortion takes place.

There is physical fear, the fear of darkness, the fear of the unknown, of losing what one has, the fear of death and of not being loved, the fear of not achieving, of not fulfilling, the fear of loneliness and of having no relationship—the small physical fears and the much more complex and subtle psychological fears. Can the mind be free of all fears, not only at the conscious level but at the deep, psychological levels? The mind must be completely merciless to find this out, otherwise one enters a world of illusion and distortion.

We all know physical pain through ill health and disease. Those pains leave a memory and that memory which is thought, says: You must not have that pain again, take great care. Thought, thinking about the past pain, projects the future pain and therefore is afraid of the future. Now when physical pain occurs, live with it and end it—do not carry it over. If you do not end it instantly, then fear comes in. That is, I have had great pain and I see the importance of not having fear. That is my vital, intense demand, that there must be no fear. When the pain comes you do not identify yourself with it and carry it over, but you go through with it completely and end it. To end that pain, you have to live with it, not say, "How can I get out of it as quickly as possible." When you have pain, can you live with it without self-pity and not complain? You do whatever is necessary to end the pain—but when it has gone it is finished. You do not carry it over as memory. It is thought that carries it over; the pain has gone, but thought—which is the response of memory—has established that memory and says "you must not have that pain again". So when you have pain, is it possible not to build a memory of it? Do you know what this means? It means to be completely aware when you have pain, to be completely attentive, so that the pain is not carried over as memory. Do it, if you are interested in it.

Then there are all the psychological fears which are much more complex; again the complexity is brought about through thought. "I want to be a great man and I am not"—so there is the pain of not achieving. Or I have compared myself with somebody who I think is superior, therefore I feel inferior and I suffer from that. All this is the measurement of thought. And I am afraid of death and the ending of everything I possess. There is the whole psychological complexity of thought. Thought is always wanting to be sure and always frightened of uncertainty, always wanting to achieve, knowing it may fail. There is a battle between the action of thought and thought itself. So can fear end completely?

Sitting here listening to the speaker, at this present moment, you are not afraid; there is no fear because you are listening. And you can't evoke fear, which would be artificial. But you can see that when you are attached or dependent, this is based on fear. You can see your attachments, your psychological dependency on your wife, your husband, your books, or whatever it is. If you watch closely you will discover that the root of that attachment is fear. Not being able to be alone, you want companionship; feeling inadequate, empty, you depend on somebody else. In that you see the whole structure of fear. Being dependent and attached, can you see the involvement of fear in it? And can you be psychologically independent of anyone? Now comes the test. We can play with words, with ideas, but when it comes to the actual fact, we withdraw. When you withdraw and do not face the fact, you are not concerned with the understanding of illusion; you would rather live in an illusion than go beyond it. Don't be a hypocrite: you love to live in an illusion, in deception, so face it. Then you will come upon fear; remain with it, don't fight it. The more you fight it, the more there is fear. But if you understand the whole nature of fear, then, as you observe, you are not only aware of the superficial, conscious fears, but also you penetrate deeply into the inner recesses of your mind. Then fear completely comes to an end and the factor of distortion ends.

If you are pursuing or demanding pleasure, that also is a factor of distortion: "I don't like this guru"; but I like that one"; "My guru is wiser than your guru"; "I will go to the remote corners of the earth to find truth"—but truth is just around the corner, here! When there is a demand for pleasure, in any form, this must be a distorting factor. Enjoyment is right, isn't it? It is beautiful to enjoy the sky, the moon, the clouds, the hills, the shadows—there are lovely things on earth. But the mind, thought, says, "I must have more and more, I must repeat this pleasure tomorrow." On this demand is based the whole habit of drink and drugs, which again is the activity of thought. You see the mountains in the evening light, the snow peaks and the shadows in the dark valley, you enjoy the beauty, the loveliness of it tremendously. Then thought says, "I must see that again tomorrow, it was so beautiful." So thought, demanding pleasure, pursues the experience of the sunset on those hills and sustains this memory; and the next time you see the sunset that memory is strengthened. Can the mind see that sunset, live with it completely at that moment and finish with it—and begin afresh tomorrow? So that the mind is always free from the known.

There is a freedom which is not measurable. You can never say, "I am free"—you understand? It is an abomination. All you can do is to enquire into the function of thought and discover for yourself if there is an action which is not measurable, which is not in the field of the known. A mind that is constantly learning has no fear and

328

perhaps such a mind can then enquire into the immeasurable.

Questioner: Can one observe without any evaluation, without any judgment, without any prejudice? Is that at all possible, or is it just another trick of the mind, a deception? You see a mountain and you recognise that it is a mountain, not an elephant. To differentiate in this way, surely, there must be judgment and evaluation?

KRISHNAMURTI: You see the mountain, you recognise it and the recognition is only possible when a memory of the mountain has been established. Obviously, otherwise you can't recognise it.

Questioner: I remember when I came to Switzerland as a small child and I saw a mountain for the first time, it was without any remembrance. It was very beautiful!

KRISHNAMURTI: Yes, Sir, when you see it for the first time you don't say, "It is a mountain". Then somebody tells you that it is a mountain and the next time you recognise it as such. Now, when you observe, there is the whole process of recognition. You don't confuse the mountain with a house or an elephant, it is a mountain. Then the difficult problem arises: to observe it non-verbally. "That is a mountain", "I like it or I don't like it", "I wish I could live up there", and so on. It is fairly easy just to observe it, because the mountains do not affect your life. But your husband, your wife, your neighbour, your son or daughter, they affect you; therefore, you cannot observe them without evaluation, without the image. This is where the problem arises—can you look at the mountain and at your wife or your husband, without a single image? See what happens! If you can observe without an image, then you are looking at them for the first time, aren't you? Then you are looking at the earth, the stars, the mountains, or the politician, for the first time. That means your eyes are clear, not dimmed with the burden of past memories. That is all. Go into it. Work at it. You will find out the enormous beauty that is in this.

Questioner: If you look at a factory that way, without being aware of what it does to the environment, you cannot act.

329

KRISHNAMURTI: On the contrary, you see that is polluting the air, belching forth smoke, so you want to do something. Don't confuse it, keep it simple. Do it, and you will see what action comes out of it.

Questioner: Is perception seeing something totally, and is it gradual or instantaneous?

KRISHNAMURTI: Can I observe all of myself totally, all the reactions, the fears, the enjoyments and the pursuit of pleasure, all that, at a glance? Or do I have to do it gradually? What do you think? If I do it little by little, look one day at one part of myself, the next day at another part, can it be done that way? Today I look at a fragment of myself and tomorrow at another; what is the relationship of the first fragment to the second one? And in the interval between the perception of the first and the second fragment, other factors have come into being. So this fragmentary examination, observing little by little, leads to a great deal of complexity; in fact, it has no value. My question then is: can I observe non-fragmentarily, totally, on the instant?

I have been conditioned to look at myself, to look at the world fragmentarily—as a Christian, a Communist, a Hindu. I have been brought up in this culture to look at the world fragmentarily. Being conditioned by this culture, I cannot possibly take a total view. My chief concern then is to be free of this culture, this education, and not whether I can see completely or not. To free the mind from fragmentation not to be a Catholic or a Protestant—to wipe away all that! I can wipe away all that instantly when I see the truth of it; I cannot see the truth of it if I love being a Hindu, because that gives me a certain position. I wear a turban and impress a lot of silly people. And I take pleasure in the past, because tradition says, "We are one of the most ancient races"; that gives me great delight. But I can only see the truth when I see the falseness of all that. The truth is in the falseness.

Questioner: You have been using words to describe a non-verbal state of mind. Is not this a contradiction?

KRISHNAMURTI: The description is never the described; I can describe the mountain, but the description is not the mountain, and if you are caught in the description, as most people are, then you will never see the mountain. There is no contradiction. Please be very careful. I did not describe the immeasurable, I said: you cannot enquire into that—whatever it is—unless the mind understands the whole process of thought. So I only described the functioning of thought in action with regard to time and knowledge; to describe the other is impossible.

SAANEN
27 JULY 1971

6

THE ACTION OF WILL AND THE ENERGY
NEEDED FOR RADICAL CHANGE

Great energy needed; its wastage. Will is resistance. Will as assertion of the "me". Is there action without choice, which is not motivated? "To look with eyes that are not conditioned." Choiceless awareness of conditioning. To see and reject the falseness. What love is not. To face the question of death. "The ending of energy as the 'me' is the capacity to look at death." Energy to look at the unknown: supreme energy is intelligence.

Questions: *We understand intellectually, but can't live it; is a man capable? How to listen? Are not feelings and emotions the cause of violence?*

ONE NEEDS a great deal of energy, vitality, interest to bring about a radical change in oneself. If we are interested in outward phenomena, we have to see what we can do with the rest of the world in the process of changing ourselves; and also we must see not only how to conserve energy, but how to increase it. We dissipate energy endlessly, by useless talk, by having innumerable opinions about everything, by living in a world of concepts, formulas and by the everlasting conflict in ourselves. I think all this wastes energy. But beyond that, there is a much deeper cause that dissipates the vital energy that is necessary not only to bring about a change in ourselves, but also to penetrate very deeply beyond the confines of our own thought.

331

The ancients said, control sex, hold your senses on a tight rein, take vows so that you don't dissipate your energy: you must concentrate your energy on God, or whatever it is. All such disciplines are also a wastage of energy, because when you take a vow, it is a form of resistance. It needs energy not only for a superficial external change, but also to bring about a deep, inward transformation of revolution. One must have an extraordinary sense of energy which has no cause, which has no motive, which has the capacity to be utterly quiet, and this very quietness has its own explosive quality. We are going to go into all that.

One sees how human beings waste their energy, in quarrels, in jealousies, in a tremendous sense of anxiety, in the everlasting pursuit of pleasure and in the demand for it; it is fairly obvious that this is a wastage of energy. And is it not also a wastage of energy to have innumerable opinions and beliefs about everything?—how another should behave, what another should do and so on. Is it not a waste of energy to have formulas and concepts? In this culture we are encouraged to have concepts according to which we live. Don't you have formulas and concepts in the sense of having images of how you should be, what should happen?—in the sense of thought which rejects "what is" and formulates "what should be"? All such endeavour is a waste of energy and I hope we can proceed from there.

What is the basic reason behind dissipation of energy? Apart from the cultural patterns that one has acquired of wasting energy, there is a much deeper question, which is: can one function, and carry on daily life without any form of resistance? Resistance is will. I know you are all brought up to use will, to control, in the sense of "you must, you must not, you should, you should not". Will is independent of the fact. Will is the assertion of the self, of the "me", independent of "what is". Will is desire; the manifestation of desire is will. We function superficially, or at great depth, in this assertion of the resistance of desire as will, which is unrelated to the "fact" but dependent on the desire of the "me", of the self.

Knowing what will is, I am asking: is it possible to live in this world without the operation of will at all? Will is a form of resistance, a form of division. "I will" against something "I will not", "I must" against "I must not". So will is building a wall in action against every other form of action. We only know action either as conforming to a formula, to a concept, or as approximating according to an ideal, and acting in relationship to that ideal, to that pattern. That is what we call action and in that there is conflict. There is imitation of what "should be", which we have projected as an ideal according to which we act; therefore there is a conflict between the act and the ideal, because in that there is always an approximation, imitation, conformity. I feel that is a total wastage of energy and I am going to show why.

I hope we are watching our own activities, our own minds, to see how we exercise will in action. To repeat, will is independent of the fact, of "what is"; it depends on the self, on what it wants—not on "what is", but on what it wants. And that want is depending on circumstances, on the environment, the culture and so on; it is divorced from the fact. Therefore there is contradiction and resistance against "what is", and that is a wastage of energy.

Action means the doing now—not tomorrow, not having acted. Action is in the present. Can there be action without an idea, without a formula, without a concept?—an action in which there is no resistance as will. If there is will there is contradiction, resistance and effort, which is a wastage of energy. So I want to find out if there is an action without any will as the assertion of the "me" in resistance.

You see, we are slaves to the present culture, we *are* the culture, and if there is to be a different kind of action, a different kind of life and so a different kind of culture altogether—not the counter-culture but something entirely different—one must understand this whole question of will. Will belongs to the old culture in which is involved ambition and drive, the whole assertion and aggression of the "me". If there is to be a totally different way of living, one has to understand the central issue, which is: can there be action without formula, concept, ideal, or belief? An action based on knowledge, which is the past, which is conditioned, is not action. Being conditioned and dependent on the past, it must inevitably create discord and therefore conflict. So I want to find out if there is an action in which there is no will at all and choice does not enter.

We said the other day, where there is confusion there must be choice. A man who sees things very clearly (not neurotically or obstinately) does not choose. So choice, will, resistance—the "me" in action—is wastage of energy. Is there an action unrelated to all this so that the mind

lives in this world, functioning in the field of knowledge
and yet free to act without the inpediment of the limitation of knowledge? The speaker says there is an action in
which there is no resistance, no interference of the past,
no response of the "me". That action is instantaneous because it is not in the field of time—time being yesterday,
with all the knowledge and experience which acts today,
so that the future is already established by the past. There
is an action which is instantaneous and therefore complete,
in which will does not operate at all. To find that out the
mind must learn how to observe, how to see. If the mind
sees according to a formula of what you *should* be, or
what I *should* be, then the action is of the past.

Now I am asking: is there an action which is not motivated, which is in the present and which does not bring
contradiction, anxiety and conflict? As I said, a mind
which has been trained in a culture which believes and
functions and acts with will, such a mind obviously cannot
act in the sense we are talking about, because it is conditioned. So can the mind—your mind—see this conditioning and be free of it so as to act differently? If my
mind is trained through education to function with will,
then it cannot possibly understand what it is to act without
will. Therefore my concern is not to find out how to act
without will, but rather to find out if my mind can be free
of its conditioning, which is the conditioning of will. That
is my concern, and I see, as I look into myself, that everything I do has a secret motive, is the outcome of some
anxiety, of some fear, of the demand for pleasure and so
on. Now can that mind free itself instantly to act differently?

So the mind must learn how to look. That, for me, is
the central problem. Can this mind, which is the result of
time, of various cultures, experiences and knowledge, look
with eyes that are not conditioned? That is, can it operate
instantly, being free of its conditioning? So I must learn to
look at my conditioning without any desire to change, to
transform, to go beyond it. I must be capable of looking at
it as it is. If I want to change it, then I bring about the action of will again. If I want to escape from it, there is
again a resistance. If I keep one part and reject others,
again it means choice. And choice, as we pointed out, is
confusion. So can I, can this mind, look without any
resistance, without any choice? Can I look at the mountains, the trees, my neighbour, my family, the politicians,

the priests, without any image? The image is the past. So the mind must be able to look. When I look at "what is" in myself and in the world, without resistance, then out of that observation there is instant action which is not the result of will. Do you understand?

I want to find out how to live and act in this world; not go off into a monastery, or escape to some Nirvana asserted by some guru who promises, "If you do this, you will get that"—all that is nonsense. Putting that aside, I want to find out how to live in this world without any resistance, without any will. I also want to find out what love is. So my mind which has been conditioned to the demand of pleasure, of gratification, of satisfaction and therefore of resistance, sees all that is *not* love. So what is love? You know, to find out what is, one must deny, put aside totally what is not. Through negation come to the positive; do not seek the positive, but come to it by understanding what it is not. That is, if I want to find out what truth is, not knowing what it is, I must be able to see what is false. If I do not have the capacity to perceive what is false, I cannot see what truth is. So I must find out what is false.

What is false? Everything is false that thought has put together—psychologically not technologically. That is, thought has put together the 'me", the self with its memories, with its aggression, with its separativeness, with its ambitions, competitiveness, imitation, fear and past memories; all that has been put together by thought. And thought has put together the most extraordinary things mechanically. So thought, as the me, which in essence no reality whatsoever, is the false. When the mind understands what is false, then the truth is there. Similarly, when the mind really enquires deeply into what is love, without saying "it is this", "it is that", but enquires, then it must see what it is not and completely drop it; otherwise you can't find the real. Is one capable of doing that? To say for instance, "Love is not ambition". A mind that is ambitious, wanting to achieve, wanting to become powerful, that is aggressive, competitive, imitative, such a mind cannot possibly understand what love is—we see that, don't we?

Now can the mind see the falseness of it? Can it see that a mind that is ambitious cannot possibly love and drop it instantly because it is false? Only when you deny the false completely, then the other is. So can we see very

335

clearly that a mind seeking gain, or achievement, either in the world, or in the so-called spiritual seeking of enlightenment, cannot love? The drive to find out, to achieve is ambition. Therefore can the mind see the falseness of it and completely drop it instantly? Otherwise you won't find out "what is", and you will never find out what love is. Love is not jealousy, is it? Love is not possessiveness, it is not dependency. Do you see that? Do not carry it over with you to the next day but drop it instantly. The dropping of it instantly does not depend on will. It depends on whether you actually see the falseness of it. When you drop that which is false, that which is not, the other is.

Now it becomes a little more difficult. Is love pleasure? Is love fulfillment? If you really want to have a mind that has love, you have to go into it very deeply. We are asking: is love pleasure, gratification, fulfilment? We said that the demand for pleasure is the continuity of thought, which pursues pleasure as desire and will, separate from "what is". We have associated love with sex, and because there is pleasure in it we have made an extraordinary thing of it. Sex has become the most important thing in life. We have tried to find some deep meaning in it, a deep reality, a sense of great union, oneness, and other transcendental things. Why has sex such significance in our life? Probably we have nothing else; maybe in every other field we are mechanical. There is nothing original in ourselves, nothing creative—not "creative" in the sense of producing pictures, songs and poems, that is a very superficial part of what is really a sense of creativeness. As we are more or less second-hand people, sex and pleasure have become extraordinarily important. That is why we call it love, and behind that mask we do all kinds of mischievous things.

So can we find out what love is? This has been a question man has always asked. Not being able to find out this he says, "Love God", "Love an idea", "Love the State", "Love your neighbour". Not that you shouldn't love your neighbour, but this has become merely a social operation; it is not the love that is always new. So love is not the product of thought, which is pleasure. As we said: thought is old, not free, it is the response of the past, and so love has no real relationship with thought. As we know, most of our life is a battle, the strain, the anxiety, the guilt, the despair, the immense sense of loneliness and sorrow, that is our life. That is actually "what is" and we are unwilling to face it. When you face it without choice and resistance, what takes place? Can you face it?—not try to overcome fear, jealousy, this or that, but actually look at it without any sense of wanting to change it, conquer it, control it, just to observe it totally, and give your whole attention to it. When you look at our daily life of travail, our daily bourgeois or non-bourgeois life, what takes place? Haven't you then tremendous energy? Energy has been dissipated in resistance, in overcoming, in going beyond it, trying to understand it, trying to change it. So when you do look at this life as it is, is there not then a transformation of "what is"? That transformation takes place only when you have this energy in which the operation of will does not exist at all.

You know, we like explanations, we like theories, we indulge in speculative philosophy and we are carried away by all that which is so obviously such a waste of time and energy. We must face what actually is: the misery, the poverty, the pollution, the wretched division of peoples and nations, the wars which we human beings have created—they haven't come into existence miraculously, each one of us is responsible for all this—we must face what actually is. And also we must face one of the most important things in life, which is death. That is one of the things that man avoids all the time. Ancient as well as modern civilisations have tried to go beyond that, to somehow conquer it to imagine there is immortality, a life after death—anything but face it. Can my mind face something of which it knows absolutely nothing? Most of you, unfortunately, if I may say so, have read so much about these things. You have probably read what Indian philosophers and teachers have said; or you have read other philosophers and had your Christian training. You are full of other people's knowledge, assertions and opinions. You are bound to be, although you may not consciously acknowledge it, it is there in the blood because you were brought up in this civilisation and culture. And here is something of which you know absolutely nothing. All you know is that you are frightened of coming to an end. And that is what death is.

Fear prevents you from looking at it, as fear has prevented you from living without anxiety, sorrow, guilt—you know all that brutal business. Fear has prevented you from living and fear prevents you from looking at what death is. Fear demands comfort and so there is the idea of rein-

337

carnation, the renewal in another life and so on. We won't go into this because what we are concerned with is, whether your mind can face the reality of an ending. That is what is going to happen, whether you are healthy, or a cripple, or fairly well off, anything can happen—old age, disease, or accident. Can the mind look at this enormous unknown question? Can you look at it as though for the first time?—having nobody to tell you what to do, knowing that to find comfort is an escape from the fact. So can you, as though for the first time, face something which is inevitable?

What is the state of mine that is capable of looking at something of which it knows absolutely nothing—except that there is organic death? The organism comes to an end through heart failure, through tension, through disease, and so on. But the psychological question is: can the mind face something, realising it knows absolutely nothing about it, look at it, live with it and understand it completely? Which means, can it look at it without any sense of fear? The moment you have fear you have choice, there is will, there is resistance, and that is a wastage of energy. The ending of energy as the "me" is the capacity to look at death.

To face something of which I know absolutely nothing, demands great energy, doesn't it? I can only do that when there is no will, no resistance, no choice, no wastage of energy. To face something unknown, there must be the highest form of energy, and when there is that total energy, is there a fear of death? Or is there a fear of continuity? It is only when I have lived a life of resistance, will and choice that there is fear of not being, or of not living. When the mind is faced with the unknown, and all these things have gone, there is tremendous energy. And when there is that supreme energy, which is intelligence, is there death? Find out.

Questioner: Sir, this morning you have questioned what the religions say, which prompts me to ask: how is it that I can understand what you say on an intellectual level. It seems to be sensible, it seems to be reasonable, and yet I lack the passion.

KRISHNAMURTI: The questioner says: what you say makes some sense intellectually, verbally, but somehow it does not penetrate, it does not go very deep, it does not

338

touch the source of things so that I can break through. It does not bring that sense of driving vitality, that sense of living with it. I am afraid that is the case with most people.
(*Interruption.*)

KRISHNAMURTI: Please don't answer. Let us examine. The gentleman says: what you say is logical, intellectually I accept it, but I don't feel it deep in my heart so as to bring about a change, a revolution in myself and to live a totally different kind of life. And I say: that is the case with most of us. We go part of the way, take the journey a little distance and then drop out. We keep up the interest for ten minutes and the rest of the time think about something else. You go away after the talk and carry on with your daily life. Now why does this happen? Intellectually, verbally, logically, you understand; but apparently it does not touch you deeply, so that you will burn out the old, like a fire. Why doesn't this happen? Is it lack of interest? Is it a sense of deep laziness, of indolence? Examine it, Sir, don't answer me. If it is lack of interest, why aren't you interested? When the house is burning—your house—when your children are going to grow up to get killed, why aren't you interested? Are you blind, insensitive, indifferent, callous? Or deep down haven't you got the energy and are therefore lazy? Examine it, don't agree or disagree. Have you become so insensitive because you have your own problems? You want to fulfil, you are inferior, you are superior, you are anxious, you have a great sense of fear—there is all that; and your problems are smothering you, therefore you are not interested in anything unless you solve your problems first. But your problems are the other man's problems, your problems are the result of this culture in which you live.

So what is it? Total indifference, insensitivity, callousness? Or is it that your whole culture and training has been intellectual, verbal? Your philosophies are verbal, your theories are the product of tremendously cunning brains and you have been brought up in that. Your whole education is based on it. Is it that thought has been given such extraordinary importance?—the clever, cunning, capable, technological mind, the mind that can measure, construct, fight and organise. You have been trained in that and you respond on that level. You say, "Yes, I agree with you intellectually, verbally, I see the logic, the sequence of

339

it." But you cannot go beyond it because your mind is caught in the operations of thought which is measurement. Thought cannot measure depth or height, but only on its own level.

So this is really an important question for everybody, because most of us agree with all this verbally, intellectually, but somehow the fire doesn't get lit.

Questioner: I think there is no change because the important things are not on the intellectual level but on another plane.

KRISHNAMURTI: That is what we said, Sir. There is no change, the gentleman says, because psychologically, economically, socially, in education, we are conditioned. We are the result of the culture in which we live. And he says as long as that is not changed in us we won't take any deep interest. So what is going to make you interested? I am asking: why is it that though you listen to all this logically, and I hope with a healthy mind, this does not light a fire so that you burn with it? Please ask yourselves, find out why you agree logically, verbally, superficially, yet it does not touch you deeply. If your money or your sex is taken away it will touch you. If your sense of importance is taken away, then you will struggle. If your gods, your nationalism, your petty bourgeois life is taken away, you will fight like cats and dogs. Which all indicates that intellectually we are capable of anything. Technologically, going to the moon, we live on the level of thought, but thought cannot possibly ignite the flame which changes man. What changes man is to face all this, to look at it and not always live on that very superficial level.

Questioner: You said this morning that when you are capable of looking at death as the absolute unknown, that includes that you are also capable of looking at life as it is, and that you are capable of action.

KRISHNAMURTI: Yes, Sir. "When you are capable." The word "capable" is a difficult word. Capacity means working, or to have capacity for something. You can cultivate capacity. I can cultivate the capacity to play golf or tennis, or to put machinery together. Now we are not using the word "capacity" in the sense of time—you understand? Capacity involves time, doesn't it? That is, I am not capable now, but give me a year and I'll be capable of speaking Italian, French or English. If you have understood capacity as time, it is not what I mean. I mean: observe the unknown without any fear, live with it. That does not need capacity. I said you will do it, if you know what is false and reject that.

Questioner: It is not a question of not knowing how to listen? You have said that to listen is one of the hardest things to do.

KRISHNAMURTI: Yes, it is one of the hardest things to do, to listen. Do you mean to say that a man who is committed to social activity and has put all his life into it, is he ever going to listen to any of this? Or a man who says, "I have taken a vow of celibacy"—will he listen to all this? No, Sir. Listening is quite an art.

Questioner: You were saying that the difficulty is on the intellectual level and that we do not allow our feelings and our emotions to come into our relations with other people. But I have the impression it is exactly the contrary. I think that the trouble in the world is caused by uncontrolled emotions and passions, probably born out of lack of understanding, but they are passions. We live a violent life.

KRISHNAMURTI: Violent, of course, that's understood. Now, do you live an emotional life which needs conquering? Emotional, excited, the enthusiasms of pleasure and sentiment—do you live in that world? And when you do live in that world and when it gets disorderly, then the intellect comes in and you begin to control it, saying "I must not"; but the intellect always dominates.

Questioner: Or it justifies.

KRISHNAMURTI: It justifies or condemns. I may be greatly emotional but the intellect comes along and says: look, be careful, try to control yourself. Intellect always dominates—which is thought—doesn't it? In my relationship with another I get angry, irritated, emotional. Then what happens? That leads to trouble, a quarrel takes place between two human beings. Then I try to control it—which is thought; because it has established a pattern for itself of what it should do, or what it should not do, saying, "I must control". So we say, "There must be control," otherwise relationship breaks down. Isn't all that a process of thinking, of intellection? The intellect plays a tremendous part in our life, that is all we are pointing out. We are not saying emotions are wrong or right, or true or false, but thought with its measurement is always judging, evaluating, controlling, overcoming, and therefore thought prevents you from looking.

SAANEN
29 JULY 1971

7

THOUGHT, INTELLIGENCE, AND
THE IMMEASURABLE

Different meanings of space. The space we think and act from; the space that thought has built. How is one to have immeasurable space? "To carry our burden and yet to seek freedom." Thought which does not divide itself is moving in experiencing. The meaning of intelligence. Harmony: mind, heart and organism. "Thought is of time, intelligence is not of time." Intelligence and the immeasurable.

Questions: *Hatha Yoga. Is there separation of observer and observed in technological work? Awareness and sleep.*

WE HAVE BEEN talking about the various contradictory states of the world, outside our skin as it were, about the tortures of the refugees, and the horrors of war, about poverty, the religious and national separations of people, and the economic and social injustice. These are not merely verbal statements but actual facts of what is going on in the world: violence, terrible disorder, hatreds, and every form of corruption. And in ourselves the same phenomenon is going on; we are at war with ourselves, unhappy dissatisfied, seeking something which we don't know about, violent, aggressive, corrupt, astonishingly miserable and lonely and suffering a great deal. Somehow we don't seem to be able to get out of this, to be free of these conditionings. We have tried every form of behaviour and therapy, of religious sanctions and their pursuits, the monastic life, a life of sacrifice, denial, suppression and blindly seeking, going from one book to another, or from one religious guru to another; or we try political reforms, and make revolutions. We have tried so many things and yet somehow we don't seem to be able to free ourselves from this terrible mess inside ourselves as well as outwardly. We follow the latest guru who offers some system, a panacea, some way to crawl out of our own misery, and that again does not seem to resolve any of our problems. I think the average person here asks: I know I am caught in the trap of civilisation, miserable, sorrowful, and leading rather a small, narrow life. I have tried this and that, but somehow all this chaos is still in me. What am I to do? How am I to get out of all this confusion?

During these talks we have gone into various things: order, fear, pain, love, death and sorrow. But at the end of these meetings most of us are where we began, with slight peripheral changes, but at the very root of our being our whole structure and nature more or less remains as it was. How is all that to be really jolted, so that when you leave this place, at least for one day, for one hour, there will be something totally new, a life that really has significance, has meaning, depth and width?

I don't know if you have noticed the mountains this morning, the river and the changing shadows, the pine trees dark against the blue sky, and those extraordinary hills full of light and shade. On a morning like this, sitting in a tent to talk about serious things seems rather absurd, when everything about us is crying with great joy, shouting to the heavens the beauty of the earth and the misery of man. But since we are here, I would like to approach the whole problem in a different way. Just listen to it and not only to the meaning of the words, not only to the description, because the description is never the described—as when you describe the hills, the trees, the rivers and the shadows, if you don't see them for yourselves, with your heart and your mind, the description has very little meaning. It is like describing food to a hungry man; he must have food, not just words and the smell of food.

I don't quite know how to put all this differently, but I

would like to explore—if you will do it with me—a different way of looking at all this, to look from a totally different dimension. Not the usual dimension of "me and you", "we and they", "my problems", "their problems", "how to end this and how to get that", how to become more intelligent, noble, but rather to see together if we can observe all these phenomena from a different dimension. Pehaps some of us are not used to that dimension, we don't know if there is actually a different dimension; we may speculate about it, we may imagine, but speculation and imagination are not the fact. So as we are only dealing with facts and not with speculations, it behoves us I think not only to listen to what the speaker is going to say, but also to try to go beyond the words and the explanations. It means you must also be sufficiently attentive and interested, sufficiently aware of the meaning of a dimension which we have probably not touched at all, to ask: can I look at that dimension this morning, not with my eyes, but with the eyes of objective intelligence and beauty and interest?

I do not know if you have ever thought about space. Where there is space there is silence. Not the space created by thought, but a space that has no frontiers at all, a space that is not measurable, that cannot be connived at by thought, a space that is really quite unimaginable. Because when man has space, *real* space, width and depth and an immeasurable sense of extension, not of his consciousness—which is merely another form of thought extending itself with its measurement from a centre—but that sense of space which is not conceived by thought, when there is that kind of space there is absolute silence.

With the overcrowding of cities, the noise, the exploding population, outwardly there is more and more restriction, there is less and less space. I do not know if you have noticed in this valley how new buildings are going up, there are more people, more and more cars polluting the air. Outwardly there is less and less space; if you go into any street in a crowded town you will notice this, especially in the East. In India you see thousands of people sleeping and living on the overcrowded pavement. And take any big town, London, New York, or where you will, there is hardly any space; the houses are small, people are living enclosed, trapped, and where there is no space there is violence. We have no space either ecologically, socially, or in our own mind; this is partly responsible for the violence, that we have no space.

344

In our own minds the space we create is isolation, a world built around ourselves. Please do observe this in yourselves and not only because the speaker is talking about it. Our space is a space of isolation and withdrawal. We don't want to be hurt any more, we have been hurt when we were young and the marks of hurt remain; so we withdraw, we resist, we build a wall around ourselves and around those whom we think we like, or love, and that gives a very limited space. It is like looking over the wall into another person's garden, or into another person's mind, but the wall is still there and in that world there is very little space. From that narrow, small, rather shoddy space we act, we think, we love, we function, and from that centre we try to reform the world, joining this or that party. Or from that narrow hold, we try to find a new guru who will teach us the latest way to enlightenment. And in our chattering minds, crowded with knowledge, rumours and opinions, there is hardly any space at all.

I do not know if you have noticed it, but if one has been observant, aware of the things around one and in oneself, has not just lived to earn money and have a bank account, this and that, one must have seen how little space one has, how crowded it is in ourselves. Please watch it in yourself. Being isolated in that little space, with enormous thick walls of resistance, of ideas and of aggression, how is one to have space that is really immeasurable? As we said the other day, thought is measurable, thought is measure. And any form of self-improvement is measurable; obviously, self-improvement is the most callous form of isolation. One sees that thought cannot bring about the vast space in which there is complete and utter silence? Thought cannot bring it, thought can only progress, evolve, in ratio to the end it projects, which is measurable. That space which thought creates, imaginatively, or of necessity, can never enter a dimension in which there is space which is not of thought. Through centuries thought has built a space that is very limited, narrow, isolated, and because of this very isolation, it creates division; where there is division there is conflict, nationally, religiously, politically, in relationship, in every way. Conflict is measurable—less conflict or more conflict, and so on.

Now the question is: how can thought enter into the other? Or can thought never enter it? I am the result of thought. All my activities, logical, illogical, and neurotic or highly educated and scientific are based on thought. "I"

345

am the result of all that, and it has space within the walls of resistance. How is the mind to change that and discover something which is of a totally different dimension? Have you understood my question? Can the two come together?—the freedom in which there is complete silence and therefore vast space, and the walls of resistance which thought has created with its narrow little space. Can the two come together, flow together? This has been the problem of man religiously when he enquires at great depth. Can I hold on to my little ego, to my little space, to the things that I have collected, to my knowledge, experiences, hopes and pleasures, and move into a different dimension where the two can operate? I want to sit on the right hand of God and yet I want to be free of God! I want to live a life of great delight, pleasure and beauty, and also I want to have joy which is not measurable, which cannot be caught by thought. I want pleasure and joy. I know the movement, the demand, the pursuit of pleasure with all its fears, travails, sorrow, agony and anxiety. And I also know that joy which is totally uninvited, which thought can never capture; if it does capture it, it again becomes pleasure and then the old routine begins. So I want to have both—the things of this world and the other world.

I think this is the problem for most of us—isn't it? To have a wonderful time in this world—why not?—and avoid all pain, all sorrow, because I also know other moments when there is great joy which cannot be touched, which is not corrupt. I want both, and that is why we are seeking: to carry all our burden and yet to seek freedom. Can I do this through will? You remember what we said the other day about will? Will has nothing whatsoever to do with the actual, with "what is". But will is the expression of desire as "me". We think somehow through will we shall come upon the other, so we say to ourselves, "I must control thought, I must discipline thought". When the "I" says, "I must control and discipline thought", it is thought which has separated itself as the "I" and controls thought as something separate. It is still thought: the "I" and the "not I". And one realises—thought being measurable, noisy, chattering, running all over the place—that thought has created the space of a little rat, a monkey that chases its own tail. So one says: how is thought to become quiet? Thought has created the technological world of chaos, of war, of national divisions, religious separations; thought has brought about misery, confusion and sorrow.

346

Thought is time, so time is sorrow. And you see all this if you have gone deeply, not at the instruction of another, but merely by observing this in the world and in yourself.

Then the question arises: can thought be completely silent and only function when necessary—when one has to use technical knowledge, in the office, when one if talking and so on—and the rest of the time be absolutely quiet? The more there is space and silence, the more it can function logically, sanely, healthily with knowledge. Otherwise knowledge becomes an end in itself and brings about chaos. Do not agree with me, see it for yourself? Thought, which is the response of memory, of knowledge, experience and time, is the content of consciousness; thought must function with knowledge, but it can only function with the highest intelligence when there is space and silence—when it functions from *there*.

There must be vast space and silence, because when there is that space and silence, beauty comes, there is love. Not the beauty put together by man, architecture, tapestries, porcelain, paintings, or poems, but that sense of beauty, of vast space and silence. And yet thought must act, must function. There is no living *there*, and then coming down. So that is our problem—I am making it a problem so that we can investigate together, so that both you and I discover something in this which is totally new. Because each time one investigates without knowing, one discovers something. But if you investigate with knowing, then you will never discover anything. So that is what we are doing. Can thought become silent? Can that thought, which must function in the field of knowledge totally, completely, objectively and sanely, can that thought end itself? That is, can thought which is the past, which is memory, which is a thousand yesterdays, can all that past, all that conditioning come totally to an end?—so that there is silence, there is space, there is a sense of extraordinary dimension.

I am asking myself and you are asking it with me: how is thought to end and not in the very ending of it get perverted, go off into some imaginative state and become rather lop-sided, neurotic and vague? How is that thought, which must function with great energy and vitality, to be at the same time completely motionless? Have you understood my question? This has been the problem of every serious religious man—not the man who belongs to some sect based on organised belief and propaganda and therefore not religious at all. Can the two operate together, can they move together—not coalesce, not join together—but move together? They can only move together if thought does not separate itself as the observer and the observed.

You see, life is a movement in relationship, constantly moving and changing. That movement can sustain itself, move freely, when there is no division between the thinker and the thought. That is, when thought does not divide itself as the "me" and the "not me", as the observer, the experiencer, and the observed, the experienced; because in that there is division and therefore conflict. When thought sees the truth of that, then it is not seeking experience, then it is moving in experienc*ing*. Aren't you doing this now?

Just now I said thought with all its knowledge, which is always accumulating, is something living; it is not a dead thing, therefore the vast space can move together with thought. When thought separates itself as the thinker, as the experiencer causing division and conflict, then that experiencer, observer, thinker, becomes the past which is stationary and therefore cannot move. The mind sees in this examination that where there is division in thought, movement is not possible. Where there is division the past comes in and the past becomes stationary, the immovable centre. The immovable centre can be modified and added to, but it is an immovable state and therefore it has no free movement.

So my next question to myself and so to you is: does thought see this, or is perception something entirely different from thought? One sees division in the world, national, religious, economic, social and all the rest of it; in this division there is conflict, that is clear. And when there is division and fragmentation in myself, there must be conflict. Then I am divided in myself as the observer and the observed, the thinker and the thought, the experiencer and the experience. That very division is created by thought, which is the result of the past—I see the truth of this. Now my question is: does thought see this, or does some other factor see it? Or is the new factor intelligence and not thought? Now what is the relationship between thought and intelligence? Do you understand my question? I am terribly interested in this personally, you can come with me or not. It is extraordinary to go into this.

Thought has created this division: the past, the present, the future. Thought is time. And thought says to itself: I see this division outwardly and inwardly, I see this division is the factor of conflict. It is not capable to go beyond it, therefore it says: I am where I began, I am still with my conflicts, because thought says, "I see the truth of division and conflict." Now does thought see that, or does a new factor of intelligence see it? If it is intelligence that sees it, what is the relationship between thought and intelligence? Is intelligence personal? Is intelligence the result of book-knowledge, logic, experience? Or is intelligence the freedom from the division of thought?—the division which thought has created. Seeing that logically and not being able to go beyond it, remains with it; it does not try to struggle with it or to overcome it. Out of that comes intelligence.

You see, we are asking: what is intelligence? Can intelligence be cultivated? Is intelligence innate? Does thought see the truth of conflict, of division and all the rest of it, or is it the quality of mind that sees the fact and is completely quiet with the fact?—completely silent, not trying to go beyond it, to overcome it, to change it, but is completely still with the fact. It is that stillness that is intelligence. Intelligence is not thought. Intelligence is this silence and is therefore totally impersonal. It does not belong to any group, to any person, to any race, to any culture.

So my mind has found that there is a silence, not something put together by thought, discipline, practice and all that horror, but a seeing thought cannot possibly go beyond itself; because thought is the result of the past and where the past is functioning it must create division and therefore conflicts. Can one see that and remain still with it? You know, it is like being completely still with sorrow. When somebody dies for whom you care, whom you have looked after, cherished, loved and been concerned with, there is the shock of loneliness, of despair, a sense of isolation, everything falls around you; can one remain with that sorrow not seeking explanations and the cause, thinking, "Why should he go and not I?" To remain completely still with it is intelligence. That intelligence can then operate in thought, using knowledge, and that knowledge and thought will not create division.

So the question arises: how is the mind, your mind, which is endlessly chattering, endlessly bourgeois—caught in a trap, struggling, seeking, following a guru and using discipline—how is that mind to be completely still?

Harmony is stillness. There is harmony between the body, the heart and the mind, complete harmony, not discord. That means the body must not be imposed upon, not disciplined by the mind. When it likes a certain kind of food, or tobacco, or drugs and the excitement of all that, to be controlled by the mind is an imposition. Whereas the body has its own intelligence when it is sensitive, alive and not spoilt; it has its own intelligence. One must have such a body, which is alive, active, not drugged. And also one must have a heart—not excitement, not sentiment, not emotion, not enthusiasm, but that sense of fulness, of depth, quality, vigour, that can only be when there is love. And one must have a mind that has immense space. Then there is harmony.

Now how is the mind to come upon this? I am sure you are all asking this, perhaps not whilst you are sitting here, but when you go home, when you walk, you will ask: how can one have this sense of complete integrity, of unity of body, heart and mind without any sense of distortion, division or fragmentation? How do you think you can have it? You see the fact of this, don't you? You see the truth of it, that you must have complete harmony in yourself, in the mind, the heart and the body. It is like having a clear window, without any scratch, unsullied; then, as you look out through the window you can see things without any distortion. How can you have that?

Now, who sees this truth? Who sees the truth that there must be this complete harmony? As we said, when there is harmony there is silence. When the mind, the heart and the organism are completely in harmony there is silence; but when one of the three becomes distorted, there is noise. Who sees this fact? Do you see it as an idea, as a theory, as something you "should have"? If you do, then it is all the function of thought. Then you will say: tell me what kind of system I must practise to get this, I will renounce, I will discipline—all that is the activity of thought. But when you see the truth of this—the truth, not what "should be"—when you see that is the fact, then it is intelligence that sees it. Therefore it is intelligence that will function and bring about this state.

Thought is of time, intelligence is not of time. Intelligence is immeasurable—not the scientific intelligence, not the intelligence of a technician, or of a housewife, or of a man who knows a great deal. Those are all within the field of thought and knowledge. It is only when the mind is completely still—and it *can* be still, you don't have to practise or control, it can be completely still—then there is harmony, there is vast space and silence. And only then the Immeasurable is.

Questioner: I have been listening to you for fifty years. You have said that one has to die every moment. This is more real to me now than it has ever been.

KRISHNAMURTI: I understand, Sir. Must you listen to the speaker for fifty years and at the end of it you understand what he says? Does it take time? Or do you see the beauty of something instantly and therefore it is? Now why do you and others take time over all this? Why must you have many years to understand a very simple thing? And it is very simple, I assure you. It only becomes complex in explanation, but the fact is extraordinarily simple. Why doesn't one see the simplicity and the truth and the beauty of it instantly—and then the whole phenomenon of life changes? Why? Is it because we are so heavily conditioned? And if you are so heavily conditioned, can't you see that conditioning instantly, or must you peel it off like an onion, layer after layer? Is it that one is lazy, indolent, indifferent, caught in one's own problem? If you are caught in one problem, that problem is not separate from the rest of the problems, they are all interrelated. If you take one problem whether it is sex, relationship, or loneliness, whatever it is—go to the very end of it. But because you can't do it, you have to listen to somebody for fifty years! Are you going to say it takes you fifty years to look at those mountains?

Questioner: I would like to know about Hatha Yoga. I know many people who practise it but they betray themselves; they live obviously in imagaination.

KRISHNAMURTI: I was told that Hatha Yoga and all the complications of it was invented about three thousand years ago. I was told this by a man who had studied the whole thing very carefully. At that time the rulers of the land had to keep their brains and their thoughts very clear and so they chewed some kind of leaf from the Himalayan mountains. As time went on the plant died out, so they had to invent a method by which the various glands in the human system could be kept healthy and vigorous. So they

351

invented Yoga exercises to keep the body healthy and thereby to have a very active, clear mind. The practice of certain exercises—asanas and so on—does keep the glands healthy and active. They also found that the right kind of breathing helps—not to achieve enlightenment, but to keep the mind, the brain cells, supplied with sufficient air, so that they function well. Then all the exploiters came along and said: if you do all these things then you will have a quiet, silent mind. Their silence is the silence of thought, which is corruption and therefore death. They said: this way you will awaken various centres and you will experience enlightenment. Of course our minds are so eager, so greedy, wanting more experiences, wanting to be better than somebody else, better looking, to have a better body, so we fall into that trap. The speaker does various exercises, about two hours a day; don't copy him, you know nothing about it! So long as one has imagination, which is the function of thought, do what you will, the mind can never be quiet, peaceful, with a sense of great inward beauty and sufficiency.

Questioner: In this harmonious, integrated state, when the mind functions strictly in a technological way, is there then this separation of the observer and the observed?

KRISHNAMURTI: I understand the question. What do you think? When there is complete harmony—real, not imaginary harmony—when the body, the heart and the mind are completely harmonious and integrated, when there is that sense of intelligence which is harmony, and that intelligence is using thought, then will there be the division of the observer and the observed? Obviously not. When there is no harmony there is fragmentation, then thought creates the division as the "me" and the "not me", the observer and the observed. This is so simple.

Questioner: You said in your second talk that one should be aware not only when awake but also during sleep.

KRISHNAMURTI: Is there an awareness when you are asleep as well as when you are awake? Do you understand the question? That is, during the day one is superficially or deeply aware of everything that is going on inwardly; one is aware of all the movements of thought, the division, the conflict, the misery, the loneliness, one's demand for pleasure, the pursuit of ambition, greed, anxiety, one is aware of the whole of that. When you are so aware during the day, does that awareness continue during the night in the form of dreams? Or are there no dreams but only an awareness?

Please listen to this: am I, are you, aware during the day of every movement of thought? Be honest, be simple: you are not. You are aware in patches. I am aware for two minutes, then there is a great blank and then again a few minutes, or half an hour later, I realise I have forgotten myself and pick it up again. There are gaps in our awareness—we are never aware continuously and we think we ought to be aware all the time. Now first of all, there are great spaces between awareness, aren't there? There is awareness, then unawareness, then awareness and so on, during the day. Which is important? To be continuously aware? Or to be aware for short periods? What is one to do with the long periods when one is not aware? Amongst those three, what do you think is important? I know what is important for me. I am not bothered about being aware for a short period, or wanting to have awareness continuously. I am only concerned with when I am not aware, when I am inattentive. I say I am very interested in why I am inattentive, and what I am to do about that inattention, that unawareness. That is my problem—not to have constant awareness. You would go crazy unless you had really gone into this very, very deeply. So my concern is: why am I inattentive and what happens in that period of inattention?

I know what happens when I am aware. When I am aware nothing happens. I am alive, moving, living, vital; in that nothing can happen because there is no choice for something to happen. Now, when I am inattentive, not aware, then things happen. Then I say things which are not true, then I am nervous, anxious, caught, I fall back into my despair. So why does this happen? Are you getting my point? Is that what you are doing? Or are you concerned with being totally aware and trying, practising to be aware all the time?

I see I am not aware, and I am going to watch what happens in that state when I am not aware. To be aware that I am not aware *is* awareness. I know when I am aware; when there is an awareness it is something entirely different. And I know when I am not aware, I get nervous, I twitch my hands, I do all kinds of stupid things. When

353

there is attention in that unawareness the whole thing is over. When at that moment of unawareness I am aware that I am not aware, then it is finished; because then I don't have to struggle nor say, "I must be aware all the time, please tell me a method to be aware, I must practise and so on"—becoming more and more stupid. So you see there is no awareness and I know I am not aware, then the whole movement changes.

Now, what happens during sleep? Is there an awareness when you are asleep? If you are aware during the day-time in patches, then that continues while you are asleep—obviously. But when you are aware, and also aware that you are inattentive, a totally different movement takes place. Then when you sleep there is an awareness of complete quietness. The mind is aware of itself. I won't go into all this, it is not a mystery, it is not something that is extraordinary. You see, when the mind is deeply aware during the day, that awareness in depth brings about a quality of mind during sleep that is absolutely quiet. During the day you have observed, you have been aware, either in patches, or you have been aware of your inatten-tion; then as you go through the day the activity of the brain has established order when you sleep. The brain de-mands order, even if that order is in some neurotic belief, in nationalism, or in this or that—but in *that* it finds an order which inevitably brings about disorder. But when you are aware during the day, and aware of your un-awareness, then at the end of the day there is order; then the brain does not have to struggle during the night to bring about order. Therefore the brain becomes rested, it is quiet. And the next morning the brain is extraordinarily alive, not a dead, corrupt, drugged thing.

SAANEN
1 AUGUST 1971

EUROPE

VIII

Five Dialogues in Saanen

THE FRAGMENTATION OF CONSCIOUSNESS

Are we aware that we look at life fragmentarily? The condition-
ing of consciousness. Do we really know its content? Is there a
division into conscious and unconscious? The observer is part of
the content of consciousness. Is there any agent outside this
conditioned content? "Tricks I play upon myself." What is
action? Since the self is fragmented, "I" cannot see life as a
totality.

KRISHNAMURTI: Could we in these dialogues work out
one problem each morning, go into it thoroughly, so that
we really understand it? This is a friendly conversation between us in which we can go into a problem together and
see if we cannot resolve the problem that we take each
morning. A dialogue is different from a dialectical argument; it is not seeking truth through opinion, or discussion, which means reasoning, logic, argument; that will not
lead us very far. Can we take one problem this morning
and go into it completely, not deviating from it but go into
it step by step, in detail, hesitatingly, not offering an
opinion—because then it is your opinion, your argument,
against somebody else's—and also not indulging in ideologies, not quoting others, but take a problem that is vital to
each one of us and work it out together? That would be
worthwhile, I feel. Shall we do that?

Questioner (1): Could we discuss order?

Questioner (2): I find that in spite of all you have said I
am still left with my inner emptiness. The urge to escape
from it prevents me from looking—I am always escaping.

Questioner (3): I wonder if the method we use together
really makes it possible for us to make a radical and last-
ing transformation? Because this method is on the conscious
level and the forces which bind us are on the uncon-

*scious level. How can we really be liberated from the
unconscious conditioning and motives? For instance, if I
may give an example, I know lots of people who have
been following you for many years, they don't judge from
the point of view of nationalities any more, but they judge
the hippies, which is the same thing.*

*Questioner (4): I have a problem in understanding aware-
ness. My mind is aware when it is going through something,
it labels it, and then I become separate from the experience. When I become aware, there is a separation between
the observed and the observer.*

Questioner (5): What is it to look at life completely?

*Questioner (6): You said, "I am the world and the world
is me." What are the simple reasons for that assertion?*

KRISHNAMURTI: Which one of these problems shall we
take this morning, so that when you and I leave the tent
we have really understood it?

Questioner: Do you look at life as good or evil?

KRISHNAMURTI: How do you actually look at life? Don't
pretend. Don't let us become theoretical, hypothetical, and
thereby slightly dishonest. Do you look at life as a whole,
or do you look at life in fragments?—all broken up. Is it
possible to look at this whole movement as a unitary
process? And can I, who have been brought up in a certain culture which conditions me, consciously or unconsciously, to look at God and the Devil—the physical
and the non-physical—can I consider this whole movement of life, or do I break it up? And when you do break
it up then, out of that, comes disorder. Now, how do you
actually look at life?

*Questioner: In most of the discussions I have heard you
start with the premise of disorder, not from the point of
view of order.*

KRISHNAMURTI: I don't posit order, I start with disorder.
We *are* in disorder, that is clear. There is war, the division
of nationalities, there is man and woman fighting each
other. We are at war with each other and in ourselves,

358

that is disorder. This is the fact. It would be absurd to posit order—there is no order!

Questioner: Is there not order in natural life?

KRISHNAMURTI: Probaby there is, in nature. But that is not my question. Our question is: can you and I look at this whole phenomenon of existence as one unitary movement, not broken up as the conscious and the unconscious?

Questioner: But that would be order.

KRISHNAMURTI: We are discussing that, I don't know where it is going to lead us. We are trying to find out through conversation whether our minds are capable of looking at life as a whole, as one unitary movement and therefore without contradiction.

Questioner: But isn't the definition of the unconscious that I am unable to look at it?

KRISHNAMURTI: We must go into this slowly. Now suppose I cannot look at life as a whole. Am I aware that I look at life fragmentarily? Let us begin with that. Are you aware, do you know that you divide life?

Questioner (1): No.

Questioner (2): Is not "life as a whole" an abstract concept?

KRISHNAMURTI: If we posit life as a unitary process, as an idea, then it is a concept. But if we realise that we live in fragments and ask whether that fragmentary division can be changed, then we may find out the other.

Questioner: It appears to me that I have to find out what I am first, before I can begin to change. I don't like hippies, and that's what I am! Possibly I can change it, if I first become what I am.

KRISHNAMURTI: Look, Sir, we are not talking about change. This morning we are trying to go into the question: how do I consider life?

Questioner: If I am fragmented I can't see it as a whole.

KRISHNAMURTI: That's it. Are we fragmented? Let's begin with that.

Questioner: Maybe fragmentation is not at the conscious level, as you said, as an artist, a scientist, a priest. The fragmentation is in the unconscious.

KRISHNAMURTI: First of all be absolutely sure that you have discarded the superficial; that you are no longer caught in the various religious and nationalistic fragmentary approaches to life. Be quite sure you have discarded all that completely; it is one of the most difficult things to do. But let's go deeper.

Questioner: If these divisions do exist on the conscious level, isn't that a fragmentation in itself, to discard them?

KRISHNAMURTI: We'll come to that. By going into the conscious and seeing how fragmentary it is, we will naturally come upon the other. Then they will come together, because we have divided life as the conscious and the unconscious, the hidden and the open. That is the psychoanalytical, the psychological point of view. To me personally that does not exist. I don't divide into conscious and unconscious. But apparently for most of us there is this division.

Now, how are you going to examine the unconscious? You have said there is this division between the conscious and the unconscious, and one may be superficially free of the divisions that culture has brought about. How are you going to examine the unconscious with all its fragmentations?

Questioner (1): Hadn't we better examine whether there is a conscious and an unconscious, and find out whether or not they exist?

Questioner (2): What is the definition of the unconscious?

KRISHNAMURTI: Apparently the definition of the unconscious is: it is what we don't know about. We think we know what superficial consciousness is, but we don't know

360

what the unconscious is. Just listen to what that gentleman said: we have made this division but is that a fact?

Questioner: If the unconscious is not a fact, after one talk at Saanen we would be liberated!

KRISHNAMURTI: There is the conscious and the unconscious. I don't say the division exists, but that's what we have taken. Do you know your conscious mind—what you think, how you think, why you think? Are you conscious of what you are doing and what you are not doing? You think you understand the conscious but you may not actually understand it. Which is the fact? Do you really know the conscious? Do you know the content of the conscious mind?

Questioner: Isn't the conscious mind, what we understand, by definition?

KRISHNAMURTI: You may understand one thing and you may not understand another. You may understand one part of the content of the conscious and another part you may not know anything about at all. So do you know the content of your conscious mind?

Questioner: If we knew it there wouldn't be this chaos in the world.

KRISHNAMURTI: Of course, naturally.

Questioner: But we don't know it.

KRISHNAMURTI: That's my point. We *think* we know it. We think we know the operations of the conscious mind, because there is a set of habits: going to the office, doing this and that. And we think we understand the content of the superficial mind. But I question it, and I also question very much whether the unconscious can ever be investigated by the conscious. If I don't know the content of the conscious mind, how can I examine the unconscious with its content? So there must be a different approach to it altogether.

Questioner (1): How do we know the unconscious exists?

361

Questioner (2): *By its manifestations.*

KRISHNAMURTI: You say, "By its manifestations." That is, consciously you may be doing something, but unconsciously the motive may be entirely different from the conscious urge.

Questioner: Negative action.

KRISHNAMURTI: Of course. Please let us try to understand each other. If the content of the conscious cannot be known completely, how can that conscious, which is superficial, which does not know itself, examine the unconscious with all its hidden content? Now you have only one means of examination, which is: to look at the unconscious consciously. Please see the importance of this.

Questioner: Isn't it true that for any inward conscious manifestation there is also a parellel outward manifestation?

KRISHNAMURTI: Obviously. Can we put it this way: do I know the content of my consciousness? Am I aware of it, do I understand it, have I observed without prejudice, without any kind of formula?

Questioner: I think the problem is deeper. What you know, what you are aware of, that is your conscious; everything you are not aware of, don't know about, that is your unconscious.

KRISHNAMURTI: I understand; that is what he said just now. Please give a few minutes thought to what somebody else has said, which is: if I don't know the content of my superficial consciousness, can that consciousness, which is not complete in the understanding of its superficiality, examine the unconscious? That is what you are doing now, aren't you? You are trying to observe the unconscious consciously. No?

Questioner (1): *This is impossible. We cannot do it.*

Questioner (2): *There is no frontier between consciousness and the unconscious.*

362

KRISHNAMURTI: Therefore what will you do? Don't indulge in theories. Look, I have been brought up with a highly traditional Brahmanical background; the tradition of it is ruthless. From morning until night you are told what to do, what not to do, what to think. From the moment you are born you are conditioned. It is done consciously every day, by the Temple, by the mother, by the father, by the environment, by the culture, which is Brahmanic. Then you move to another conditioning, and again to another conditioning. There is conditioning after conditioning. All this is laid upon you by society, by civilisation, by accident, or by intention. Now, how are you going to divide this and that?—they are all interrelated. I may reject the Brahmanical tradition very quickly, or I may not, or I may think I have done it, yet still be caught in it. How am I to understand this whole content?

Questioner: I am that content.

KRISHNAMURTI: Of course, consciousness is its content! Please see that. My consciousness is made up of the Brahmanical tradition, the theosophical tradition, the World Teacher—all that; the content of all this consciousness *is* that. Now can I look at this whole content as one, or do I have to look at it fragmentarily? Wait, see the difficulty first. Is there a content so deep down that I don't know it? Can I forever only know the superficial content? That is the problem. Now how am I to uncondition the mind which has such a content?

Questioner: You said that you were taking the example of a Brahmanical conditioning, which is still looking at it fragmentarily. But your relationship with a father, or a mother, or with somebody who was awfully nervous, or who frustrated you—this would be even more important. If you ask, "How do I uncondition the mind, or how do I uncondition myself", I would say: how do I change?

KRISHNAMURTI: It is the same thing, Sir.

Questioner: For instance, I believe that first you must become what you are.

KRISHNAMURTI: What are you? You are all that conditioning. Are you aware of all your conditioning? Before we talk about change, first we must ask: am I aware of my conditioning? Not only superifically but in the deep down layers. As the gentleman pointed out, I may be caught in a Christian, Communist, or Brahmanical tradition; but also I have lived in a family where the mother may have been brutal or nervous. Fortunately in the family in which this person grew up, there were thirteen children and nobody cared!

Questioner: I have the feeling that I am unconditioning myself by listening to you.

KRISHNAMURTI: That's it, just listen, that is what I want to get at. Let's move!

Questioner: Attention must uncondition the mind.

KRISHNAMURTI: No, Madam. That is speculation. Just let us follow this please. I am all my content: the content is my consciousness, the content is experience, knowledge, tradition, upbringing, the nervous father, the brutal or the nagging mother. All that is the content which is "me". Now am I aware of this content? Don't shrug your shoulders and say "I don't know"; otherwise you can't move forwards. If you are not aware—I am afraid you are not, if I may point out—then how do we proceed?

Questioner: The mind is aware that it is conditioned. It sees the conditioning.

KRISHNAMURTI: I understand. Look, I can see part of my conditioning; I can see I am conditioned as a Communist or a Muslim, but there are other parts of this. Can I investigate consciously the various fragments which compose the "me", the content of my consciousness? Can I consciously look at all this?

Questioner: But we are not separate from it.

KRISHNAMURTI: I understand. How am I to look at the various contents of my consciousness? Or is that a totally wrong process?

Questioner: It must be.

364

KRISHNAMURTI: We are going to find out, don't say, "It must be."

Questioner: I don't see how one can envisage all of these parts. It seems that if one can hold oneself to what one is seeing actually around one in the foreground of one's sight, without judgment or preconception as to how one should look at it, then one begins to see even the subconscious.

KRISHNAMURTI: I understand. But you have not yet answered my question, which is: can you look at the content of your consciousness?—you being part of that content. If you cannot know the content of your consciousness, how can you say, "I am right", or "I am wrong", "I loathe this or that", "This is good", or "That is bad", "The hippies are nice", "The hippies are not nice"? You are not in a position to judge at all. So, can you know the content of your own consciousness?

Questioner: What is aware of the conditioning? That is the important thing, surely.

KRISHNAMURTI: So let's go on a little bit. Does one realise one's consciousness is its content? Do you understand my statement? The content makes up consciousness. So consciousness is not separate from its content: the content *is* consciousness. Is that absolutely clear? Now, what do you do then? The fact is, the content makes up your consciousness; being a Communist, a Christian, a Buddhist, the influence of the father, the mother, the pressures of civilisation, whatever it is, all that is the content. Do you say, "That is a fact"? Begin with that. Keep to it. Then what do you do?

Questioner: I see that the usual process of my trying to act on what I see, is in itself a fragmentation; and when that is seen clearly, I stop acting on what I see.

KRISHNAMURTI: No, you are missing my point.

Questioner: We cannot do anything—there is nothing to be done.

KRISHNAMURTI: Wait: don't move from there.

365

Questioner: This process must lead to the world order.

KRISHNAMURTI: That's just it. The world order, or dis-order, is the content of my consciousness, which is in disorder. Therefore I said, "I am the world, the world is me." The "me" is made up of all the different parts of the content, and so is the world. The fact is, the content of my consciousness is consciousness. How do I proceed from there to unravel the various contents, examine them, throw out some, keep some. Who is the entity that is examining? That entity, which seems separate, is part of my consciousness, which is the result of the culture in which I have been brought up. The second fact is: if there is an entity which examines each fragment of that content, then that examiner is part of the content, and that examiner has separated himself from the content for various psychological reasons of security, safety, protection; and also it is part of the culture. So on examination I find that I am playing a trick I am deceiving myself. Do you see this?

The division as the examiner, as the observer, separating himself from the content, analysing, rejecting or keeping—all that is also the result of the content. Do I see this very clearly? If I do, then what is action? I am faced with this problem. I am tremendously conditioned, and part of this conditioning is the desire to be secure. A child needs to be secure; the brain needs to be completely secure so as to function healthily. But that brain, wanting to be secure, may find security in some neurotic belief or in some neurotic action. So it has found security in tradition and holds on to it. And it has found security in this division as the observer and the observed, because that is part of the tradition; because if I reject the observer I am lost!

So I am now faced with the fact that division as the observer and the observed, or whatever movement I make, is part of the content. Are you clear on this? Then what is there to be done? We are not discussing the conscious or the unconscious, because it is part of this. We say the conscious mind observes at a certain level but there are deeper motives, deeper intentions, deeper vitalities, and the whole of that is the content of my consciousness, which is the world consciousness.

So what am I to do? My mind realises that it must be free from conditioning, otherwise I am a slave to that; I see there will be wars, there will be antagonism, there will be division. So the mind, being intelligent, says it must uncondition itself at any price. How is this to be done without the division as the analyser and the analysed?—knowing the content *is* consciousness, and that any effort I make to get out of it is still part of that content. Do you understand? Then what is one to do, faced with this?

Questioner: Either accept the world as it is, or totally reject it—we can't accept it as it is.

KRISHNAMURTI: Who are you to accept it? Why should you accept it or reject it? It is a fact. There is the sun. Do you accept it or reject it. It is there! You are faced with this and if you reject it, who is the person who is rejecting it? The person is part of that consciousness he is rejecting; only it is a part that does not suit him. And if he accepts, he will accept the part that suits him.

Questioner: But it is even more difficult than that; because if you are only conditioned to be a Hindu, you might not even know it. To go back to what you said before about a neurotic pattern: one may be fixed in a neurotic pattern and not know it.

KRISHNAMURTI: That's why I am going to show you something, Sir.

Questioner: How can I reject it?

KRISHNAMURTI: You can't reject anything. There it is! Now what is the action that takes place when you observe that you can't do anything?

Questioner: You stop. You feel that all this consciousness is not really it, and you might be a monster. And getting the feeling that you are this, you stop. But the process goes on, you can't help it.

KRISHNAMURTI: No. The process goes on only when I have not understood the content of my consciousness: whether it is neurotic, or not, whether it is homosexual or not—the content—all that is implied. And if I choose one part and hold on to it, that is the very essence of neurosis. So any action on my part—which is part of the content of my consciousness—cannot be unconditioned; it cannot be done that way.

367

Then what am I to do? Have you got it? I will not reject or accept it. That is a fact.

Questioner: Everything you do only strengthens the division.

KRISHNAMURTI: Therefore, what do you do?

Questioner: You can't do anything.

KRISHNAMURTI: Wait, you are too quick! You don't know what it means not to do a thing!

Questioner: May I just say what Freud said: you must bring what is in the unconscious into the conscious.

KRISHNAMURTI: I am not interested in what Freud says.

Questioner: I am.

KRISHNAMURTI: Why?

Questioner: Because it is a fact. You can see it in nature.

KRISHNAMURTI: Are you quoting Freud, or have you observed it yourself? Is it your own experience when you say that the unconscious pops up and acts, or that the unconscious prevents action? You are still thinking in terms of division—the conscious and the unconscious. I am not thinking in those terms at all.

Questioner: There isn't really a division.

KRISHNAMURTI: But you still say: the unconscious pops up.

Questioner: It's just a word—like "will".

KRISHNAMURTI: Oh no, when we use the word "unconscious" we are using it with the definite meaning that there is something which is not conscious. To me that is a statement of fragmentation. So if you know that you are fragmented that way, why do you hold on to it?

Questioner: Our unconscious works!

KRISHNAMURTI: Of course it does. Someone says he is heterosexual; deep down he is probably homosexual. We are always contradicting ourselves, always hypocrites. So I say all this is part of consciousness: tradition, Freud, holding on to it, not holding on to it, dislike of the hippies and liking the squares—it is all the same. So I am saying to you, the whole of the content is my consciousness. I will not choose one part, and not the other; not hold on to one part because that pleases me, or because I am conditioned that way.

Questioner: But when you say "the religious mind"—you talk about that ...

KRISHNAMURTI: I am afraid I do.

Questioner: ... you also make a division.

KRISHNAMURTI: Ah, no, I say when there is no division of *any* kind, not only superifcially, but in the content of consciousness itself, as the observer and the observed, when there is nothing of that, then there is the quality of the religious mind. That has been made very clear.

Now please just listen. When we say the content makes up consciousness—whether Freudian philosophy, or your particular experience—*everything* is included in that. The poor man in India has never heard of Freud, or Christ, but the man who has been brought up with the mythology of Christ, says: that is a fact. And the poor villager with *his* God, says: *that* is a fact. Both are the content of one's consciousness. Surely Sir?

Questioner: It is not clear.

KRISHNAMURTI: You see, you refuse to let go of the particular fragment to which you are holding on. This is what I have to fight when I go to India, because for centuries they have been brought up with the idea that there is an Atman and Brahman, God. And they believe most fundamentally that enlightenment is only possible when these two come together. And I say it is nonsense, both are invented by thought.

Now I have come to this point: I see for myself that any movement within that content is still part of the content. I know it completely, it is as clear as that sunshine, it

369

is an absolute fact. Then I say to myself: now, how is the mind to free itself from its conditioning?

Questioner: You will have to go beyond the conditioning.

KRISHNAMURTI: No, to "go beyond" means still being part of it.

Questioner: But you can go beyond yourself when you are listening.

KRISHNAMURTI: Yes, quite right.

Questioner: Because I feel that you have lost your conditioning, I am going to listen to you, actually listen.

KRISHNAMURTI: I understand, Sir. You don't know me, please don't say, "you are unconditioned"; you don't know what it means, so please don't judge.

Questioner: We don't want to get rid of our conditioning.

KRISHNAMURTI: Keep it and live with it, be in turmoil, be in misery, have wars! If you like it, hold on to it. And that is what is happening! The Arab holds on to his conditioning and that is why he is fighting the Israelis. And the Israelis hold on to theirs. That is the world. I have my particular anchor and I won't let go. So knowing all this, what is the mind to do?

Questioner: I become very quiet. I don't do anything.

KRISHNAMURTI: Do you follow that statement? He says: when I am faced with this fact that I am wholly conditioned, I become silent. I can play tricks upon myself and say I am unconditioning myself—which is part of my training, which is part of the content. He says, "I become silent". Is that so?

Questioner: I can't help bringing in the "I".

KRISHNAMURTI: That's just it. He means really that it is a means of saying "I". Now what happens when you are faced with something about which you can't do anything? Until now you have thought, because of your conditioning, that you could do something, that you could change, that you could manipulate, that you could alter things; but it is still part of the same field, moving from one corner of the field to another. When you realise that any movement within that field is a conditioned movement, what takes place? When the Arab and the Israeli say: look, I am conditioned and you are conditioned, what takes place? Go on, Sir, what takes place?

Questioner: Then it is possible to live here.

KRISHAMURTI: I realise I am totally conditioned and that any tricks I can play upon myself are part of my conditioning. Changing from being a Catholic to becoming a Hindu, from being a Hindu to Communism, then back to Zen, and from Zen to Krishnamurti and so on *(Laughter)*—it is part of my conditioning, it is part of this whole content. What happens when I realise this?

Questioner: The process stops itself.

KRISHNAMURTI: Has it stopped with you? Don't theorise!

Questioner: It is a fact. It stops by itself.

KRISHNAMURTI: It is much more complex than that. You are too quick, you are not going with it. You want a result.

Questioner: The mind that sees this, is not the same mind that started the enquiry.

KRISHNAMURTI: That's it. Go slowly, sir. What has taken place to a mind that started enquiring into its content and has discovered the extraordinary divisions, the contradictions, the fragmentation, the assertions, the aggression, all that; what happens to such a mind.

Questioner: It becomes very clear. It wins space, it is in another state.

KRISHNAMURTI: Then Sir, I will put to you a different question. What is your action in daily life—not just in a crisis—when you realise this fact?

Questioner: Maybe we don't realise this.

371

KRISHNAMURTI: That's my point. Either you realise this as a fact, and that fact fundamentally changes the whole structure of your consciousness, or you don't realise it. If you don't realise it—as apparently you don't—and merely say, "I understand", it means nothing. When you are confronted with this fact, what is your action in daily life? Relate the two, then you will get the answer. That is: I realise that I am conditioned as a Hindu. I realise that I have been brought up in peculiar circumstances—the world teacher—the devotion, candles, worship, all that; facing the world, property, money, position, prestige—and I see all that is part of the content, part of "me". What is the relationship of that perception to my daily life? Unless I relate it, it remains verbal, theoretical, nonsensical. So I must relate it. If you can't answer it, then you have not realised it, then you are playing with words.

Questioner: It appears to me that every time you ask a question, there is a problem of everyone trying to find the answer. In the question should be the realisation that you can't answer.

KRISHNAMURTI: Of course not, Sir. I am asking it because *you* have to ask that question.

Questioner: That's right. It's the person who asks the question who always looks for the answer.

KRISHNAMURTI: That is what I am saying. Whether you are attached to one neurosis or another, when you realise all this conditioning, what does that realisation do to your daily activities?

Questioner: Does all effort on the part of the self cease?

KRISHNAMURTI: You are going to find out. When you say, "I have understood it", if there is a division between that realisation and your daily action, then there is conflict. That conflict is disorder, in which we live, both the world and you and another. So what takes place when there is a real perception of the truth, like "fire burns", "poison kills"? When you realise this fact as vitally as that, then what is your action in that realisation in your daily life?

Questioner: This realisation keeps me aware in daily life—that is all that is needed.

KRISHNAMURTI: Oh no, Madam. It is nothing of the kind.

Questioner: It must totally change my way of living.

KRISHNAMURTI: Find out, Sir. Of course it does. I am not being patronising, I am just asking you: do you realise it, in the sense that when you have toothache there is an absolute realisation of pain—you do something about it? You don't theorise about it, you go to the nearest drugstore, or to the dentist, there is action. In the same way, when the mind realises totally that you are conditioned, that your consciousness is its content—and that any movement you make is still part of that consciousness—trying to get out of it, accepting it, or rejecting it, is still part of it—then how does the realisation of that truth affect your life?

The realisation of the truth of that fact is going to act. You understand? And that truth, being highly intelligent, will act according to the moment.

Questioner: But can you realise that, when you are still caught in your fears and your desires?

KRISHNAMURTI: You can't. You are trying to overcome one fragment which is fear, by another fragment. That way you cannot get rid of it, so there must be a different approach to that fragment which you call fear. And the approach is this: *To do absolutely nothing* about fear. Can you?

I can't do anything about the noise of that train going by, therefore I listen to it. I cannot do a thing about the roar of that train. Therefore I don't put up a resistance to it, I listen. There is noise but it does not affect me. In the same way when I realise that I am neurotic, that I am holding on to a particular way of belief, a particular way of action, that I am homosexual, or whatever it is, that I have tremendous prejudices, I just listen to it totally. I do not resist it, I listen to it totally, completely, with my heart.

We started out by asking if I can look at the whole movement of life as a unitary process. The killing, the refugees, the war in the Middle East, the Catholics, the Protestants, the scientists, the artists, the businessmen, private life, public life, my family, your family—there is endless division. The division has brought about such disorder in the world and in myself. Can I look at all this as a marvellous single movement? I can't, that is a fact. I can't, because I am fragmented in myself. I am conditioned in myself. So my concern then, is not to find out how to live a unitary life, but to see if the fragmentation can come to an end. And that fragmentation only comes to an end when I realise that all my consciousness is made up of these fragments. My consciousness is the fragmentation. And when I say, "There must be integration, it must be brought together", it is still part of that trick I am playing upon myself. So I realise that. I realise it as a truth, like fire burns, you can't deceive me, it is a fact, and I am left with it. And I have to find out how it operates in my daily life—not guess, play, theorise. Because I have seen the truth of it, that truth is going to act. If I don't see it and pretend I have seen it, then I am going to make a hideous mess of my life.

SAANEN
4 AUGUST 1971

2

IS INTELLIGENCE AWAKE?

What is the relationship between intelligence and thought? The limitations of conditioned thinking. No new movement can take place if the "old brain" is constantly in operation. "I have been going South, thinking I was going North." The perception of the limitations of the old is the seed of intelligence. Is the "new" recognisable? The different dimension can only operate through intelligence.

KRISHNAMURTI: We were discussing the question of the conscious and the unconscious, and the content of consciousness. Shall we go on with that, or would you like to discuss another problem this morning?

374

Questioner (1): Go on with that.

Questioner (2): I would like to discuss more about the relationship between intelligence and thought, and between silence and death.

Questioner (3): I don't know if we have finished with what we discussed yesterday, and if we really went to the bottom of the question of motivation in one's life.

KRISHNAMURTI: I wonder if we cannot discuss this question of consciousness more deeply by considering what is the relationship between intelligence and thought; and perhaps we can also go into the problem of silence and its relationship to death. But before we go into that, there are several things involved in what we were discussing yesterday. I do not know if you have gone deeply into it yourself: what you have understood, how much of it is a reality?

We said yesterday, that most of us are conditioned by the culture, by the environment, by food, clothes, religion and so on. The conditioning is the content of consciousness and consciousness is the conditioning. What relationship has thought to that conditioning? Can there be intelligence where there is conditioning?

If one has examined and observed oneself objectively, not with any kind of condemnation or judgment, one realises that one is conditioned superficially and in great depth. There is deep conditioning, which may be the result of the family, the racial accumulation, the influences which have not been obvious but nevertheless have penetrated very deeply. Is it at all possible for the mind ever to be free of all that? When it is conditioned, can the mind uncondition itself totally? Or can the mind prevent itself—not through resistance—from ever being conditioned? There are these two things which we have to examine this morning in relation to thought and intelligence, and also with regard to silence and death. If we can, we shall go into this, cover this whole field.

Why does the mind ever get conditioned? Is it so sensitive, so capable of being hurt? It is a tender, delicate thing, and in relationship it gets invariably hurt, invariably conditioned. Is it possible for that conditioning ever to be washed away? One realises the mind, the brain itself, is conditioned, evolved through centuries upon centuries and the brain is the storehouse of memories. You can watch it yourself, you don't have to read philosophical or psychological books—at least I don't, though you may. The brain which has evolved through time—which is the past, which is the accumulation of memory, experience, knowledge—responds instantly to any challenge according to its conditioning, superficially or in depth. I think this is clear.

Now can that response from the past be delayed so that there is an interval between the challenge and the response? I am taking a very superficial conditioning: one has been brought up in a particular culture, in a particular belief or pattern, and when that is questioned there is an instant response according to the background of the particular saying, "You are another", or getting angry with you, or this or that. Now when you call me a fool, can there be an interval, a space, before I respond? So that the brain is quiet enough to respond in a different way.

Questioner: Or to observe its own response.

KRISHNAMURTI: The brain responds all the time according to its conditioning, according to various forms of stimuli: it is always active. The brain is the response of time, of memory; in the brain the whole past is contained. If the brain can hold itself and not respond immediately, then there is a possibility of a new response.

The brain operates in the old habits established by the culture we live in, by the past racial inheritance and so on; that responds all the time, to any stimulus—judging, evaluating, believing, not believing, discussing, protecting, denying and so on. The brain cannot be denied its past knowledge; it must have that, otherwise it can't function. So I am asking whether that brain—which is the old—will allow itself to be quiet so that a new part can operate. When you flatter me, the old brain says, "How lovely." But can the old brain listen to what you say and not respond, so that perhaps a new movement can take place? That new movement can only take place when there is silence, when the machinery is not operating in terms of the past. Is that clear—clear in the sense of watching yourself, otherwise it is no fun? I am not explaining this for myself, we are working together.

I find, when one examines one's activities, that the old brain is always responding according to its limited knowledge, to its tradition, its racial inheritance, and when that is operating nothing new can come about. Now I want to find out whether that old brain can be quiet so that a new movement can take place. I can do that when I am in relationship with another, watching the old brain in operation, and when it understands the truth that it must be quiet in order that a new operation can take place.

The brain is not forcing itself to be quiet. If it is forcing itself to be quiet then it is still in operation of the past. In that there is division, there is conflict, there is discipline and all the rest of it. But if the old brain understands, or sees the truth—that as long as it is in constant response to any stimulus, it must operate along the old lines—if the old brain sees the truth of that, then it becomes quiet. It is the truth that brings about quietness—not the intention to be quiet.

You see, this question is very interesting because one finds there are certain brains that are never conditioned. You may say, how do you know? I only know because it has happened to the speaker. You may believe it, or disbelieve it! Just take the fact.

I am asking why the brain must always function in this old pattern. If it does not function in its old pattern, it sets up a new pattern according to its memories in opposition to the old. We only use a very small part of the brain and that small part is the past. There is a part of the brain which has not functioned at all, which is open, empty, new. Do you know anything about it? Don't agree to this. You only know the old brain in operation, when you are at all conscious of it. Now I am asking whether that old brain can be still to stimuli, so that a new response can come. And the next question is: how can that brain, which has been so conditioned, hold back a little? Can I go on?

Questioner: It is very clear.

KRISHNAMURTI: And one finds the brain does hold back when there is the necessity, the urgency, when this question is vital—so that a new quality of mind, of the brain, which has never been touched, operates. This happens, this is not only my experience. Any top-level scientist who is free from the desire for success, or position, must have asked this question, because how does he discover new things? If the old brain is in operation all the time it can't discover anything new. So it is only when the old brain is quiet that something new is seen, and in that quiet state something new is discovered. This is a fact.

Now, without forcing the brain, how can that quietness come and the brain be voluntarily quiet? It can discover something new only when it sees the truth that the old cannot find anything new and therefore the old becomes quiet. The truth makes it quiet; it does not wish to be quiet. Is that very clear? Then, can that quietness operate all the time?—and the old conditioning with its knowledge operate only when it is necessary. Have you understood my question?

Questioner: You say, "Operate all the time"? Will that not bring conflict?

KRISHNAMURTI: Please listen, Sir. I want to find out, I am enquiring, I am not saying, "It must be quiet". I see the old brain must operate, otherwise I can't speak English, drive a car, or recognise you. The old brain must operate functionally. But, also, as long as it is not quiet, no new thing can be seen. Are you following?

Audience: Yes.

KRISHNAMURTI: I am asking myself: what is the relationship between the new quality of the brain, which functions in quietness, and the old? The old *is* thought—right? The old is the collection of memories and any response according to these memories is thought. That thought must function, otherwise you can't do anything.

Questioner: Aren't you making a division?

KRISHNAMURTI: No, it is not a division. It is like a house, it is a whole, but there are no divisions in it.

We have discovered two things. That the old brain—we'll call it that for the moment—is the conditioned brain which has accumulated knowledge through centuries upon centuries. We are not dividing it as the old and the new, we just want to convey the meaning that there is this whole structure of the brain, one part of which is the old—which doesn't mean it is separate from the new—it is different. Now I am saying to myself: I see that if the old brain is in operation nothing new can be discovered. The new can be discovered only when the old is quiet. And the old can only be quiet when it sees the truth that the new

378

cannot be discovered by the old. Now we have this fact: the old must naturally be quiet to discover something new.

Questioner (1): Is the discovery made by the new or the old?

Questioner (2): By neither of them.

KRISHNAMURTI: Answer it, Sirs! My brain says, "I really don't know, I am going to find out." You have asked a question, which is: does the old brain recognise the new, or does the new use the old?

The old brain is quiet because it has understood completely that it can never discover anything new. We won't even use the word "discover". No new movement can take place if the old is constantly in operation. The old sees the fact of that and is quiet. And a new movement, a new happening takes place. Is that happening recognised by the old, or does it open the door for the new to utilise it?

Look Sirs, this is really quite important, even though you don't follow it, because I want to find a totally new way of living. I realise the old way of living is terrible, ugly, brutal. I must find a new dimension which is unrelated to the old. Any movement on the part of the old to discover a different dimension is not possible. Realising this, it becomes quiet. Now what takes place in that quietness? Let's proceed along that way. What takes place when the old brain has understood that it cannot find a new dimension?

Questioner: The unknown?

KRISHNAMURTI: No, don't invent. Unless you experience this, don't guess.

Questioner: There is space.

KRISHNAMURTI: Now wait a minute. When the old brain is quiet, the gentleman says, there is space. Let's examine it. What do you mean by space?

Questioner: Emptiness.

379

KRISHNAMURTI: Please don't invent, don't guess, observe. Is your old brain quiet?

Questioner (1): No.

Questioner (2): If the old brain is quiet, can you ask that question?

KRISHNAMURTI: I am asking you. It may be a wrong question, but we must find out.

Questioner: The part of the brain which is not used starts operating.

KRISHNAMURTI: Just listen to what he is saying. When the old brain is quiet, perhaps a new part of the brain which has not been used comes into operation. That is, we are only functioning with a very small part of our brain and when that small part of the brain is quiet, the rest of the brain may be active. Or, it has been active all the time but we don't know it because that one part which has accumulated knowledge, tradition, time, is always super-active, and therefore we don't know the other part at all; it may have its own activity. Are you following this?

This is really a very interesting question. Please give your minds to this a little bit; don't say, "I don't understand" and just drop it. Apply yourselves! You see, having used the old brain so much we have never considered any other part of the brain, and what part is, which may have a quality of a different dimension. I say that quality of a different dimension can be discovered when the old brain is really quiet. That's my point. You follow? When the old brain is completely quiet, not *made* quiet, but has naturally understood that it must be quiet and therefore *is* quiet, then we can find out what takes place.

Now, I am going to investigate—not you—because your old brain is not quiet. Would you agree to that? It has not understood the necessity of being completely quiet under any stimulus, except of course physical stimuli—that is, if you put a pin into my leg it will respond. But as nobody is pricking my leg with a pin the old brain can be quiet.

I want to find out what is the quality of the new brain—that quality which the old brain cannot recognise? Because the old brain cannot recognise anything which it has not experienced, which is not the outcome of memory.

380

Therefore what the old brain recognises is still the old. Is that clear? So I am asking: what is the new? The old brain does not know anything about it, therefore it can only say: I really don't know. Let's proceed from there—do some of you follow this? The old brain says, "I can't touch this and I really don't know." Because I cannot touch it, because I cannot recognise it, I am not going to be deceived by it. I know absolutely nothing about the new dimensions of this new brain. When the old brain is quiet and incapable of recognition, it can only say, "I really don't know." Can the old brain remain in that state of *not* knowing? It has said, "All my life I have functioned with knowledge and recognition." In functioning that way it has said, "I know" in terms of what I do not know, of that which I will learn, but always within the pattern of knowing. Now it says, "I really don't know", because something new is taking place. The new cannot be recognised, therefore I have no relationship to it yet. I am going to find out.

Now what is the nature of not knowing? Is there fear when there is a state of not knowing?—which is death. You follow, Sirs? When the old brain actually says, "I don't know", it has relinquished all knowing. It has relinquished altogether the intention of knowing, of wanting to know. So there is a field in which the old brain cannot function, because it does not know. Now what is that field? Can it ever be described? It can be described only when the old brain recognises and verbalises it to communicate. So there is a field in which the old brain cannot possibly enter; this is not an invention, this is not a theory, this is a fact when the old brain says, "I really don't know anything about this." Which means there is not intention to learn about the new. You see the difference, Sirs?

So now I want to find out non-verbally, because the moment I use a word I am back in the old. Therefore is there an understanding of something new non-verbally?—in the sense of not inventing a new word, or intending to describe it so as to capture it and hold it. So I am just enquiring, the mind is looking at something which it does not know at all. Is that possible? It has always looked in terms of learning about it, resisting it, avoiding it, escaping from it, or overcoming it. Now it is doing nothing of the kind. Do you understand? If this is not possible you cannot understand the other.

What is the something which the old brain cannot understand and therefore cannot possibly know or acquire knowledge about? Is there such a thing? Or is it just an invention of the old brain wanting something new to happen? If it is the old brain wanting something new to happen, it is still part of the old brain. Now I have examined it completely, so that the old brain has understood its structure and nature and therefore is absolutely still, not wanting to know. That is where the difficulty lies.

Is there something real, not imagined, not invented, which is not a theory? Something which the old brain cannot possibly understand, or recognise, or want to understand? Is there anything like that? For the speaker there is—but that has no value, he may be deluding himself. It has value only in the sense that it is for you to discover it. So you have to find out what is the relationship of the new—if you see the new—to the old, which must operate in life objectively, sanely, non-personally, therefore efficiently. Does the old capture the new so that there is a different life? Or does the new operate in a way that the old cannot possibly recognise, and that operation is the new way of living?

Go slowly, take time, look! This old brain, with its consciousness, has lived for thousands of years; the consciousness of this old brain is its content. Its content may have been acquired superficially or in depth and that is the old brain with all the knowledge, with all the experience of centuries of human endeavour, of evolution. When it is functioning within that field of consciousness it can never discover anything new. That is an absolute fact, not a theory. We know nothing about freedom, about what love is, what death is; we know nothing except jealousy, envy, fear, which are all part of the old content. Then this old brain, realising its utter limitation, becomes quiet, because it has found it has no freedom. And because it has found no freedom, a new part of the brain is in operation. I don't know if you see that.

Look! I have been going South, thinking I was going North, and suddenly I discover that. At the moment of discovery there is a total reversion—not of the old, it is a complete reversal. The movement is neither to the North nor South, it is in a totally different direction. That is, at that moment of discovery there is a totally different movement, which is freedom.

Questioner: Could you discuss the difference between the intensity to find out, and the desire of the old for the new.

KRISHNAMURTI: The desire of the old for the new is still the old; therefore the desire for the new, or the experience of the new—call it enlightenment, God, what you like—is still part of the old; therefore that's out.

Questioner (1): *Krishnaji, do you realise that you have been speaking of the highest philosophy and that we, here in this tent, are not even able to have the smallest relationship with each other.*

Questioner (2): *Who are we?*

KRISHNAMURTI: We have been through that—we are monkeys! Look, Sir, this is not talking of the "highest philosophy", it is the pure thing. Do you realise actually, not theoretically, that you have no relationship one with another, that your relationship with another cannot exist as long as the old brain is in operation, because the old brain functions in images, pictures, past incidents; when the past happenings, images, knowledge, are strong, then relationship comes to an end—obviously. If I have built an image about you—who are my wife, or my friend, my girl or whatever it is—that image, that knowledge, which is the past, obviously prevents relationship. Relationship means direct contact immediately in the present, at the same level, with the same intensity, with the same passion. And that passion, that intensity at the same level, cannot exist if I have an image about you and you have an image about me. So it is for you to see if you have an image about somebody else. Obviously you have; therefore apply yourself, *work* to find out—that is, if you really want a relationship with another, which I doubt. We are all so terribly selfish, enclosed; if you really want a relationship with another, you have to understand this whole structure of the past—which is what we have been doing. And when that is gone, you have a relationship which is totally new all the time. And that new relationship is love—not the old, beating the drum!

Now what is the relationship of that quality, of that dimension which is the new, which is not known, which cannot be captured by the old, to my daily life? I have discovered that dimension, it has happened because I have seen that the old brain can never be free and so is incapable of finding out what truth is. Therefore the old brain says: my whole structure is of time and I function only with regard

383

to that which has time—machinery, language, all the rest of it—so that part will be completely still. So what is the relationship between the two? Has the old any relationship with freedom, love, the unknown? If it has relationship with the unknown, then it is part of the old—you follow? But if the unknown has relationship with the old, then it is quite a different proposition. I don't know if you see that?

My question is: what is the relationship between these two, and who wants relationship? Who is demanding this relationship? Is the old demanding it? If the old demands it, then it is part of the old, therefore it has no relationship with the other. I don't know if you see the beauty of this. The old has no relationship with freedom, with love, with this dimension. But that new dimension, love, can have a relationship with the old, but not the other way round. Do you see it, Sirs?

So the next step then is: what is the action in daily life, when the old has no relationship with the new, but the new is establishing relationship as it moves in life. The mind has discovered something new. How is the new going to operate in the field of the unknown, in which functions the old brain with all its activities?

Questioner: Would that be where intelligence comes in?

KRISHNAMURTI: Now wait Sir, perhaps you are right. When the old brain sees that it can never understand what freedom is: when it sees that it is incapable of discovering something new, that very perception *is* the seed of intelligence, isn't it? That *is* intelligence? "I cannot do." I thought I could do a lot of things, and I can, in a certain direction, but in a totally new direction I cannot do anything. The discovery of that is intelligence, obviously.

Now what is the relationship of that intelligence to the other? Is the other part of this extraordinary sense of intelligence? I want to find out what we mean by that word "intelligence"; the mind must not be caught by words. Obviously the old brain, all these centuries, thought it could have its God, its freedom, it could do everything it wanted. And suddenly it discovers that any movement of the old brain is still part of the old; therefore intelligence is the understanding that it can only function within the field of the known. The discovery of that is intelligence, we say. Now what is that intelligence? What is its relationship to life, to a dimension which the old brain does not know?

You see, intelligence is not personal, is not the outcome of argument, belief, opinion or reason. Intelligence comes into being when the brain discovers its fallibility, when it discovers what it is capable of, and what not. Now what is the relationship of that intelligence with this new dimension? I would rather not use the word "relationship".

The different dimension can only operate through intelligence; if there is not that intelligence it cannot operate. So in daily life it can only operate where intelligence is functioning. Intelligence cannot function when the old brain is active, when there is any form of belief and adherence to any particular fragment of the brain. All that is lack of intelligence. The man who believes in God, the man who says, "There is only one Saviour", is not intelligent. The man who says, "I belong to this group", is not intelligent. When one discovers the limitation of the old, the very discovery of that is intelligence, and only when that intelligence is functioning can the new dimension operate through it. Full stop. Have you got it?

Questioner: May I put another question? I don't completely agree with you. What you say about intelligence applies only to primary intelligence. But we need also secondary intelligence; that is, the ability to integrate what is new with the old.

KRISHNAMURTI: That is what takes place when there is not intelligence. I won't use the word "integrate"; the new operates when there is that intelligence which is not only primary but fundamental.

Questioner: But you see, in your talk today I always heard the word "primary". I think what you call "new", is in a certain sense primary. If I play a game, throwing a coin, I cannot predict what will appear and one says one's game here is a random event. I want to know what you think about the relation of what you call "completely new" with what is random in the sense I have explained it.

KRISHNAMURTI: I understand. The professor asks, what is the relationship of randomness, of chance, to something totally new. There are events in one's life that appear to happen by chance, events that occur at random. Is that happening new, totally unexpected? Or is it the result of unexamined, hidden, unconscious events?

I happen to meet you by chance. Is that chance at all, or has it happened because certain unconscious, unknown, events have brought us together? We may consider this chance, but it is not chance at all. I meet you, I did not know you existed, and in the meeting something has taken place between us. That may be the result of a great many other events of which we are not conscious, and we may then say, "This is a random event, this is an unexpected chance, this is totally new." It may not be that. Is there a chance in life at all?—a happening which has not a cause. Or have all events in life their basic, deep, causes, which we may not know and therefore we say, "Our meeting happens by chance, it is a random event." The cause undergoes a change when there is an effect. The effect becomes a cause. There is the cause and the effect which becomes the cause of the next effect. So cause-effect is a constant chain; it is not one cause, one effect, it is undergoing constant change. Each cause, each effect, changes the next cause, the next effect. So as this is going on in life, is there anything which is unexpected, chance, a random event? What do you say?

Questioner: The very concept of randomness is based on causality.

KRISHNAMURTI: Causality? I don't think life works that way. The cause becomes effect and the effect becomes cause—you can see this in life. So we can never say, "Cause and effect", there it is! The professor asked about the relationship of the unknown—not in the sense of a new dimension—to a chance event.

Questioner: The unknown is outside the world of relativity.

KRISHNAMURTI: You can discuss it. I know nothing about all this, I am talking about human relationships, human beings, not mathematical problems and chance events and mathematical order. All that does not seem to affect our daily living. Here we are concerned to bring about a change in that daily living—the way we behave.

And if our behaviour is based on that past it still brings conflict and misery; that is what we are talking about.

SAANEN
5 AUGUST 1971

3

FEAR

The link between pleasure and fear; the role of thought. Thought cannot reduce the uncertain unknown to terms of knowledge. Need to see the structure of fear. Psychologically, tomorrow may not exist. What does, "To live wholly in the present" imply?

Questioner (1): *I would like to discuss fear and death and their relationship to intelligence and thought.*

Questioner (2): *Could you go into the statement: the world is me and I am the world?*

Questioner (3): *Could we discuss—but not theorise—about what happens after death if it is actually possible to die to things known?*

KRISHNAMURTI: Fear is a complex problem and we have to enquire into it, not come with any preconceived ideas, but really penetrate into this whole question of fear. Now first of all, in enquiring into this problem, we are not trying to deal with it as collective fear, nor are we discussing it as group-therapy to get rid of fear. We are going to find out what fear means and what are its nature and structure; whether the fear deep down at the very root of our being can be understood, and whether the mind can ever be free from fear. How do you approach this problem? Have you got any kind of fear—physical or psychological? If you have psychological fears—we shall come back to the physical fears a little later—how do you deal with them?

Suppose I am afraid that I shall lose my position, my

387

prestige: I depend on an audience, on you, to bolster me up, I depend on you to give me vitality by talking. I am afraid, as I grow older, I may become senile. I will be faced with nothing and I am afraid. What is this fear? Or I am afraid that I depend on you—a man or a woman—and that dependency makes me attached to you, so I am afraid to lose you. Or I am afraid because I have done something in the past, which I regret or am ashamed of, and I don't want you to know; so I am afraid of your knowing it and I feel guilty. Or I feel terribly anxious about death, about living, about what people say, or don't say, how they look at me. I have a deep sense of foreboding, anxiety, a sense of inferiority. And in this anxiety about death, living a life that has no meaning, I seek assurance from somebody through human relationship. Or out of my anxiety I seek a sense of security in a certain belief, a certain ideology, in God, and so on.

Also I am afraid that I shan't be able to do everything I want to do in this life. I have not the capacity nor the intelligence, but I am tremendously ambitious to achieve something; so I am frightened of that too. And of course I am afraid of death; and I am afraid of being lonely, of not being loved; so I want to establish a relationship with another in which this fear, this anxiety, this sense of loneliness, this separation, does not exist. Also I am afraid of the dark, of the elevator—innumerable neurotic fears!

What is this fear? Why are you, why is anybody, afraid? Is it based on not wanting to be hurt? Or is it that one wants complete security, and not being able to find it—this sense of complete safety, of protection, physically, emotionally, psychologically—one becomes terribly anxious about living?—so there is this sense of uncertainty. Now why is there fear?

One of our major problems is fear, whether we are aware of it or not, whether we run away from it or try to overcome it, try to withstand it, develop courage and all the rest of it, there is still fear. I am asking myself, I am asking you, whether the mind is so delicate, so sensitive, that from childhood on it does not want to be hurt. And not wanting to be hurt one builds a wall. One is very shy, or aggressive; before you attack I am ready to attack you verbally, or with thought. I have been hurt so much in my life, everybody hurts me—everybody treads on one's toes—and I don't want to be hurt. Is that one of the reasons why fear exists?

You have been hurt, haven't you? And out of that hurt you do all kinds of things. We resist a great deal, we don't want to be disturbed; out of that feeling of hurt we cling to something which we hope will protect us. Therefore we become aggressive towards anything that attacks what we are holding on to for protection.

As a human being sitting here, wanting to resolve this problem of fear, what is it that you are frightened of? Is it physical fear—fear of physical pain? Or a psychological fear of danger, of uncertainty, of being hurt again? Or of not being able to find total, complete security? Is it fear of being dominated, and yet we are dominated? So what is it that you are frightened of? Are you aware of your fear?

Questioner: I fear the unknown.

KRISHNAMURTI: Now listen to that question. Why should one be afraid of the unknown, when you know nothing about it? Please enquire into it.

Questioner: I have an image of what has happened to me and there is the fear that it might happen again.

KRISHNAMURTI: But is it the fear of letting go the known? Or fear of the unknown? You understand? Fear of letting go the things I have gathered—my property, my wife, my name, my books, my furniture, my good looks, my capacities—to let go the things that I know, that I have experienced: is that the fear? Or is it fear of the future, the unknown?

Questioner: I find that my fear generally is of what will happen, not of what is happening.

KRISHNAMURTI: Shall we go into that?

Questioner: It isn't that one is frightened of what might happen tomorrow, but of losing one's own recognitions, one's satisfactions, today.

KRISHNAMURTI: Look, the gentleman asked a question which was: "I am not frightened of yesterday or of today, but I am frightened of what might happen tomorrow, in the future." Tomorrow may be twenty-fours hours away or a year, but I am frightened of that.

Questioner: But the future is the result of all the expectations one has because of the past.

KRISHNAMURTI: I am frightened of the future, how shall I deal with this? Don't explain it to me, I want to find out what to do with this fear. I am frightened what might happen: I might get ill, I might lose my job, a dozen things might happen to me, I may go insane, lose all the things which I have stored up. Now please enquire.

Questioner: I think perhaps it is not the future that we fear but rather the uncertainty of the future, new events which cannot be predicted. If the future were predictable there would be no fear, we should know what would happen. Fear is a sort of defence of the body against something completely new, against the whole uncertainty of what life is.

KRISHNAMURTI: "I am afraid of the future because the future is uncertain." I don't know how to deal with this uncertainty, with my whole being, therefore I am afraid. Fear is an indication of this uncertainty of the future, is that it?

Questioner: That's only a part of it. There are other fears too.

KRISHNAMURTI: Sir, we are taking one fear; we will discuss various forms of fears presently. The gentleman says, "I am not really frightened of anything except of the future. The future is so uncertain, I don't know how to meet it. I haven't the capacity to understand not only the present, but also the future." So it is this sense of uncertainty that indicates fear. Whatever the explanation be, the fact is I am frightened of tomorrow. Now how shall I deal with it? How shall I be free of that fear?

Questioner: Looking at one's response to the uncertainty of the future it seems it might be inadequate.

KRISHNAMURTI: I am frightened of tomorrow. of what might happen. The whole future is uncertain, there might be an atomic war, there might be an ice age—I am frightened of all that. How am I to deal with it? Help me, don't theorise about it, don't give me explanations!

Questioner (1): Need uncertainty breed fear?

Questioner (2): We are frightened because we are pretending, playing games, and we are afraid, of being exposed.

KRISHNAMURTI: But you are not helping me! Aren't you frightened of the future, Sir?—stick to this.

Questioner: Yes, perhaps.

KRISHNAMURTI: Now, how are you going to deal with it?

Questioner: By living in the present.

KRISHNAMURTI: I don't know what that means.

Questioner (1): For me it has been helpful to realise what I have been afraid of in the past, and why I have been afraid, and to submit this to examination. This helps me to face the future.

Questioner (2): First of all we have got to understand what we mean by the future.

KRISHNAMURTI: That's what I am trying to find out.

Questioner: The first thing we have to do is not to be afraid of being frightened.

KRISHNAMURTI: Oh, that is a cliché, that doesn't help me!

Questioner: One has to realise you can't help me out: fear is always there. One has to understand fear is going to be a life companion.

KRISHNAMURTI: Sir, you have not fed me. You have given me a lot of words, ashes. I am still frightened of tomorrow.

Questioner (1): That is just the problem. You can't help anyone.

Questioner (2): Can't you wait for tomorrow and let things come, see what happens?

Questioner (3): I know the necessity for physical security, but I want to understand my need for psychological security.

KRISHNAMURTI: He means that, Sir. He probably has some security physically, but psychologically he is frightened of tomorrow. He has got a little bank account, a little house and all the rest of it, he is not frightened about that; he is frightened of what might happen in the future.

Questioner (1): Is is possible to live with your uncertainty?

Questioner (2): If we knew what was going to happen, we should not be afraid.

Questioner (3): Sitting here I am not afraid, but thinking about tomorrow I get frightened.

KRISHNAMURTI: Thought does it.

Questioner: Thought does it. When we are frightened now, it is a fact. If we accept the fact and if we live totally in the present, we forget the future.

KRISHNAMURTI: Right, let's look. I want to find out what causes this fear of tomorrow. What is tomorrow? Why does tomorrow exist at all? You understand? I am going to answer it.

I want to find out how thought arises, how fear arises. I think about tomorrow, and the past has given me a sense of security; though there may have been a great many uncertainties in the past, on the whole I have survived. Up to now I am fairly safe, but tomorrow is very uncertain and I am frightened. So I am going to find out what causes this fear of tomorrow. The response of my whole being to that insecurity of tomorrow being uncertain, is fear. So I want to find out why fear arises when I think about the future. Which means, the future may be all right, but my thinking about it makes the uncertainty. I don't know the future, it may be marvellous, or it may be deadly, it may be terrible, or most beautiful, I don't know; thought is not certain about the future. So thought, which has always been seek-

392

ing certainty, is suddenly faced with this uncertainty. So why does thought create fear? You follow?

Questioner: Because thought divides and creates a distance between past and future, and fear enters into this space.

KRISHNAMURTI: The questioner says, "Thought separates the future from the past and divides what might be. This separation of 'what is' and 'what might be' is part of this fear." If I did not think about tomorrow, there would be no fear, I would not know the future, I would not even care. Because I think about the future—the future which I don't know, the future which is so uncertain—my whole response, psychologically as well as physically, is to say, "My God, what is going to happen?" So thought breeds fear.

Questioner: Is thought the only psychological function that is able to bring about fear? There are some other irrational functions like feeling; that might bring about fear as well.

KRISHNAMURTI: I am taking that one particular thing, there are other factors too.

Questioner (1): There is fear of the unknown, fear of tomorrow; it is based on attachment to a belief, or some formula. The fear can be understood if I see why I am attached to a particular convention or belief.

Questioner (2): What about fear of existence?

KRISHNAMURTI: All these are involved, are they not? The attachment to a belief, to a formula, to a certain ideological concept which I have built for myself, all these are part of this fear. Now I want to find out by seeing what is fear.

I said to you earlier I have done something in the past of which I am ashamed, or of which I am frightened: I don't want it to recur. Thinking about what I have done in the past breeds fear, doesn't it? Thinking about what might happen in the future also breeds fear. So I see—I may be wrong—that thought is responsible for the fear, both of the past and of the future. And thought is also responsible for fear by projecting an ideal, a belief, and holding on to that belief and wanting certainty out of that belief; it is all the operation of thought, isn't it? So I have to understand why thought thinks about the future, why thought goes back to some event which has brought fear. Why does thought do this?

Questioner: Thought can help itself by imagining all the possibilities of terrible things that could happen in the future, so it can make some plans to prevent these things happening. It tries to protect itself by imagining.

KRISHNAMURTI: Thought also helps you to protect yourself, through insurance, through building a house, avoiding wars; thought cultivates fear and also protects, doesn't it? We are talking about thought creating fear, not how it protects. I am asking why thought breeds this fear; thought also breeds pleasure, doesn't it?—sexual pleasure, the pleasure of the sunset which happened yesterday and so on. So thought gives a continuity to pleasure and also to fear.

Questioner: Man, seeking pleasure, follows the choice of his thoughts by discriminating. "This would be good" and "That would be bad". And fear seems to come directly from what man does to make the good things happen and to avoid the bad.

KRISHNAMURTI: Surely the whole process is based on thought, isn't it?

Questioner: Fear comes from the discriminating aspect of thought.

KRISHNAMURTI: Yes, but it is still thought, saying, "This is good, this I will keep, this reject." The whole movement of thought is the demand for pleasure and discrimination in that, saying, "This will give me pleasure, that will not." So the whole movement of fear and pleasure, the demand, and the continuity of both, depends on thought, doesn't it?

Questioner: But how can you be free from it?

KRISHNAMURTI: Wait, first let's get this thing going.

Questioner: Thought is fear.

KRISHNAMURTI: We are going to find out. I am safe today. I know I am going to have my meals, there is a house, there is a room; but I don't know what is going to happen tomorrow. Yesterday I had a great deal of pleasure in various forms, and I want those pleasures repeated tomorrow. So thought both sustains fear and gives a continuity to the pleasure which I had yesterday.

Then my question is: how am I going to prevent the continuity of fear, but yet let pleasure continue? I want pleasure, want it as much as possible, all the time in the future; and also I have had fears, I want to get rid of them and I don't want future fears. So thought is working in both directions. Sir, this is your job, not mine, look at it!

Questioner: This gives thought a kind of energy.

KRISHNAMURTI: Thought is energy.

Questioner: This gives thought a dfferent kind of energy.

KRISHNAMURTI: Go into it, it is both.

Questioner: It is accumulating memories.

KRISHNAMURTI: The memories that have been pleasurable I hold on to, and the memories that have been painful—which are fear—I want to throw out. But I don't see the root of all this is thought.

Questioner (1): Thought seems to resist its termination—fear and pleasure seem to be somewhat similar—but that state where thought doesn't exist eludes me.

Questioner (2): Do what you are doing so totally, that you think about the thing that is giving you pleasure while it is happening, and don't think about the things which may not happen.

KRISHNAMURTI: Don't say: not to think about those things which might not happen. How am I to prevent myself from thinking about them?

Questioner: Think about what is happening, rejoice!

KRISHNAMURTI: So I force myself to think about things that are happening and not about things that don't happen?

Questioner: Think about what is happening.

KRISHNAMURTI: But my mind is always watching what might happen. Doesn't this happen to you? Let's be quite simple and honest. We want to think about the things that are happening, but thought also keeps an eye on what might happen. And when I am not thinking about this, that pops up!

Questioner: Sir, the feeling "I am" has nothing to do with pleasure and nothing to do with fear and thought. I think only "I am". I don't have fear. This feeling "I am" has nothing at all to do with thought.

KRISHNAMURTI: When you say "I am"—what do you mean by those words?

Questioner: The feeling to be present, to be sitting here, and there is no fear in it.

KRISHNAMURTI: That is not the problem, Sir.

Questioner: First of all we must find out if certainty exists, then there won't be fear.

KRISHNAMURTI: How shall I find out?

Questioner: I see the whole process of thought as a trap.

KRISHNAMURTI: Go into it; each person pursues something else. Let me state what I feel the problem is.

I am frightened of tomorrow because tomorrow is uncertain. So far I have been fairly certain in my life; though there have been occasions on which I have been frightened, somehow I have got over them. But the sense of fear of tomorrow, which is so uncertain—atomic war, the casual wars that might explode into all kinds of horrors, losing money—I am in a state of convulsion about the future. Now what am I to do? I want to be free, if I can, of the fear both of the past and the future, of the fears deep down and the superficial fears.

Don't give me explanations, "Do this", "Don't do that." I want to find out what fear is; whether it is fear of darkness, of uncertainty whether it is the fear of attachment, holding on to something, or to some person or idea. I want to find out what is the root of it, how to escape from it, not how to smother it. I want to see the structure of fear. If I can understand that, then something else can take place. So I am going to investigate what fear is. Let me go on a little while, may I?

Fear exists for me because I am thinking about tomorrow; despite your assurance that tomorrow is perfectly all right, I still feel fear. Now why am I thinking about tomorrow? Is it because the past has been so good, has given me a great deal of knowledge and this has become my security, and I have no knowledge about the future? If I could understand the future and reduce that to my knowledge, then I would not be frightened. Can I understand the future as knowledge, as experience, so that it becomes part of my knowledge, of which I shan't be frightened?

I see also, that I want a great deal of pleasure, sexual pleasure, the pleasure of achieving, fulfilling, of being somebody. I want those pleasures, which I have had, repeated. And when I get bored with them I want wider, deeper pleasures. My principle drive is pleasure—in every direction. So I want to avoid fear and I want more pleasure. This is what we all want. Is pleasure separate from fear? Or are they the two sides of the same coin? I must find out, not say "Yes" or "No", I must put my teeth into it and find out whether pleasure does breed fear and whether fear is the result of my demand for pleasure. You have understood my question?

Questioner: But pleasure could be something else, a learning process.

KRISHNAMURTI: No, that pleasure is also painful; but I will overcome that in order to have more pleasure. Haven't you noticed this in your life, how we want pleasure?

Questioner: Yes.

KRISHNAMURTI: That's all I am talking of. We are demanding, pursuing pleasure; everything is based on this. And when that is not fulfilled, I become uncertain. So I am asking myself whether pleasure and fear don't go together. I never question pleasure, I never say, "Should I have so much pleasure?" "Where does it lead?" but I want more of it, in heaven, on earth, in my family, in sex—it is driving me in everything. And fear is there also. Look at it please, don't stick to your particular opinion, for God's sake move from it! Find out!

So follow this: I want certainty of tomorrow, and certainty can only exist where there is knowledge, when I say, "I know". Can I know anything except the past? The moment I say "I know" it is already the past. When I say "I know my wife", I know her in terms of the past. In the past there is certainty and in the future there is uncertainty. So I want to draw the future into the past so that I will be completely safe. I see fear arises where thought is operating; if I did not think about tomorrow there would be no fear.

Questioner: Fear seems to me to be something instinctive. I feel that fear is an energy, that some force is there.

KRISHNAMURTI: You see, each of us has an opinion. Each of us is quite sure we know how to deal with fear. We explain it, we give causes, we think we understand it, and yet at the end of it we are frightened. I want to go behind all that and find out why fear exists at all. Is it the result of thought thinking about the future? Because the future is very uncertain and thought is based on the memory of the past. Thought is the response of memory, accumulated as knowledge, as centuries of experience, and out of that comes thought. Thought says, "Knowledge is my security". And now you are telling me to be free of tomorrow, which is uncertain; if I know what tomorrow is, there will be no fear. What I am craving for is certainty of knowledge. I know my past, I know what I did ten years or two days ago. I can analyse it, understand it, live with it; but I don't know tomorrow and therefore not knowing it makes me afraid. Not knowing means: not having knowledge of. Now can thought have knowledge about something which it does not know?

So there is fear. Thought trying to find out the future, and not knowing what its content is, it is afraid. Why is thought thinking of tomorrow, about which it knows nothing? It wants certainty, but there may be no certainty. Please answer my question, not your question.

Questioner: The living system needs to think about to-morrow, this is a fundamental rule of life: it needs some sort of prediction.

KRISHNAMURTI: I said that, Sir.

Questioner: We must follow this rule of life. There are psychological disturbances due to imagination which project awful fears, as you say, but it is impossible to prevent human beings from thinking in a logical fashion.

KRISHNAMURTI: If I may say so, we did say thought is necessary to protect physical survival. That is part of our life, that is what we are doing all the time.

Questioner: I don't agree, I think thought is not necessary for survival. Animals have the instinct for survival without the fear which is our trouble.

KRISHNAMURTI: Madam, we are mixing up two things. Please, we tried to explain this at the beginning.

Questioner: She's right; human thought replaces instinct.

KRISHNAMURTI: I agree with you. One must know that to-morrow the house will be there. Physical survival and planning for the future are essential, aren't they? Without that we can't survive.

Questioner (1): When you see it all so clearly, fear has no time.

Questioner (2): Thought thinks of living in the present, and must also think of tomorrow.

KRISHNAMURTI: The weather is hot, I must plan to buy some trousers that will be cool. That means planning for tomorrow. I have to go to India in the winter. I shall plan, which is the future. We are not denying that, on the contrary. What we are talking about is the fear of uncertainty.

Questioner: We have no confidence in ourselves.

KRISHNAMURTI: That I really don't understand. Who is "yourself" for you to have confidence in? Are you such a marvellous human being to have confidence in yourself?

Questioner: Why not?

KRISHNAMURTI: What is yourself?

Questioner: Humanity.

KRISHNAMURTI: What is humanity? The good and the bad, the wars—we have been through all that. We are concerned with fear. We must use thought to survive. But to survive, thought has divided the world as my country, your country, my government, your government, my God, your God, my guru and your guru: thought has created this. Though it wants to plan to survive, thought has divided the world which destroys itself, of which I am part. So I have to understand the nature of thought, where it is necessary, and where it is diabolical, where it is destructive and where it creates fear—that is my problem.

I said thought must function, otherwise you can't survive; but in the desire to survive it has divided and is therefore destructive. I see thought must function clearly, objectively, without any distortion. So my question is: why does thought think about tomorrow? It has to think about tomorrow in one direction, but why does thought think about the future and breed fear?

Questioner: To be safe.

KRISHNAMURTI: You see, thought must think about tomorrow in order to be safe, that is clear. And also you see that thought, thinking about tomorrow, creates fear. Now why?

Questioner (1): Because we want to continue.

Questioner (2): Because we are tied to pleasure.

KRISHNAMURTI: We haven't solved this problem because we refuse to leave our particular little opinions, judgments and conclusions. Let's abolish them and think anew.

For me it is very simple. Thought must create fear because thought cannot ever find security in the future.

Thought has security in time; tomorrow has no time. Tomorrow exists in the mind as time, but tomorrow may not exist at all, psychologically. And because of that uncertainty, thought projects what it wants for tomorrow: safety, what I have acquired, what I have achieved, what I possess, all that. And that too is completely uncertain. So can thought be quiet about the future? That's my point. Can thought be quiet, which means: function where it is necessary for physical protection; and therefore no divisions into nationalities, no separate Gods, no warmongers. Let thought be quiet so that time as tomorrow does not exist.

Therefore I have to understand what it is to live now. I don't understand what it is to live now, nor have I understood what it is to live in the past, therefore I want to live in the future, which I don't know, as I don't know what the present is. So I am asking, can I live completely, wholly, today? I can only do that when I have understood the whole machinery and the functioning of thought, and in the very understanding of the reality of thought there is silence. And where the mind is quiet there is no future, no time.

SAANEN
AUGUST 1971

4

FEAR, TIME AND THE IMAGE

Chronological and psychological time. The dilemma of knowledge. The dilemma of thought and the image. Can one find the root of fear? "The mind that can never be hurt."

Questioner (1): You have covered enough ground couldn't we consolidate? I am not quite sure in myself about the relation between thought and fear; could we discuss this some more?

401

Questioner (2): When thought meets the unknown, it doesn't know what to do. Now if you have thought without time, if there is no time, then there is no fear.

KRISHNAMURTI: Would you like to talk about that?

Audience: Yes.

KRISHNAMURTI: What is time? I had to be here this morning in spite of the bad weather at half past ten and I was. If I did not come on time, I would keep you all waiting. There is time by the watch—yesterday, today and tomorrow. There is time to cover a certain distance—between here and the moon, to go from here to Montreux, and so on. There is also time to cover the distance between the image of myself—or the image I have projected of myself—and what "I should be", and the distance between what "I am" and what "I should like to be", between fear and the ending of fear. We must understand this.

Questioner: Can you give practical examples as you go along?

KRISHNAMURTI: I am not good at giving practical examples. What I am saying is fairly simple. I am not a philosopher, I don't spin theories.

So there is time as yesterday, today and tomorrow; and there is time—at least we think there is time—between what I am and what I should be, between the fact of fear and the eventual ending of fear. Both are time, aren't they?—chronological time, and time as invented by thought. "I am this" and "I should change to that" and to cover that distance between what I am and what I should be I need time. That also is time. It will take me many days, or many weeks, to do certain exercises properly, to loosen up my muscles—to do that I need time; I shall take perhaps three days, or a week: that's time.

So when we talk about time, let us be clear what we are talking about. There is chronological time, as yesterday, today and tomorrow; and there is the time which we think is necessary to achieve an ending to fear. Time is part of fear, isn't it? I am afraid of the future—not of what might happen in the future but of the idea of the future, the idea of tomorrow. So there is psychological time and chronolog-

402

ical time. We are not talking about chronological time, time by the watch. What we are talking about is, "I am all right now, but I am afraid of the future, of tomorrow." Let's call that psychological time.

Now I am asking, is there such a thing as psychological time at all, or is it merely an invention of thought? "I shall meet you tomorrow, under a tree, near the bridge"—that is chronological time. "I am afraid of tomorrow and I don't know how to meet that fear of tomorrow"—that is psychological time, isn't it?

Questioner: How about if I say, "Why must this beautiful thing come to an end?"

KRISHNAMURTI: That is also psychological time, isn't it? I feel a particular relationship to something beautiful and I don't want it to end. There is the idea that it might come to an end and I won't like it to end, and I am afraid of it. So that's one part of the structure of fear.

The other is, I have known security, certainty, and tomorrow is uncertain and I am afraid of that—that is psychological time, isn't it? I have lived a life of quasi-security, but tomorrow is dreadfully uncertain and I am frightened of it. Then arises my problem: how am I not to be afraid? All that is involved, surely, is it not, in psychological time? The knowledge of yesterday, of many thousand yesterdays, has given to the brain a certain sense of security, knowledge being experience, remembrance, memories. In the past there has been security for the brain; tomorrow there may be no security at all, I might be killed.

Knowledge as time gives to the brain a sense of security. So knowledge is of time. But I have no knowledge of tomorrow, therefore I am afraid. If I had knowledge of tomorrow I would not be afraid. So knowledge breeds fear, and yet I must have knowledge. You are following? I must have knowledge to go from here to the station, I must have knowledge to speak English, or French, or whatever it is; I must have knowledge to carry out any kind of function. I have accumulated knowledge about myself as the experiencer, and yet that experiencer is frightened of tomorrow because he does not know tomorrow.

Questioner: What about repetition?

KRISHNAMURTI: It is the same thing, it is mechanical. After all, knowledge is repetitive. I add to it or take away from it, but it's a machinery of accumulation.

Questioner: What about the people who have terrible tragedies, who have seen people slaughtered and tortured?

KRISHNAMURTI: What has that got to do with what we are talking about?

Questioner: Well, you see, they remain with that fear.

KRISHNAMURTI: We are talking about the relationship between thought and fear.

Questioner: But even so, people have been telling me how their fear remains in them and they can't get rid of it because for them man is a beast.

KRISHNAMURTI: It is the same problem, surely. That is, I have been hurt, by a snake or by a human being. That hurt has left a deep mark on my brain and I am afraid of snakes or of human beings—which is the past. Also I am afraid of tomorrow. It is the same problem, isn't it?—only one is in the past, the other is in the future.

Questioner: It's only difficult when you say, "Knowledge of yesterday has given security." Some people find the knowledge of yesterday has given them insecurity.

KRISHNAMURTI: Knowledge gives security and it also gives insecurity, doesn't it? I have been hurt by human beings in the past—that's knowledge. That remains deeply rooted and I loath human beings, I am frightened of them.

Questioner: One isn't speaking of psychological knowledge but of physical torture.

KRISHNAMURTI: Yes, physical torture which is again in the past.

Questioner: But you know that in the present people go on doing it.

KRISHNAMURTI: You are mixing up two facts. We are talking about fear and its relationship to thought. There are physical tortures going on in the world, people are extraordinarily brutal and I like to think about it and get terribly excited. I feel morally righteous about it and I can't do anything, can I? Sitting in this tent I can't do anything about what is happening in another place. But I like to get neurotically excited about it, and to say, "It's terrible what human beings are doing." No? What can I actually do? Join a group that is going to stop this torture of human beings? Make a demonstration in front of somebody?— and yet the torture will go on. What I am concerned with is how to change the human mind so that it will not torture human beings physically or psychologically in any way. But if I am neurotic I like to keep on thinking, "How terrible this world is."

Now let's come back. I am afraid of what human beings have done to me, or to another human being, and that knowledge is a scar in the brain. That is, knowledge of the past not only gives certainty but also uncertainty, that I may be hurt tomorrow, therefore I am afraid. Now why does the brain retain the memory of that hurt of yesterday? In order to protect itself from future hurts? Let's think it out. That means, I am always facing the world with that hurt and therefore I have no relationship with another human being, because the hurt is so deep. And I resist every human relationship because I might get hurt again. Therefore there is fear. Knowledge of the past hurt brings fear of future hurt. So knowledge brings fear—yet I must have knowledge.

Knowledge has been accumulated through time. Scientific, technological knowledge, knowledge of a language and so on need time. Knowledge, which is the product of time, must exist, otherwise I can't do anything, I can't communicate with you. But also I see that knowledge of a past hurt says, "Be careful not to be hurt in the future." So I am afraid of the future.

So how am I, who have been scarred very deeply, how am I to be free of that and not project that knowledge into the future, saying, "I am afraid of the future." There are two problems involved, aren't there? There is the scar of pain, of hurt, and the knowledge of it makes me afraid of tomorrow. Can the mind be free of that scar? Now let's examine that.

I am sure most of us have some kind of psychological

scars. Haven't you?—of course. We are not talking about the physical scars which affect the brain—we can leave that aside for the moment. There are the psychological scars of hurt. How is the mind, the brain, to be free of them? Must it be free of them? Is not the memory of being hurt a protection against the future? Verbally, in many ways you have hurt me; there is a memory of it. If I forget that, I come innocently to you next morning and you hurt me again. So what am I to do? Think it out, Sirs, go on.

Questioner: Isn't it important for me to find out why I am psychologically capable of being hurt?

KRISHNAMURTI: It is fairly simple. We are very sensitive, there are a dozen reasons. I have an image about myself and I don't want you to hurt that image. I think I am a great man, you come along and put a pin into it and it hurts me. Or I feel terribly inferior and I meet you, who feel extraordinarily superior, and I get hurt. You are clever, I am not—I get hurt. You are beautiful, I am not. The knowledge of being hurt, not only physically but psychologically, inwardly, has left a mark on the brain as memory. Memory is knowledge. Why should I be free of that knowledge? If I am free, you are going to hurt me again. Therefore that knowledge acts as a resistance, as a wall. And what happens in relationship between human beings when there is this wall between you and me?

Questioner: We can't meet.

KRISHNAMURTI: Exactly. So what do we do? Go on Sir, pursue it!

Questioner: Take away the wall.

KRISHNAMURTI: But you are going to hurt me.

Questioner: It's only the image that is hurt.

KRISHNAMURTI: No, Sir. Look, I come to you quite innocently. The root-meaning of that word "innocent" is that you cannot be hurt. So I come to you open, friendly, and you say something to me which hurts me. Doesn't this happen to all of you? And what takes place? That leaves a mark—that's knowledge. What is wrong with that knowledge? That knowledge acts as a wall between you and me. Of course! Therefore what shall I do?

Questioner: You've got to break through.

KRISHNAMURTI: First look at it, don't say, "Break through" —just look at it. You've hurt me and the knowledge of that remains. If I have no knowledge of it, you will hurt me again; and if I have that knowledge strengthened, it acts as a wall between you and me. Therefore between you and me there is no relationship. So knowledge of the past prevents a relationship between you and me. What shall I do?

Questioner: Examine it.

KRISHNAMURTI: I have examined it, I have taken ten minutes in the examination of it and I see that examination, that analysis is totally useless.

Questioner: Is this where time comes in?

KRISHNAMURTI: I have taken ten minutes—analysis implied ten minutes—and that ten minutes is a waste.

Questioner: If there were no time . . .

KRISHNAMURTI: I have used time. Don't say there is no time.

Questioner: But if there were no time.

KRISHNAMURTI: I don't know, that's a supposition. I have taken ten minutes to see why I am hurt, to examine the hurt, to see the necessity of keeping that hurt as knowledge. I have asked myself: if I remove that hurt, won't you hurt me again? And I see, as long as that hurt remains, there is no relationship between you and me. All that has taken more than a quarter of an hour. And I see I have achieved nothing at the end of it. So I have found analysis has no value at all. What shall I do, having been hurt and remembering that hurt prevents all relationship?

Questioner: We have to accept being hurt.

KRISHNAMURTI: No, I'm neither accepting nor rejecting, I'm looking. I don't accept or reject anything. My question then is, "Why am I hurt?" What is this thing that is being hurt?

Questioner: The knowledge of being a fool in fact.

KRISHNAMURTI: Sir, say something that's actual, don't imagine and then verbalise. First find out what it is that is being hurt. When I say I am hurt because you call me a fool, what is it that is being hurt?

Questioner: Your pride. The knowledge of being a fool is there.

KRISHNAMURTI: No, Madam, it is not only that, please look at it, it is much deeper than that. I am hurt because you called me a fool. Why should I be hurt?

Questioner: Because of the image I have of myself.

KRISHNAMURTI: Which means I have an image of myself as not being a fool. And when you call me a fool, or a blackguard, or a whatever it is, I get hurt because of my image. Why do I have an image about myself? As long as I have an image about myself I'm going to be hurt.

Questioner: Why do I have to care about the image that the other has of me, whatever that may be?

KRISHNAMURTI: The other has an image of me as a fool, or he has the image of me as a great intellect—it's the same thing, you follow? Now why do I have an image about myself?

Questioner: Because I don't like what I am.

KRISHNAMURTI: No, first why do you have it? Because you don't like yourself as you are? What are you? Have you looked at yourself without an image? Let's be simple. I have an image about you as being very clever, bright, intelligent, awake, enlightened—a tremendous image. And comparing myself with you I am dull. Measuring myself against you I find I am inferior—obviously. That makes me feel I am very dull, very stupid, and from that feeling

408

of inferiority, of stupidity, I have many other problems. Now why do I compare myself with you at all? Is it that we have been brought up from childhood to compare? In schools we compare, through the giving of marks, through examinations. The mother says, "Be as bright as your elder brother." There is this terrible comparison going on all the time throughout life. And if I don't compare, where am I? Am I dull? I don't know. I have called myself dull in comparing myself with you, who are not dull, but if I don't compare, what happens?

Questioner: I become myself.

KRISHNAMURTI: What is "yourself"? Just see the cycle we go through, repeating these things over and over again without understanding them. So I come back to this: why do I have to have an image about myself—good, bad, noble, ignoble, ugly or dull. Why do I have an image about anything?

Questioner: It's a means of conscious acting. A man who is conscious and aware must automatically become involved in comparison.

KRISHNAMURTI: Sir, I am asking: why do I compare? Comparison implies not only conflict but imitation, doesn't it?

Questioner: But surely it is necessary to evaluate.

KRISHNAMURTI: Watch it please—comparison implies conflict and imitation, doesn't it? That's one side of it. In comparing myself with you I feel I am dull, therefore I must struggle to be as clever as you are. There is conflict and I then imitate what you are. That's implied in comparison: conflict and imitation. But also I see I must compare between this cloth and that cloth, this house and that house, measure whether you are tall or short, measure the distance between here and another place. You follow? But why do I have an image about myself? Because if I have an image about myself it's going to be hurt.

Questioner: Perhaps this image doesn't exist at all.

KRISHNAMURTI: That's right, go on, investigate it. Why do I have an image about myself as something or nothing?

Questioner: I want to be secure, that depends on how secure the image is.

KRISHNAMURTI: You are saying that you are seeking security in an image. Is that it? That image has been put together by thought. So you find security in the image which thought has built, and in that image thought is seeking security. Thought has created an image because it wants security in that image, so thought is seeking security in itself. Which is: thought is seeking security in the image which it has built, and that image is the product of thought; thought is memory, which is the past. So thought has built this image about itself? No?

Questioner: Sir, may I ask what to do with education? Because even parents start to compare their own children and say, "This child is cleverer."

KRISHNAMURTI: I know. Parents are the most dangerous human beings! *(Laughter)* They destroy their children, because *they* are uneducated.

So the image is built by thought and thought is seeking security; so thought has invented an image in which it finds security, but it is still thought and thought is the response of memory, of yesterday. What has happened? Knowledge of yesterday has created this image. How am I not to be hurt? Not being hurt implies not having any kind of image—obviously. Now, how am I to prevent images?—images of the future, of which I am going to be frightened. Thought is time, thought is fear of the image of tomorrow in which there is no certainty. How is the mind, or the brain, not to have images at all and yet not be hurt? The moment it is hurt, it is going to have an image. And being hurt, it protects itself with another image.

So my question is: apart from the physical aspect, where it has to protect itself against danger, polluted air, wars, etc., where protection is necessary—can the brain not be hurt at all? Which means, not to have any kind of image. Not to be hurt implies having no resistance. Having no resistance means having no image. Not to be hurt means vitality, energy, and that energy is dissipated when

I have images. That energy is dissipated when I compare myself with you,—compare my image with your image. That energy is dissipated in conflict, in trying to become your image, which I have projected for myself. That energy is wasted when I am imitating the image which I have projected about you. So the dissipation of energy is this factor. And when I am energetic, which can only take place when there is attention, I am not hurt. I don't know whether you are following all this? Let's understand it differently.

One observes that one is hurt. One is hurt because basically one has an image about oneself. That image has been built through the various forms of culture, education, civilisation, tradition, nationality, economic conditions and social injustice. That image is the past and therefore knowledge. Thought—whether it is my thought or the collective thought—has imprinted on the brain this sense of comparing an image with another image. The mother, the schoolteacher, the politician does it, as well as the mythology of the Christians; the whole civilisation is based on building this image. And there it is, in the brain, which is thought. Now one discovers, one understands, that as long as one has an image, there must be hurt.

Questioner: The image is the hurt, isn't it?

KRISHNAMURTI: So can the brain be free of all images and therefore never be hurt? That means to be free of the knowledge of the past as image. Knowledge of the past is essential to speak a language; but as long as there is knowledge as an image, put together by thought, which is the "me"—which is the greatest image—and as long as I have the greatest image in "me", you have a perfect right to put pins into it. And you do!

So can the brain never be hurt? Sirs, find this out for yourselves and live a life in which the brain is never hurt! Then only can you have relationship. But if in the relationship you are hurting me and I am hurting you, it comes to an end. And if in that relationship between you and me there is hurt and that relationship comes to an end, then I go to find another relationship—divorce you and join somebody else. And again there is going to be hurt. We think by changing a relationship we are going to be completely invulnerable. But all the time we are being hurt.

Questioner: If the images are gone, between what is the relationship? Relationship means a relevant word, and if the images are gone, what is the relationship between man and wife?

KRISHNAMURTI: Why are you asking me? Find out if your image has gone, not because you want to ask me a question which I should answer. Find out if the images, which you have, have gone; then you will find out what your relationship is with another. But if I say, "It is love", it is just a theory. Throw it out, that has no meaning. But if you said: "I know I am hurt, all my life I have been hurt." Don't you know this?—a series of inward tears, a series of anxieties. These images exist!

Our question is: can the brain never be hurt at all? And that you have to apply yourself to, not just talk about it. Go after it, say, "Have I got an image?" Obviously you have, otherwise you and I wouldn't be sitting here. And if you have an image, examine it, go into it and see the futility of analysis, because that prevents you from action. Whereas if you say now, "I move with the image", to move with the image means the thought that is building this; and thought is knowledge. So can the brain be full of knowledge in one direction and have no knowledge in the other? That means complete silence. You understand, Sir? To be completely silent, and out of that silence to use knowledge. You won't see this.

Questioner: What place is there for established relationship? Is there such a thing?

KRISHNAMURTI: Go to the Registrar and get married. That establishes legally a relationship, and what goes on, my God! And what goes on also not legally! So it's your torture.

To come back, what is the relationship of thought to fear? We said, thought springs from knowledge of the past, knowledge is the past. In that knowledge thought has found security: I know my house, I know you, I am this, I am conditioned or not conditioned. I have asserted what I am in knowledge. But tomorrow I don't know, I am afraid of tomorrow. And also I am afraid of the knowledge which I have of the past, because I see there is also tremendous insecurity. If I live in the past, as most of us do, I am already dead and that feeling of living in the past

412

is suffocating, and I don't know how to get rid of it and I am frightened of that, as I am frightened of tomorrow. So I am frightened of living and I am frightened of dying. What am I to do with the fears I have? Or is there only one fear? Apart from the physical fears and psychosomatic fears, is there only one fear, taking different forms?

Questioner: Is it the fear of nothingness, of the void?

KRISHNAMURTI: Is it the fear of not being? The fear of not having any image: the being is the image, isn't it? Let's apply our minds and see actually whether the mind can be free of fear, both of the physical fears and the psychological fears which are much deeper, more neurotic. Let's apply ourselves, put our teeth into it, because one sees that when there is fear of any kind it is the most appalling thing. One lives in darkness, in a sense of void, disassociated, having no relationship, everything becomes ugly. Haven't you fear?—not only of the past, but also of the future; not only the fears of which one is conscious, but deep down.

Now when you look at this whole phenomenon of fear, at the various forms of fear, physical and psychological, with all their divisions, in all their varieties, when you see the whole structure of fear, what is the root of it all? Unless I discover the root of it, I shall go on manipulating the parts, modifying the parts. So I must find the root of it. What do you think is the root of all fears?—not just of one particular form of fear. Please don't answer me. Be sure for yourself, what is the root of it, discover it, unfold it, look at it.

Questioner: Sir, I would like to say that as an exercise we should hurt each other. I would like to hurt you, and you should hurt these people; because of the conditions here—I feel the whole atmosphere is polite—you don't want to hurt these people.

KRISHNAMURTI: The gentleman says, this atmosphere is polite, a bore. I don't want to hurt you and you don't want to hurt me; therefore it's a form of politeness and it doesn't amount to anything. Is that so? I don't mind your hurting me.

Questioner (1): I think relationship is not just sitting here and listening to you. I think if I hurt you, there would be a relationship between you and me, because then I have destroyed part of the image.

Questioner (2): That's nonsense! Is it possible for you to continue, as we have so little time?

KRISHNAMURTI: You see, Sir, it's not a reaction, he is telling you something, he says, look: we have been through all this. We have examined the images—you having one, I having one, you hurting and I hurting, we've been through all that; it's not politeness.

Questioner: But you described images and we did not look into the images.

KRISHNAMURTI: You were supposed to. How do you know?

Questioner: Maybe the others did.

KRISHNAMURTI: How do you know? You see, how do I know that you have not washed away your images? It's my conceit which says you have not. Who am I to tell you whether you have, or not. It's up to you. So let's go back.

I want to find out about fear—not the parts of the various fears—but I really want to find out the root of it. Is it "not being"?—which is the "becoming", you follow? That is, "I am becoming something", "I want to be something". I have been hurt and I want to be free of hurts. All our life is this process of "becoming". Aggression is part of this becoming. And the "not becoming" is an immense fear; "not being" is a fear, isn't it? Is that the root of it?

Questioner: Sir, I try to find out the root of fear. I see I can't think about the fear, so the mind becomes silent so that I can just feel that fear; and then all I feel is a deep, inner tension; but I can't get beyond that point.

KRISHNAMURTI: But why is one tense about it? I just want to find out. Why should I have any tension about it? Because if there is tension I want to go beyond it, I am so eager, so greedy! Sir, just look. We think, don't we, each one of us, in terms of becoming—becoming enlightened,

414

breaking down the images: "You don't listen to my image", "I don't listen to your image"—you follow? This whole process is a form of "becoming" or "being". When the "being" is threatened—which is "not becoming"—there is fear. Right?

What is there to become? I can understand that I can become healthier, I can grow my hair longer, but psychologically, what is there to become? What is becoming? Changing images? Changing one image for another image?—obviously. But if I have no image at all and I see the reason for not having one logically, I also see the truth, that images prevent relationship, whether it is the hurt image, or a pleasant image—it is both, obviously. If I have a pleasant image about you, you are my friend, if I have an unpleasant image about you, you are my enemy. So not to have images at all! Work this out, *apply it*, not just accept it, but actually apply it. Enquire and apply and live it. Then one finds—if you do apply, do work at it—there is a mind, there is a brain, that can never be hurt, because there is nothing to be hurt.

SAANEN
8 AUGUST 1971

5

INTELLIGENCE AND THE RELIGIOUS LIFE

What is a religious life? Relationship between meditation and the quiet mind. Thought as measure; the action of measurement. How can the immeasurable be understood? Intelligence as the relationship between the measurable and the immeasurable. The awakening of intelligence. Choiceless awareness. Learning, not accumulating knowledge.

Questioner (1): *Can we discuss the observer and the observed and their relation to awareness?*

Questioner (2): *May we discuss what it really means to lead a religious life?*

415

Questioner (3): *Could we talk about intelligence and meditation?*

KRISHNAMURTI: Now what is a religious life? In talking that over, we shall come upon this question of the observer and the observed, intelligence and meditation and the rest of it. I don't know if it interests you at all to find out what religion means. Not the accepted meaning of that word, the belief in some saviour, in some form of God, in some ritual and so on, which is all propaganda and for me has no value whatsoever—that is not a religious life. Are you quite sure we all see that fact? You may not belong to any sect or group, or any community that believes—or doesn't believe—in God. That belief—or unbelief—in God is another form of fear: the mind wanting some kind of security, certainty; because our life in so uncertain, so confused, so meaningless, we want something to believe in. So can we also put aside the hope that something outside, a superior agency, exists? To enquire, all that must obviously be put aside.

Thoughts can imagine anything—gods or no gods, angels or no angels—it can produce every form of neurotic perception, idea and conclusion. Knowing that intelligently, man then says: how can thought be quiet, so that the mind is free to enquire? Thought is capable of inventing, or imagining every form of conclusion, of projecting an image in which the human mind finds security; that security, that image, becomes an illusion—the Saviour, the Brahma, the Atman, the experiences you have through various forms of discipline and so on. So the problem is: can thought become completely still? Some say you can make it still only through a system which a teacher has invented through discipline and control. Can a system, discipline, conformity, make the mind really quiet? Or doesn't following a system, practising day after day, make the mind mechanical?—and being mechanical, then you can control it like any other machine. But the brain is not quiet, it has been shaped and conditioned by the system which it has practised. Such a brain, being mechanical, can be controlled and thinks such control is quietness, stillness. Obviously it is not. Please don't just accept what the speaker is saying. But do we all see the necessity of having a completely quiet mind? For when the mind is quiet it can see and hear much more, see things as they are—not invent, not imagine.

416

So can the mind become completely still without coercion, without compulsion, without discipline?—discipline being will, resistance, suppression, conformity, fitting into a pre-established pattern. If you do that, you are forcing the mind through conflict to conform to the pattern established by the system. So discipline in the ordinary sense of the word is out. The word discipline means to learn; not to conform, not to suppress, not to control, but to learn.

Can the whole structure of the brain and the mind be completely quiet without any form of distortion by will, by desire, by thought? That is the problem and knowing it, people have said, "It is not possible." Therefore they went in the other direction, used control, and discipline, did all kinds of tricks. In Zen meditation they sit, paying attention, watching, and if they go to sleep they are struck to keep awake. This kind of tremendous discipline is mechanical and therefore controllable; it is done in the hope of achieving an experience which will be true.

In his search for some super-transcendental experience man has said: the mind must be absolutely quiet to receive something which it has never experienced before; he has never tasted the smell, the quality of it, therefore the mind must be still. And they have said there is only one way of making the mind still: to force it. When there is the operation of will in bringing about a quiet mind, there is distortion. A mind which is distorted cannot possibly see "what is". Are we doing this?—that is, not exercising will, not forcing the mind to be mechanical through any form of discipline or system, in which are included all the tricks of Yoga—which is totally wrong. Those people who teach physical exercises make it into a perfect racket.

So seeing all that, can the mind become completely still—the mind and the brain, because it is very important that the brain be completely quiet. The brain, which is the result of time, with all its knowledge, experience and so on, is always active to every stimulus, responding to every impression, to every influence, and can that brain also be quiet?

Questioner: Why should it be quiet? It has a lot of different functions.

KRISHNAMURTI: It must be active within the field of knowledge, because that is its function. If I did not know

417

that a cobra was a most poisonous snake I would play with it and get killed. The knowledge that it is poisonous is self-protection, therefore knowledge must exist—technologically, in every way. That knowledge has been acquired, but we are not interfering with it, we don't say, "You must not have knowledge", on the contrary, you *must* have knowledge of the world, of the facts. But that knowledge has to be used impersonally.

So the brain has to be quiet; if it makes any movement, its movement will be in the direction of security, because it can only function in security, whether that security be neurotic, rational, or irrational. The brain has to have that quality of sensitivity so that it can function in knowledge, fully, completely, efficiently, sanely, healthily, and not from the point of view of "My country", "For my people", "For my family", "For me". But also there must be that quality of sensitivity which makes the brain completely quiet—that is the problem. I have explained, described the problem, but it has nothing whatsoever to do with the fact. The fact is whether you, listening to this, have put aside every form of organised belief, every form of wanting more and more experience. Because if you are desirous of wanting more experience, then the desire is in operation, which is will.

So the fact is, if you are interested in pursuing a religious life, you have to do this, which means leading a really serious life—no drugs, all that is out. And also there must be no seeking or demanding experience. Because when you are seeking experience—transcendental, or whatever you like to call it—you are seeking because you are bored with the daily experiences of life and you want to have an experience which is beyond this. And when you are experiencing what one calls a transcendental, or a different level of experience, in that there is the experiencer and the experienced; there is the observer who is experiencing and the observed which is the experience. So there is division, there is conflict: you want more and more experience. That also must be completely set aside, because when you are enquiring, experience has no place.

One sees clearly that it is absolutely necessary that the brain, the mind, the whole system, the organism, must be quiet. As you can see, if you want to listen to something like music, your body, your mind is still—you are listening. And if you are listening to somebody who is talking, your body becomes quiet. When you want to understand something, the mind, the brain, the body, the whole organism, become quiet naturally. Look how you are all sitting quietly! You are not forcing yourself to sit quietly, because you are interested to find out. That very interest is the flame that makes the mind, the brain, the body, quiet.

Now what relationship has meditation to a quiet mind? The word meditation means to measure: that is the root meaning of it. Thought alone can measure, thought is measurement. Please, this is important to understand. One really should not use the word "meditation" at all. Thought is based on measure, and the cultivation of thought is the action of measurement—technologically and in life. Without measurement there could be no modern civilisation. To go to the moon you must have the infinite capacity to measure.

Although measurement is essential, is obviously necessary, how can thought—which is measurable, which is measure—not enter? Let us put it round the other way. When there is this absolute quietness of the mind, of the whole organism, including the brain, measurement as thought ceases. Then one can enquire if there is such a thing as the immeasurable. The measurable is thought, and as long as thought is functioning the immeasurable cannot be understood. Therefore it has been said: control, beat down thought. And the whole Asiatic world went into the immeasurable, neglecting the measurable. You are following this?

Still using the word "meditation", what relationship has that to a very still mind? Can thought be really quiet, which means for the body, the mind and the heart to be in complete harmony?—yet seeing the truth that thought is measurable and that all the knowledge which thought has produced is essential. And also seeing the truth that thought, which is measurable, can never understand the immeasurable.

So if one has gone as far as that, then what relationship has this quality of the immeasurable with daily life? Are you all asleep? Are you all being mesmerised by the speaker?

We know thought is measure, we know all the mischief that thought has done in human life, the misery, the confusion, the division between people. "You believe and I don't believe," "Your God is not my God": thought has brought about havoc in the world. Thought is also knowledge, so thought is necessary. To see the truth of that, and that thought can never investigate the immeasurable, is to see that thought can never experience it as an experiencer and the experienced. So when thought is absolutely quiet, then there is a state, or a dimension, in which the immeasurable has its own movement. Now what relationship has that to daily life? Because if it has no relationship, then I shall live a life very carefully measuring my morality, my activity, according to the measurement of thought, but it will be very limited.

So what is the relationship of the unknown to the known? What is the relationship between the measurable and that which is not measurable? There must be a liaison: and that is intelligence. Intelligence has nothing whatsoever to do with thought. You may be very clever, very good at arguing, very learned. You may have experienced, lived a tremendous life, been all over the world, investigating, searching, looking, accumulating a great deal of knowledge, practised Zen or Hindu meditation. But all that has nothing whatsoever to do with intelligence. Intelligence comes into being when the mind, the heart, and the body are really harmonious.

Therefore—follow this, Sirs—the body must be highly sensitive. Not gross, not overindulging in eating, drinking, sex, and all the rest that makes the body coarse, dull, heavy. You have to understand all that. The very seeing the fact of that makes you eat less, gives the body its own intelligence. If there is an awareness of the body, which is not being forced, then the body becomes very, very sensitive, like a beautiful instrument. The same with the heart; that is, it is never hurt and can never hurt another. Not to hurt and not to be hurt, that is the innocency of the heart. A mind which has no fear, which demands no pleasure— not that you cannot enjoy the beauty of life, the beauty of trees, of a beautiful face, looking at children, at the flow of water, at the mountains and the green pastures—there is great delight in that. But that delight, when pursued by thought, becomes pleasure.

The mind has to be empty to see clearly. So the relationship between the immeasurable, the unknown and the known, is this intelligence, which has nothing whatsoever to do with Buddhism, with Zen, with me or with you; it has absolutely nothing to do with authority or tradition. Have you got that intelligence? That is the only point that matters. That intelligence will operate in this world morally. Morality then is order, which is virtue. Not the virtue or the morality of society, which is totally immoral.

So that intelligence brings about order, which is virtue, a thing that is living, that is not mechanical. Therefore you can never practise being good, you can never practise trying to become humble. When there is that intelligence, it naturally brings about order and the beauty of order. This is a religious life, not all the fooling around with it.

Listening to the speaker have you understood this?—not verbally or intellectually, but actually seen the truth of this? If you see the truth of it, it will act. If you see the truth that a snake is dangerous, you act. If you see the danger of a precipice, the fact, the truth of it, you act. If you see the truth of arsenic, of poison, you act. So do you see this, or do you still live in the world of ideas? If you live in the world of ideas, of conclusions, then that's not truth, that's just a projection of thought.

So that is the real question: listening to this, as you have for the last three weeks, in which we have talked about all the varieties of human existence, of suffering, pain and pleasure, of sex and immorality, social injustice, national divisions, wars, and all the rest—do you see the truth of this, and therefore is there that intelligence which operates?—not "me" operating. When you say, "I must be myself", which is the slogan or the cliché of the modern generation, when you examine these words, "I must be myself", what is myself? A lot of words, a lot of conclusions, traditions, reactions, memories, a bundle of the past; and yet you say, "I want to be myself", which is too childish.

So having listened to all this, is there the awakening of that intelligence? And if there is that awakening of intelligence, then it will operate, then you don't have to say, "What am I to do?" Perhaps there have been a thousand persons here during these three weeks who have listened. If they really live that, do you know what is going to happen? We should change the world. We shall be the salt of the earth.

Questioner: Do I understand correctly, that for thought to cease the mind has to see deeply the truth of the poison of seeking security. Is that what you said?

421

KRISHNAMURTI: Partly, Sir.

Questioner: The difficulty seems to be, that this part doesn't see, so the mind doesn't see it, and in order for the mind to see something there has to be quiet—it seems like a vicious circle. The difficulty is that it has not seen it.

KRISHNAMURTI: No, Sir. First of all, why should a mind be quiet, why shouldn't it go on chattering? When the mind is chattering, you can't see anything very clearly, can you? You can't listen to anybody clearly. If you are looking at a mountain, seeing its beauty, your mind naturally has to be quiet; which means you have to give attention to that moment, to seeing. That's all. That is, if you listen to the fact that thought is measure, that thought has divided human beings, that thought has brought about wars—if you see the truth of it—not the explanation, the justification—you just see the fact of what thought has done. Obviously to see that fact your mind must be quiet. So it's not a vicious circle at all, Sir.

Questioner: May I ask you a question? You often talk about the beauty of the mountains and the stillness of the mind when looking at the beauty of a cloud. Can the mind be still when looking at something horrible?

KRISHNAMURTI: Just listen carefully, observe the dark and the light, the slum and the non-slum. Can you watch that? Can there be an awareness in which these divisions don't exist? Is there an awareness in which the division between poverty and riches does not exist? Not the fact that there is not the division, with all its injustice, immorality, all that—but an awareness in which this division doesn't exist? That is, can the mind observe the beauty of the hill and the squalor, and not prefer, or incline to one, opposed to the other? That means an awareness in which choice doesn't exist. You can do this. Not that poverty should go on—you would *do* something, politically, socially and so on; but the mind could be freed from division, from this classical division between the rich and the poor, between beauty and ugliness, from the opposites and all the rest of it.

Questioner: I should like to ask you, is there a difference for you between thought and speculation?

KRISHNAMURTI: Why should there be a difference between thought and speculation? Who is speculating—isn't thought speculating? Isn't thought theorising that there is God, that there is no God, about how many angels can sit on a pin-head, and so on? It is the whole business of thought to speculate—there is no difference, it is the same.

Questioner: One can be aware objectively of a tree, of a mountain, of a person. Can thought observe its own movement? Is there awareness of itself, and is one aware of being aware?

KRISHNAMURTI: Yes: is there an awareness of thought watching itself?

Questioner: I don't like the word "watch".

KRISHNAMURTI: All right: an awareness of itself. Now wait a minute, just look. Have you understood the question? You can be aware of the tree, of the hill, of your sitting there; there is an awareness of that. Is there an awareness that you are aware that you are being aware? Please see the question. You can be aware of the tree, the cloud, the colour of your shirt, and you can be aware objectively. You can also be aware of how your thought is operating. But is there an awareness of being aware?

When you are aware of a tree, as an observer, is that awareness? The tree is there and you are aware of that tree. You then become the observer and that becomes the observed, and you say, "That's not it." In that there is a division, as the observer and the observed. It is the same with the cloud, the same with you sitting there, and the person speaking, sitting on a platform and observing. In that too there is a division. In this too there is the observer watching you, the observed; in that there is division. One can be aware of thought. I am going step by step. Being aware of thought, in that also there is a division; the one who is aware separating himself from thought.

Now you are asking a question, which is: does awareness know, or it it aware of itself, without an observer? Of course not, the moment there is no observer, there is no awareness of being aware. Obviously, Sir, that's the whole point! The moment I am aware that I am aware, I'm *not* aware. Remain with it, Sir, for two minutes remain with it! The moment I am aware that I am hum-

423

ble, humility is not. The moment I am aware that I am happy, happiness is not.

So if I am aware that I am aware, then that is not awareness; in that there is division between the observer and the observed. Now you are asking a question, which is: is there an awareness in which division as the observer and the observed comes to an end? Obviously awareness means that—awareness means that the observer is not.

Questioner: Can one be aware of the tree without the observer, without that space?

KRISHNAMURTI: Look at it. When you look at a tree, there is space between you and the tree. Wait Sir, we are going step by step. When you look at that tree, there is a distance between you and the tree, there is the space, there is division. That division takes place when there is the observer who has an image of that tree as the oak, or the pine. So the knowledge, the image, separates the observer from the observed, from the tree. Please look at it. Can you look at that tree without the image? If you look at that tree without the image, without saying, "That is an oak", "That is beautiful or not beautiful", without like or dislike, then what takes place? What takes place when there is no observer, but only the observed? Go on, Sir, tell me what takes place—I'm not going to tell you!

Questioner (1): There comes about union.

Questioner (2): Oneness.

KRISHNAMURTI: Oneness means the same thing.

Questioner: Awareness.

KRISHNAMURTI: No don't invent, don't speculate.

Questioner: When I am aware of the tree I have a feeling ...

KRISHNAMURTI: I'm coming to that, Sir. Please listen to it step by step. I said to you: when you look ordinarily at a tree, there is the division between you and the tree. You are the observer and the tree is the observed. That's a fact.

424

You, with your image, with your prejudices, with your hopes and all the rest of it—that is the observer. Therefore as long as that exists as the observer, there must be division between you and the tree. When the observer is not, but only the object, what takes place?—don't imagine, do it!

Questioner (1): There is stillness . . . thought does not work any more.

Questioner (2): We become the tree.

KRISHNAMURTI: You become the tree—my God, I hope not! Become the elephant! *(Laughter)* Do please listen. Do it. Look at a tree and see if you can look at it without any image. That is fairly easy. But to look at yourself without an image, to look at yourself without the observer, that's much more difficult. Because what you see is unpleasant or pleasant, you want to change it, you want to control it, you want to shape it, you want to do something about it.

So can you look at yourself without the observer, as you can if you look at the tree? Which means to look at yourself with complete attention. When there is complete attention there is no image. It is only when your mind is thinking, "I wish I had a better 'me' ", or "I am going to do so and so"—then when you are looking, there is inattention.

Questioner: Am I wrong if I say that we are in a state of awareness all the time? It's thought that invents the division.

KRISHNAMURTI: Oh, no! That is another speculation of thought, that we are aware all the time. We are in a state of awareness only at moments, then we go off to sleep. The moments when we go off to sleep, the moments when we are inattentive, that is what is important, not when we are aware.

Questioner: Are we aware of the infinite affection you express when you translate intelligence into human life?

KRISHNAMURTI: It's up to you, Sir!

425

Questioner: When I am aware of my image, and my image goes, then isn't that awareness in itself?

KRISHNAMURTI: When I am aware of my image, does the image exist? It doesn't.

Questioner: Then that is awareness in itself.

KRISHNAMURTI: That's right, awareness in itself without any choice. Sir, what is important in all this, is not what one has heard, but what one is learning. Learning is not accumulation of knowledge. When you go away from here, you will have various ideas about awareness, love, truth, fear and all the rest of it. Those very ideas are going to prevent learning. But if you are aware a little bit, then you are learning and then intelligence can operate through learning in daily life.

SAANEN
10 AUGUST 1971

ENGLAND

IX

Two Talks at Brockwood

1

THE RELATIONSHIP TO AWARENESS
OF THOUGHT AND THE IMAGE

The uses and limitations of thought. Images: the authority of the image. "The more sensitive one is, the greater the burden of images." Analysis and images. Psychological order; causes of disorder: opinion, comparison, images. Possible dissolution of images. Formation of images. Attention and inattention. "It is only when the mind is inattentive that the image is formed." Attention and harmony: mind, heart, body.

I THINK IT would be worth while to talk over together the question of violence, which is becoming worse and spreading right through the world; this is really a part of the whole human conditioning. Can man ever be free either of the superficial social conditioning of a particular culture, or of the much deeper conditioning, which is the whole collective sorrow, the violence, the destructive despairs and their activities of which most of us are unconscious? It is like a cloud which one has inherited, in which one lives. Apparently one finds it tremendously difficult to free oneself from it all.

Wherever one goes, all over the world, one observes that the superficial cultures don't penetrate very deeply into human consciousness. But the great clouds of sorrow—I don't like to use the word "evil"—that destructive violence, the antagonisms and conflicts seem to be deeply rooted in all of us. Can one be utterly free of this? If that is essential, then how is one to set about it? Superficially we may be highly cultured, polite, slightly indifferent, but deep down I think most of us are unaware that there is a great inheritance of this vast, complex conflict, misery and fear. If one is at all conscious of it one asks: is it possible to be entirely free of it, so that the mind is a totally different kind of instrument? I do not know if you have thought about this at all—or perhaps it seems that the superficial conditioning is so important that one is always

429

struggling against it. If one has been through that and has put it away, then there are all these deep layers which are for the most part unconscious. How is one to become aware of those? Is it at all possible to be completely rid of them?

Perhaps we could discuss how to be aware of these terrible things which man has inherited or cultivated. Whatever the explanations be, the fact is that we are deeply violent, that we are caught in sorrow. There is this cloud of fear and obviously this brings about a great deal of mischief and confusion in action. I think that is fairly obvious. How is one to be aware of all this, and is it possible to go beyond it?

The organised religions throughout the world have laid down certain rules, disciplines, attitudes and beliefs. But have they resolved human suffering and the deep-rooted anxieties, guilts and all the rest of it? So we can put aside all religious beliefs, hopes and fears. One is aware of what is taking place in the world, of the nature of religious organisations with their heads, gurus and saviours and all their mythology. If one has set aside all that, because one has understood it and seen the futility, the falseness of it and is free of it, then certain facts remain: sorrow, violence, fear and great anxiety.

If I am conscious of all that, how am I to be free of it, so that I have a different kind of brain, a different kind of action, a different attitude towards life, a different way of living? The more intelligent, enquiring and intellectually aware one is of this, the more serious one becomes and there is also the demand that the mind must be totally free of all this mess that human beings have created and carry about with them endlessly. I think that is the basic problem; not that there is not social injustice and poverty, wars, violence, the division between nationalities and so on. All that can be solved, I feel, when human beings really understand this whole problem of existence. Then they can tackle all the confusion and wars from a different dimension.

The human mind *wants* to find that dimension. It *has* to find it to solve all this misery. If you are serious, not playing with words, speculating or indulging in theoretical supposition, ideas and hypotheses, but are actually confronted not only with your own, but with this human suffering, how are you to end all this? The demand for constant security is much more a demand for psychological security, which is much deeper than physiological security; because we want psychological security, to give over all our thoughts and hope to some teacher, to some saviour, to some belief. How shall I, knowing all this, understand and be free of this constant effort, struggle and misery?

How are we to be aware of all that? What does this awareness or perception mean? How do I know that I am in sorrow?—not only I, but every human being in the world, of which I am part; how do I know that there is this sorrow? Is it a verbal recognition or is it an acceptance of an idea that there is sorrow of which I am part? Or is there a conscious awareness that sorrow is a fact? When I say to myself: there is tremendous sorrow in the world, of which I am part—as I am the world and the world is me—that is a fact. It is not an idea, not a sentiment, not an emotional assertion; it is an absolute fact that I am the world and the world is me. Because we have made this world we are responsible for it. All my thoughts, my activities, my fears, my hopes, are the hopes and fears of the world. There is no division between the world and me. The community is me, the culture is me and I am that culture; so there is no division. I don't know if you see and feel that?

Knowing that I am the world and that there must be a radical revolution in the world—not through bombs, that leads nowhere—I realise there must be a revolution in the very psyche and in the mind itself. So that one lives differently, thinks differently, acts in a totally different manner altogether. How am I to free the mind that is responsible for all this?—the mind being thought. It is thought that has brought about the division between people, the wars, the structure of religious belief. And thought has also put together the technology that makes for the convenience of everyday existence: electricity, the railway, the technological knowledge that enables one to go to the moon; it is thought that has done all this. This thought which has gathered so much information, so much knowledge, how is it to be free from the whole structure and nature of sorrow and fear?—and yet function efficiently, with sanity, in the field of knowledge without bringing about division and antagonism between man and man. You see the problem?

How then is thought to prevent this division? Because where there is division there is conflict, not only outwardly but inwardly. Am I making the problem clear?—it's your problem, it's the problem of human beings. One sees what thought has done, being cunning, extraordinarily capable, it has gathered technological knowledge which cannot possibly be put aside; thought must be exercised to function at all. And yet thought has brought about violence, and thought is not love. So one has to have the clarity of thought in function, and yet be aware that thought does breed all the misery in the world. How can we be aware of the whole implication of thought—which is the measurable—and also of a dimension in which thought as the measureable does not exist at all? First, is it clear what thought has done in the world, both beneficial and destructive? How is thought to function efficiently, healthily and not create division between people?

The collective memory of man responds as thought—which is the past. It may project into the future, but it still has its roots in the past and from there it functions. We see that in operation and we say that is necessary. But why does thought divide people? Why should I be conditioned as a Muslim—which is the result of thought—and you be conditioned as a Communist, also as a result of thought? Some people think that only violence can produce a sociological change, and others say: that is not the way. So thought is always creating divisions and where there is division there is conflict. So what is the function of thought?

Knowing that thought can only function in the field of knowledge, can thought invent or come upon a different dimension in which there is no division created by thought? Personally, I am very interested in this, because I have seen all over the world that thought has created such marvellous things and yet has brought about such misery, such confusion, such an enormous amount of sorrow. Can thought completely operate in one direction and be totally silent in another, so that it does not create a division? After having put that question to myself—and I hope you are putting it to yourself—is it possible for thought to say, "I won't go beyond the technological world, knowledge and daily existence", and not enter into that dimension in which there is no division? Is it possible for thought to separate itself like that or are we putting the wrong question altogether? Can thought see its own limitations and bring about a different intelligence? If thought sees its own limitation, is there not a different kind of intelligence in operation? Then is there not an awakening of intelligence which is above and beyond thought?

Questioner: When thought is seeing itself, that must not be thinking.

KRISHNAMURTI: I don't know, Sir.

Questioner: Hasn't thought come up with systems to destroy itself?

KRISHNAMURTI: First see our difficulty, don't let's find an easy answer, see the enormous implications in this. Man has lived by thought. We exercise thought every day, every minute. We must have thought; without it there is no action, you can't live. You can't destroy thought. To destroy thought implies a thought which is superior and says "I must destroy my lower thought"—it is all within the field of thought. This is what the Indians have done. They have said: thought is very limited, there is a superior thought, the Atman, the Brahman, the thing above; keep thought silent and then the other will operate. The very assertion of that is thought, isn't it? Here you say "The soul"—it is still part of thought. So thought has produced this extraordinary world of technology, which thought uses for the convenience of human beings and for their destruction. It is thought that has invented the saviours, the myths, the gods; it is thought that has produced violence, that becomes jealous, anxious, fearful.

So is there a field which is not measurable by thought? Can that field operate within the field of thought, without thought breaking up into fragmentations? If thought is operating all the time, then the mind is functioning with the knowledge which is the past. Knowledge *is* the past—I can't have knowledge of tomorrow, and knowledge is thought. If the only way to live is always within the field of thought, then the mind can never be free and man must always live in sorrow, in fear, in division, therefore in conflict. Realising that, man has said there must be an outside agency—as God—who will help me to overcome all this fragmentation of thought. But that God, that Atman—or other forms of hope—is still the invention of thought not finding security in this world, which invents or believes or projects an idea which it calls God, which is secure. I see this. If thought is to be the only field in which human beings can live, then they are doomed. This is not my invention, this is what is actually going on.

Have I made the problem clear? The human mind demands freedom from guilt, suffering, confusion, of these endless wars and violence, and thought cannot produce freedom. It can invent the idea of freedom, but that is not freedom. So the human mind must find the answer. It can only do that when it has understood the nature of thinking and has seen its capacity and has found a state of the immeasurable in which thought does not function at all. This is what is called meditation. People have done this; but again, their meditation is part of the furthering of thought. They say "I must sit quietly, my thoughts must be controlled." Knowing the limitation of thought, they say "I must discipline it", "I must hold it in check, not let it wander". They discipline themselves tremendously, but they have not got that other dimension, because thought cannot enter into that.

The really serious people have enquired deeply into this. And yet, thought has been their major instrument and therefore they have never solved this problem. They have invented things, they have speculated. And poor fools like us accept these speculations, the philosophies, the teachers, the whole gamut of it. Obviously there must be a different kind of meditation, a different kind of perception, that is seeing and not evaluating. To see the operations of thought, all its inward and outward movement without giving it any direction or forcing it in any way, just to observe it completely without any choice, that is a different kind of perception. We see, but we always give it a direction. We say "This must not be", "This should be", "I shall overcome it". All that is the old way of responding to any action, feeling or idea. But to observe without any direction, without any pressure, without any distortion—is that possible at all? If I can see myself as I am without any condemnation or saying "I'll keep this and I'll reject that", then perception has a different quality. Then it becomes a living thing, not the repetitive pattern of the past.

So in the very act of listening, as you are doing now, you see the truth that to really perceive there must be no directive or persuasion or compulsion. In that observation, you will see that thought does not enter at all. Which means, in that perception, in that seeing, there is complete attention. Where there is no attention there is a distortion. Now when you are listening to this, if you see the truth of it, that acts.

Questioner: Sir, in that state one sees oneself absolutely powerless and also amoral, and thought always feels and knows its own power. Thought always enters where there is interest, fear and anxiety.

KRISHNAMURTI: Sir, isn't fear and anxiety the result of thought?—thought has produced fear!

Questioner: Sometimes it comes unexpectedly.

KRISHNAMURTI: That may be, but whether it is unexpected or not, it's thought that has produced fear—no? Thought has produced this immense sorrow.

Questioner: What about children's fears?

KRISHNAMURTI: Surely, isn't that based on their lack of security? Children need complete security and the parents cannot give it because they are interested in their own little selves. They are quarrelling, they are ambitious, so they cannot give the security the child demands—which is love.

So we come back to the same question. Thought has produced fear, there is no question about it. Thought has produced the aching loneliness in oneself, thought has said "I must fulfil, I must be, I am little, I must be big". Thought has brought about jealousy, anxiety, guilt. Thought *is* that guilt. Not: thought makes for guilt, thought *is* guilt. How can I observe myself and the world, of which I am part, without any interference of thought in that observation, so that out of the observation a different action can come which does not produce fear, regrets and all the rest of it. So I must learn to observe myself and the world and my actions quite differently. There must be a learning of observation in which thought does not interfere at all because the moment thought interferes it leads to distortion, it becomes biased. Perception is in the present; you can't perceive tomorrow. You perceive *now*, and when thought interferes in that perception—thought being the response of the past—it must distort the present; this is logical.

Questioner: Surely, to be aware we have to think.

KRISHNAMURTI: Wait, look at it. What does awareness mean? I am aware that you are sitting there and that I am sitting up here, I am aware that I am sitting on a chair etc. Then thought says "I am a better person than somebody who is sitting below, because I am talking". Thought gives me prestige—do you follow? Is that awareness, or is it merely the continuous movement of thought? Can you see a tree without the operation of thought, without the image of the tree?—the image being thought that says: that is an oak.

In observing a tree what takes place? There is the space between the observer and the tree, there is distance; then there is the botanical knowledge, the like or dislike of that tree. I have an image of a tree and that image looks at that tree; is there a perception without the image? The image is thought; thought is the knowledge of that tree. When there is perception with an image, there is no direct perception of the tree. Is it possible to look at the tree without the image? That is fairly simple, but it becomes much more complex when I look at myself without any image about myself. Can there be an observation of myself without any image? I am full of my images. I am this, I am not that, I should be this, I should not be that, I must become, I must not become—do you follow? Those are all images and I am looking at myself with one of the images—not with the whole group of images.

So what is looking? If there is no image then what is seeing? If I have no images at all about myself—which one has to go into very deeply—then what is there to see? There is absolutely nothing to see, and one is frightened of that. That is: one is absolutely nothing. But we can't face that, therefore we have those images about ourselves.

The human mind demands freedom. Freedom is essential, it is even demanded politically, but you don't demand freedom from all images. Thought has created these images for various sociological, economic and cultural reasons. These images are measurable: the greater, the lesser. One asks: can thought observe without distortion? Obviously it can't. There is a distorting factor in thought, because thought is the response of the past. Is there an observation without the interference of thought?—that means without the interference of any image. You can find this out; it's not a question of just accepting or believing. You can look at your wife or your husband, the tree, the cloud, or the person sitting next to you, without any image.

436

Questioner: Is there such a thing as an unconscious image one might not be aware of?

KRISHNAMURTI: Yes, there is, of course. Please listen to my question: how am I to be aware of the many unconscious images that I have stored up?

Questioner: Krishnaji, as long as one is trying to be aware, one creates things to be aware of.

KRISHNAMURTI: That is what I am saying. You cannot try to be aware, you cannot determine to be aware; to be aware is not the result of exercising will. Either you see or you don't see, either you listen to what we are talking about now, or you don't listen. But if you listen with your image, then of course you don't listen at all.

The question is really very interesting. I can understand the conscious images, the superficial knowledge that I have, that is fairly simple and clear. But how am I to be aware of the deep, hidden images which have such a powerful influence on the whole way of life?

Questioner: We find out by how we behave, by how these images come up, sometimes in sleep.

KRISHNAMURTI: Which means: through my behaviour I begin to discover the unconscious images that have been stored up—one image after the other, you follow? I behave towards you differently than towards another, because you are more powerful, you have greater prestige than the other man. Therefore my image of you is greater and I despise the other; so it means going through one image after another. Is there a central fact that creates these images consciously as well as deeply? If I can find that out, then I don't have to go through image after image, or discover the images through dreams?

Through my behaviour I discover my unconscious images; that's a form of analysis, isn't it? Will analysis resolve these images? These images are created by thought, and analysis is thought. Through thought I hope to destroy the images that thought has created, so I am caught in a vicious circle. How do I deal with this? Are your images revealed through dreams? Isn't that another form of analysis? Why should you dream at all? Dreams are a continuation of my daily activity, aren't they? I lead rather a confused life—uncertain, miserable, lonely, frightened, comparing myself with somebody else who is more beautiful, more intelligent; that is my life during the waking hours and when I sleep, all that goes on. I dream of all the things I have been through; it is the continuation of how I have been living during the daytime. If there is a revelation of myself through dreams, that is a form of analysis. Therefore I am depending on dreams to reveal the hidden images, and the dependence on dreams makes me less and less awake during the waking hours—no?

Questioner: Thought and sub-thought create images and these are useful on a certain level.

KRISHNAMURTI: We have said that, there are useful images which must function, which we must have, there are highly dangerous images which one must totally abolish—obviously. That is what this whole discussion is about.

Questioner: Is there not only one question?—not whether thought can be silent when necessary but: can there be only silence?

KRISHNAMURTI: That means, Sir: can there be silence from which thought can operate, doesn't it?

Questioner: It is not a question whether thought can operate or not, but can there be only silence?

KRISHNAMURTI: Can thought be completely silent? Who is putting that question? Is thought putting that question?

Questioner: Obviously.

KRISHNAMURTI: So thought is asking itself whether it can be quiet.

How will it find out? Can it *do* anything to be silent? It can't can it? Can thought say to itself: I must be quiet? That is not being quiet! Then what is silence which is not the product of thought? Is there a silence which is not the result of thought? Which means, can thought come to an end by itself, without asking to come to an end? Isn't that what is implied when you listen to something, when you see clearly? When you are completely attentive, in that attention there is silence, isn't there? Complete attention

drifted apart culturally, socially, intellectually and religiously.

Meditation is quite a complex problem, we have to go into it slowly and approach it from different angles, bearing in mind all the time that a psychological revolution is absolutely necessary for a different kind of world, a different kind of society, to come into being. I do know how strongly you feel about this. Probably most of us, being bourgeois, comfortable with our little incomes, our family and so on, would rather remain as we are and not be disturbed. But events, technology, and all those things that are happening in the world, are producing great changes outwardly. Yet inwardly most of us remain more or less as we have been for centuries. That revolution can only take place at the very centre of our being and requires a great abundance of energy; meditation is the release of that total energy and we are going to talk that over.

We have got a great many ideas about what meditation is and what it should be; we import it from the East, or interpret it according to our own particular religious inclination, as contemplation, acceptance, prayer, keeping the mind still or open—we have all kinds of fanciful ideas about it. And especially lately, people have come from India propagating meditations of various forms.

First of all, how is one to have this quality of energy which is without friction? We know mechanical energy, which is friction mechanically, and the friction in us which produces energy through conflict, through resistance, through control and all the rest of it. So there is a kind of energy caused by mechanical friction. Is there another kind of energy which has no friction whatsoever and is therefore completely free and immeasurable? I think meditation is the discovery of that. Unless one has great abundance of energy, not only physically but much more so psychologically, our action will never be complete, it will always produce friction, conflict and struggle. Seeing the various forms of meditation, of Zen, of Yoga brought over from India, and the various contemplative groups of monks and so on, in all that, there is the idea of control, acceptance of a system, practising a repetition of words, which is called mantra, and various forms of breathing, hatha yoga and so on. I suppose you know all this.

So first of all let us dispose of them altogether by investigating. Not accepting what they say, but investigating it,

441

seeing the truth or the falseness of it. There is this repetition of words, of sentences, mantras, a set of phrases given by a guru, being initiated, paying money to learn a peculiar phrase to be repeated by you secretly. Probably some of you have done that and you know a great deal about it. That is called mantra yoga, and is brought over from India. I don't know why you pay a single penny to repeat certain words from somebody who says, "If you do this you will achieve enlightenment, you will have a quiet mind." When you repeat a series of words constantly, whether it is *Ave Maria* or various Sanscrit words, obviously your mind becomes rather dull and you have a peculiar sense of unity, of quietness, and you think that will help to bring about clarity. You can see the absurdity of it, because why should you accept what anybody says about these matters—including myself? Why should you accept any authority about the inward movement of life? We reject authority outwardly; if you are at all intellectually aware and observant politically you reject these things. But apparently we accept the authority of somebody who says, "I know, I have achieved, I have realised." The man who says he knows, he does *not* know. The moment you say you know, you don't know. What is it you know? Some experience which you have had, some kind of vision, some kind of enlightenment? I dislike to use that word "enlightenment". Once you have experienced that, you think you have attained some extraordinary state; but that is past, you can only know something which is over and therefore dead. When these people come over and say they have realised, "Do this" or "Do that" for so much money, this is obviously absurd. So we can dispose of that.

We can also dispose of this whole idea of practising a system, a method. When you practise a method in order to achieve enlightenment, or bliss, or to have a quiet mind, or to achieve a state of tranquility, whatever it is, it obviously makes the mind mechanical, you repeat over and over again. This not only implies suppression of your own movement and understanding, but also conformity and the endless conflict involved in practising a particular system. The mind likes to conform to a system because then it gets crystallised and it is easy to live that way. So can we dispose, now, of all systems of meditation? But you won't, because our whole structure of habit is based on that demand to find a method, so that we can just follow and live

442

a monotonous, dull life of routine; not to be disturbed, that is what we want, and so we accept authority.

One has to find out for oneself, not through anybody. We have had the authority of the priest for centuries upon centuries, the authority of teachers, saviours and masters. If you really want to find out what meditation is, you have to set aside all authority completely and totally; not the authority of law, of the policeman—law, legislation, you may understand later, when your own mind is orderly and clear. Now what is meditation? Is it control of thought? And if it is, who is the controller of thought? It is thought itself, isn't it? Our whole culture, both in the East and in the West, is based on control of thought and concentration, in which only one thought can be pursued to the end. Why should one control at all? Control implies imitation, conformity, it implies the acceptance of a pattern as the authority, according to which you are trying to live. That pattern is set by the society, by the culture, by somebody who you think has knowledge, enlightenment and so on. According to that pattern one tries to live, suppressing all one's own feelings and ideas, trying to conform. In that there is conflict, and conflict is essentially a wastage of energy.

So concentration, which so many advocate in meditation, is totally wrong. Are you accepting all this, or are you just listening out of boredom? Because we must go into this question, whether thought can function where necessary, without any form of control. Can thought function when necessary as knowledge, in action, and be completely still at other times? That is the real issue. The mind which is cluttered up with so many activities of thought and is therefore uncertain, is trying to find clarity in that confusion, forcing itself to control, to conform to an idea; it therefore brings about more and more confusion within itself. I want to find out whether the mind can be quiet and only function when necessary.

Control, because it implies conflict, is a great waste of energy; that is important to understand, because I feel meditation must be a releasing of energy in which there is not the slightest friction. How is a mind to do this? How is it to have such energy in which every form of friction comes to an end? In enquiring into that, one must understand oneself completely, there must be total self-knowing—not according to any psychologist, philosopher or teacher, or the pattern set by a particular culture—but to know oneself right through, both at the conscious level as well as at the deeper levels, is that possible? When there is complete understanding of oneself, then there is the ending of conflict—and that is meditation.

Now, how am I to know myself? I can only know myself in relationship; the observation of myself takes place only when there is response and reaction in relationship; there is no such thing as isolation. The mind is isolating itself all the time in all its activities, building a wall round itself in order not to be hurt, not to have any discomfort, unhappiness, or trouble; it is isolating itself all the time in its self-centred activity. I want to know "myself" as I want to know how to get from here to a particular town; that is, clearly, watching everything that is involved in myself, my feelings, my thoughts, my motives, conscious or unconscious. How is that possible? The Greeks, the Hindus, the Buddhists have said: know yourself. But apparently that is one of the most difficult things to do. We are going to find out this morning how to look at ourselves; because once you know yourself completely, that prevents all friction, and therefore out of that comes this quality of energy which is totally different. So to find out how to observe oneself, one must understand what is meant by observing.

When we observe objective things like trees, clouds, the things outside of us, there is not only the space between the observer and the observed—the physical space—there is also the space of time. When we look at a tree there is not only physical distance, but there is also psychological distance. There is the distance between you and the tree, the distance created by the image as knowledge: that is an oak tree, or an elm. That image between you and the tree separates you.

But when the quality of the mind of the observer is without the image, which is imagination, then there is quite a different relationship between the observer and the observed. Have you ever looked at a tree without a single word of like or dislike, without a single image? Have you noticed what then takes place? Then, for the first time, you see the tree as it is and you see the beauty of it, the colour, the depth, the vitality of it. A tree, or even another person, is fairly easy to observe; but to observe *oneself* that way—that is to observe without the observer—is much more difficult. So one must find out who is the observer.

I want to watch myself, I want to know myself as

444

deeply as possible. What is the nature, the structure of that observer who is watching? That observer is the past, isn't it?—the past knowledge which he has collected and stored up; the past being the culture, the conditioning. That is the observer who says, "This is right, this is wrong, this must be, this must not be, this is good, this is bad." So the observer is the past and with those eyes of the past we try to see what we are. Then we say, "I don't like this, I am ugly", or "This I will keep". All these discriminations and condemnations take place. Can I look at myself without the eyes of the past? Can I watch myself in action, which is in relationship, without any movement of the past? Have you ever tried this? (I don't suppose you have.)

When there is no observer then there is only the observed. Please see this: I am envious, or I overeat, I am greedy. The normal reaction is, "I must not overeat", "I must not be greedy", "I must suppress", you know all that follows. In that there is the observer trying to control his greed, or his envy. Now when there is an awareness of greed without the observer, what takes place? Can I observe that greed without giving it a name, as "greed"? The moment I name it I have already fixed it as greed in my memory which says: I must get over it, I must control. So is there an observation of greed without the word, without justifying it, without condemning it? Which means, can I observe this thing called greed without any reaction whatsoever?

To so observe is a form of discipline, isn't it? Not imposing any particular pattern, which means conformity, suppression and all the rest of it, but to observe the whole series of actions without condemning, justifying or naming —just to observe. Then you will see the mind is no longer wasting energy. It is then aware and therefore it has energy to deal with that which it is observing.

Questioner: May I ask, Sir, whether the "me" observing the "me" without naming it as the "me", is the same as observing the past, also without naming it as the past?

KRISHNAMURTI: Quite right, Sir, that's it. But once you understand the whole mechanism it does not become difficult. Once you see the truth of it, then that truth, that fact, acts. One can do that at the conscious level. There are a great many unconscious responses, motives, inclinations, tendencies, inhibitions and fears. How is one to deal with all that? Must one go through analysing layer after layer of hidden accumulations, exposing all that through dreams? How is all that to be exposed totally so that knowing oneself becomes complete?

Apparently it cannot be done by the conscious mind. I can't investigate consciously the unconscious, the hidden. Can you? Don't say "no"—see the difficulty of it, because I don't know what is hidden, and the hidden may intimate through dreams, but the dreams need to be interpreted and that will take a lot of time, won't it?

Questioner: I think it is possible under certain drugs to know myself—there is no conflict.

KRISHNAMURTI: Does any drug really expose the totality of the content of consciousness, or does it bring about chemically a certain state of mind, which is totally different from the understanding of oneself? I have watched many people in India taking drugs and I have also watched students at universities in America, and others, who have been taking psychedelic drugs. These drugs do affect the mind, the brain cells themselves—they destroy the brain. If you have talked to those who have taken drugs, you see they can't reason, they can't pursue a logical sequence of thought. I am not asking you not to take drugs, it's up to you; but you can see the effect of it on people. They have no sense of responsibility, they think they can do anything they like—and how many hospitals are full of people who are mentally unbalanced through drugs. We are talking of something which is non-chemical. If LSD, or any other drug, could bring about a state of mind in which there is no conflict, and at the same time one could maintain complete responsibility and a logical sequence of thought and action, that would be marvellous.

We are asking: how is one to expose the whole hidden content at one glance? Not through a series of dreams, not through analysis, all that implies time and wastage of energy. This is an important question because I want to understand myself—myself being all my past, the experiences, the hurts, the anxieties, the guilt, the various fears. How am I to comprehend all that immediately? To understand all that immediately gives immense energy. Now how do you do that? Is that an impossibility? We have to ask the impossible question to find a way out of it. Unless we ask the most impossible question we shall always be dealing with what is possible, and what is possible is very little. So I am asking the most impossible question, which is: to have this whole content of consciousness exposed and understand it, see it totally, without time—which means without analysis, exploration and seeing layer after layer, which is an expenditure of time. How is the mind to observe this whole content with one look?

If that question is put to you, as it is being put now, if you are really listening to that question, what is your response? You obviously say "I can't do it". You really don't know how to do it. Are you waiting for somebody to tell you? If I say to myself, "I don't know", am I waiting for somebody to inform me—am I expecting an answer? When I am expecting an answer, then I already know. Are you following this? When I say, "I don't know, I *really* don't know"—I am not waiting for anybody to tell me, I am not expecting anything because nobody can answer it. So I actually don't know. What is the state of the mind that says "I really don't know"? I can't find it in any book, I can't ask anybody, I can't go to any teacher or priest, I really don't know. When the mind says "I do not know", what is the state of the mind? Please, don't answer me. Do look at it, because we always say we know. I know my wife, I know mathematics, I know this, I know that. We never say, "I really don't know". I am asking: what is the state of the mind that honestly says, "I don't know"? Don't verbalise immediately. When I really mean I don't know, the mind has no answer. It is not expecting anything from anybody. It is not waiting, it is not expecting. So what happens? Is it not completely alone? It is not isolated—isolation and aloneness are two different things. In that quality of aloneness there is no influence, there is no resistance, it has shed itself from all the past, it says, "I really don't know." Therefore the mind has emptied itself of all its content. Have you understood this?

I have asked the impossible question and I have said, "I don't know." Therefore the mind empties itself of everything, of every suggestion, every probability, every possibility; so the mind is completely active and empty of all the past—which is time, analysis, the authority of somebody. So it has exposed all the content of itself by denying the content. Do you understand now? As we said, meditation can only begin with the total understanding of myself; that is part of the beginning of meditation. Without understanding myself the mind can deceive itself, it can have

447

illusions according to its particular conditioning. When you know your conditioning and are free of it, then there is no possibility of any kind of illusion, and that is absolutely essential because we can deceive ourselves so easily. So when I investigate into myself, I see that consciousness is emptying itself of all its content through knowing itself, not by denying anything, but by understanding the whole content; that brings about great energy, which is necessary, because that energy transforms completely all my activity. It is no longer self-centred and therefore the cause of friction.

Meditation is a way of putting aside altogether everything that man has conceived of himself and of the world. So he has a totally different kind of mind. Meditation also means awareness, both of the world and of the whole movement of oneself, to see exactly what is, without any choice, without any distortion. Distortion takes place the moment you bring in thought. Yet thought has to function, but when there is an observation and thought interferes with that observation as image, then there is distortion and illusion. So to observe actually what is, in oneself and in the world, without any distortion, a quiet, very still mind is necessary. One knows that it is necessary to have a quiet mind, therefore there are various systems to help you to control it, and all that means friction. If you want to observe passionately, with intensity, the mind inevitably becomes quiet. You don't have to force it—the moment you force it, it is not quiet, it is dead. Can you see this truth, that to perceive anything you must look?—and if you look with prejudice you cannot see. If you see that, your mind is quiet.

Now what takes place in a quiet mind? We are enquiring not only into that quality of energy in which there is no friction, but also into how to bring about a radical change within oneself. One's self is the world and the world is oneself—the world is not the fruit separate from me: I am the world. It is not just an idea, but an actual fact, that I am the world and the world is "me". So there is a radical revolution, a change in me that will inevitably effect the world, because I am part of the world.

In this enquiry into what meditation is, I see that any wastage of energy is caused by friction in my relationship with another. Is it possible to have a relationship with another in which there is no friction whatsoever? That is possible only when I understand what love is, and the understanding of what love is, is the denial of what love is not. Jealousy, ambition, greed, self-centred activity, obviously all that is not love. When in the understanding of myself there is the total setting aside of all that which is not love, then it is. The observation takes a second, the explanation and the description takes a long time, but the act of observation is instantaneous.

In this observation I have found no system, no authority, no self-centred activity, therefore there is no conformity, no comparison of myself with another; to observe all this the mind must be extraordinarily quiet. If you want to listen to what is being said just now, you have to give attention, haven't you? You can't listen if you are thinking about something else. If you are bored with this, I can get up and go, but to force yourself to listen is absurd. If you are really interested in it passionately, intensely, then you listen completely, and to listen completely the mind must be quiet—this is very simple. All this is meditation; not just sitting for five minutes by yourself, crosslegged, breathing properly—that is not meditation, that is self-hypnosis.

I want to find out what is the quality of the mind that is completely still and also what takes place when it is still. I have observed, I have recorded, I have understood and I have finished with that. But there is another enquiry: what is the state of the mind, of the brain cells themselves? The brain cells store up the memories that are useful, that are necessary for their self-protection, memories of what might lead to danger. Haven't you noticed this? I suppose you read a lot of books? Personally I don't, therefore I can look into myself and find out, watch myself, not according to somebody—but just watch. I am asking myself what is the quality of such a mind, what has happened to the brain? The brain records, that is its function. It functions only through memory which protects it, otherwise it can't function. The brain may find security in some neurosis; it has found security in nationalism, in a belief in the family, in having possessions, which are all various forms of neurosis. The brain must be secure to function and it may choose to find that security in something that is false, unreal, illusory, neurotic.

When I have examined myself thoroughly, all this disappears. There is no neurosis, no belief, no nationality, no desire to hurt anybody, nor to recall all the hurts. So the brain then is a recording instrument, without thought using it as the "me" in operation. So meditation implies not only the body being still but also the brain being quiet. Have you ever watched your brain in operation? Why you think certain things. Why you react to others, why you feel desperately lonely, unloved, with nothing to rely on, no hope—you know this tremendous sense of loneliness? Though you may be married, have children and live in a group, there is this feeling of complete emptiness. Seeing it, one tries to escape from it, but if you remain with it, do not escape from it, just look at it completely without condemning it or trying to overcome it, but observe it actually as it is, then you will see that what you considered to be loneliness ceases to be.

So the brain cells record, and thought as the "me"—my ambitions, my greed, my purposes, my fulfilment—comes to an end. Therefore the brain and the mind become extraordinarily quiet and only function when necessary. Therefore your brain, your mind, enters into quite a different dimension of which there is no description; because the description is not the described. What we have done this morning is description, explanation, but the word is not the thing, when one realises that then one is free of the word. The quiet mind then enters into the immeasurable.

All our life is based on thought which is measurable. It measures God, it measures its relationship with another through the image. It tries to improve itself according to what it thinks it should be. So unnecessarily we live in a world of measurement, and with that world we want to enter into a world in which there is no measurement at all. Meditation is the seeing of what is and going beyond it— seeing the measure and going beyond the measure. What takes place when the brain, the mind and the body are really quiet and harmonious—when the mind, the body and the heart are completely one? Then one lives a totally different kind of life.

Questioner: What is intuition?

KRISHNAMURTI: One has to be very careful of that word. Because I like something unconsciously, I say I have an intuition about it. Don't you know all the tricks one plays upon oneself through that word? When you see things as they are, why do you want intuition? Why do you want any form of hunch, in intimation? We are talking of understanding oneself.

Questioner: When one is aware of one's sexual appetites, they seem to disappear. Can that awareness, that attention, be maintained all the time?

KRISHNAMURTI: Watch the danger of this question. "When I am aware of my sexual desires they seem to disappear." So awareness is a trick which will help me to make things, which I don't like, disappear. I don't like anger, therefore I am going to be aware of it and perhaps it will disappear. But I do like my fulfilment, I want to become a great man, and I won't be aware of that. I believe in God and I worship the State, but I won't be aware of all the dangers involved in that, although it separates, it destroys, it tortures people. So I am going to be aware of the things that are most unpleasant, but unaware of all those things which I want to keep. Awareness is not a trick, it is not something that will help me to dissolve the things we don't want. Awareness means to observe the whole movement of like and dislike, of your suppressions. If you are old-fashioned you don't talk about sex, you suppress it, but you go on thinking about it—one has to be aware of all that.

Questioner: Sir, can we by understanding our minds, be aware when we are asleep?

KRISHNAMURTI: This is really a complex question. How am I to be aware that I am asleep? Is there an awareness of what is going on during sleep? Am I aware during the day of all the movements that are going on within me, of all the reactions? If I am not aware during the day, how am I going to be aware at night when I sleep? If you are aware during the day, watching, attentive to how much you eat, what you say, what you think, of your motives, then have you anything to be aware of during the night? Please find out. If you are not aware, except of that which is going on as a recording in the brain, what takes place? I have spent my day actively, being aware, watching what I eat, what I think, what I feel, how I talk to others. Jealousy, envy, greed, violence—I have been completely aware of all that; which means I have brought order there, not according to any plan. I have lived a disordered life of not being aware; when I become aware

451

of all this, there is order. So when the body goes to sleep, what takes place? Generally the brain tries to bring about order while you are asleep, because during the conscious waking hours you have lived a disordered life and the brain needs order. I don't know if you have watched it—the brain cannot function properly, healthily if there is no order. So if during the day there has been order, the brain is not trying to bring about order when you sleep, through dreams, through intimations and so on—it becomes quiet. It may record, but it is quiet and so there is a possibility of renewal, a possibility of a mind no longer fighting and struggling; therefore the mind becomes extraordinarily young, fresh and innocent, in the sense that it won't hurt and will not be hurt.

Questioner: When a man has a message, the relationship between that man and his followers is usually that of a teacher. The teacher often has powers, and his message is a system. Why don't you consider yourself a teacher and your message a system?

KRISHNAMURTI: I have made this fairly clear, haven't I? Don't follow anybody and don't accept anybody as a teacher, except when you yourself become your own teacher and disciple.

BROCKWOOD PARK
12 SEPTEMBER 1971

452

ENGLAND

X

A discussion with a small group at Brockwood

Violence and the "me"

1

VIOLENCE AND THE "ME"

Does change imply violence? To what extent do we reject violence? Violence and energy: observing violence. What is the root of violence? Understanding the "me"; the "me" that wants to change is violent. Does the "me" or intelligence see? The implications of seeing.

KRISHNAMURTI: When we go into any problem or issue we ought to go into it completely and thoroughly, taking one thing at a time, not vaguely talk about many things. So if we could take one real human problem and talk it over together completely and seriously, I think it would be worthwhile. So what shall we talk about?

Questioner (1): *Education.*

Questioner (2): *Our lack of awareness.*

Questioner (3): *Love.*

Questioner (4): *Sir, sometimes, due to nervous fatigue, the mind seems to lose its sensitivity. I was wondering what we could do to cope with such a situation.*

KRISHNAMURTI: Could we take a problem like violence? It seems to me it is spreading all over the world; could we see what the implications are, and whether the human mind can really solve the social and also the inward problems, without any kind of violence?

As one observes, in every part of the world there are revolts and revolutions in order to change the social structure. Obviously the structure has to be changed; is it possible to change it without violence?—because violence begets violence. Through revolt one party can assume the power of government, and having achieved this, it will maintain itself in power through violence. It is fairly obvious that this is what is happening throughout the world. So we are asking whether there is a way of bringing about a change in the world and in ourselves which does not breed violence. I should have thought this would be a very serious problem for each one of us. Would you like to discuss this? What do you say?

Questioner: Yes, let's discuss violence.

KRISHNAMURTI: But let us go into it really deeply, not just superficially, because in talking this over we should bear in mind that it must also alter our ways of life. I do not know if you want to go so deeply into this. My question is, whether the outside world, the social structure, the injustice, the divisions, the appalling brutality, wars, revolts and all the rest of it, can be changed, as well as the inward struggle that is going on perpetually. Can all that be changed without violence, without conflict, without opposition, without forming one party as opposed to another party, not only outwardly, but also without the inward division?—bearing in mind that division is the source of conflict and of violence. How is one to bring about this change, both outwardly and inwardly? I should have thought that would be the most important issue that we have to face. What do you say, Sirs? How do we discuss this?

Questioner: Shall we start with violence in a small child?

KRISHNAMURTI: Shall we start with the children? With the student, or with the educator?—which is ourselves. Let us talk it over together, don't let me do all the talking.

Questioner (1): We should start with the educator.

Questioner (2): With ourselves. I see violence in ourselves every day.

KRISHNAMURTI: Where would you begin to resolve this problem? In all parts of the world, even in Russia where some of the intellectuals and writers are revolting against the tyranny, revolts are going on; they want freedom, they want to stop wars. Where would you start with this problem? Stopping wars in Vietnam, or in the Middle East?

Where does one begin to understand this problem? At the periphery, or at the centre?

Questioner: In oneself, in one's life.

KRISHNAMURTI: Where would you begin? With oneself, with one's own home, or out there?

Questioner: Why not in both places? If one can bring about some superficial change, that may resolve a certain superficial problem. I see no reason why that shouldn't take place, as well as individual enquiry.

KRISHNAMURTI: Are we concerned with superficial changes, with a superficial reformation? And therefore— which may be necessary—put our energies, thought, affection and care in outward, superficial reformation? Or do we begin at a wholly different level?—not as the opposite of it.

Questioner: Are the two exclusive?

KRISHNAMURTI: I did not say they were exclusive. I said they were not opposite.

Questioner: I don't see it being a case of either one thing or the other. One can see very clearly that one can achieve saving a hundred lives by some superficial action. I see no contradiction.

KRISHNAMURTI: I agree. There are many people who are pursuing superficial activities, thousands of them! Do we exclude that and entirely concern ourselves with our own house, or, in the very concern for our house, is the other included too? It is not an exclusion, or an opposition, or the avoidance of the one, and laying emphasis on the other.

Questioner: Well, Sir, I won't persist, but it does seem that very often people listen to you—myself included—who have thought that individual enquiry was extremely important to resolve the immediate problem to the exclusion of, say, political action, which at its own level may resolve some particular issues, though not fundamental ones. But I see no reason why they shouldn't go on in parallel.

457

KRISHNAMURTI: I quite agree, Sir. Do we deal with the fundamental issues?

Questioner: It is obviously the important thing.

KRISHNAMURTI: So, where shall we begin? Which is the fundamental issue?

Questioner: The individual. The mass is the extension of the individual.

KRISHNAMURTI: It is very clear, isn't it? We want change, both outwardly and inwardly, superficially and deeply. One does not exclude the other: I must have food in order to think! Without dividing, what is the fundamental issue? Where shall we tackle it? Where shall we put our teeth into it?

Questioner: What is the cause of violence?

KRISHNAMURTI: Shall we discuss that?

Questioner: Why do we want to change?

KRISHNAMURTI: That is a good question, too. Why should we change at all?

Another Questioner: Because we don't seem to be getting anywhere in our present state.

KRISHNAMURTI: And even if you got somewhere in your present state wouldn't you want to change? Now, please, let us come back.

Questioner: In our present state we seem to have very little possibility of moving; we are caught in our own individual ways, by some event, over and over again. There is this lack of movement in which we are always caught in life in some way or another and therefore violence arises.

KRISHNAMURTI: Shall we find out what are the causes of violence? Each one will have a different opinion; even the experts disagree on the causes of violence, volumes have been written about it! Shall we go on explaining the causes, or *see* violence as it is—as a fundamental issue in

458

human relationship. And find out whether it should perpetuate itself, or be changed, or modified. What is the fundamental issue involved in violence?

Questioner: We are apparently issued with a sort of animal brain, that is the main cause, I think we are naturally violent unless we can jump out of it. Half the time politicians are behaving just like chickens in a farmyard.

KRISHNAMURTI: I know! *(Laughter)*

Questioner: Is it possible to look at the individual state of mind to find out whether we are intrinsically violent within ourselves, in the very mode of mental activity—whether this dualistic movement is itself violent?

KRISHNAMURTI: So, Sir, what would you consider to be violence?

Questioner (1): I think it is self-involvement, selfishness.

Questioner (2): Separation.

Questioner (3): Reaction to fear.

KRISHNAMURTI: We have been educated to be violent. Our animal nature and the activity of the human brain etc. are violent and dividing; we all know this. Self-centred activities, to be aggressive, opposing, resisting, asserting, all that makes for violence.

Questioner: There is also part of oneself that is repelled by violence and another part which likes it, thrives on it.

KRISHNAMURTI: Yes. There is part of oneself which resists violence, is appalled by violence. Then, where are we?

Questioner: The desire to go into the problem of violence is only a partial seeing. I mean, one does not totally want to resolve the problem of violence.

KRISHNAMURTI: Doesn't one?

Questioner: No.

KRISHNAMURTI: Let's find out. Is it possible to resolve the question of violence totally?

Questioner (1): Isn't rebelling against violence a kind of violence? I should think it could be very destructive.

Questioner (2): If the mind, with its conditioning, is violent to start with, then the outcome is bound to be violence.

KRISHNAMURTI: So, what shall we do then, Sir?

Questioner: Would it be wise to just watch the violence without splitting, or separating?

KRISHNAMURTI: The gentleman raised the question: do we really want to be free of all violence? Answer that question. Do we? Which means to have no conflict, no dualistic activity within oneself, no resistance, no opposition, no aggression, no ambition to *be* somebody, not to assert one's opinion and oppose other opinions. All that implies a form of violence. Not only the violence of self-discipline, but also the violence that makes me twist my particular desires in order to conform to a pattern, to make it moral, or whatever it is; all these are forms of violence. Will is violence. Do we want to be free of all this? And can a human being live, being free from it?

Questioner: It seems that in the process we call our life, tension is necessary. We have to distinguish, it seems, between tension and violence. I am reminded of the story of the languishing herrings who didn't really come to life until some dog-fish were put into the tank. When does normal tension as a process of life cease, and violence begin? Do we make a distinction here?

KRISHNAMURTI: So you see tension is necessary?

Questioner: In everything there is polarity.

KRISHNAMURTI: Please, Sir, let us find out. Does a human being—us here—want to be free of *all* violence?

Questioner (1): This seems to me a very difficult question because there are such a lot of contradictions in us. One

460

says at this moment that one does not want violence; the scene changes, and in an hour's time one is violent, one is caught. One is broken up into so many facets.

Questioner (2): Someone may seriously attempt to bring attention to violence within, but how does such a person react when he is confronted with violence outside?

KRISHNAMURTI: Wait, Sir, that is a later question. Do we here see the importance of being totally free of all violence? Or would we like to keep certain parts of it? Is it possible to be completely free of all violence?—that means to be free of all irritation, all anger, of any form of anxiety, and of resistance to anything.

Questioner: I think there is a difference between you positing that question and an individual saying "I want to be free of all violence". Because the one is a dispassionate looking at the question, the other one is a movement— again a violent movement.

KRISHNAMURTI: That is just it!

Questioner: It seems to me to be a real thing, or a reasonable thing, to look at the question rather than try to resolve violence. To me they are two different things.

KRISHNAMURTI: Then, what is the question, sir?

Questioner: Is it possible to be completely free of violence?

KRISHNAMURTI: That is all.

Questioner: It is quite different from seeking to be free of violence.

KRISHNAMURTI: Quite! Then what do I do?—is it possible?

Questioner (1): If one sees the pattern of one's daily life, one sees that it seems that without some form of violence— or maybe what this gentleman calls tension—one could perhaps never carry through one distinct job in the face of the pressures and difficulties that often surround one in society. We talk about freedom from violence when we are angry, or afraid, as if we were trapped, but I feel that per-

haps there is always some violence in our lives. It is difficult to conceive living, doing some job and so on, without some kind of drive which I feel is violence.

Questioner (2): Isn't there a difference between tension and violence? It seems that violence being resistance and aggression, is deadening; it tries to stop something. Whilst tension is moving with what you are doing. It seems to me we have to have an understanding of the difference between violence and tension.

KRISHNAMURTI: Sir, can we pursue that question: is it possible for a human being to be completely free of violence? We have understood what we mean by violence, more or less.

Questioner (1): I don't think we have. If there is no difference between violence and energy, then I wouldn't want to be free of violence.

Questioner (2): If we could see our violence the whole time, there would be no violence.

KRISHNAMURTI: No, Sir. Before we come to that point, as a human being, have I said to myself: is it possible to live without violence?

Questioner: One obviously does not know.

KRISHNAMURTI: So let us enquire, Sir, let us find out.

Another Questioner: Wouldn't the only way to find out be to do it?

KRISHNAMURTI: Not only do it, but enquire, go into it, watch it, be aware of this whole movement of resistance. Knowing the danger of violence, seeing the outward effects of it, the divisions, the horrors, and so on, I ask myself: is it possible for me to be free of *all* violence? I really don't know. So I am going to enquire, I want to find out, not verbally, but passionately! Human beings have lived with violence for thousands of years and I want to find out whether it is possible to live without violence. Now where shall I begin?

Questioner: Would you first try to understand what vi-olence is?

KRISHNAMURTI: I know very well what it is: anger, jeal-ousy, brutality, revolt, resistance, ambition, all the rest of it. We don't have to define endlessly what violence is.

Questioner: I don't really see ambition as violence.

KRISHNAMURTI: No?

Another Questioner: Is it possible to see how it arises in oneself, when it comes up, when it reaches the surface?

KRISHNAMURTI: Sir, must I wait till anger comes up, and then be aware of that anger and say, "I am violent"? Is that what you propose, Sir?

Questioner: The movement leading up to it is very rarely caught by us.

Another Questioner: Should we understand thought?—the sudden thoughts?

KRISHNAMURTI: Sir, it is such a vast problem, don't let us take little bits of it, let us observe it at the very core. What makes the mind violent in me, in this human body, in this person? What is the source of this violence? Watch it in yourself.

Another Questioner: Is it my desire to achieve something, to gain something, to be something? I want to look and see how much of the violence that I knew I had, I could give up—and still survive within acceptable limits. That would be my first step.

KRISHNAMURTI: Within acceptable limits—and that may also be violent.

Questioner: Yes, I would expect I should still have a degree of violence.

KRISHNAMURTI: I am asking myself whether it is possible to live *without* violence and I say: what is the root of this?

463

If I could understand that, perhaps I would know how to live without violence. What is the root of it?

Questioner: The feeling of revolution, of separation.

KRISHNAMURTI: You say the root of this violence is separation, division, the "me". Can the mind live without the "me"? Please go on, let us enquire.

Questioner: Is it true that as long as there is an objective, or desire of any kind, there is the seed of violence?

KRISHNAMURTI: Of course! That is the whole point. We must go step by step into this. Please, Sirs, go on!

Questioner: Does not this pose the question: is it possible to live without any objective?

KRISHNAMURTI: Yes. Is it possible to live without any objective, without any principle, without any aim, without any purpose?

Questioner: The purpose is life.

KRISHNAMURTI: The opposite of that is to drift. Therefore we must be careful that we don't think in terms of the opposite. If I have no objective, then I am just drifting. So I must be very careful when I say, "To have an objective is a form of violence"; to have no objective may be to drift.

Questioner: But this is irrelevant, Sir, because whether one drifts or not isn't the question. The question is: is it possible to live without violence?

KRISHNAMURTI: I'm only warning, Sir, not to go into the opposite. Now, is it possible to live without direction? Direction means resistance, means no distraction, no distortion, it means a continuous drive towards a goal. Why do I want a purpose, an end? And that end, the goal, the purpose, the principle, the ideal—is it true? Or is it a thing which the mind has invented because it is conditioned, because it is afraid, because it is seeking security, both outwardly and inwardly and therefore invents something and pursues that, hoping to have security?

464

Another Questioner: At times one has perhaps had intimations of this other thing and those intimations seem to give a drive.

KRISHNAMURTI: Yes, one may have an intimation of it, but that isn't good enough for me. I'm going to find out whether it is possible to live without violence, and that is a *passionate* thing. It is not just an ideological fancy. I really want to find out.

Questioner: The trouble is, I don't really feel this question.

KRISHNAMURTI: You don't feel it?

Questioner: Not enough to reach out, to go towards it.

KRISHNAMURTI: Why don't you? Why not? The whole issue of existence is this!

Questioner: I think this is a problem for most of us.

KRISHNAMURTI: Good God! They are burning, they are destroying, and you say, "I am sorry, it doesn't really interest me!"

Questioner (1): If the question of violence interests you, I think you are already assisting the burning and enjoying it. I think if you didn't have violence in yourself, you wouldn't be really interested.

Questioner (2): Sir, what is the meaning of the word "violence"? Would you include things such as enthusiasm for something, drive, pep? Would you call these things violence?

KRISHNAMURTI: Not what would I call it, Sir—what do you call it?

Questioner: I don't know . . .

KRISHNAMURTI: I am not an oracle, let us find out. Let us stick to this question. Is it possible for me to live *completely* without violence?

Questioner: We are caught in a terrible trap.

KRISHNAMURTI: We are caught in it; do we remain in it?

Questioner: No, but we have a body and a self to preserve. It is very difficult.

KRISHNAMURTI: What shall I do?—please, answer my question! To me this is of tremendous importance. The world is burning. Don't say, "My body is weak, this is difficult, it is not possible, I must be a vegetarian, I must not kill." I am asking: is it possible? And to find that out, I must find out what the *source* of this violence is.

Questioner: I think it is being divided. If I am divided I must be violent. I feel I will be destroyed, therefore I am afraid.

KRISHNAMURTI: Therefore we accept violence?

Questioner: No, but we want to destroy the thing we are afraid of.

KRISHNAMURTI: Sir, would you put it this way: if you could find the source, the root of this violence, and if that root could wither away, you might live a totally different kind of life. So, wouldn't it be worthwhile to find out what is the root of it, and whether it can wither away?

Questioner: Probably it is connected with fear.

KRISHNAMURTI: I am not interested in fear. I want to end violence because I see violence begets violence. This violence is an endless process. You know what is happening in the world. So I ask myself: is it possible to end violence? Before I can answer that question, I must find out what is the root of all these innumerable branches.

Another Questioner: But we can't do it by thinking about it.

KRISHNAMURTI: We are going to find out. We are going to think about it and see the futility of thought, and then go outwards. But we must exercise our intelligence, our thought.

466

Questioner: So long as I want to do anything, there is violence to a greater or lesser degree.

KRISHNAMURTI: I understand this. I just said, look: is it possible to live without violence? And to find that out, there must be an enquiry into the root of it.

Questioner: What I am trying to say is, that the whole structure of life as we know it, is wanting to do this, wanting to do that—everything involves violence.

KRISHNAMURTI: Of course, Sir, that's agreed.

Questioner: Paradoxically, might one consider self-preservation?

KRISHNAMURTI: You see, you are all not bringing up the main, fundamental issue.

Questioner: Sir, you keep talking about the root, but living in a town, the way life is at the moment, violence in human society is just like the air one has to breathe, it is like a fog that envelops everything. The question about the root of it doesn't spring to my mind. One sees violence in an animal-like way, one knows of people being frightened and behaving in a certain way, but one is only aware of a series of reactions.

KRISHNAMURTI: I understand all that, Sir. I am asking you: what is the root of this?

Questioner: The self.

KRISHNAMURTI: The self! All right. If the "me" is the root of all this, what shall I do? Having discovered the "me" wanting this, not wanting that, the "me" wanting a purpose and running after it, the "me" that resists, that has a battle with itself, if that is the root of violence—which for me *is* the root—then what shall I do with it?

Questioner: You cannot do anything.

KRISHNAMURTI: Wait, Sir! Do I accept it? Do I live in this battle, with this violence?

467

Questioner: I feel, Sir, that if you say, "I am violent", you haven't got to the root of the problem.

KRISHNAMURTI: No, you haven't. Quite right.

Questioner: Because one can go on saying "I am violent" endlessly.

KRISHNAMURTI: Agreed. I see the "me" with all its branches is the cause of violence; it is the "me" that separates: you and me, we and they; the Blacks and the Whites, the Arabs and the Israelis, and so on.

Questioner: Rationally, you could say: eliminate the "me".

KRISHNAMURTI: How is the mind to eliminate its own structure, which is based on the "me"? Sir, do look at the issue. The "me" is the root of all this; the "me" is identified with a particular nation, with a particular community, with a particular ideology or religious fancy. The 'me" identifies itself with a certain prejudice, the "me" says "I must fulfil"; and when it feels frustrated, there is anger and bitterness. It is the "me" that says, "I must reach my goal, I must be successful", that wants and doesn't want, that says "I must live peacefully", and it is the "me" that gets violent.

Questioner: Though it seems to be an entity, to me it is more of an action, or an activity. Is this word not misleading us?

KRISHNAMURTI: No, it isn't. It does not mean it is something solid, like the trunk of a tree. It is a movement, it is a living thing. One day it feels marvellous, the next day it is in great depression. One day it is passionate, lustful, the next day it is worn out and says, "Let me have some peace." It is a constantly moving, active thing. How is this movement to transform itself into another movement, without becoming violent? First, let us get the question right. We said: this is a movement, it is a living thing, it is not static, it is not something dead, it is adding to itself all the time, and taking away from itself all the time. This is the "me". And when the "me" says, "I must get rid of the 'me'," wanting to have another "me", it is still violent; the "me" that says: "I am a pacifist, I live peacefully", the me

468

that seeks truth, the me that says "I must live beautifully, non-violently", is still the "me" which is the cause of violence.

What will the mind do with this living thing? And the mind itself is the "me". Do you understand the question? Any movement on the part of the "me" to get rid of itself, to say "I must wither away", "I must destroy myself", "I must gradually get rid of myself", is still that same movement of the "me", is still the "me" which is the root of violence. Do we realise that? Do we really see that? Not theoretically, but actually realise the truth of it, that any movement of the "me" in any direction, is the action of violence. Do I actually, sensuously, intelligently, see the truth of it, know the feel of it? If the mind does not, it can go on playing with words for ever.

Questioner: Does the mind consist only of the "me"? Are they identical?

KRISHNAMURTI: When the mind is not occupied with the "me", it is not the "me". But most of us are occupied with the "me", consciously or unconsciously.

Questioner: We seem to be able to give up all kinds of thoughts and as the "me" is put together by thought, why can't we discard it?

KRISHNAMURTI: No, Sir, it is impossible to discard anything, except perhaps smoking cigarettes. Please, let us stick to this one thing: do I actually see that in the action of the "me", negative or positive, there is a form of violence. It *is* violence. If I don't see it, why not? What is wrong with my eyesight, with my feeling? Is it that I am afraid what will happen if I see it? Or am I bored with the whole thing? Please, come on, Sirs!

Questioner: Sometimes one is carried away, and therefore . . .

KRISHNAMURTI: No, Sir, no. It is not a question of being carried away. Not to be violent—I want to find this out!

Another Questioner: We can't rake up the energy to keep the mind on the subject.

KRISHNAMURTI: No, Sir. If you say you haven't the energy, the collecting of that energy is again a form of the "me", which says "I must have more energy in order to tackle this". Any movement of the "me", which is thought, conscious or unconscious, is still the "me". Do I really see the truth of this?

Questioner: Is there something behind the "me" which in essence is not of thought?

KRISHNAMURTI: Do listen to that question; don't say, "We don't know or we do." Is there anything behind the "me" which is not of the me?

Questioner: If there is, and we think about it, it is yet again part of the "me".

KRISHNAMURTI: Who is putting this question? Surely it is the "me"!

Questioner: Why not? Thought is a tool, why not use it?

KRISHNAMURTI: No, you can't say "Why not"—it is still the movement of the "me".

Questioner: You have asked: do we really see that any movement of the "me" is violence? I think the only reason that we can't see it, is because we reject violence.

KRISHNAMURTI: Oh, no. Either you see it or you don't see it. It isn't a question of something that prevents you from seeing. I don't see my affection for my dog, or for my wife, or husband, for the beauty of it is part of me; because I think that is a most marvellous state.

Questioner: Sir, by definition you have virtually said that life is violence, movement, change.

KRISHNAMURTI: As we live now, life, living, is a form of violence.

Questioner: Is life possible without change, without movement?

470

KRISHNAMURTI: That's what we are asking. The life we lead is a life of violence, which is caused by the "me", and we are saying: do we see that any movement of the "me" in any direction, conscious or unconscious, is a form of violence? If I don't see it, why don't I see it? What is wrong?

Questioner: It seems to me it is the "me" that is seeing it.

KRISHNAMURTI: Wait. Is it the "me" that sees it?

Questioner: Is it intelligence?

KRISHNAMURTI: I don't know, you find out! What is it that sees that the "me" is the root of all mischief? Sir, please watch it. Who sees it?

Questioner: I don't see it. I'm afraid to give up everything I've ever known.

KRISHNAMURTI: So you don't want to see that the "me" is responsible for this hideous mess. Because one says: I don't care if the world goes bust, but I want to have my little corner. Therefore I don't see the "me", the root of all mischief.

Questioner: Would you say there is another "me", other than the thinking process with an object in view? When I think towards something, towards an object, to me this is the "me", and there is no other "me" except that process.

KRISHNAMURTI: Obviously.

Questioner: But you said it isn't the thing that sees the significance of the question.

KRISHNAMURTI: No. We said, this "me" is a living thing, a movement. All the time it is adding to itself and taking away from itself. And this "me", this movement, is the root of all violence. Not only this "me" as something static which invents the soul, which invents God, Heaven and punishment—it is the whole of that.

We are asking: does the mind realise that the "me" is the cause of this mischief? The mind—use the word intelligence if you like—which sees the whole map of violence,

471

all the intricacies, sees it by observing, this mind says: that is the root of all evil. So the mind now asks: is it possible to live without the "me"?

Questioner: The process of seeing is different from the process of moving in a certain direction towards something.

KRISHNAMURTI: Right. The process of seeing is entirely different. It is not a process. I won't use that word. The seeing is seeing *now*; it is not a process of seeing. Seeing is acting. Now, does the mind see this whole map of violence and the root of it? And what is it that sees? If the "me" sees it, then it is afraid to live differently, then the "me" says, "I must protect myself, I must resist this, I am afraid". Therefore the "me" refuses to see the map. But the seeing is not the "me".

Questioner: Seeing has no purpose, has it?

KRISHNAMURTI: There is no purpose in seeing the map; it just sees.

Questioner: But, immediately I say that I see it . . .

KRISHNAMURTI: Wait! Do we realise that the mind which is observing this entire map is entirely different from the "me" which sees it and is afraid to break from it? There are two different observations: the "me" seeing, and "seeing". The "me" seeing must inevitably be afraid, and must therefore resist and say, "How shall I live?" What shall I do? Must I give this up? Must I hold on?" and so on. We said: any movement of the "me" is violence. But there is a mere seeing of the map, which is entirely different. Is this clear? Now, which is it that you are doing?

Questioner: The "me" is seeing.

KRISHNAMURTI: You say the "me" is seeing—therefore it is afraid.

Another Questioner: Of course, it is afraid.

KRISHNAMURTI: What will you do, knowing any movement of the "me" is still furthering that fear?

Questioner: I don't know.

KRISHNAMURTI: Ah! What do you mean by, "You don't know"?

Questioner: To me, the "me" is all I know.

KRISHNAMURTI: No, Sir, we have made it very clear. Do listen to this. There are two actions of seeing. Seeing the map non-directionally, non-purposively, just seeing, and the "me" seeing—the "me" with its purpose, with its drive, with its directive, with its resistances. It sees and is afraid to do this, or that.

Questioner: Are you using the word "see" now in the way in which you normally speak of being aware?

KRISHNAMURTI: I am just using the word "seeing" for a change, that's all.

Questioner: Sir, you tell me there is a state in which you can see without the "me", but I have never experienced this.

KRISHNAMURTI: Do it now, Sir! I am showing it to you! There is the "me" that looks at this whole map of violence and therefore is afraid and resists. And there is another seeing which is not of the "me", which just observes, non-objectively, non-purposively, and says, "I just see it".

But this is simple, isn't it? I see you have got a green shirt; I don't say, "I like it" or "I dislike it", I just see it. But the moment I say, "I like it", it is already the "me" saying "I like it"; and therefore all the rest of it follows. This is sufficiently clear—verbally at least.

Questioner: Could we go into the question of why this looking without the "me" is so very difficult and happens so rarely.

KRISHNAMURTI: I don't think it is difficult. Don't say it is difficult; then you are stuck, then you have blocked yourself.

Questioner: Could one summarise this by saying that in one case there is a seeing without purpose, and in the other case purpose is involved?

KRISHNAMURTI: Yes, that's all. Can I look without direction? When I look with a direction, it is the "me". What is the difficulty in this, may I ask?

Another Questioner: Usually we have the illusion that looking, with a direction is looking.

KRISHNAMURTI: Looking with a direction is *not* looking, obviously.

Questioner: There is a difference between looking and seeing. If one is looking, one is involved.

KRISHNAMURTI: Don't let's complicate it. We said: does the mind see the whole map, without any direction?

Questioner: The map is selected from both directions.

KRISHNAMURTI: No, no. Just look. This whole structure of the "me" *is* violence; the structure being the way I live, the way I think, the way I feel, my whole reaction to everything is a form of violence which is the "me". That is all in the category of time. The "seeing" has no time—you are seeing it. The moment I see with time there is fear.

Questioner: There is seeing, and the thing seen. When once you have seen something is it the old mind that has seen?

KRISHNAMURTI: Yes. Now do find out, Sir, how do you see? Do you see non-purposively, or purposively? Do you see in terms of time? That is, do you say, "It is too difficult, it is too complex, what am I to do?" Or do you see without time?

If you say, "I don't see it without time," the next question is, "Why? What is the difficulty?" Is it physical blindness, or is it psychological disinclination to look at anything as it is? Is it because we have never looked at anything directly, are always trying to avoid, to escape? Therefore, if we are escaping, let us see that—not try to find out how to resist escape.

BROCKWOOD PARK
6 JUNE 1970

ENGLAND

XI

*Conversation between J. Krishnamurti
and Professor David Bohm*

On intelligence

ON INTELLIGENCE

Conversation between J. Krishnamurti
and Professor David Bohm.

Thought is of the order of time; intelligence is of a different order, different quality. Is intelligence related to thought? Brain the instrument of intelligence; thought as a pointer. Thought, not intelligence, dominates the world. Problem of thought and the awakening of intelligence. Intelligence operating in a limited framework can serve highly unintelligent purposes. Matter, thought, intelligence have a common source, are one energy; why did it divide? Security and survival: thought cannot consider death properly. "Can the mind keep the purity of the original source?" Problem of the quietening of thought. Insight, the perception of the whole, is necessary. Communication without the interference of the conscious mind.

Professor Bohm:[1] About intelligence, I always like to look up the origin of a word as well as its meaning. It is very interesting; it comes from *inter* and *legere* which means "To read between". So it seems to me that you could say that thought is like the information in a book and that intelligence has to read it, the meaning of it. I think this gives a rather good notion of intelligence.

KRISHNAMURTI: To read between the lines.

Bohm: Yes, to see what it means. There is also another relevant meaning given in the dictionary which is: mental alertness.

KRISHNAMURTI: Yes, mental alertness.

Bohm: Well, this is very different from what people have in mind when they measure intelligence. Now. considering many of the things you have said, you would say intelli-

[1] David Bohm, Professor of Theoretical Physics at Birkbeck College, London University; author of *Causality & Chance in Modern Physics, Quantum Theory, The Special Theory of Relativity.*

gence is not thought. You say thought takes place in the old brain, it is a physical process, electrochemical; it has been amply proved by science that all thought is essentially a physical, chemical process. Then we could say perhaps that intelligence is not of the same order, it is not of the order of time at all.

KRISHNAMURTI: Intelligence.

Bohm: Yes, intelligence reads "between the lines" of thought, sees the meaning of it. There is one more point before we start on this question: if you say thought is physical, then the mind or intelligence or whatever you want to call it, seems different, it is of a different order. Would you say there is a real difference between the physical and intelligence?

KRISHNAMURTI: Yes. Are we saying that thought is matter? Let us put it differently.

Bohm: Matter? I would rather call it a material process.

KRISHNAMURTI: All right; thought is a material process, and what is the relationship between that and intelligence? Is intelligence the product of thought?

Bohm: I think that we can take for granted that it is not.

KRISHNAMURTI: Why do we take it for granted?

Bohm: Simply because thought is mechanical.

KRISHNAMURTI: Thought is mechanical, that is right.

Bohm: Intelligence is not.

KRISHNAMURTI: So thought is measurable; intelligence is not. And how does it happen that this intelligence comes into existence? If thought has no relationship with intelligence then is the cessation of thought the awakening of intelligence? Or is it that intelligence, being independent of thought, not of time, therefore exists always?

Bohm: That raises many difficult questions.

478

KRISHNAMURTI: I know.

Bohm: I would like to put this in a framework of thinking that one could connect with any scientific views that may exist.

KRISHNAMURTI: Yes.

Bohm: Either to show that it fits or doesn't fit. So you say intelligence may be there always.

KRISHNAMURTI: I am asking—is it there always?

Bohm: It may or may not be. Or it is possible that something interferes with intelligence?

KRISHNAMURTI: You see the Hindus have the theory that intelligence, or Brahman, exists always and is covered over by illusion, by matter, by stupidity, by all kinds of mischievous things created by thought. I don't know if you would go as far as that.

Bohm: Well, yes; we don't actually see the eternal existence of intelligence.

KRISHNAMURTI: They say peel all this off, that thing is there. So their assumption is that it existed always.

Bohm: There is difficulty in that, in the word "always".

KRISHNAMURTI: Yes.

Bohm: Because "always" implies time.

KRISHNAMURTI: That is right.

Bohm: And that is just the trouble. Time is thought—I would like to put it that thought is of the order of time— or perhaps it is the other way round—that time is of the order of thought. In other words thought has invented time, and in fact thought *is* time. The way I see it is, that thoughts may sweep over the whole of time in one moment; but then thought is always changing without noticing that it is changing physically—for physical reasons, that is.

479

KRISHNAMURTI: Yes.

Bohm: Not rational reasons.

KRISHNAMURTI: No.

Bohm: The reasons do not have to do with something total, but they have to do with some physical movement in the brain; therefore . . .

KRISHNAMURTI: . . . they depend on environment and all kinds of things.

Bohm: So as thought changes with time its meaning is no longer consistent, it becomes contradictory, it changes in an arbitrary way.

KRISHNAMURTI: Yes, I'll follow that.

Bohm: Then you begin to think, everything is changing, everything changes, and one realises "I am in time". When time is extended it becomes vast, the past before I was, further and further back and also forward in the future, so you begin to say time is the essence of all, time conquers everything. First the child may think, "I am eternal"; then he begins to understand that he is in time. The general view that we get to is, that time is the essence of existence. This I think is not only the common sense view but also the scientific view. It is very hard to give up such a view because it is an intense conditioning. It is stronger even than the conditioning of the observer and the observed.

KRISHNAMURTI: Yes, quite. Are we saying that thought is of time, thought is measurable, thought can change, modify, expand? And intelligence is of a different quality altogether?

Bohm: Yes, different order, different quality. And I get an interesting impression of this thought with regard to time. If we think of the past and the future, we think of the past as becoming the future; but you can see that that can't be, that it is just thought. Yet one gets the impression that past and future are present together and there is movement in another way; that the whole pattern is moving.

KRISHNAMURTI: The whole pattern is moving.

Bohm: But I can't picture how it moves. In some sense it is moving in a perpendicular direction to the direction between past and future. That whole movement—then I begin to think that movement is in another time.

KRISHNAMURTI: Quite, quite.

Bohm: But that gets you back into the paradox.

KRISHNAMURTI: Yes, that is it. Is intelligence out of time and therefore not related to thought, which is a movement of time?

Bohm: But thought must be related to it.

KRISHNAMURTI: Is it? I am asking. I think it is unrelated.

Bohm: Unrelated? But there seems to be some relation in the sense that you distinguish between intelligent thought and unintelligent thought.

KRISHNAMURTI: Yes, but that requires intelligence: to recognise unintelligent thought.

Bohm: But when intelligence reads thought, what is the relationship?

KRISHNAMURTI: Let us go slowly . . .

Bohm: And does thought respond to intelligence? Doesn't thought change?

KRISHNAMURTI: Let us be simple. Thought is time. Thought is movement in time. Thought is measurable and thought functions in the field of time, all moving, changing, transforming. Is intelligence within the field of time?

Bohm: Well, we've seen that in one sense it can't be. But the thing is not clear. First of all, thought is mechanical.

KRISHNAMURTI: Thought is mechanical, that is clear.

481

Bohm: Secondly, in some sense there is a movement which is of a different direction.

KRISHNAMURTI: Thought is mechanical; being mechanical it can move in different directions and all the rest of it. Is intelligence mechanical? Let's put it that way.

Bohm: I would like to ask the question, what does mechanicalness mean?

KRISHNAMURTI: All right: repetitive, measurable, comparative.

Bohm: I would say also dependent.

KRISHNAMURTI: Dependent, yes.

Bohm: Intelligence—let us get it clear—intelligence cannot be dependent on conditions for its truth. Nevertheless, it seems that in some sense intelligence doesn't operate if the brain is not healthy.

KRISHNAMURTI: Obviously.

Bohm: In that sense intelligence seems to depend on the brain.

KRISHNAMURTI: Or is it the quietness of the brain?

Bohm: All right, it depends on the quietness of the brain.

KRISHNAMURTI: Not on the activity of the brain.

Bohm: There is still some relation between intelligence and the brain. We once discussed this question many years ago, when I raised the idea that in physics you could use a measuring instrument in two ways, the positive and the negative. For example, you can measure an electric current by the swing of the needle in the instrument, or you can use the same instrument in what is called the Wheatstone bridge, where the reading you look for is a null reading; a null reading indicates harmony, balance of the two sides of the whole system as it were. So if you are using the instrument negatively, then the non-movement of the instrument is the sign that it is working right. Could we say the brain may have used thought positively to make an image of the world . . .

KRISHNAMURTI: . . . which is the function of thought—one of the functions.

Bohm: The other function of thought is negative, which is by its movement to indicate non-harmony.

KRISHNAMURTI: Yes, non-harmony. Let us proceed from there. Is intelligence dependent on the brain—have we come to that point? Or when we use the word "dependent" what do we mean by that?

Bohm: It has several possible meanings. There may be simple mechanical dependence. But there is another kind: that *one* can't exist without the *other*. If I say, "I depend on food to exist", it doesn't mean that everything I think is determined by what I eat.

KRISHNAMURTI: Yes, quite.

Bohm: So I propose that intelligence depends for its existence on this brain, which can indicate non-harmony, but the brain does not have anything to do with the content of intelligence.

KRISHNAMURTI: So if the brain is not harmonious, can intelligence function?

Bohm: That is the question.

KRISHNAMURTI: That is what we are saying. It cannot function if the brain is hurt.

Bohm: If the intelligence doesn't function, is there intelligence? Therefore it seems that intelligence requires the brain in order to exist.

KRISHNAMURTI: But the brain is only an instrument.

Bohm: Which indicates this harmony or disharmony.

KRISHNAMURTI: But it is not the creator of the other.

483

Bohm: No.

KRISHNAMURTI: Let us go into this slowly.

Bohm: The brain doesn't create intelligence but it is an instrument which helps intelligence to function. That is it.

KRISHNAMURTI: That's it. Now if the brain is functioning within the field of time, up and down, negatively, positively, can intelligence operate in that movement of time? Or must that instrument by quiet for the intelligence to operate?

Bohm: Yes. I would put it possibly slightly differently. The quietness of the instrument *is* the operation of intelligence.

KRISHNAMURTI: Yes, that is right. The two are not separate.

Bohm: They are one and the same. The non-quietness of the instrument is the failure of the intelligence.

KRISHNAMURTI: That is right.

Bohm: But I think it would be useful to go back into questions which tend to be raised in the whole of scientific and philosophical thinking. We would ask the question: is there some sense in which intelligence exists independently of matter? You see that some people have thought that mind and matter have some separate kind of existence. This is one question that comes up. It may not be relevant, but I think the question should be considered in order to help to make the mind quiet. The consideration of questions that cannot be clearly answered is one of the things that disturbs the mind.

KRISHNAMURTI: But you see, Sir, when you say, "Help to make the mind quiet", will thought help the awakening of intelligence? It means that, doesn't it? Thought and matter and the exercise of thought and the movement of thought, or thought saying to itself, "I will be quiet in order to help the awakening of intelligence". Any movement of thought is time, *any* movement, because it is measurable, it is functioning positively or negatively, harmoniously, or dishar-

484

moniously, in this field. And realising that thought may say unconsciously, or unknowingly, that "I would be quiet in order to have this or that", then that is still within the field of time.

Bohm: Yes. It is still projecting.

KRISHNAMURTI: It is projecting it to capture it. So how does this intelligence take place—not how—when does it awaken?

Bohm: Once again the question is in time.

KRISHNAMURTI: That is why I don't want to use the words "when", "how".

Bohm: You might perhaps say the condition for it to awaken is the non-operation of thought.

KRISHNAMURTI: Yes.

Bohm: But that is the same as the awakening, it is not merely the condition. You can't even ask if there are conditions for intelligence to awaken. Even to talk about a condition is a form of thought.

KRISHNAMURTI: Yes. Let us agree, any movement of thought in any direction, vertical, horizontal. in action or non-action, is still in time—any movement of thought.

Bohm: Yes.

KRISHNAMURTI: Then what is the relationship of that movement to this intelligence which is not a movement, which is not of time. which is not the product of thought? Where can the two meet?

Bohm: They don't meet. But there is still a relation.

KRISHNAMURTI: That is what we are trying to find out. Is there any relationship at all, first? One thinks there is a relationship, one hopes there is a relationship, one projects a relationship. Is there a relationship at all?

Bohm: That depends what you mean by relationship?

KRISHNAMURTI: Relationship: being in contact with, recognition, a feeling of being in touch with.

Bohm: Well, the word relationship might mean something else.

KRISHNAMURTI: What other meaning has it?

Bohm: For example there is a parallel, isn't there? The harmony of the two. That is, two things may be related without contact, but by simply being in harmony.

KRISHNAMURTI: Does harmony mean a movement of both in the same direction?

Bohm: It might also mean in some way keeping in the same order.

KRISHNAMURTI: In the same order: same direction, same depth, same intensity—all that is harmony. But can thought ever be harmonious?—thought as movement, not static thought.

Bohm: I understand. There is that thought which you abstract as static, in geometry let us say, that may have some harmony; but thought as it actually moves is always contradictory.

KRISHNAMURTI: Therefore it has no harmony in itself. But intelligence has harmony in itself.

Bohm: I think I see the source of the confusion. We have the static products of thought that seem to have a certain relative harmony. But that harmony is really the result of intelligence, at least it seems so to me. In mathematics we may get a certain relative harmony of the product of thought, even though the actual movement of thought of a mathematician is not necessarily in harmony, generally won't be in harmony. Now that harmony which appears in mathematics is the result of intelligence, isn't it?

KRISHNAMURTI: Proceed, Sir.

Bohm: It is not perfect harmony because every form of mathematics has been proved to have some limit; that is why I call it only relative.

KRISHNAMURTI: Yes. Now, in the movement of thought is there harmony? If there is, then it has relationship with intelligence. If there is no harmony but contradictions and all the rest of it, then thought has no relationship with the other.

Bohm: Then would you say that we could do entirely without thought?

KRISHNAMURTI: I would put it round the other way. Intelligence uses thought.

Bohm: All right. But how can it use something which is disharmonious?

KRISHNAMURTI: Expression, communication, using thought which is contradictory, which is not harmonious, to create things in the world.

Bohm: But still, there must be harmony in some other sense, in what is done with thought, in what we have just described.

KRISHNAMURTI: Let us go slowly in this. Can we first put into words, negatively or positively, what is intelligence, what is not intelligence? Or is that impossible because words are thought, time, measure and so on?

Bohm: We can't put it in words. We are trying to point. Can we say that thought can function as the pointer to intelligence, and then its contradiction doesn't matter.

KRISHNAMURTI: That is right. That is right.

Bohm: Because we are not using it for its content, or its meaning, but rather as a pointer which points beyond the domain of time.

KRISHNAMURTI: So thought is a pointer. The content is intelligence.

Bohm: The content which it points to.

KRISHNAMURTI: Yes. Can we put this thing entirely differently? May we say, thought is barren?

Bohm: Yes. When it moves by itself, yes.

KRISHNAMURTI: Which is mechanical and all the rest of it. Thought is a pointer, but without intelligence the pointer has no value.

Bohm: Could we say that intelligence reads the pointer? If the pointer has nobody to see it then the pointer doesn't point.

KRISHNAMURTI: Quite. So intelligence is necessary. Without it thought has no meaning at all.

Bohm: But could we not say: that if thought is not intelligent it points in a very confused way?

KRISHNAMURTI: Yes, in an irrelevant way.

Bohm: Irrelevant, meaningless and so on. Then with intelligence it begins to point in another way. But then somehow thought and intelligence seem to fuse in a common function.

KRISHNAMURTI: Yes. So we can ask: what is action in relationship to intelligence? Right?

Bohm: Yes.

KRISHNAMURTI: What is action in relation to intelligence, and in the carrying out of that action is thought necessary?

Bohm: Yes; well, thought is necessary and this thought points obviously towards matter. But it seems to point both ways—back towards intelligence as well. One of the questions which always comes up is: should we say that intelligence and matter are merely a distinction within the same thing, or are they different? Are they really separate?

KRISHNAMURTI: I think they are separate, they are distinct.

Bohm: They are distinct, but are they actually separate?

KRISHNAMURTI: What do you mean by the word "separate"? Not related, not connected, with no common source?

Bohm: Yes. Do they have a common source?

KRISHNAMURTI: That is just it. Thought, matter and intelligence, have they a common source? *(Long pause).* I think they have.

Bohm: Otherwise there could be no harmony, of course.

KRISHNAMURTI: But you see thought has conquered the world. You understand?—conquered.

Bohm: Dominates the world.

KRISHNAMURTI: Thought, the intellect, dominates the world. And therefore intelligence has very little place here. When one thing dominates, the other must be subservient.

Bohm: One asks, I don't know if it is relevant, how that came about.

KRISHNAMURTI: That is fairly simple.

Bohm: What would you say?

KRISHNAMURTI: Thought must have security; it is seeking security in all its movement.

Bohm: Yes.

KRISHNAMURTI: But intelligence is not seeking security. It has no security. The idea of security doesn't exist in intelligence. Intelligence itself is secure, not, "It seeks security."

Bohm: Yes, but how did it come about that intelligence allowed itself to be dominated?

KRISHNAMURTI: Oh, that is fairly clear. Pleasure, comfort, physical security, first of all physical security: security in relationship, security in action, security . . .

Bohm: But that is the illusion of security.

KRISHNAMURTI: Illusion of security, of course.

Bohm: You could say that thought got out of hand and ceased to allow itself to be orderly, ordered in general by intelligence, or at least to stay in harmony with intelligence, and began to move on its own accord.

KRISHNAMURTI: On its own accord.

Bohm: Seeking security and pleasure and so on.

KRISHNAMURTI: As we were saying the other day when we were talking together, the whole Western world is based on measure; and the Eastern world tried to go beyond that. But they used thought to go beyond it.

Bohm: Tried to anyway.

KRISHNAMURTI: Tried to go beyond the measure by exercising thought; therefore they were caught in thought. Now security, physical security, is necessary and therefore physical existence, physical pleasures, physical well-being became tremendously important.

Bohm: Yes, I was thinking about that a little. If you go back to the animal, then there is instinctive response towards pleasure and towards security: that would be right. But now when thought comes in, it can dazzle the instinct and produce all sorts of glamour, more pleasure, more security. And the instincts are not intelligent enough to deal with the complexity of thought, therefore thought went wrong, because it excited the the instincts and the instincts demanded more.

KRISHNAMURTI: So thought really created a world of illusion, miasma, confusion, and put away intelligence.

490

Bohm: Well, as we said before, that has made the brain very chaotic and noisy and intelligence is the silence of the brain; therefore the noisy brain is not intelligent.

KRISHNAMURTI: The noisy brain is not intelligent, of course!

Bohm: Well that more or less explains the origin of the thing.

KRISHNAMURTI: We are trying to find out what is the relationship, in action, of thought and intelligence. Everything is action or inaction. And what is the relationship of that to intelligence? Thought does produce chaotic action, fragmentary action.

Bohm: When it is not ordered by intelligence.

KRISHNAMURTI: And it is not ordered by intelligence in the way we all live.

Bohm: That is because of what we have just said.

KRISHNAMURTI: It is fragmented activity; it is not an activity of a wholeness. The activity of wholeness is intelligence.

Bohm: Intelligence also has to understand the activity of thought.

KRISHNAMURTI: Yes, we said that.

Bohm: Now would you say that when intelligence understands the activity of thought, then thought is different in its operation?

KRISHNAMURTI: Yes, obviously. That is, if thought has created nationalism as a means of security and then one sees the fallacy of it, the seeing of the fallacy of it is intelligence. Thought then creates a different kind of world in which nationalism doesn't exist.

Bohm: Yes.

KRISHNAMURTI: And also division, war, conflict and all the rest.

Bohm: That is very clear. Intelligence sees the falseness of what is going on. When thought is free of this falseness it is different. Then it begins to be a parallel to intelligence.

KRISHNAMURTI: That is right.

Bohm: That is, it begins to carry out the implications of intelligence.

KRISHNAMURTI: Therefore thought has a place.

Bohm: That is very interesting because thought is never actually controlled or dominated by intelligence. thought always moves on its own. But in the light of intelligence, when the falseness is seen. then thought moves parallel or in harmony with intelligence.

KRISHNAMURTI: That is right.

Bohm: But there is never anything that forces thought to do anything. That would suggest that intelligence and thought have this common origin or substance, and that they are two ways of calling attention to a greater whole.

KRISHNAMURTI: Yes. One can see how politically, religiously, psychologically, thought has created a world of tremendous contradiction, fragmentation, and the intelligence that is the product of this confusion then tries to bring order in this confusion. It is not that intelligence which sees the falseness of all this. I don't know if I am making myself clear. You see, one can be terribly intelligent although one is chaotic.

Bohm: Well, in some ways.

KRISHNAMURTI: That is what is happening in the world.

Bohm: But I suppose it is rather hard to understand that at this moment. You could say that in some limited sphere it seems that intelligence is able to operate, but outside it doesn't.

KRISHNAMURTI: We are, after all, concerned with living, not with theories. One is concerned with a life in which intelligence operates. Intelligence which is not of time, which is not of measure, which is not the product or the movement of thought, or of the order of thought. Now a human being wants to live a different kind of life. He is dominated by thought, his thought is always functioning in measurement, in comparison, in conflict. He asks, "How am I to be free of all this in order to be intelligent?" "How can the 'me', how can 'I' be the instrument of this intelligence?"

Bohm: Obviously it can't be.

KRISHNAMURTI: That is just it!

Bohm: Because this thought in time is the essence of unintelligence.

KRISHNAMURTI: But one is thinking in terms of that all the time.

Bohm: Yes. That is thought projecting some sort of phantasy of what intelligence is, and trying to achieve it.

KRISHNAMURTI: Therefore I would say that thought must be completely still for the awakening of intelligence. There can't be a movement of thought and yet the awakening of that.

Bohm: That is clear on one level. We consider thought to be actually mechanical and this may be seen on one level—but still the mechanism continues.

KRISHNAMURTI: Continues, yes . . .

Bohm: . . . through instincts and pleasure and fear and so on. The intelligence has to come to grips with this question of the pleasures, the fears, the desires, which make thought continue.

KRISHNAMURTI: Yes.

Bohm: And you see there is always a trap: this is our concept or image of it, which is partial.

KRISHNAMURTI: So as a human being I would be concerned only with this central issue. I know how confused, contradictory, disharmonious one's life is. Is it possible to change that so that intelligence can function in my life, so that I live without disharmony, so that the pointer, the direction is guided by intelligence? That is perhaps why the religious people, instead of using the word intelligence, have used the word God.

Bohm: What is the advantage of that?

KRISHNAMURTI: I don't know what the advantage is.

Bohm: But why use such a word?

KRISHNAMURTI: It came from primitive fear, fear of nature, and gradually out of that grew the idea that there is a superfather.

Bohm: But that is still thought functioning on its own, wthout intelligence.

KRISHNAMURTI: Of course. I am just recalling that. They said trust God, have faith in God, then God will operate through you.

Bohm: God is perhaps a metaphor for intelligence—but people didn't generally take it as a metaphor.

KRISHNAMURTI: Of course not, it is a terrific image.

Bohm: Yes. You could say that if God means that which is immeasurable, beyond thought . . .

KRISHNAMURTI: . . . it is unnameable, it is immeasurable, therefore don't have an image.

Bohm: Then that will operate within the measurable.

KRISHNAMURTI: Yes. What I am trying to convey is, that the desire for this intelligence, through time, has created this image of God. And through the image of God, Jesus, Krishna, or whatever it is, by having faith in that—which is still the movement of thought—one hopes that there will be harmony in one's life.

Bohm: And this sort of image because it is so total produces an overriding desire, urge; that is, it overrides rationality ... everything.

KRISHNAMURTI: You heard the other day what the archbishops and bishops were saying, that only Jesus matters, nothing else matters.

Bohm: But it is the same movement whereby pleasure overrides rationality.

KRISHNAMURTI: Fear and pleasure.

Bohm: They override; no proportion can be established.

KRISHNAMURTI: Yes, what I am trying to say is: you see the whole world is conditioned this way.

Bohm: Yes, but the question is what you have hinted at: what is this world which is conditioned this way? If we take this world as existing independently of thought, then we have fallen into the same trap.

KRISHNAMURTI: Of course, of course.

Bohm: That is, the whole conditional world is the result of this way of thinking, it is both the cause and the effect of this way of thinking.

KRISHNAMURTI: That is right.

Bohm: And this way of thinking is disharmony and chaos and unintelligence and so on.

KRISHNAMURTI: I was listening to the Labour Party Conference at Blackpool—how clever, some of them very serious, double talk and all that, thinking in terms of Labour Party and Conservative Party. They don't say, "Let all of us get together and see what is the best thing for human beings."

Bohm: They are not capable.

KRISHNAMURTI: That is it, but they are exercising their intelligence!

Bohm: Well, in that limited framework. That is what our trouble has always been; people have developed technology and other things in terms of some limited intelligence, which is serving highly unintelligent purposes.

KRISHNAMURTI: Yes, that is just it.

Bohm: For thousands of years that has been going on. Then of course the reactions arise: the problems are much too big, too vast.

KRISHNAMURTI: But it is really very simple, extraordinarily simple, this sense of harmony. Because it is so simple it can function in the most complex field.

KRISHNAMURTI: Let us go back. We said the source is common to both thought and intelligence . . .

Bohm: Yes, we got that far.

KRISHNAMURTI: What is that source? It is generally attributed to some philosophical concept, or they say that source is God—I am just using that word for the moment—or Brahman. That source is common, is the central movement which divides itself into matter and intelligence. But that is just a verbal statement, it is just an idea, which is still thought. You can't find it through thought.

Bohm: That raises the question: if you find it then what are "you"?

KRISHNAMURTI: "You" don't exist. "You" can't exist when you are asking what is the source. "You" are time, movement, environmental conditioning—you are all that.

Bohm: In that question the whole of this division is put aside.

KRISHNAMURTI: Absolutely. That is the point, isn't it?

Bohm: There is no time . . .

KRISHNAMURTI: Yet we still say, "I am not going to exercise thought." When the "me" enters it means division: so understanding the whole of this—what we have been talking about—I put away the "me" altogether.

Bohm: But that sounds like a contradiction.

KRISHNAMURTI: I know. *I* can't put it away. It takes place. Then what is the source? Can it ever be named? For instance the Jewish religious feeling is that it is not nameable: you don't name it, you can't talk about it, you can't touch it. You can only look. And the Hindus and othes say the same thing in a different way. The Christians have tripped themselves up over this word Jesus, this image, they have never gone to the source of it.

Bohm: That is a complex question: it may be that they were trying to synthesise several philosophies, Hebrew, Greek, and Oriental.

KRISHNAMURTI: Now I want to get at this: what is the source? Can thought find it? And yet thought is born from that source; and also intelligence. It is like two streams moving in different directions.

Bohm: Would you say matter is also born from that source more generally?

KRISHNAMURTI: Of course.

Bohm: I mean the whole universe. But then the source is beyond the universe.

KRISHNAMURTI: Of course. Could we put it this way? Thought is energy, so is intelligence.

Bohm: So is matter.

KRISHNAMURTI: Thought, matter, the mechanical, is energy. Intelligence is also energy. Thought is confused, polluted, dividing itself, fragmenting itself.

Bohm: Yes, it is multiple.

KRISHNAMURTI: And the other is not. It is not polluted. It cannot divide itself as "my intelligence" and "your intelligence". It is intelligence, it is not divisible. Now it has sprung from a source of energy which has divided itself.

Bohm: Why has it divided itself?

KRISHNAMURTI: For physical reasons, for comfort . . .

Bohm: To maintain physical existence. So a part of intelligence has been changed in such a way as to help to maintain physical existence.

KRISHNAMURTI: Yes.

Bohm: It has developed in a certain way.

KRISHNAMURTI: And gone on in that way. Both are energy. There is only one energy.

Bohm: Yes, they are different forms of energy. There are many analogies to this, although it is on a much more limited scale. In physics you could say light is ordinarily a very complex wave motion, but in the laser it can be made to move all together in a very simple and harmonious way.

KRISHNAMURTI: Yes. I was reading about the laser. What monstrous things they are going to do with it.

Bohm: Yes, using it destructively. Thought may get something good but then it always gets used in a broader way that is destructive.

KRISHNAMURTI: So there is only energy, which is the source.

Bohm: Would you say energy is a kind of movement?

KRISHNAMURTI: No, it is energy. The moment it is a movement it goes off into this field of thought.

Bohm: We have to clarify this notion of energy. I have also looked up this word. You see, it is based on the notion of work; energy means, "To work within."

KRISHNAMURTI: Work within, yes.

498

Bohm: But now you say there is an energy which works, but no movement.

KRISHNAMURTI: Yes. I was thinking about this yesterday—not thinking—I realised the source is there, uncontaminated, non-movement, untouched by thought, it is there. From that these two are born. Why are they born at all?

Bohm: One was necessary for survival.

KRISHNAMURTI: That is all. In survival this—in its totality, in its wholeness—has been denied, or put aside. What I am trying to get at is this, Sir. I want to find out, as a human being living in this world with all the chaos and suffering, can the human mind touch that source in which the two divisions don't exist?—and because it has touched this source, which has no divisions, it can operate without the sense of division. I don't know if I am conveying this?

Bohm: But how is it possible for the human mind *not* to touch the source? Why does it not touch the source?

KRISHNAMURTI: Because we are consumed by thought, by the cleverness of thought, by the movement of thought. All their gods, their meditations—everything is that.

Bohm: Yes. I think this brings us to the question of life and death. This relates to survival; because that is one of the things that gets in the way.

KRISHNAMURTI: Thought and its field of security, its desire for security, has created death as something separate from itself.

Bohm: Yes, that may be the key point.

KRISHNAMURTI: It is.

Bohm: You can look at it this way. Thought has constructed itself as an instrument for survival. Now therefore . . .

KRISHNAMURTI: . . . it has created immortality in Jesus, or in this or that.

Bohm: Thought cannot possibly contemplate its own death. So if it tries to do so, it always projects something else, some other broader point of view from which it seems to look at it. If anybody tries to imagine that he is dead, then he is still imagining that he is alive and looking at himself as dead. You can always complicate this in all sorts of religious notions; but it seems to be built into thought that it cannot possibly consider death properly.

KRISHNAMURTI: It cannot. It means ending itself.

Bohm: That is very interesting. Suppose we take the death of the body, which we see outwardly; the organism dies, it loses its energy and therefore it falls apart.

KRISHNAMURTI: It is really that the body is the instrument of the energy.

Bohm: So let us say the energy ceases to imbue the body and therefore the body no longer has any wholeness. You could say that with thought also; the energy in some ways goes to thought, as to the body—is that so?

KRISHNAMURTI: That is right.

Bohm: You and other people have often used the phrase: "The mind dies to the whole of thought." That way of putting it is puzzling at first, because you would think it was thought that should die.

KRISHNAMURTI: Quite, quite.

Bohm: But now you are saying that it is the mind that dies, or the energy that dies to thought. The nearest I can see to what that means is, that when thought is working it is invested with a certain energy by the mind or the intelligence; and when thought is no longer relevant, then the energy goes and thought is like a dead organism.

KRISHNAMURTI: That is right.

Bohm: Now it is very hard for the mind to accept this. The comparison between thought and the organism seems so poor, because thought is insubstantial and the organism is substantial. So the death of the organism appears to be something far more than the death of thought. Now this is a point that is not clear. Would you say that in the death of thought we have the essence of the death of the organism as well?

KRISHNAMURTI: Obviously.

Bohm: Although it is on a small scale, as it were, it is of the same nature?

KRISHNAMURTI: As we said, there is energy in both, and thought in its movement is of this energy, and thought cannot see itself die.

Bohm: It has no way of imagining, or projecting, or conceiving its own death.

KRISHNAMURTI: Therefore it escapes from death.

Bohm: Well, it gives itself the illusion.

KRISHNAMURTI: Illusion of course. And it has created the illusion of immortality or a state beyond death, a projection of its own desire for its own continuity.

Bohm: Well, that is one thing, that thought may have begun by desiring the continuity of the organism.

KRISHNAMURTI: Yes, that is right, and then gone on beyond it.

Bohm: Gone beyond that, to desire its own continuity. That was the mistake, that was where it went wrong. It regarded itself as an extension, not merely an extension, but the essence of the organism. At first thought is functioning merely in the organism and then thought begins to present itself as the essence of the organism.

KRISHNAMURTI: That's right.

Bohm: Then thought begins to desire its own immortality.

KRISHNAMURTI: And thought itself knows, is very well aware that it is not immortal.

Bohm: It knows it only outwardly, though. I mean, it knows it as an outward fact.

KRISHNAMURTI: Therefore it creates immortality in pictures, images.

KRISHNAMURTI: I listen to all this as an outsider and I say to myself, "This is perfectly true, so clear, logical, sane; we see it very clearly, both psychologically and physically." Now my question, observing all this, is: can the mind keep the purity of the original source? The original pristine clarity of that energy which is not touched by the corruption of thought? I don't know if I am conveying it?

Bohm: The question is clear.

KRISHNAMURTI: Can the mind do it? Can the mind ever discover that?

Bohm: What is the mind?

KRISHNAMURTI: The mind, as we now say, or organism, thought, the brain with all its memories, experiences and all that, which is all of time. And the mind says, "Can I come to this?" It cannot. Then I say to myself, "As it cannot, I will be quiet." You see the tricks it has played.

Bohm: Yes.

KRISHNAMURTI: I will learn how to be quiet; I will learn how to meditate in order to be quiet. I see the importance of having a mind that is free of time, free of the mechanism of thought, I will control it, subjugate it, put away thought. But it is still the operation of thought. That is very clear. Then what is it to do? Because a human being lives in this disharmony, he must enquire into this. And that is what we are doing. As we begin to enquire into it, or in enquiring, we come to this source. Is it a perception, an insight, and has that insight nothing whatsoever to do

502

with thought? Is insight the result of thought? The conclusion of an insight is thought, but insight itself is not thought. So I have got a key to it. Then what is insight? Can I invite it, cultivate it?

Bohm: You can't do any of that. But there is a kind of energy that is needed.

KRISHNAMURTI: That is just it. I can't do any of that. When I cultivate it, it is desire. When I say I will do this or that, it is the same. So insight is not the product of thought. It is not in the order of thought. Now, how does one come upon this insight? *(Pause)* We *have* come upon it because we denied all that.

Bohm: Yes, it is there. You can never answer that question, how you come upon anything.

KRISHNAMURTI: No. I think it is fairly clear, Sir. You come upon it when you see the whole thing. So insight is the perception of the whole. A fragment cannot see this, but the "I" sees the fragments, and the "I" seeing the fragments sees the whole, and the quality of a mind that sees the whole is not touched by thought; therefore there is perception, there is insight.

Bohm: Perhaps we will go over that more slowly. We see all the fragments; could we say the actual energy, activity, which sees those fragments is whole?

KRISHNAMURTI: Yes, yes.

Bohm: We don't manage ever to see the whole because . . .

KRISHNAMURTI: . . . we are educated—and all the rest of it.

Bohm: But I mean, we wouldn't anyway see the whole as something. Rather, wholeness is freedom in seeing all the fragments.

KRISHNAMURTI: That is right. Freedom to see. The freedom doesn't exist when there are fragments.

Bohm: That makes a paradox.

KRISHNAMURTI: Of course.

Bohm: But the whole does not start from the fragments. Once the whole operates then there are no fragments. So the paradox comes from supposing that the fragments are real, that they exist independently of thought. Then you would say, I suppose, that the fragments are there with me in my thoughts, and then I must somehow do something about them—that would be a paradox. The whole starts from the insight that these fragments are in a way nothing. That is the way it seems to me. They are not substantial. They are very insubstantial.

KRISHNAMURTI: Insubstantial, yes.

Bohm: And therefore they don't prevent wholeness.

KRISHNAMURTI: Quite.

Bohm: You see, one of the things that often causes confusion is that, when you put it in terms of thought, it seems that you are presented with the fragments that are real, substantial reality. Then you have to see them, and nevertheless you say, as long as the fragments are there, there is no wholeness so that you can't see them. But that all comes back to the one thing, the one source.

KRISHNAMURTI: I am sure, Sir, really serious people have asked this question. They have asked it and tried to find an answer through thought.

Bohm: Yes, well it seems natural.

KRISHNAMURTI: And they never saw that they were caught in thought.

Bohm: That is always the trouble. Everybody gets into this trouble: that he seems to be looking at everything, at his problems, saying, "Those are my problems, I am looking." But that looking is only thinking, but it is confused with *looking*. This is one of the confusions that arises. If you say, don't think but look, that person feels he is already looking.

KRISHNAMURTI: Quite. So you see, this question has arisen and they say, "All right, then I must control thought, I must subjugate thought and I must make my mind quiet so that it becomes whole, then I can see the parts, all the fragments, then I'll touch the source." But it is still the operation of thought all the time.

Bohm: Yes, that means the operation of thought is unconscious for the most part and therefore one doesn't know it is going on. We may say consciously we have realised that all this has to be changed, it has to be different.

KRISHNAMURTI: But it is still going on unconsciously. So can you talk to my unconscious, knowing my conscious brain is going to resist you? Because you are telling me something which is revolutionary, you are telling me something which shatters my whole house which I have built so carefully, and I won't listen to you—you follow? In my instinctive reactions I push you away. So you realise that and say, "Look, all right, old friend, just don't bother to listen to me. I am going to talk to your unconscious. I am going to talk to your unconscious and make that unconscious see that whatever movement it does is still within the field of time and so on." So your conscious mind is never in operation. When it operates it must inevitably either resist, or say, "I will accept"; therefore it creates a conflict in itself. So can you talk to my unconscious?

Bohm: You can always ask how.

KRISHNAMURTI: No, no. You can say to a friend, "Don't resist, don't think about it, but I am going to talk to you." "We two are communicating with each other without the conscious mind listening."

Bohm: Yes.

KRISHNAMURTI: I think this is what really takes place. When you were talking to me—I was noticing it—I was not listening to your words so much. I was listening to you. I was open to you, not to your words, as you explained and so on. I said to myself, all right, leave all that. I am listening to you, not to the words which you use, but to the meaning, to the inward quality of your feeling that you want to communicate to me.

Bohm: I understand.

KRISHNAMURTI: That changes me, not all this verbalisation. So can you talk to me about my idiocies, my illusions, my peculiar tendencies, without the conscious mind interfering and saying, "Please don't touch all this, leave me alone!" They have tried subliminal propaganda in advertising, so that whilst you don't really pay attention, your unconscious does, so you buy that particular soap! We are not doing that, it would be deadly. What I am saying is: don't listen to me with your conscious ears but listen to me with the ears that hear much deeper. That is how I listened to you this morning, because I am terribly interested in the source, as you are. You follow, Sir? I am really interested in that one thing. All this is the explicable, easily understood—but to come to that thing together, feel it together! You follow? I think that is the way to break a conditioning, a habit, an image which has been cultivated. You talk about it at a level where the conscious mind is not totally interested. It sounds silly, but you understand what I mean?

Say for instance I have a conditioning; you can point it out a dozen times, argue, show the fallacy of it, the stupidity—but I still go on. I resist, I say what it should be, what shall I do in this world otherwise, and all the rest of it. But you see the truth, that as long as the mind is conditioned there must be conflict. So you penetrate or push aside my resistance and get to that, get the unconscious to listen to you, because the unconscious is much more subtle, much quicker. It may be frightened, but it sees the danger of fear much quicker than the conscious mind does. As when I was walking in California high in the mountains: I was looking at birds and trees and watching, and I heard a rattler and I jumped. It was the unconscious that made the body jump; I saw the rattler when I jumped, it was two or three feet away, it could have struck me very easily. If the conscious brain had been operating it would have taken several seconds.

Bohm: To reach the unconscious you have to have an action which doesn't directly appeal to the conscious.

KRISHNAMURTI: Yes. That is affection, that is love. When you talk to my waking consciousness, it is hard, clever, subtle, brittle. And you penetrate that, penetrate it with your look, with your affection, with all the feeling you have. That operates, not anything else.

BROCKWOOD PARK
7 OCTOBER 1972

J. KRISHNAMURTI